SOLUTIONS MANUAL

AUDITING

SOLUTIONS MANUAL

Alvin A. Arens
Price Waterhouse
Auditing Professor
Michigan State University

James K. Leobbecke
Kenneth A. Sorenson
Peat Marwick Professor of Accounting
University of Utah

With Contributing Authors

Randal J. Elder
Syracuse University

Mark S. Beasley
North Carolina State University

AUDITING
AN INTEGRATED APPROACH

Eighth Edition

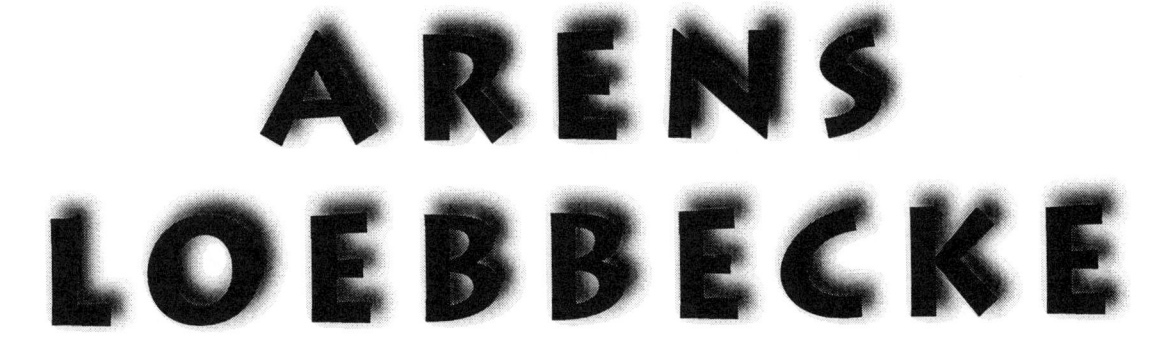

ARENS
LOEBBECKE

Prentice Hall, Upper Saddle River, NJ 07458

Acquisitions editor: Annie Todd
Associate editor: Kathryn Sheehan
Project editor: Richard Bretan
Manufacturer: Daamen, Inc.

© 2000 by Prentice Hall, Inc.
Upper Saddle River, New Jersey 07458

All rights reserved. No part of this publication may be
reproduced, in any form or by any means,
without permission in writing from the publisher.

Printed in the United States of America

10　9　8　7　6　5　4　3　2　1

ISBN 0-13-086748-9

Prentice-Hall International (UK) Limited, London
Prentice-Hall of Australia Pty. Limited, Sydney
Prentice-Hall Canada Inc., Toronto
Prentice-Hall Hispanoamericana, S.A., Mexico
Prentice-Hall of India Private Limited, New Delhi
Prentice-Hall of Japan, Inc., Tokyo
Prentice-Hall (Singapore) Pte Ltd
Editora Prentice-Hall do Brasil, Ltda., Rio de Janeiro

CONTENTS

Chapter 1 1-1

Chapter 2 2-1

Chapter 3 3-1

Chapter 4 4-1

Chapter 5 5-1

Chapter 6 6-1

Chapter 7 7-1

Chapter 8 8-1

Chapter 9 9-1

Chapter 10 10-1

Chapter 11 11-1

Chapter 12 12-1

Chapter 13 13-1

Chapter 14 14-1

Chapter 15 15-1

Chapter 16 16-1

Chapter 17 17-1

Chapter 18 18-1

Chapter 19 19-1

Chapter 20 20-1

Chapter 21 21-1

Chapter 22 22-1

Chapter 23 23-1

Chapter 24 24-1

Chapter 25 25-1

Chapter 1

The Demand for Audit and Assurance Services

■ **Review Questions**

1-1 The relationship among audit services, attestation services, and assurance services is reflected in Figure 1-1 on page 6 of the text. An assurance service is an independent professional service to improve the quality of information for decision makers. An attestation service is a form of assurance service in which the CPA firm issues a written conclusion about an assertion made by a third party. Audit services are a form of attestation service, in which the auditor expresses a written conclusion about the degree of correspondence between information and established criteria.

The most common form of audit service is an audit of historical financial statements, in which the auditor expresses a conclusion as to whether the financial statements are presented in conformity with generally accepted accounting principles. An example of an attestation service is a report on the effectiveness of an entity's internal control over financial reporting. There are many possible forms of assurance services, including services related to business performance measurement, health care performance, and information system reliability.

1-2 An independent audit is a means of satisfying the need for reliable information on the part of decision makers. Factors of a complex society which contribute to this need are:

1. Remoteness of information
    a. Owners (stockholders) divorced from management
    b. Directors not involved in day-to-day operations or decisions
    c. Dispersion of the business among numerous geographic locations and complex corporate structures
2. Biases and motives of provider
    a. Information will be biased in favor of the provider when his or her goals are inconsistent with the decision maker's goals.
3. Voluminous data
    a. Possibly millions of transactions processed daily via sophisticated computerized systems
    b. Multiple product lines
    c. Multiple transaction locations
4. Complex exchange transactions
    a. New and changing business relationships lead to innovative accounting and reporting problems
    b. Potential impact of transactions not quantifiable, leading to increased disclosures

1-3
1. *Risk-free interest rate* This is approximately the rate the bank could earn by investing in U.S. treasury notes for the same length of time as the business loan.
2. *Business risk for the customer* This risk reflects the possibility that the business will not be able to repay its loan because of economic or business conditions such as a recession, poor management decisions, or unexpected competition in the industry.
3. *Information risk* This risk reflects the possibility that the information upon which the business risk decision was made was inaccurate. A likely cause of the information risk is the possibility of inaccurate financial statements.

Auditing has no effect on either the risk-free interest rate or business risk. However, auditing can significantly reduce information risk.

1-4 The four primary causes of information risk are remoteness of information, biases and motives of the provider, voluminous data, and the existence of complex exchange transactions.

The three main ways to reduce information risk are:

1. User verifies the information.
2. User shares the information risk with management.
3. Audited financial statements are provided.

The advantages and disadvantages of each are as follows:

	ADVANTAGES	DISADVANTAGES
USER VERIFIES INFORMATION	1. User obtains information desired. 2. User can be more confident of the qualifications and activities of the person getting the information.	1. High cost of obtaining information. 2. Inconvenience to the person providing the information because large number of users would be on premises.
USER SHARES INFORMATION RISK WITH MANAGEMENT	1. No audit costs incurred.	1. User may not be able to collect on losses.
AUDITED FINANCIAL STATEMENTS ARE PROVIDED	1. Multiple users obtain the information. 2. Information risk can usually be reduced sufficiently to satisfy users at reasonable cost. 3. Minimal inconvenience to management by having only one auditor.	1. May not meet needs of certain users. 2. Cost may be higher than the benefits in some situations, such as for a small company.

1-5 To do an audit, there must be information in a *verifiable form* and some standards (*criteria*) by which the auditor can evaluate the information. Examples of established criteria include generally accepted accounting principles and the Internal Revenue Code. Determining the degree of correspondence between information and established criteria is determining whether a given set of information is in accordance with the established criteria. The information for Jones Company's tax return is the federal tax returns filed by the company. The established criteria are found in the Internal Revenue Code and all interpretations. For the audit of Jones Company's financial statements the information is the financial statements being audited and the established criteria are generally accepted accounting principles.

1-6 The primary evidence the internal revenue agent will use in the audit of the Jones Company's tax return include all available documentation and other information available in Jones' office or from other sources. For example, when the internal revenue agent audits taxable income, a major source of information will be bank statements, the cash receipts journal and deposit slips. The internal revenue agent is likely to emphasize unrecorded receipts and revenues. For expenses, major sources of evidence are likely to be cancelled checks, vendors' invoices and other supporting documentation.

1-7 This apparent paradox arises from the distinction between the function of auditing and the function of accounting. The accounting function is the recording, classifying and summarizing of economic events to provide relevant information to decision makers. The rules of accounting are the criteria used by the auditor for evaluating the presentation of economic events for financial statements and he or she must therefore have an understanding of generally accepted accounting principles (GAAP), as well as generally accepted auditing standards (GAAS). The accountant need not, and frequently does not, understand what auditors do, unless he or she is involved in doing audits, or has been trained as an auditor.

1-8

	AUDITS OF FINANCIAL STATEMENTS	COMPLIANCE AUDITS	OPERATIONAL AUDITS
PURPOSE	To determine whether the overall financial statements are presented in accordance with specified criteria (usually GAAP)	To determine whether the client is following specific procedures set by higher authority	To evaluate whether operating procedures are efficient and effective
USERS OF AUDIT REPORT	Different groups for different purposes—many outside entities	Authority setting down procedures, internal or external	Management of organization
NATURE	Highly standardized	Not standardized, but specific and usually objective	Highly nonstandard; often subjective
PERFORMED BY:			
CPAs	Almost universally	Occasionally	Frequently
GAO AUDITORS	Occasionally	Frequently	Frequently
IRS AUDITORS	Never	Universally	Never
INTERNAL AUDITORS	Frequently	Frequently	Frequently

1-9 Five examples of specific operational audits that could be conducted by an internal auditor in a manufacturing company are:

1. Examine employee time cards and personnel records to determine if sufficient information is available to maximize the effective use of personnel.
2. Review the processing of sales invoices to determine if it could be done more efficiently.
3. Review the acquisitions of goods, including costs, to determine if they are being purchased at the lowest possible cost considering the quality needed.
4. Review and evaluate the efficiency of the manufacturing process.
5. Review the processing of cash receipts to determine if they are deposited as quickly as possible.

1-10 The major differences in the scope of audit responsibilities are:

1. CPAs perform audits in accordance with generally accepted auditing standards of published financial statements prepared in accordance with generally accepted accounting principles.
2. GAO auditors perform compliance or operational audits in order to assure the Congress of the expenditure of public funds in accordance with its directives and the law.
3. IRS agents perform compliance audits to enforce the federal tax laws as defined by Congress, interpreted by the courts, and regulated by the IRS.
4. Internal auditors perform compliance or operational audits in order to assure management or the board of directors that controls and policies are properly and consistently developed, applied and evaluated.

1-11 The four parts of the Uniform CPA Examination are: Auditing, Accounting and Reporting, Financial Accounting and Reporting, and Business Law.

■ Multiple Choice Questions From CPA Examinations

1-12 a. (3)   b. (2)   c. (2)   d. (3)
1-13 a. (2)   b. (3)   c. (4)   d. (3)

■ Discussion Questions And Problems

1-14 a. The relationship among audit services, attestation services and assurance services is reflected in Figure 1-1 on page 6 of the text. Audit services are a form of attestation service, and attestation services are a form of assurance service. In a diagram, audit services are located within the attestation service area, and attestation services are located within the assurance service area.

   b. 1. (1) Audit of historical financial statements
       2. (2) An attestation service other than an audit service; or
          (3) An assurance service that is not an attestation service
              (*WebTrust* developed from the AICPA Special Committee on Assurance Services, but the service meets the criteria for an attestation service.)
       3. (2) An attestation service other than an audit service
       4. (2) An attestation service other than an audit service
       5. (3) An assurance service that is not an attestation service
       6. (2) An attestation service that is not an audit service
          (Review services are a form of attestation, but are performed according to Statements on Standards for Accounting and Review Services.)
       7. (2) An attestation service other than an audit service

1-15 a. The interest rate for the loan that requires a review report is lower than the loan that did not require a review because of lower information risk. A review report provides moderate assurance to financial statement users, which lowers information risk. An audit report provides further assurance and lower information risk. As a result of reduced information risk, the interest rate is lowest for the loan with the audit report.

b. Given these circumstances, Vial-tek should select the loan from City First Bank that requires an annual audit. In this situation, the additional cost of the audit is less than the reduction in interest due to lower information risk. The following is the calculation of total costs for each loan:

LENDER	CPA SERVICE	COST OF CPA SERVICES	ANNUAL INTEREST	ANNUAL LOAN COST
Existing loan	None	0	$ 142,500	$ 142,500
First National Bank	Review	$12,000	$ 127,500	$ 139,500
City First Bank	Audit	$ 20,000	$ 112,500	$ 132,500

c. Vial-tek may desire to have an audit because of the many other positive benefits that an audit provides. The audit will provide Vial-tek's management with assurance about annual financial information used for decision-making purposes. The audit may detect errors or fraud, and provide management with information about the effectiveness of controls. In addition, the audit may result in recommendations to management that will improve efficiency or effectiveness.

1-16 a. The services provided by Consumers Union are very similar to assurance services provided by CPA firms. The services provided by Consumers Union and assurance services provided by CPA firms are designed to improve the quality of information for decision makers. CPAs are valued for their independence, and the reports provided by Consumers Union are valued because Consumers Union is independent of the products tested.

b. The concepts of information risk for the buyer of an automobile and for the user of financial statements are essentially the same. They are both concerned with the problem of unreliable information being provided. In the case of the auditor, the user is concerned about unreliable information being provided in the financial statements. The buyer of an automobile is likely to be concerned about the manufacturer or dealer providing unreliable information.

c. The four causes of information risk are essentially the same for a buyer of an automobile and a user of financial statements:

(1) *Remoteness of information* It is difficult for a user to obtain much information about either an automobile manufacturer or the automobile itself without incurring considerable cost. The automobile buyer does have the advantage of possibly knowing other users who are satisfied or dissatisfied with a similar automobile.

1-16 (Continued)

- (2) *Biases and motives of provider* There is a conflict between the automobile buyer and the manufacturer. The buyer wants to buy a high quality product at minimum cost whereas the seller wants to maximize the selling price and quantity sold.
- (3) *Voluminous data* There is a large amount of available information about automobiles that users might like to have in order to evaluate an automobile. Either that information is not available or too costly to obtain.
- (4) *Complex exchange transactions* The acquisition of an automobile is expensive and certainly a complex decision because of all the components that go into making a good automobile and choosing between a large number of alternatives.

d. The three ways users of financial statements and buyers of automobiles reduce information risk are also similar:
- (1) *User verifies information him or herself* That can be obtained by driving different automobiles, examining the specifications of the automobiles, talking to other users and doing research in various magazines.
- (2) *User shares information risk with management* The manufacturer of a product has a responsibility to meet its warranties and to provide a reasonable product. The buyer of an automobile can return the automobile for correction of defects. In some cases a refund may be obtained.
- (3) *Examine the information prepared by Consumer Reports* This is similar to an audit in the sense that independent information is provided by an independent party. The information provided by *Consumer Reports* is comparable to that provided by a CPA firm that audited financial statements.

1-17 a. The following parts of the definition of auditing are related to the narrative:
- (1) Virms is being asked to issue a report about qualitative and quantitative information for trucks. The trucks are therefore the *information* with which the auditor is concerned.
- (2) There are four *established criteria* which must be evaluated and reported by Virms: existence of the trucks on the night of June 30, 1999, ownership of each truck by Regional Delivery Service, physical condition of each truck and fair market value of each truck.
- (3) Susan Virms will *accumulate* and *evaluate* four types of *evidence*:
  - (a) Count the trucks to determine their existence.
  - (b) Use registrations documents held by Oatley for comparison to the serial number on each truck to determine ownership.
  - (c) Examine the trucks to determine each truck's physical condition.
  - (d) Examine the blue book to determine the fair market value of each truck.

1-17 (Continued)

        (4)   Susan Virms, CPA, appears qualified, as a *competent, independent person*. She is a CPA, and she spends most of her time auditing used automobile and truck dealerships and has extensive specialized knowledge about used trucks that is consistent with the nature of the engagement.

        (5)   The *report results* are to include:
- (a) which of the 35 trucks are parked in Regional's parking lot the night of June 30.
- (b) whether all of the trucks are owned by Regional Delivery Service.
- (c) the condition of each truck, using established guidelines.
- (d) fair market value of each truck using the current blue book for trucks.

b.   The only parts of the audit which will be difficult for Virms are:

    (1)   Evaluating the condition, using the guidelines of poor, good, and excellent. It is highly subjective to do so. If she uses a different criterion than the "blue book," the fair market value will not be meaningful. Her experience will be essential in using this guideline.

    (2)   Determining the fair market value, unless it is clearly defined in the blue book for each condition.

1-18 a. The major advantages and disadvantages of a career as an IRS agent, CPA, or an internal auditor are:

EMPLOYMENT	ADVANTAGES	DISADVANTAGES
INTERNAL REVENUE AGENT	1. Extensive training in individual, corporate, gift, trust and other taxes is available with concentration in area chosen. 2. Hands-on experience with sophisticated selection techniques.	1. Experience limited to taxes. 2. No experience with operational or financial statement auditing. 3. Training is not extensive with any business enterprise.
CPA	1. Extensive training in audit of financial statements, compliance auditing and operational auditing. 2. Opportunity for experience in auditing, tax consulting, and management consulting practices. 3. Experience in a diversity of enterprises and industries with the opportunity to specialize in a specific industry.	1. Exposure to taxes and to the business enterprise may not be as in-depth as the internal revenue agent or the internal auditor. 2. Likely to be less exposed to operational auditing than is likely for internal auditors.
GAO AUDITOR	1. Increasing opportunity for experience in operational auditing. 2. Exposure to highly sophisticated statistical sampling and computer auditing techniques.	1. Little exposure to diversity of enterprises and industries. 2. Bureaucracy of federal government.
INTERNAL AUDITOR	1. Extensive exposure to all segments of the enterprise with which employed. 2. Constant exposure to one industry presenting opportunity for expertise in that industry. 3. Likely to have exposure to compliance, financial and operational auditing.	1. Little exposure to taxation and the audit thereof. 2. Experience is limited to one enterprise, usually within one or a limited number of industries.

b. Other auditing careers that are available are:
- Auditors within many of the branches of the federal government (e.g., Atomic Energy Commission)
- Auditors for many state and local government units (e.g. state insurance or bank auditors)

1-19 The most likely type of auditor and the type of audit for each of the examples are:

EXAMPLE	TYPE OF AUDITOR	TYPE OF AUDIT
1.	IRS	Compliance
2.	GAO	Operational
3.	Internal auditor or CPA	Operational
4.	CPA or Internal auditor	Financial statements
5.	GAO	Operational
6.	CPA	Financial statements
7.	GAO	Financial statements
8.	IRS	Compliance
9.	CPA	Financial statements
10.	Internal auditor or CPA	Compliance
11.	Internal auditor or CPA	Financial statements
12.	GAO	Compliance

1-20 a. The conglomerate should either engage the management advisory services division of a CPA firm or its own internal auditors to conduct the operational audit.

b. The auditors will encounter problems in establishing criteria for evaluating the actual quantitative events and in setting the scope to include all operations in which significant inefficiencies might exist. In writing the report, the auditors must choose proper wording to state that no financial audit was performed, that the procedures were limited in scope and that the results reported do not necessarily include all the inefficiencies that might exist.

■ Internet Problem Solution: Assurance Services

1-1 This problem requires students to work with the AICPA assurance services website.

   a. Considering the assurance needs of customers and the capabilities of CPAs, the Special Committee on Assurance Services developed business plans for six assurance services with potential revenues of over $1 billion each. Chapter 1 of the textbook discussed two of these services, Elder Care and Business Performance Measurement.

   1. What are the other four services for which business plans have been developed?

   > Risk Assessment, Information Systems Reliability, Electronic Commerce, and Health Care Performance Measurement.

   2. Go to the business plan for the assurance service that most interests you (any one of the six). What are the major aspects or sections of the business plan (i.e., does the plan address market potential, competition, etc.?)

   > Each business plan provides background information, describes the service, assesses market potential, discusses issues such as competition and why CPAs should offer the service, identifies practice tools available and steps that CPAs must take to begin offering the services.

   b. The Special Committee's report on Assurance Services discusses competencies needed by assurance providers today and in the coming decade. Briefly describe the 5 general competencies needed in the next decade. (**Hint**: Go to the "site map" in the AICPA's Assurance Services Internet area and look for "Competencies.")

The Committee identified the following five major imperatives regarding future competencies, each of which implies increasing emphasis on the competencies noted:

   1. *Customer focus.* Assurers need to understand user decision processes and how information should enter into those processes. Increasing emphasis is needed on: Understanding of user needs, communication skills, relationship management, responsiveness and timeliness.
   2. *Migration to higher value-added information activities.* To provide more value to client/decision makers and others, assurers need to focus less on activities involved in the conversion of business events into information (e.g., collecting, classifying, and summarizing activities), and more on activities involved in the transformation of information into knowledge (e.g., analyzing, interpreting, and evaluating activities) that effectively drives decision processes. This will require: Analytical skills, business advisory skills, business knowledge, model building (including sensitivity analysis), understanding the client's business processes, measurement theory (development of operational definitions of concepts, design of appropriate measurement techniques, etc.).

1-1 (Continued)

3. *Information technology (IT).* Assurance services deal in information. Hence, the profound changes occurring in information technology will shape virtually all aspects of assurance services. As information specialists, assurers need to embrace information technology in all of its complex dimensions. Embracing IT means understanding how it is transforming all aspects of business. It also means learning how to effectively use new developments in hardware, software, communications, memory, encryption, etc., in everything assurers do as information specialists, not only in dealing with clients, but also in dealing with each other as individuals, teams, firms, state societies, and national professional organizations. To fully embrace IT, the assurer needs to go beyond the competency entitled "Technology" shown in the Committee's sub-report "The Profession's Current Competencies" and consider the new developments identified above.

4. *Pace of change and complexity.* Assurance services will take place in an environment of rapid change and increasing complexity. Assurers need to invest heavily in life-long learning in order to maintain up-to-date knowledge and skills. They will require: Intellectual capability, learning and rejuvenation.

5. *Competition.* Growth in new assurance services will depend less on franchise/regulation and more on market forces. Assurers need to develop their marketing skills—the ability to see clients' latent information and assurance needs and rapidly design and deploy cost-effective services to meet those needs—in order to effectively compete for market-driven assurance services. Required skills include: Marketing and selling, understanding customer needs, designing and deploying effective solutions.

(**Note**: Internet problems address current issues using Internet sources. Because Internet sites are subject to change, Internet problems and solutions are subject to change. Current information on Internet problems is available at www.prenhall.com/arens/).

Chapter 2

The CPA Profession

■ Review Questions

2-1 The four major services that CPAs provide are:

1. *Assurance services* Assurance services are independent professional services that improve the quality of information for decision makers. Assurance services include attestation services, which are any services in which the CPA firm issues a written communication that expresses a conclusion about the reliability of a written assertion that is the responsibility of another party. The three categories of attestation services are audits of historical financial statements, reviews of historical financial statements, and other attestation services.
2. *Accounting and bookkeeping services* Accounting services involve preparing the client's financial statements from the client's records. Bookkeeping services include the preparation of the client's journals and ledgers as well as financial statements.
3. *Tax services* Tax services include preparation of corporate, individual, and estate returns as well as tax planning assistance.
4. *Management consulting services* These services range from suggestions to improve the client's accounting system to computer installations.

2-2 The major characteristics of CPA firms that permit them to fulfill their social function competently and independently are:

1. *Organizational form* A CPA firm exists as a separate entity to avoid an employer-employee relationship with its clients. The CPA firm employs a professional staff of sufficient size to prevent one client from constituting a significant portion of total income and thereby endangering the firm's independence.
2. *Conduct* A CPA firm employs a professional staff of sufficient size to provide a broad range of expertise, continuing education, and promotion of a professional independent attitude and competence.
3. *Peer review* This practice evaluates the performance of CPA firms in an attempt to keep competence high.

2-3 The AICPA is the organization that sets professional requirements for CPAs. The AICPA also conducts research and publishes materials on many different subjects related to accounting, auditing, management advisory services, and taxes. The organization also prepares and grades the CPA examinations and provides continuing education to its members.

2-4 The purpose of the AICPA *Standards for Attestation Engagements* is two-fold: First, it provides a framework to be followed by standard-setting bodies within the AICPA in developing detailed standards on specific types of attestation services. Second, it provides a framework for guidance to practitioners when no such specific standards exist. Both generally accepted auditing standards and compilation and review standards are consistent with the broader attestation standards.

2-5 *Generally accepted auditing standards* are ten general guidelines to aid auditors in fulfilling their professional responsibilities. These guidelines include three general standards concerned with competence, independence, and due professional care; three standards of field work including planning and supervision, study and evaluation of internal control, and the gathering of competent evidential matter; and four standards of reporting which require a statement as to presentation in accordance with generally accepted accounting principles, inconsistency observed in the current period in relation to the preceding period, adequate disclosure, and the expression of an opinion as to the fairness of the presentation of the financial statements.

Generally accepted accounting principles are specific rules for accounting for transactions occurring in a business enterprise. Examples may be any of the opinions of the FASB.

2-6 Auditors can obtain adequate technical training and proficiency through formal education in auditing and accounting, adequate practical experience, and continuing professional education. Auditors can demonstrate their proficiency by becoming licensed to practice as CPAs, which requires successful completion of the Uniform CPA Examination. The specific requirements for licensure vary from state to state.

2-7 For the most part, generally accepted auditing standards are general rather than specific. Many practitioners along with critics of the profession believe the standards should provide more clearly defined guidelines as an aid in determining the extent of evidence to be accumulated. This would eliminate some of the difficult audit decisions and provide a source of defense if the CPA is charged with conducting an inadequate audit. On the other hand, highly specific requirements could turn auditing into mechanical evidence-gathering, void of professional judgment. From the point of view of both the profession and the users of auditing services, there is probably a greater harm from defining authoritative guidelines too specifically than too broadly.

2-8 Quality controls are established by individual CPA firms to help ensure that their firm meets its professional responsibilities to clients. Quality controls are the procedures used by a CPA firm that help it meet its professional responsibilities to clients. Quality controls are therefore established for the entire CPA firm as opposed to individual engagements.

2-9 The element of quality control is personnel management. The purpose of the requirement is to help assure CPA firms that all new personnel should be qualified to perform their work competently. A CPA firm must have competent employees conducting the audits if quality audits are to occur.

2-10 A peer review is a review, by CPAs, of a CPA firm's compliance with its quality control system. A mandatory peer review means that such a review is required periodically. Firms who choose to join the SEC Practice Section (SECPS) or Private Companies Practice Section (PCPS) must have such a review at least once every three years. A CPA firm is not required to become a member of either section, however. An AICPA member firm who is not a member of either the SECPS or the PCPS is also required to have a less extensive peer review every three years.

Peer reviews can be beneficial to the profession and to individual firms. By helping firms meet quality control standards, the profession gains if reviews result in practitioners doing higher quality audits. A firm having a peer review can also gain if it improves the firm's practices and thereby enhances its reputation and effectiveness, and reduces the likelihood of lawsuits. Of course peer reviews are costly. There is always a trade off between cost and benefits. A CPA firm also gives up some independence of activities when it is reviewed by another CPA firm.

2-11 The two divisions of practice that a CPA firm may belong to are the SEC Practice Section and the Private Companies Practice Section. A firm may belong to one section, both sections, or neither.

Proponents of this division believe that this will improve the quality of practice by CPA firms and that it will improve self-regulation. Critics state that it establishes two classes of CPAs and implies a lower performance quality for firms that are not members of the SEC Practice Section.

2-12 The purpose of the Securities and Exchange Commission is to assist in providing investors with reliable information upon which to make investment decisions. Since most reasonably large CPA firms have clients that must file reports with the SEC each year (all companies filing registration statements under the securities acts of 1933 and 1934 must file audited financial statements and other reports with the SEC at least once each year), the profession is highly involved with the SEC requirements.

The SEC has considerable influence in setting generally accepted accounting principles and disclosure requirements for financial statements because of its authority for specifying reporting requirements considered necessary for fair disclosure to investors. In addition, the SEC has power to establish rules for any CPA associated with audited financial statements submitted to the Commission.

■ **Multiple Choice Questions From CPA Examinations**

2-13 a. (1)   b. (2)   c. (3)   d. (3)

2-14 a. (2)   b. (2)   c. (3)

■ **Discussion Questions And Problems**

2-15 The comments on the problem do summarize the beliefs of many practitioners about quality control and peer review. The arguments against quality control and peer review are stated in the comments and can be summarized as five arguments:

1. Relative cost for local firms is excessively high.
2. Smaller firms have less need for quality control because of partner involvement.

2-15 (Continued)
3. Eliminates the major competitive advantage of local firms which is a simple and efficient organizational structure.
4. Quality control standards are not needed because they have already been implemented by quality firms.
5. Three other things already provide assurance of adequate quality: a competitive economic environment, legal liability, and auditing standards.

To support these comments, it can be argued that the profession has functioned well with relatively little controversy and criticism. A major reason many practitioners choose the profession is the relative freedom to operate their professional practice as they see fit.

a. The arguments against these comments are primarily as follows:

1. It will not be costly for most local firms to implement quality control requirements because the Private Companies Practice Section allows for simplified quality control standards.
2. There is no need to eliminate the simple organizational structure now enjoyed by many CPA firms. Requirements for quality CPA firms are relatively few, especially those choosing not to join the SEC Practice Section.
3. Certain critics of the profession have argued strongly against self-regulation of the profession. Many CPAs believe that only through self-regulation will it be possible to minimize government interference. Even if the five elements of quality control are in existence, the quality control and peer review requirements may be necessary to avoid government interference.
4. For those firms that already have the five elements of quality control in their practice, the additional implementation costs should be minimal. Those lacking such elements will incur more cost, but presumably are lacking in certain elements needed for a high quality practice.
5. Partner involvement on engagements does not necessarily assure that all quality control requirements have been met. For some smaller firms, top partners may spend relatively little time on audits and therefore not be as knowledgeable about auditing as may be necessary.

b. There is no correct answer to this question. Different people reach different conclusions, depending on the weights put on each of the five arguments stated in part a. for and against quality control and peer reviews. The authors believe that both quality control and peer review are worth the cost.

2-16
a. Engagement performance
b. Personnel management
c. Personnel management
d. Engagement performance
e. Independence, integrity, and objectivity
f. Monitoring
g. Acceptance and continuation of clients and engagements
h. Personnel management
i. Personnel management

2-17 a. Rossi and Montgomery's primary ethical consideration is their professional competence to perform all of the audit work for filing with the SEC. In addition, if Rossi and Montgomery have performed bookkeeping services for Mobile Home, they will not be independent under the SEC independence requirements.

b. The filing with the SEC, in addition to normal audited financial statements, will require completion and registration with the SEC of Form S-1 which includes an audited summary of operations for the last five fiscal years as well as many additional schedules and descriptions of the business. Each quarter subsequent to the filing, Form 10-Q must be filed; and within 90 days of the end of each fiscal year Form 10-K must be filed with the SEC.

In addition, Form 8-K must be filed whenever significant events have occurred which are of interest to public investors. These forms must be filed in conformity with Regulation S-X which requires considerable disclosures in addition to those normally required in audited financial statements.

The firm should also be a member of the SEC Practice Section and meet its requirements in order to accept the engagement. Membership is not required, however.

2-18

BRIEF DESCRIPTION OF GAAS	HOLMES' ACTIONS RESULTING IN FAILURE TO COMPLY WITH GAAS
GENERAL STANDARDS	
1. The audit is to be performed by a person or persons having adequate technical training and proficiency as an auditor.	1. It was inappropriate for Holmes to hire the two students to conduct the audit. The audit must be conducted by persons with proper education and experience in the field of auditing. Although a junior assistant has not completed his formal education, he may help in the conduct of the audit as long as there is proper supervision and review.
2. In all matters relating to the assignment, an independence in mental attitude is to be maintained by the auditor or auditors.	2. To satisfy the second general standard, Holmes must be without bias with respect to the client under audit. Holmes has an obligation for fairness to the owners, management, and creditors who may rely on the report. Because of the financial interest in whether the bank loan is granted to Ray, Holmes is independent in neither fact nor appearance with respect to the assignment undertaken.
3. Due professional care is to be exercised in the performance of the audit and the preparation of the report.	3. This standard requires Holmes to perform the audit with due care, which imposes on Holmes and everyone in Holmes' organization a responsibility to observe

2-18 (Continued)

BRIEF DESCRIPTION OF GAAS	HOLMES' ACTION RESULTING IN FAILURE TO COMPLY WITH GAAS
	the standards of field work and reporting. Exercise of due care requires critical review at every level of supervision of the work done and the judgments exercised by those assisting in the audit. Holmes did not review the work or the judgments of the assistants and clearly failed to adhere to this standard.
STANDARDS OF FIELD WORK 1. The work is to be adequately planned and assistants, if any, are to be properly supervised.	1. This standard recognizes that early appointment of the auditor has advantages for the auditor and the client. Holmes accepted the engagement without considering the availability of competent staff. In addition, Holmes failed to supervise the assistants. The work performed was not adequately planned.
2. A sufficient understanding of internal control is to be obtained to plan the audit and to determine the nature, timing, and extent of tests to be performed.	2. Holmes did not obtain an understanding of internal control, nor did the assistants obtain such an understanding. There appears to have been no audit at all. The work performed was more an accounting service than it was an auditing service.
3. Sufficient, competent evidential matter is to be obtained through inspection, observation, inquiries, and confirmations to afford a reasonable basis for an opinion regarding the financial statements under audit.	3. Holmes acquired no evidence that would support the financial statements. Holmes merely checked the mathematical accuracy of the records and summarized the accounts. Standard audit procedures and techniques were not performed.
STANDARDS OF REPORTING 1. The report shall state whether the financial statements are presented in accordance with generally accepted accounting principles.	1. Holmes' report made no reference to generally accepted accounting principles. Because Holmes did not conduct a proper audit, the report should state that no opinion can be expressed as to the fair presentation of the financial statements in accordance with generally accepted accounting principles.

2-18 (Continued)

BRIEF DESCRIPTION OF GAAS	HOLMES' ACTION RESULTING IN FAILURE TO COMPLY WITH GAAS
2. The report shall identify those circumstances in which such principles have not been consistently observed in the current period in relation to the preceding period.	2. Holmes' improper audit would not enable him to determine whether generally accepted accounting principles were consistently applied. Holmes' report should make no reference to the consistent application of accounting principles.
3. Informative disclosures in the financial statements are to be regarded as reasonably adequate unless otherwise stated in the report.	3. Management is primarily responsible for adequate disclosures in the financial statements, but when the statements do not contain adequate disclosures the auditor should make such disclosures in the auditor's report. In this case both the statements and the auditor's report lack adequate disclosures.
4. The report shall either contain an expression of opinion regarding the financial statements taken as a whole or an assertion to the effect that an opinion cannot be expressed. When an overall opinion cannot be expressed, the reasons therefor should be stated. In all cases where an auditor's name is associated with financial statements, the report should contain a clear-cut indication of the character of the auditor's work, if any, and the degree of responsibility the auditor is taking.	4. Although the Holmes report contains an expression of opinion, such opinion is not based on the results of a proper audit. Holmes should disclaim an opinion because he failed to conduct an audit in accordance with generally accepted auditing standards.

■ **Internet Problem Solution: CPA Vision Project (http://www.cpavision.org)**

2-1 The CPA Vision Project is all about helping the "CPA profession stay on top of the change curve." With input from CPAs across the nation, the CPA Vision Process has created a comprehensive and integrated vision of the profession's future.

1. What characteristics and professional services come to mind when you hear the term CPA? What is the general public's stereotype of CPAs?

    Students' responses will vary to this question.

2. Find the Vision Statement and fill in the missing words. (Answers are underlined)

    VISION STATEMENT: CPAs are the <u>trusted</u> professionals who enable people and organizations to <u>shape</u> their future. Combining insight with integrity, CPAs deliver value by ...

    - Communicating the total picture with <u>clarity and objectivity</u>,
    - <u>Translating</u> complex information into critical knowledge,
    - Anticipating and creating opportunities, and
    - Designing pathways that transform vision into <u>reality</u>.)

3. Briefly describe the eight forces impacting the profession.

    1. *Non-CPA Competitors.* The number of new, non-CPA competitors, not bound by the profession's code of standards and ethics, is increasing at an alarming rate.
    2. *Decline of new CPAs.* The number of students and young people electing to join the CPA profession has dramatically declined.
    3. *Technology Displacement.* Many of the traditional, essential skills of CPAs are being replaced by new technologSies that are increasing in number and being rapidly developed, often from unexpected sources.
    4. *Borderless World.* As the world becomes borderless, the marketplace is demanding more complex, real-time advice and services, presenting unlimited opportunities for CPAs to expand their skills, competencies, and services.
    5. *Leadership Imperative.* Corporations are conducting business in a world of commerce that is global, technological, instantaneous, and increasingly virtual. The leadership they require from both internal and external advisors requires new insights, new skills, and extraordinary agility.
    6. *Technological Advances.* Technology will continue to challenge and reshape our lifestyles, work patterns, educational experiences, and communication styles and techniques. Technology will rewrite the "rules of business," leaving those far behind who will not harness it and effectively integrate it.
    7. *Market Value Shifts.* The perceived value of some of the profession's cornerstone services-accounting, auditing, and tax preparation-is declining in the marketplace.

2-1 (Continued)

8. *Pressure to Transform Finance from Scorekeeper to Business Partner.* The CPA in business is being challenged to deliver value to the organization and help create a sustainable competitive advantage.

4. The CPA Vision Project suggests that "the increasing complexities of the global environment and the commodity characteristics of traditional services mandate that the CPA profession migrate up the economic value chain." What is meant by "moving up the economic value chain," and how are CPAs going to accomplish this? (**Hint:** look in the final report.)

Suggested Answer: Moving up the economic value chain means moving from providing low value products (i.e., a well defined product based upon the ability to perform a particular task) to higher value products and services (i.e., services that will permit the profession to thrive in a knowledge-based, global economy). The higher on the economic value chain the higher the revenue. "The more a product or service is refined and defined, the less market value it will have. For example: tax preparation services have been commodified and automated to the point that they can largely be prepared electronically. Tax form preparation is a Platform 1 service - a foundation service. The higher economic value of this information lies in understanding what the foundation service implies-the "where do we go from here" and the "so whats" of business and finance. Higher Platform services, such as estate and financial planning are where higher economic benefits exist for the future of the profession. Higher Platform services are, and will increasingly be, the most valued services and functions, and therefore will command higher fees and salaries. Traditional services are the foundation from which CPAs can leverage to higher value services." The report describes 7 platforms.

Obviously, to move up the value chain CPAs need to develop expertise for and market higher value services. For some this may represent "thinking out of the box." It appears the CPA Vision Project and the Committee on Assurance Services covered in Chapter 1 have come to similar conclusions.

(**Note**: Internet problems address current issues using Internet sources. Because Internet sites are subject to change, Internet problems and solutions are subject to change. Current information on Internet problems is available at www.prenhall.com/arens/).

Chapter 3

Audit Reports

■ **Review Questions**

3-1 Auditor's reports are important to users of financial statements because they inform users of the auditor's opinion as to whether or not the statements are fairly stated or whether no conclusion can be made with regard to the fairness of their presentation. Users especially look for any deviation from the wording of the standard unqualified report and the reasons and implications of such deviations. Having standard wording improves communications for the benefit of users of the auditor's report. When there are departures from the standard wording, users are more likely to recognize and consider situations requiring a modification or qualification to the auditor's report or opinion.

3-2 The unqualified audit report consists of:

1. *Report title* Auditing standards require that the report be titled and that the title include the word *independent*.
2. *Audit report address* The report is usually addressed to the company, its stockholders, or the board of directors.
3. *Introductory paragraph* The first paragraph of the report does three things: first, it makes the simple statement that the CPA firm has done an *audit*. Second, it lists the financial statements that were audited, including the balance sheet dates and the accounting periods for the income statement and statement of cash flows. Third, it states that the statements are the responsibility of management and that the auditor's responsibility is to express an opinion on the statements based on an audit.
4. *Scope paragraph*. The scope paragraph is a factual statement about what the auditor did in the audit. The remainder briefly describes important aspects of an audit.
5. *Opinion paragraph*. The final paragraph in the standard report states the auditor's conclusions based on the results of the audit.
6. *Name of CPA firm*. The name identifies the CPA firm or practitioner who performed the audit.
7. *Audit report date*. The appropriate date for the report is the one on which the auditor has completed the most important auditing procedures in the field.

The same seven parts are found in a qualified report as in an unqualified report. There are also often one or more additional paragraphs explaining reasons for the qualifications.

3-3 The purposes of the scope paragraph in the auditor's report are to inform the financial statement users that the audit was conducted in accordance with generally accepted auditing standards, in general terms what those standards mean, and whether the audit provides a reasonable basis for an opinion.

3-3 (Continued)
The information in the scope paragraph includes:

1. The auditor followed generally accepted auditing standards.
2. The audit is designed to obtain *reasonable assurance* about whether the statements are free of *material* misstatement.
3. Discussion of the audit evidence accumulated.
4. Statement that the auditor believes the evidence accumulated was appropriate for the circumstances to express the opinion presented.

3-4 The purpose of the opinion paragraph is to state the auditor's conclusions based upon the results of the audit evidence. The most important information in the opinion paragraph includes:

1. The words "in our opinion" which indicate that the conclusions are based on professional judgment.
2. A restatement of the financial statements that have been audited and the dates thereof or a reference to the introductory paragraph.
3. A statement about whether the financial statements were presented fairly and in accordance with generally accepted accounting principles.

3-5 The auditor's report should be dated February 17, 2000, the date on which the auditor completed the most important auditing procedures in the field.

3-6 An unqualified report may be issued under the following five circumstances:

1. All statements—balance sheet, income statement, statement of retained earnings, and statement of cash flows—are included in the financial statements.
2. The three general standards have been followed in all respects on the engagement.
3. Sufficient evidence has been accumulated and the auditor has conducted the engagement in a manner that enables him or her to conclude that the three standards of field work have been met.
4. The financial statements are presented in accordance with generally accepted accounting principles. This also means that adequate disclosures have been included in the footnotes and other parts of the financial statements.
5. There are no circumstances requiring the addition of an explanatory paragraph or modification of the wording of the report.

3-7 When adherence to generally accepted accounting principles would result in misleading financial statements there should be a complete explanation in a separate paragraph. The separate paragraph should fully explain the departure and the reason why generally accepted accounting principles would have resulted in misleading statements. The opinion should be unqualified, but it should refer to the separate paragraph during the portion of the opinion in which generally accepted accounting principles are mentioned.

3-8 An unqualified report with an explanatory paragraph or modified wording is the same as a standard unqualified report *except* that the auditor believes it is necessary to provide additional information about the audit or the financial statements. For a qualified report, either there is a scope limitation (condition 1) or a failure to follow generally accepted accounting principles (condition 2). Under either condition, the auditor concludes that the overall financial statements are fairly presented.

Two examples of an unqualified report with an explanatory paragraph or modified wording are:

1. The entity changed from one generally accepted accounting principle to another generally accepted accounting principle.
2. A report involving the use of other auditors.

3-9 When another CPA has performed part of the audit, the primary auditor issues one of the following types of reports based on the circumstances.

1. No reference is made to the other auditor. This will occur if the other auditor audited an immaterial portion of the statement, the other auditor is known or closely supervised, or if the principal auditor has thoroughly reviewed the other auditor's work.
2. Issue a shared opinion in which reference is made to the other auditor. This type of report is issued when it is impractical to review the work of the other auditor or when a portion of the financial statements audited by the other CPA is material in relation to the total.
3. The report may be qualified if the principal auditor is not willing to assume any responsibility for the work of the other auditor. A disclaimer may be issued if the segment audited by the other CPA is highly material.

3-10 Even though the prior year statements have been restated to enhance comparability, a separate explanatory paragraph is required to explain the change in generally accepted accounting principles in the first year in which the change took place.

3-11 Changes that affect the consistency of the financial statements may involve any of the following:

a. Change in accounting principle
b. Change in reporting entity
c. Corrections of errors involving accounting principles.

An example of a change that affects consistency would be a change in the method of computing depreciation from straight line to an accelerated method. A separate explanatory paragraph is required if the amounts are material.

Comparability refers to items such as changes in estimates, presentation, and events rather than changes in accounting principles. For example, a change in the estimated life of a depreciable asset will affect the comparability of the statements. In that case, no explanatory paragraph for lack of consistency is needed, but the information may require disclosure in the statements.

3-12 The three conditions requiring a departure from an unqualified opinion are:

1. *The scope of the audit has been restricted.* One example is when the client will not permit the auditor to confirm material receivables. Another example is when the engagement is not agreed upon until after the client's year-end when it may be impossible to physically observe inventories.
2. *The financial statements have not been prepared in accordance with generally accepted accounting principles.* An example is when the client insists upon using replacement costs for fixed assets.
3. *The auditor is not independent.* An example is when the auditor owns stock in the client's business.

3-13 A *qualified opinion* states that there has been either a limitation on the scope of the audit or a departure from GAAP in the financial statements, but that the auditor believes that the overall financial statements are fairly presented. This type of opinion may not be used if the auditor believes the exceptions being reported upon are extremely material, in which case a disclaimer or adverse opinion would be used.

An *adverse opinion* states that the auditor believes the overall financial statements are so materially misstated or misleading that they do not present fairly in accordance with GAAP the financial position, results of operations, or cash flows.

A *disclaimer of opinion* states that the auditor has been unable to satisfy him or herself as to whether or not the overall financial statements are fairly presented because of: a significant limitation of the scope of the audit, or a nonindependent relationship under the *Code of Professional Conduct* between the auditor and the client.

Examples of situations that are appropriate for each type of opinion are as follows:

OPINION TYPE	EXAMPLE SITUATION
Disclaimer	Material physical inventories not observed and the inventory cannot be verified through other procedures.
	Lack of independence by the auditor.
Adverse	A highly material departure from GAAP.
Qualified	Inability to confirm the existence of an asset which is material but not extremely material in value.

3-14 The common definition of materiality as it applies to accounting and, therefore, to audit reporting is:

A misstatement in the financial statements can be considered material if knowledge of the misstatement would affect a decision of a reasonable user of the statements.

3-14 (Continued)
Conditions that affect the auditor's determination of materiality include:

- Potential users of the financial statements
- Dollar amounts of the following items: net income before taxes, total assets, current assets, current liabilities, and owners' equity
- Nature of the potential misstatements—certain misstatements, such as fraud, are likely to be more important to users of the financial statements than other misstatements.

3-15 Materiality for lack of independence in audit reporting is easiest to define. If the auditor lacks independence as defined by the *Code of Professional Conduct*, it is always considered highly material and therefore a disclaimer of opinion is always necessary. That is, either the CPA is independent or not independent. For failure to follow GAAP, there are three levels of materiality: immaterial, material, and highly material.

3-16 The auditor's opinion may be qualified by scope limitations caused by client restrictions or by limitations resulting from conditions beyond the client's control. The former occurs when the client will not, for example, permit the auditor to confirm material receivables or physically observe inventories. The latter may occur when the engagement is not agreed upon until after the client's year-end when it may not be possible to physically observe inventories or confirm receivables.

A disclaimer of opinion is issued if the scope limitation is so material that the auditor cannot determine if the overall financial statements are fairly presented. If the scope limitation is caused by the client's restriction the auditor should be aware that the reason for the restriction may be to deceive the auditor. For this reason, a disclaimer is more likely for client restrictions than for conditions beyond anyone's control.

When there is a scope restriction that results in the failure to verify material, but not pervasive accounts, a qualified opinion may be issued. This is more likely when the scope limitation is for conditions beyond the client's control than for restrictions by the client.

3-17 A report with a scope and an opinion qualification is issued when the auditor can neither perform procedures that he or she considers necessary nor satisfy him or herself by using alternative procedures, due to the existence of conditions beyond the client's or the auditor's control, but the amount involved in the financial statements is not highly material. An important part of a scope and opinion qualification is that it results from not accumulating sufficient audit evidence, either because of the client's request or because of circumstances beyond anyone's control.

A report qualified as to opinion only results when the auditor has accumulated sufficient competent evidence but has concluded that the financial statements are not correctly stated. The only circumstance in which an opinion only qualification is appropriate is for material, but not highly material, departures from GAAP.

3-18 The three alternative opinions that may be appropriate when the client's financial statements are not in accordance with GAAP are an unqualified opinion, qualified as to opinion only and adverse opinion. Determining which is appropriate depends entirely upon materiality. An unqualified opinion is appropriate if the GAAP departure is immaterial (standard unqualified) or if the auditor agrees with the client's departure from GAAP (unqualified with explanatory paragraph). A qualified opinion is appropriate when the deviation from GAAP is material but not highly material; the adverse opinion is appropriate when the deviation is highly material.

3-19 The AICPA has such strict requirements on audit opinions when the auditor is not independent because it is important that stockholders and other third parties be absolutely assured that the auditor is unbiased throughout the entire engagement. If users develop the attitude that auditors are not independent of management, the value of the audit function will be greatly reduced, if not eliminated.

3-20 When the auditor discovers more than one condition that requires a departure from or a modification of a standard unqualified report, the report should be modified for each condition. An exception is when one condition neutralizes the other condition. An example would be when the auditor is not independent and there is also a scope limitation. In this situation the lack of independence overshadows the scope limitation. Accordingly, the scope limitation should not be mentioned.

■ **Multiple Choice Questions From CPA Examinations**

3-21 a. (2)   b. (3)   c. (3)   d. (3)

3-22 a. (2)   b. (3)   c. (1)

■ **Discussion Questions and Problems**

3-23 a. The opinion paragraph is not intended to be a certification or a guarantee of the accuracy and correctness of the financial statements, but rather is intended to be an expression of professional judgment based upon a reasonable audit of the statements and underlying records.
       b. "Our audit was performed to detect material misstatements in the financial statements" is flawed because the purpose of the audit is to determine whether financial statements are fairly stated, not to specifically search for material errors and fraud. It also fails to recognize the standards used by the auditor to conduct the engagement.
          "We conducted our audit in accordance with generally accepted auditing standards" identifies the auditor's responsibilities for conduct of the audit, accumulation of evidence and reporting requirements. It is a much broader statement than the alternative clause. It also implies that if the auditor has conducted the audit in accordance with generally accepted auditing standards but does not uncover certain material errors or fraud, the auditor is unlikely to have responsibility for failing to do so.
       c. "Correctly stated" implies absolute accuracy, whereas the alternative report states that no material misstatements exist.

3-23 (Continued)

    d. The reference to generally accepted accounting principles specifies rules which were followed in accounting for the transactions to date; whereas "the true economic conditions" does not identify the specific accounting procedures applied to produce the financial statements.

    e. The name of the CPA firm rather than that of the individual practitioner should appear on the accountant's report because it is the entire firm which accepts responsibility for the report issued.

3-24 a. Items that need not be included in the auditor's report are:

1. That Excelsior is presenting comparative financial statements. (Both years' statements will be referred to in the audit report.)
2. Specific description of the change in method of accounting for long-term construction contracts need not be included in the report since it is discussed in the footnotes. The auditor's report must state that there is a change in accounting principles and refer to the footnote.
3. The fact that normal receivable confirmation procedures were not used should not be disclosed since the auditor was able to satisfy him or herself through alternate audit procedures.
4. The lawsuit need not be discussed in the report since it has been included in a footnote. [*Note*: prior to the issuance of SAS 79, the auditor would have been required to add an explanatory paragraph to the audit report that referred to the footnote.]

    b. The following deficiencies are in Roscoe's report:

1. The audit report is neither addressed nor dated and it does not contain a title. The audit report date should be the last day of field work.
2. The balance sheet is as of a specific date, whereas the income statement and the statement of retained earnings are for a period of time. The scope paragraph should identify the period of time (usually one year).
3. There are comparative statements, but the audit report identifies and deals with only the current year's financial statements. An opinion must also be included for the prior period financial statements.
4. There is no separate introductory paragraph that states the financial statements audited, dates, and the responsibilities of management and the auditor.
5. There is no separate scope paragraph that describes what an audit is. Two required sentences are completely omitted: "An audit includes examining, on a test basis, evidence supporting the amounts and disclosures in the financial statements. An audit also includes assessing the accounting principles used and significant estimates made by management, as well as evaluating the overall financial statement presentation."
6. The audit was made in accordance with generally accepted *auditing* standards rather than *accounting* standards.
7. The word material is excluded from the scope paragraph (free of material misstatement).

3-24 (Continued)

8. An additional paragraph should be included which describes the dividend restrictions and the refusal of the client to present a statement of cash flows.
9. The opinion paragraph states that accounting principles were consistent with those used in the prior year. The opinion paragraph should make no reference to consistency.
10. The opinion paragraph excludes the required phrase, "in all material respects."
11. The opinion paragraph includes the words "generally accepted auditing standards" rather than the phrase "generally accepted accounting principles."
12. A separate paragraph should be included stating that generally accepted accounting principles were not consistently applied.
13. The opinion should be qualified rather than being unqualified. Qualifications are caused by the:
    a. failure to present a statement of cash flows.
    b. failure to disclose the dividend restrictions.

3-25

(a) CONDITION	(b) MATERIALITY LEVEL	(c) TYPE OF REPORT	COMMENTS
1. Scope of the audit has been restricted	Highly material	Disclaimer	Because the client refuses to allow the auditor to expand the scope of his audit, a disclaimer of opinion is appropriate rather than a qualified as to scope and opinion.
2. Scope of the audit has been restricted	Highly material	Disclaimer	The auditor cannot issue an unqualified opinion on the income statement or the statement of cash flows because a disclaimer of opinion is necessary for the beginning balance sheet. The auditor may issue an unqualified opinion on the ending balance sheet and a disclaimer of opinion on the income statement, statement of cash flows, and the beginning balance sheet.
3. Scope of the audit has been restricted	Highly material	Unqualified	The auditor is able to satisfy him or herself that with the use of alternative procedures, a qualified opinion is not necessary.
4. Failure to follow GAAP	Highly material or material. We need additional information regarding the auditor's preliminary judgment about materiality	Adverse (if highly material) or Qualified (if material)	The materiality of twenty percent of net earnings before taxes would be sufficient for many auditors to require an adverse opinion. That materiality question is a matter of auditor judgment.
5. Lack of independence	Not applicable	Disclaimer	Lack of independence by audit personnel on the engagement mandates a disclaimer for lack of independence.
6. None	Not applicable	Unqualified	The company has made a decision to follow a different financing method which is adequately disclosed. There is no change of accounting principle.

3-26

(a) CONDITION	(b) MATERIALITY LEVEL	(c) TYPE OF REPORT	COMMENTS
1. Failure to follow GAAP	Material	Qualified opinion only —except for	The standards require the use of a qualified opinion for the failure to include a statement of cash flows.
2. Substantial doubt about going concern	Material	Unqualified — explanatory paragraph	There is a question about the ability of the company to continue as a going concern. The auditor therefore must issue an unqualified report with a separate explanatory paragraph.
3. Report involving other auditors	Highly material	Unqualified —modified wording	This is a shared audit report in which the auditor will identify the portion of work done by the other auditor in the introductory paragraph and still issue an unqualified opinion. The absolute dollar amounts of assets and revenues, not percentages, must be stated in the introductory paragraph.
4. Scope of the audit has been restricted	Highly material	Disclaimer	The client has restricted the scope of the auditor and the auditor was not able to satisfy him or herself by alternative procedures. Because it was a client restriction rather than a condition beyond the client's control causing the limitation, and because the limitation is highly material, a disclaimer is appropriate.
5. None	Not applicable	Unqualified — standard wording	There is no indication questioning the ability of the business to continue operations. The auditor does not automatically add an explanatory paragraph simply because there is a risky business.
6. None	Immaterial	Unqualified — standard wording	The amount is immaterial. The facts are adequately disclosed in the footnote.

3-27

(a) CONDITION	(b) MATERIALITY LEVEL	(c) TYPE OF REPORT	COMMENT
1. Failure to follow GAAP	Highly material or material, depending upon the amount of the loss and the auditor's preliminary judgment about materiality	Adverse (if highly material) or (4) Qualified opinion only —except for (if material)	Disclosure of this information is required in a footnote. Failure to do so is a violation of GAAP and is likely to result in a qualified opinion, or it could be so material that it requires an adverse opinion.
2. Scope of the audit has been restricted.	Not applicable	Unqualified— standard wording	Because the auditor was able to obtain alternative evidence, no scope qualification is necessary. If there were such a qualification, it would be a qualified scope and opinion or a disclaimer, depending on materiality.
3. Failure to follow GAAP.	Material	Qualified opinion only —except for	Retail Auto Parts has used a replacement cost inventory rather than lower of cost or market. It is not sufficiently material to require an adverse opinion.
4. Failure to follow GAAP.	Highly material	Adverse	FASB No. 2 requires the expending in the current period of all research and development costs regardless of the benefit in future years. Given the materiality of the amount, an adverse opinion would be required.

3-27 (Continued)

(a) CONDITION	(b) MATERIALITY LEVEL	(c) TYPE OF REPORT	COMMENT
5. Scope of the audit has been restricted.	Highly material or material, depending upon the auditor's preliminary judgment about materiality	Disclaimer (if highly material) or Qualified scope and opinion (if material)	Because the auditor was unable to satisfy himself about beginning inventories, it would be necessary to issue either a qualified or disclaimer of opinion on the income statement and statement of cash flows as well as the beginning balance sheet. The use of a qualified or disclaimer would depend upon materiality. An unqualified opinion could be issued for the current period balance sheet.
6. Scope of the audit has been restricted.	Highly material	Disclaimer	Failure of the client to allow the auditor to inspect the minutes book would be a material client-imposed restriction. Due to the importance of the minutes book, a disclaimer would be necessary. The certified copy of all resolutions and actions would not be a satisfactory alternative procedure.
7. None	Not applicable	Unqualified—standard wording	The change of estimated life is a change of condition and not a change in accounting principles. Therefore, an unqualified opinion is appropriate since there is adequate disclosure.

3-28

ITEM NO.	TYPE OF CHANGE	SHOULD AUDITOR'S REPORT BE MODIFIED?
1	An accounting change involving a change from one generally accepted accounting principle to another generally accepted accounting principle.	Yes
2	An accounting change involving a change in an accounting estimate.	No
3	An error correction not involving an accounting principle.	No
4	An accounting change involving a correction of an error in principle which is accounted for as a correction of an error.	Yes
5	An accounting change involving a change in the reporting entity which is a special type of change in accounting principles.	Yes
6	An accounting change involving both a change in accounting principle and a change in accounting estimate. Although the effect of the change in each may be inseparable and the accounting for such a change is the same as that for a change in estimate only, an accounting principle is involved.	Yes
7	Not an accounting change but rather a change in classification.	No
8	An accounting change from one generally accepted accounting principle to another generally accepted accounting principle.	Yes

3-29 a. Unqualified. It is a shared audit opinion. Therefore, an unqualified opinion with modified wording is appropriate.

b. In our opinion, based on our audits and the report of other auditors, the consolidated financial statements referred to above present fairly, in all material respects, the financial position of Farmers Group, Inc. as of December 31, 1999 and 1998, and the results of its operations and its cash flows for the years then ended, in conformity with generally accepted accounting principles.

3-30 The following opinion should be issued:

> Because there were significant deficiencies in internal control that resulted in the lack of detailed records and other supporting data being available for our audit, the scope of our work was not sufficient to enable us to express, and we do not express, an opinion on these financial statements.

The opinion paragraph should immediately follow the paragraph that discusses the scope restriction.

3-31
a. Failure to follow GAAP
b. The answer depends on the level of materiality: *material* - qualified, except for; *highly material* - adverse.

> It cannot be immaterial because in such a circumstance there would be no explanatory paragraph.

c. Assuming the opinion is qualified, it is as follows:

> In our opinion, except for the effects of charging goodwill and certain other intangible assets acquired in two separate acquisitions directly to shareholders' equity, as discussed in the preceding paragraph, the financial statements referred to above present fairly, in all material respects, the financial position of California First Bank and subsidiaries as of December 31, 1998 and 1997, and the results of its operations and its cash flows for the years then ended in conformity with generally accepted accounting principles.
>
> CPA Firm Name
> Los Angeles, California
> Date (end of field work)

3-32 Deficiencies in the staff accountant's tentative report include the following:

1. Report title must include the word independent.
2. The report should generally be addressed to the board of directors or stockholders, not to the audit committee.
3. The introductory paragraph should state, "we have audited," not "we have examined."
4. When the principal auditor decides to make reference to the audit of another auditor, the report should indicate clearly in the introductory paragraph all the division of responsibility regarding the portions of the financial statements audited by each. Also, the opinion paragraph should state that the opinion is based in part on the reports of other auditors. Neither of these were done.
5. When the principal auditor decides to make reference to the audit of the other auditor, the report should disclose the dollar amounts of the portion of the financial statements audited by the other auditor. This was not done.
6. The second paragraph is an inappropriately worded scope paragraph. It should be stated as follows:

3-32 (Continued)

> We conducted our audits in accordance with generally accepted auditing standards. Those standards require that we plan and perform the audit to obtain reasonable assurance about whether the financial statements are free of material misstatement. An audit includes examining, on a test basis, evidence supporting the amounts and disclosures in the financial statements. An audit also includes assessing the accounting principles used and significant estimates made by management, as well as evaluating the overall financial statement presentation. We believe that our audits and the report of other auditors provide a reasonable basis for our opinion.

7. Although the introductory paragraph referred to an audit of the financial statements for the years ended December 31, 1998 and 1997, an opinion was expressed only on the 1998 financial statements.
8. The statement of cash flows was not identified in the opinion paragraph, and financial statements were not referred to in the opinion paragraph as "consolidated."
9. The explanatory sentence for consistency should follow the opinion paragraph, not precede it. Also, the second sentence in the third paragraph should be omitted.
10. There is no inclusion of the phrase, "in all material respects" in the opinion paragraph.

3-33 The auditor's report on his audit of the financial statements of the Young Manufacturing Corporation includes the following deficiencies:

1. The audit report has no title. It should include a phrase such as "independent auditor's report."
2. The audit report is addressed to the president. It is usually more appropriate to address it to the stockholders or board of directors.
3. The date of the auditor's report should be the date of the completion of the auditor's field work, not the balance sheet date.
4. The report includes only two paragraphs. It should be three paragraphs if it is standard wording, or more if there is a violation of GAAP, which there is.
5. There must be reference to both the 1999 and 1998 financial statements in the scope and opinion paragraphs, including a statement about the degree of responsibility the auditor is taking for each year's statements.
6. The auditor's report is deficient because the dates of the balance sheet and the period covered by the income statement are not given. These dates should be given so that the reader will clearly understand that the opinion is limited to specific financial statements. Clarification as to the statements covered by the opinion is imperative because comparative financial statements are presented.
7. The title "Balance Sheet" is used in the report, but "statements of condition" is used as the title of the financial statement. Different titles should not be used because a criterion of professional work is that uniform and accurate terminology be used.

3-33 (Continued)

8. Although the auditor's report states that he audited the Statement of Income and Retained Earnings, the attached financial statements do not include the Retained Earnings statement. All financial statements referred to in the auditor's report should be appended to the report.

   The difference of $66,481 between the opening and closing balances of the Retained Earnings account is not reconcilable to the reported net income for the year of $52,924. Because an amount of $13,557 in the Retained Earnings account is not accounted for, the auditor's report should contain at least a qualification on the grounds of inadequate disclosure. If the audit disclosed that the $13,557 is a net amount of charges and credits to the Retained Earnings account, some of which bear directly upon the current year's income statement, the auditor may be compelled to render an adverse opinion.

9. There is no reference in the introductory paragraph to the responsibilities of the auditor and management.

10. The mandatory standard scope paragraph is excluded.

11. Two items in the Statements of Condition, "Accounts receivable" and "Inventories," are listed as "pledged," but no footnotes or comments disclose the nature or extent of the commitments. The item "other liabilities" probably represents the liability for which the assets serve as security; its nature should be appropriately disclosed in the statements. Also, the terms of the long-term mortgage should be disclosed. Therefore, the auditor should disclose this information in a separate paragraph in the report and his opinion should be appropriately qualified.

12. The auditor's report is written in the first person apparently because the auditor is an individual practitioner. Although some CPAs contend that it is inappropriate for an individual to practice under a style that denotes a partnership, individual practitioners generally use "we" rather than "I" in writing their reports. The "we" used in the report is the so-called "editorial we" and it is used because it is more formal, impersonal, and carries more dignity. As used in auditor's reports "we" is not to be taken in its literal (plural) sense.

13. The opinion paragraph should contain the phrase "in our opinion" to clearly disclose that the statement as to fair presentation is a professional opinion, not a statement of fact.

14. A statement of cash flows is not included in the financial statements nor is it mentioned in the audit report's introductory and opinion paragraphs. A qualified opinion is required when no statement of cash flows is included.

15. The phrase "in all material respects" is not included in the opinion.

16. There should be no reference to consistency in the opinion paragraph.

17. The opinion paragraph should include no reference to what is done on the audit. That should be in the scope paragraph.

18. As stated above, the opinion paragraph should not be unqualified, because of the missing statements of retained earnings and cash flows and the omitted footnotes.

■ Internet Problem Solution: Research Annual Reports

3-1 The U.S. Securities and Exchange Commission (SEC) makes available in electronic form via the Internet most of the forms and reports it receives from publicly traded companies through its EDGAR Database of Corporate Information. This problem explores information available on the SEC's website.

    a. The EDGAR website provides definitional information for SEC-required forms. Please describe what the following SEC filings are:

- **Form S-1** is the basic registration form used to register securities for a public offering – it is required by the Securities Act of 1933.
- **Form 10-K** is the annual report that most reporting companies file with the Commission. It provides a comprehensive overview of the registrant's business. The report must be filed within 90 days after the end of the company's fiscal year. This form is required by the Securities Exchange Act of 1934.
- **Form 10-KSB** is the annual report filed by reporting "small business issuers." It provides a comprehensive overview of the company's business, although its requirements call for slightly less detailed information than required by Form 10-K. The report must be filed within 90 days after the end of the company's fiscal year.

    b. Search the EDGAR database for the Form 10-K filings of the four companies listed below as well as one company of your own choosing. Within the 10-K filings locate the independent auditor's report and identify what type of opinion it is (e.g., unqualified, qualified, disclaimer, adverse) and what type of explanatory paragraph, if any, the report contains (e.g., consistency, going concern, emphasis). (**Hint**: you may be able to search the 10-K by using your Internet browser's "find" command commonly located in the "Edit" menu. Consider using a search term such as "auditor.")

        1. Microsoft Corporation

            (Answer: Standard Unqualified, see report on Companion Website)

        2. Gumtech International, Inc.:

            (Answer: Qualified, see report on Companion Website)

        3. Smart Games Interactive Inc.:

            (Answer: Unqualified with a going concern explanatory paragraph, see report on Companion Website)

        4. Phar-Mor, Inc.:

            (Answer: Qualified Scope and Opinion Report Due to Scope Restriction, and emphasis of matter explanatory paragraph. See report on the Companion Website.)

(**Note**: Internet problems address current issues using Internet sources. Because Internet sites are subject to change, Internet problems and solutions may change. Current information on Internet problems is available at www.prenhall.com/arens/.)

Chapter 4

Professional Ethics

■ **Review Questions**

4-1 The six core ethical values described by the Josephson Institute are:

1. Trustworthiness
2. Respect
3. Responsibility
4. Fairness
5. Caring
6. Citizenship

There are many other potential sources of ethical values, including laws and regulations, church doctrines, codes of professional ethics, and individual organizations' codes of conduct.

4-2 An ethical dilemma is a situation that a person faces in which a decision must be made about the appropriate behavior. There are many possible ethical dilemmas that one can face, such as finding a wallet containing money, or dealing with a supervisor who asks you to work hours without recording them.

An ethical dilemma can be resolved using the six-step approach outlined on p. 78 of the text. The six steps are:

1. Obtain the relevant facts.
2. Identify the ethical issues from the facts.
3. Determine who is affected by the outcome of the dilemma and how each person or group is affected.
4. Identify the alternatives available to the person who must resolve the dilemma.
5. Identify the likely consequence of each alternative.
6. Decide the appropriate action.

4-3 There is a special need for ethical behavior by professionals to maintain public confidence in the profession, and in the services provided by members of that profession. The ethical requirements for CPAs are similar to the ethical requirements of other professions. All professionals are expected to be competent, perform services with due professional care, and recognize their responsibility to clients. The major difference between other professional groups and CPAs is independence. Because CPAs have a responsibility to financial statement users, it is essential that auditors be independent in fact and appearance. Most other professionals, such as attorneys, are expected to be an advocate for their clients.

4-4

PART	PURPOSE
1. Principles of Professional Conduct	1. Provide ideal standards of ethical conduct and help practitioners understand the ideal conduct of a CPA.
2. Rules of conduct	2. Provide minimum standards of ethical conduct stated as specific rules.
3. Interpretation of the rules of conduct	3. Provide formal interpretations of the rules of conduct to answer questions that frequently arise about the rules of conduct.
4. Ethical rulings	4. Provide more detailed guidance to practitioners about interpretation of the rules of conduct for less commonly raised questions.

4-5 *Independence in fact* exists when the auditor is actually able to maintain an unbiased attitude throughout the audit, whereas *independence in appearance* is dependent on others' interpretation of this independence and hence their faith in the auditor.

Activities which may not affect independence in fact, but which are likely to affect independence in appearance are: (Notice that the first two are violations of the *Code of Professional Conduct*.)

1. Ownership of a financial interest in the audited client.
2. Directorship or officer of an audit client.
3. Performance of management advisory or bookkeeping or accounting services and audits for the same company.
4. Dependence upon a client for a large percentage of audit fees.
5. Engagement of the CPA and payment of audit fees by management.

4-6 Independence in auditing means taking an unbiased viewpoint. Users of financial statements would be unlikely to rely on the statements if they believed auditors were biased in issuing audit opinions.

4-7 The rules concerning stock ownership by partners and non-partners:

Partners can never own stock in an audit client. Staff, in a multi-office CPA firm, can own stock when they are assigned to a different office than the one conducting the audit *and* when they are not involved in the audit. Staff in a one-office firm can never own stock in an audit client.

Partner violation - A partner in the San Francisco office owns one share of stock of a client whose audit is conducted by the New York office.

Staff violation - Staff in the New York office owns one share of stock in a client whose audit is conducted by that office.

4-8 The AICPA takes the position that CPA firms can provide management services for an audit client as long as the firm's staff are competent to perform the services and do not subordinate their judgment to management's. Providing additional services to clients is frequently a valuable by-product of the audit. To prohibit such services would be a disservice to both CPA firms and clients.

4-9 Ways to reduce the appearance of the lack of independence are: the use of an audit committee to select auditors made up of directors who are not a part of management; a requirement that all changes of auditors and reasons therefore be reported to the SEC or other regulatory agency; and approval of the CPA firm by stockholders at the annual meeting.

4-10 A CPA firm has several options when it decides it is not competent to perform an audit:

1. Withdraw from the engagement.
2. Obtain the expertise through continuing education and self studies.
3. Hire someone who has the expertise.
4. Work on a consulting basis with another CPA firm.

4-11 A fee based upon the amount of time it takes to complete is *not* a violation of Rule 302. Rule 302 on contingent fees states that professional services for clients receiving assertion opinions shall not be offered or rendered under an agreement whereby no fee will be charged unless a specific finding or result is attained, or where the fee is otherwise contingent upon the findings or results of such services. The purpose of the rule is to prevent sacrificing the quality of audits because of the pressure felt by the auditor in producing the required audit outcome. An example would be the fee being dependent upon the issuance of an unqualified opinion or the obtaining of a loan by a client.

4-12 The following are exceptions to the confidentiality requirement for the CPA's working papers:

1. The confidentiality requirement cannot interfere with the member's obligation to follow generally accepted auditing standards or generally accepted accounting principles.
2. A member must comply with a validly issued subpoena or summons enforceable by order of a court.
3. A review of a member's professional practice under AICPA or state CPA society or state Board of Accountancy authorization is permitted.
4. A member must respond to any inquiry made by the ethics division or trial board of the Institute or a duly constituted investigative or disciplinary body of a state CPA society or Board of Accountancy.

4-13 Audits should be maintained at a high level of quality even if solicitation, advertising, and competitive bidding are allowed for several reasons:

1. Professionals do high quality work because it is a characteristic of being a professional.
2. A reputation of doing high quality work usually pays off in more clients and a more profitable practice.
3. Potential legal liability is also a deterrent to substandard work.
4. The *Code of Professional Conduct* requires a high quality of performance.

4-14 A member is permitted to advertise by Rule 502 except in a false, misleading, or deceptive manner. Interpretation 502-2 clarifies the meaning of false, misleading or deceptive acts, including activities that:

1. Create false or unjustified expectations of favorable results.
2. Imply the ability to influence any court, tribunal, regulatory agency or similar body or official.
3. Contain a representation that specific professional services will be performed for a stated fee, when it was likely at the time of the representation that such fees would be substantially increased and the prospective client was not informed of that likelihood.
4. Contain any other representations that would be likely to cause a reasonable person to misunderstand or be deceived.

When engagements are obtained through the efforts of third parties, Interpretation 502-5 indicates that the member has the responsibility to ascertain that all promotional efforts are within the bounds of the Rules of Conduct.

4-15 Prohibiting paying commissions to obtain clients who receive attestation services in Rule 503 is intended to discourage overly aggressive obtaining of clients by giving "finders' fees" to banks and others in a position to give business rather than on the basis of competitive and other qualifications. Prohibiting receiving commissions for referrals to other CPAs or other providers of services where attestation services are provided is intended to discourage referrals to others on the basis of a "sales commission" rather than the competition of those offering services. Commissions when attestation services are *not* provided are permitted to encourage competition for these types of services.

4-16 A CPA may practice in one of the following forms:

1. A proprietorship
2. A general partnership
3. A general corporation (if permitted by state law)
4. A professional corporation
5. Limited liability company (if permitted by state law)
6. Limited liability partnership (if permitted by state law)

4-17 There are major differences between the nature of the enforcement by the AICPA and a state Board of Accountancy.

- AICPA enforcement: A weighty social sanction since violations are published in the CPA Newsletter. However, AICPA enforcement by itself will not prevent a CPA from practicing public accounting. The AICPA can remove a practitioner from AICPA membership, but not eliminate the right to practice.
- State Board of Accountancy enforcement: A state Board of Accountancy may revoke a practitioner's license to practice public accounting.

■ Multiple Choice Questions From CPA Examinations

4-18   a.   (1)   b.   (3)   c.   (1)

4-19   a.   (1)   b.   (3)   c.   (3)

■ Discussion Questions And Problems

4-20   a.   Rule 101 - Independence. Violation. John Brown is in violation because he is assigned to the office conducting the audit. (This is a one-office CPA firm.)
b. Rule 102 - Integrity and Objectivity. Violation. This rule states that in tax practice, a member may resolve doubt in favor of his or her client as long as there is reasonable support for his or her position. In the example case, the client has provided no support for the unusual deductions. Phyllis Allen has violated Rule 102 by not requiring reasonable support for the deductions.
c. Rule 201 - General Standards. Violation. Interpretation 201-1 states that a member who accepts a professional engagement implies that he or she has the necessary competence to complete the engagement according to professional standards. Bacon has violated the rule since he does not have the expertise to review the work of the consultant hired by Bacon. Bacon should have suggested that the company hire the consultant directly.
d. Rule 301 - Confidential Client Information. Violation. The client should have been notified that the review was to take place, and an attempt made to obtain the client's permission for such review because the review was not a part of an AICPA, state CPA society or Board of Accountancy review program. The firms violated Rule 301 by not obtaining consent from the client for the review.
e. Rule 501 - Acts Discreditable. No violation. The rule is vague and the interpretation would be made by the state Board of Accountancy. In most states this will be a civil action and would not likely be a violation.
f. Rules 101 (Independence) and 102 (Integrity and Objectivity). Violation. Appearance of independence has been impaired by Bill Wendal's agency's financial dealing with his audit clients and participation in a business which impairs his objectivity. It is also a conflict of duties to recommend his own firm to review the adequacy of the existing insurance coverage of existing clients.

4-20 (Continued)

    g. Rule 101 - Independence. No violation. If the services performed conform to the requirements of Interpretation 101-3, independence of Rankin would not be considered to be impaired. There would be a violation of SEC rules if the client is publicly held.

4-21 a. No violation as long as Williams does *not* perform or give advice on management functions of the organization. See Interpretation 101-4.

    b. Violation. Rule 505 states that all owners of the firm shall be persons who actively provide services to the firm's clients. There is a violation of rule 505 because administrative personnel are responsible *primarily* for office administration, and do not directly provide services to the firm's clients. In addition, there may be a violation if the state in which the firm operates does not allow incorporation of CPA firms.

    c. No violation. 101-3 permits the performance of other services for clients. Before a member performs such services, he or she must carefully evaluate the potential effect of such services on independence. The member should establish a clear understanding with the client, and should not be responsible for preparing source documents, originating data, or performing any management functions.

    d. Violation if the services performed are attestation related, otherwise, no violation. A CPA is not permitted to pay a commission to obtain a client for attestation related services. (Rule 503) This rule is intended to discourage obtaining clients on the basis of a commission to a decision maker, rather than on the basis of the quality of the attestation services or fee to the client.

    e. No violation. Former Rule 401 and 502 would have prohibited this.

    f. No Violation. This is normal practice and is done as a part of almost all audits.

    g. No violation. Rule 502 on advertising permits the use of promotional efforts designating specialties or areas of practice as long as the advertising is not false, misleading or deceptive.

    h. No violation. The only questionable part of the information is the statement by the tax article that Gutowski is a tax expert. It may be difficult for Gutowski to demonstrate that he is in fact an expert, but the interpretations of Rule 502 no longer preclude him from making such a statement.

    i. Violation. Rule 301 does not distinguish between audit, tax, and management advisory services-related working papers. He has therefore violated the rules.

    j. No violation. There are no longer rules restricting such practice.

4-22 a. An audit committee is a special committee formed by the board of directors and made up of board members. It is ideally a group of outside directors who have no active day-to-day operations role and who are a liaison between the independent auditor and the board of directors. The audit committee assists and advises the full board of directors, and, as such, aids the board in fulfilling its responsibility for public financial reporting.

4-22 (Continued)
    b. The functions of an audit committee may include the following:

1. Select the independent auditor; discuss audit fee with the auditor; review auditor's engagement letter.
2. Review the independent auditor's overall audit plan (scope, purpose, and general audit procedures).
3. Review the annual financial statements before submission to the full board of directors for approval.
4. Review the results of the audit including experiences, restrictions, cooperation received, findings, and recommendations. Consider matters that the auditor believes should be brought to the attention of the directors or shareholders.
5. Review the independent auditor's evaluation of the company's internal controls.
6. Review the company's accounting, financial, and operating controls.
7. Review the reports of internal audit staff.
8. Review interim financial reports to shareholders before they are approved by the board of directors.
9. Review company policies concerning political contributions, conflicts of interest, and compliance with federal, state, and local laws and regulations, and investigate compliance with those policies.
10. Review financial statements that are part of prospectuses or offering circulars; review reports before they are submitted to regulatory agencies.
11. Review independent auditor's observations of financial and accounting personnel.
12. Participate in the selection and establishment of accounting policies; review the accounting for specific items or transactions as well as alternative treatments and their effects.
13. Review the impact of new or proposed pronouncements by the accounting profession or regulatory bodies.
14. Review the company's insurance program.
15. Review and discuss the independent auditor's management letter.

    c. Management is frequently under considerable pressure from stockholders and the board of directors to maintain high earnings for the company. In some cases this may in turn motivate management to put pressure on auditors to permit a violation of accounting principles and therefore affect the reported earnings and disclosures in the financial statements. The board of directors has a greater responsibility to the stockholders for fairness in reported earnings. Directors, especially those who are outside directors, have less responsibility for high reported earnings.

       Directors are also, therefore, less likely to put pressure on auditors to deviate from high professional standards. The audit committee can therefore deal with the auditor in a less biased manner than can management. In addition, the board of directors has a legal responsibility to review the policies and actions of management, therefore there is considerable incentive for them to work closely with the auditor. A small committee of outside directors from the audit committee are therefore equipped to help the

4-22 (Continued)

      auditor to maintain a more independent relationship with the client. If management exerts any pressure on the auditor, the auditor is likely to discuss that with the audit committee and thereby resolve the problem.

   d. The criticism of audit committees has been made by many smaller CPA firms. There may be some validity to the comment. At the same time, audit committees do have a responsibility to help a company control costs. Therefore if the cost of a smaller audit firm is significantly less than a large firm, assuming equal quality, the audit committee would be obligated to use the less expensive firm.

      Practically, the criticism has little impact. Only larger companies with outside directors are likely to form an audit committee. Typically these companies cannot be served adequately by small CPA firms, especially if the client has multiple offices in different cities or nations. The criticism would likely be somewhat more valid if audit committees were used by small companies. Even then there is little evidence to support the statement that audit committee members' primary concern is to reduce their exposure to legal liability. Hopefully they have the best interest of the company in mind.

4-23 a. The changes in the rules of conduct concerning advertising, competitive bidding, offers of employment and encroachment are all a result of intervention by the federal government with the rule setting of the AICPA. The changes are aimed at protecting the rights of employees and those wishing to compete with existing CPAs.

      The increased competition is likely to strain the relationship between competing CPA firms and is also likely to result in a more competitive practicing environment. It may well also increase the opportunities for professionals to set up their own practices in competition with other CPA firms who are not serving a given set of clients.

   b. The likely benefits to clients and users of financial statements may be reduced audit costs due to competition. That may come about through urging firms to be more efficient and to charge more competitive fees even if the same level of service is provided. If there is excess competition, the effect may be to reduce the quality of audits and thereby result in inaccurate accounting information. Hopefully, legal liability and professional responsibility will prevent that.

   c. This is a highly subjective question for which there is no clear cut solution. The effect appears to be a reduction of audit fees through increased competitive bidding and aggressive solicitation by many firms. Large CPA firms appear to continue to do well financially but many professionals believe that being a partner in a national CPA firm is far more difficult and demanding than before. One effect of the rules has been the expansion of large CPA firms into the areas once dominated by smaller firms. At the same time, there is now greater competition between the larger firms for larger clients and therefore a more competitive environment.

      Smaller CPA firms are prospering throughout the United States. There are however high levels of competition between different smaller CPA firms and also between large and small CPA firms. It is the opinion of the authors that although competition has increased, there are still significant opportunities for both large and small CPA firms in the U.S.A. We see no evidence that either of the groups is dominating the other.

4-23 (Continued)

Young professionals beginning their career may receive more on the job pressures because of the competitive environment. There is some evidence of that by the continued high turnover in personnel working for CPA firms. It is unquestionably easier for a young professional to begin his own practice. They can more easily solicit business and start a professional practice. They will of course be competing in a somewhat more competitive environment.

A company obtaining audits and users of financial statements will both benefit if competition has the effect of lowering audit costs without reducing quality. It is difficult to determine whether that is actually happening, but it appears to be. Overall, the desirability of these changes depends upon one's point of view. These changes are likely to make the profession more competitive. The effect on smaller CPA firms, audit fees, audit quality and competition among firms is less certain.

4-24
a. Independence is essential for an auditor because users of financial statements expect an unbiased viewpoint in the CPA's attestation to the fairness of the financial statements. If users believe that auditors are not independent, the value of the audit function is eliminated.

b. Most other professions (attorneys, doctors, dentists, etc.) represent their clients and perform services intended primarily to assist their clients. For this reason no assumption of independence is required. The importance of independence for CPAs is similar to that for judges. For both, a nonadvocacy position is essential.

c. Independence in appearance is how independent the auditor appears to outsiders such as users of financial statements. Independence in fact refers to whether the auditor has maintained an attitude of independence throughout the engagement. For example an auditor could possibly maintain an attitude of independence in fact even though he or she held shares of stock in a company and performed the audit (the auditor would have violated Rule 101). However, the auditor would not likely be independent in appearance in such a situation. Both independence in appearance and fact are essential and the *Code of Professional Conduct* concerns both.

d.
1. He has violated the *Code of Professional Conduct*. Rule 101 prohibits any direct ownership by a partner or shareholder.
2. Such a small ownership is unlikely to have any impact on a partner's objectivity in evaluating the financial statements. It is unlikely to affect the partner's independence in fact.
3. Such ownership could affect the appearance of independence and therefore impact the reputation and credibility of auditors. Additionally these strict requirements eliminate any controversy as to the line between a material and immaterial ownership. It also shows outsiders the importance of independence to auditors and therefore hopefully improves the reputation of the profession.

4-24 (Continued)

e.

INDEPENDENCE IN FACT	INDEPENDENCE IN APPEARANCE	CONSEQUENCES
1. May cause the auditor to permit misstatements to enhance personal wealth.	Users may perceive that auditors would permit misstatements to enhance personal wealth.	Minor, if any.
2. Person doing this audit may not do the audit work carefully because he or she did the bookkeeping.	Users may perceive that the auditor may not independently audit his or her own work.	Some clients find it less expensive to have bookkeeping services performed by an outside service. It is often less expensive to have this done by the auditor because the auditor will already be knowledgeable about the business.
3. There may be an absence of a careful independent check of the entries or preparation of the statements because they were originally prepared by the auditor.	Users may believe that the auditor may not independently audit his or her own work or that of a staff person from his or her firm.	Many clients lack technical expertise in auditing. Having services performed by the auditor is sometimes the least costly alternative.
4. The auditor may be reluctant to criticize or not rely on an accounting system that was originally recommended by the CPA firm. Additionally, if the CPA firm obtains considerable revenue from management advisory services, the CPA firm may fear the loss of the client and therefore be controlled by management.	Users may perceive either of the two concerns discussed under independence in fact.	A CPA firm gains considerable knowledge about a client and its business during the audit. Due to this knowledge, management services can often be provided by the same CPA firm at a lower cost than alternative sources such as other CPA firms or management consultants.

4-24 (Continued)

INDEPENDENCE IN FACT	INDEPENDENCE IN APPEARANCE	CONSEQUENCES
5. The audit team may become complacent due to familiarity and not carefully evaluate potential misstatements.	Users may perceive the possibility of complacency.	Knowledge gained by the audit team about a client's business is essential to evaluate when misstatements in the financial statements are likely and to plan the audit. It is costly for a new audit team to obtain that knowledge.
6. The CPA firm may become complacent due to familiarity and not carefully evaluate potential misstatements.	Users may perceive the possibility of complacency.	The same conclusions reached in 5 about the audit team is applicable to CPA firms. The cost of a new CPA firm of obtaining the knowledge is even greater because of confidentiality requirements and communication difficulties between CPA firms.
7. The auditor may be unwilling to disagree with management for fear of being terminated.	Users may perceive that the auditor is unwilling to disagree with management.	Someone has to select the auditor. Management is usually in the best position to evaluate the effectiveness and cost of alternative auditors.

    f.   The AICPA *Code of Professional Conduct* prohibits only e(1). The SEC prohibits e(1) and e(2), but e(3) would also be considered a violation if the adjusting entries were so extensive that they are, in essence, bookkeeping services.

4-25 The *Code of Professional Conduct* and interpretations are not clear as to what constitutes a violation in these three situations. A central point is that Marie Janes must maintain independence in fact and appearance because she is not an employee of the company and must not give the impression that she is one.

4-25 (Continued)

(a) RULES OF CONDUCT VIOLATED?	(b) APPROPRIATE ACTION?
1. Marie Janes has likely not violated the rules; the discount is available to customers on a widespread basis. Presumably many of the employees of the CPA firm buy automobiles from the agency.	1. Marie Janes should discuss the discount with the firm's managing partner if she intends or wants to buy the automobile. She should certainly not feel compelled to buy the automobile but she should also not automatically turn it down. The situation would be entirely different if the sale were limited to employees. In such a case it would likely be a violation.
2. If Marie Janes were to eat there on an ongoing basis that would likely be a violation of the rules of conduct. It would not likely be a violation if she occasionally eats with employees she is dealing with at the audit.	2. Marie Janes should eat elsewhere if it is practical to do so but if the only practical place for her to eat is the lunch room, she should make arrangements with her firm to make certain that the company is reimbursed for the expenses.
3. Accepting such a gift is likely to be a violation of the rules of conduct. That gift is reasonably large and would be considered by many employees as equivalent to a bonus.	3. Ideally Janes should not accept the gift and state that since she is not an employee, she would prefer not to take it. If she believes that it would be embarrassing to the company, she should graciously accept it and return it with an explanation of her reasons as soon as practical.

■ Cases

4-26 Forming a corporation of the nature of the one formed by Gilbert is no longer expressly prohibited by the interpretations of Rule 505. However, the corporation is in violation of the ownership requirements under Rule 505. A majority of the firm's financial interests and voting rights must belong to CPAs. Since 50% of the stock is owned by Bradley, who is not a CPA, there is a violation of Rule 505.

The failure to issue a qualified or adverse opinion for the client's failure to disclose the existence of and terms of the lien against assets is a violation of Rule 203 of the *Code of Professional Conduct*. Adequate footnotes are an integral part of the financial statements and a pledging of an asset of the nature described requires disclosure.

Finally, Gilbert is in violation of Rule 301 for disclosing confidential client information to the insurance company without Grandtime's permission.

4-27 The answers to these questions are more judgmental than most others in the chapter. They may, in some cases, be a violation of the spirit of the *Code* if the CPA is acting in a certain manner, and they may not be a violation if the CPA is acting in a different manner. For example, in 4, if Davis is sending business executives in small companies to his small loan company, there's likely to be a violation of the rule of conduct. On the other hand if he recommends the small loan company along with several others, only for those clients who truly need the services of a small loan company, he is not likely to be in violation. (Changing the facts throughout the discussion may increase the value of the case.)

1. This would not be a violation of the rules of conduct or interpretations. It is common and acceptable for a CPA firm to inform a member of management of the availability of limited partnerships. Similarly it is common for management to inform the CPA firm of such investment opportunities. In many cases the limited partners do not know of the other investors in the limited partnership. If the CPA and owner of Marshall Marine Co. either earn or lose significant sums in the investment, it should have no effect on their relationship or on the audit of Marshall Marine Co.

2. Contingent fee arrangements between the CPA and the client are a violation of the rules for clients receiving attestation services. However, Rule 302 specifically states that fees are not regarded as being contingent if fixed by courts or other public authorities or, *in tax matters, if determined based on the results of judicial proceedings and the findings of government agencies.*

    This situation involves tax matters the results of which are determined by judicial proceedings, therefore there is no violation.

3. Rule 502 permits advertising as long as it is not false, misleading, or deceptive. The advertising expressly states two facts: 14 of 36 of the largest savings and loans companies are audited by their firm and second, the average audit fee, as a percentage of total assets, is lower than any of the other CPA firms in the city. Contel must be able to support those factual statements. Assuming he can, there is no violation. However, it may be difficult to support the comparison to the fees of other firms.

4. There is no violation because Rule 504--Incompatible Occupations no longer exists. There may have been a violation under old Rule 504 if Davis or his employees consistently sent clients of Davis to the small loan company and/or encouraged them to make loans from such company.

5. There may well be a material indirect interest in the other clients. Elbert owns a material amount of stock and if the mutual fund in turn invests a large portion of its money in an audit client of Elbert, Elbert in essence has a material investment in an audit client.

    Simply because the mutual fund's investment has increased dramatically in the audit client does not mean there is a material investment, however. For example, it may have increased from one percent to three percent of the total holdings of the mutual company. Nevertheless Elbert must evaluate whether the holding could be a material indirect investment under Rule 101.

4-27 (Continued)

6. It is essential that Finigan retain both an attitude of independence in fact and in appearance. It is not possible to determine if Finigan is maintaining an attitude of independence in fact, given her involvement in the company, but it is certainly possible that she is. Finigan is not necessarily violating the *Code of Professional Conduct*. She does the audit, tax return, bookkeeping and management services work for the client, but that is not a violation.

    It is questionable whether Finigan is maintaining an attitude of independence in appearance, especially given the comments by Gilligan. It is essential that she maintain an attitude of independence throughout all her work. So she must be careful that she is not on the side of Gilligan without consideration of her professional responsibilities in conducting the audits and in all other aspects of her professional responsibilities.

4-28

a. It's an ethical dilemma for Barbara because she has a decision to make about what behavior is appropriate. If she throws the schedules away, as suggested by her supervisor, she may not be carrying out her professional responsibility to the public or the client. If she does not throw the schedules away, she will likely cause a confrontation between herself and her supervisor.

b.
   (1) Relevant facts: A number of misstatements were discovered. The aggregate of all discovered and undiscovered misstatements may be material. The audit supervisor wants Barbara to throw away some of her work.
   (2) Ethical issues: Is it ethical to throw away the schedules containing some small misstatements when her supervisor instructs her to do so?
   (3) Who is affected and how?

WHO IS AFFECTED?	HOW?
Barbara	1. Being asked to ignore misstatements is a possible violation of Rule 102. 2. Performance evaluation may be affected. 3. Future with firm may be affected.
Jack	1. Future with firm may be affected. 2. Performance evaluation may be affected.
Green, Thresher & Co., CPAs	1. If audit is completed late, they may lose the engagement. 2. May be sued if material misstatements are not detected. 3. Client may be unhappy with auditor if misstatements are subsequently discovered.
Delaney Fabrics	1. May not have opportunity to correct misstatements if they are not brought to light. 2. May be required to adjust financial statements if misstatements exist.

4-28 (Continued)
- (4) Alternatives
  - (a) Throw away schedules.
  - (b) Inform Jack that she will not throw schedules away.
  - (c) Talk to manager or partner about Jack's request.
  - (d) Refuse to work on the engagement.
  - (e) Quit the firm.
- (5) Consequences
  - (a) The misstatements may be discovered subsequently and the firm may lose the client, or be sued. Even if the misstatements are not material, the client may be justifiably upset because the problems giving rise to the misstatements may have been solved sooner.
  - (b) Barbara informs Jack that she won't throw away schedules. This may result in a confrontation. She may get an unfavorable review.
  - (c) If she talks to the manager or partner, they may admire Barbara's attempt to be ethical, or they may think she is out of line for bypassing Jack's authority without discussing the matter with him in detail.
  - (d) If she refuses to continue on the engagement, it will not look good on Barbara's record. She may be labeled as "hard to get along with."
  - (e) If she quits, she will likely miss out on some potentially valuable experiences in public accounting.
- (6) Appropriate Action

  Only Barbara can decide. One reasonable approach is for Barbara to start by discussing the matter further with Jack. She should listen carefully to his reasoning and express her reservations about throwing the schedules away. She should not subordinate her judgment to Jack, as this would be a violation of Rule of Conduct 102. If Jack satisfies her that it is acceptable to throw the schedules away (this seems unlikely in the circumstances), then she may be justified in doing so. However, if she still has reservations, she should inform Jack that she intends to contact a manager or partner.

4-29
a. Practitioners voluntarily agree to abide by the *Code* as they enter public practice. It is imperative that individuals at least comply with the minimum standards specified by the *Code of Professional Conduct*, despite pressures one may face. Concealing a known material misstatement in a client's financial statements is clearly a violation of a practitioner's responsibility to society.

b. Bob Smith in essence condoned Oake's behavior by doing nothing. His inaction is worthy of sanction by his firm, the AICPA, and the state Board of Accountancy.

c. At a minimum, practitioners must draw the line by complying with the Rules of Conduct specified in the *Code of Professional Conduct*. Violations of the *Code* are not acceptable. Hopefully, most practitioners strive to uphold the ethical principles specified in the *Code of Professional Conduct*.

4-30
1. Relevant Facts
   a. Frank believes the revenue recognition method is inappropriate.
   b. The partner believes the revenue recognition method is appropriate.
2. Ethical issue: Is it ethical for Frank to conceal his disagreement with the partner by not writing a statement which follows the requirements of SAS 22 (AU 311)?
3. Who is affected and how?

WHO IS AFFECTED?	HOW?
Frank	1. Promotion, future pay, and ability to meet personal financial obligations may be affected. 2. His relationship with partners and clients may also be affected.
Partner	1. Promotion, future pay, and ability to meet personal financial obligations may be affected. 2. Her relationship with partners and clients may also be affected.
The firm, Bright & Lorren	1. The firm faces potential liability if an improper decision is made regarding revenue recognition. 2. May lose the audit client.
The client, Machine International	1. Decision may affect the client's ability to obtain financing. 2. Decision may affect stockholder perceptions of management performance.
Users of Machine International's Financial Statements	1. Decision may affect individual decisions related to investments in Machine International.

4. Alternatives
   a. Write a statement and inform other partners if engagement partner refuses to include the statement in the working papers.
   b. Agree with the partner.
5. Consequences
   a. If Frank agrees with the partner, a potentially inappropriate accounting method may lead to an unqualified opinion on materially misstated financial statements.
   b. Other partners may be upset with Frank for failing to disclose his feelings on the matter.
   c. The firm could be sued and suffer losses.
   d. On the other hand, perhaps the partner is right and the revenue recognition method is appropriate.
   e. If Frank writes the statement and expresses his disagreement, he may be labeled as "hard to get along with." However, most firms which do high-quality audit work encourage practitioners at all levels to express their views on matters which require professional judgment such as the appropriateness of a given accounting principle.

4-30 (Continued)

6. Appropriate action:

Frank should express his opinion, leaving room for the possibility that he may be wrong. He should be respectful of the position of all other partners in the firm. Most, if not all, of the other partners in the firm would probably appreciate Frank's willingness to express his opinion regarding the inappropriateness of the revenue recognition method used by the client.

■ Internet Problem Solution: AICPA Code of Professional Conduct—Ethics Rulings and Case

4-1 a. Imagine a CPA has provided extensive advisory services for a client. In that connection, the member has attended board meetings, interpreted financial statements, forecasts and other analyses, counseled on potential expansion plans, and counseled on banking relationships. Would the independence of the member be considered to be impaired under these circumstances?

What is your opinion on the above question? The answer to many such questions can be found in Ethic Rulings associated with the AICPA Code of Professional Conduct. The AICPA publishes the Code, interpretations and rulings on its website (http://www.aicpa.org/about/code/index.htm). What did the AICPA rule in this instance? To find out, locate Ethics Ruling #8 in "ET Section 191 - Ethics Rulings on Independence."

The AICPA ruled that the independence of the member would not be considered to be impaired because the member's role is advisory in nature.

b. The Illinois CPA Society's website includes an area on CPA Ethics (http://www.icpas.org/ethindex.htm). Visit the cite, and complete the following exercises:

1. Who may file a complaint against a CPA licensed to practice in the state of Illinois?

    Anyone...Society member, non-member, taxpayer, public-at-large, student, etc.

2. In the ethics area of the Illinois CPA Society website, the society includes several ethics cases based on past complaints. Read and consider the case, "Stop Thief! The Case of the Almost Stolen Clients." What lesson can be learned from this case?

    The case actually has a section called "LESSONS LEARNED," which reads, "While we all like to make our resumes as informative as possible, make sure the information is correct, and that you don't pretend to be who you are not. Information that is false, misleading, or deceptive can get you into big trouble!"

(**Note**: Internet problems address current issues using Internet sources. Because Internet sites are subject to change, Internet problems and solutions are subject to change. Current information on Internet problems is available at www.prenhall.com/arens/).

Chapter 5

Legal Liability

■ **Review Questions**

5-1 Several factors that have affected the increased number of lawsuits against CPAs are:

1. The growing awareness of the responsibilities of public accountants on the part of users of financial statements.
2. An increased consciousness on the part of the SEC regarding its responsibility for protecting investors' interests.
3. The greater complexities of auditing and accountancy due to the increasing size of businesses, the globalization of business, and the intricacies of business operations.
4. Society's increasing acceptance of lawsuits.
5. Large civil court judgments against CPA firms which have encouraged attorneys to provide legal services on a contingent fee basis.
6. The willingness of many CPA firms to settle their legal problems out of court.
7. The difficulty courts have in understanding and interpreting technical accounting and auditing matters.

5-2 The most important positive effects are the increased quality control by CPA firms that is likely to result from actual and potential lawsuits and the ability of injured parties to receive remuneration for their damages. Negative effects are the energy required to defend groundless cases and the harmful impact on the public's image of the profession. Legal liability may also increase the cost of audits to society, by causing CPA firms to increase the evidence accumulated.

5-3 Business failure is the risk that a business will fail financially and, as a result, will be unable to pay its financial obligations. Audit risk is the risk that the auditor will conclude that the financial statements are fairly stated and an unqualified opinion can therefore be issued when, in fact, they are materially misstated.

When there has been a business failure, but not an audit failure, it is common for statement users to claim there was an audit failure, even if the most recently issued audited financial statements were fairly stated. Many auditors evaluate the potential for business failure in an engagement in determining the appropriate audit risk.

5-4 The prudent person concept states that a person is responsible for conducting a job in good faith and with integrity, but is not infallible. Therefore, the auditor is expected to conduct an audit using due care, but does not claim to be a guarantor or insurer of financial statements.

5-5 The difference between fraud and constructive fraud is that in fraud the wrongdoer intends to deceive another party whereas in constructive fraud there is a lack of intent to deceive or defraud. Constructive fraud is highly negligent performance.

5-6 Many CPA firms willingly settle lawsuits out of court in an attempt to minimize legal costs and avoid adverse publicity. This has a negative effect on the profession when a CPA firm agrees to settlements even though it believes that the firm is not liable to the plaintiffs. This encourages others to sue CPA firms where they probably would not to such an extent if the firms had the reputation of contesting the litigation. Therefore, out-of-court settlements encourage more lawsuits and, in essence, increase the auditor's liability because many firms will pay even though they do not believe they are liable.

5-7 An auditor's best defense for failure to detect a defalcation is an audit properly conducted in accordance with GAAS. SAS 82 (AU 316) states that the auditor should assess the risk of material misstatements of the financial statements due to fraud. Based on this assessment, the auditor should design the audit to provide *reasonable assurance* of detecting material misstatements due to fraud. SAS 82 also states that because of the nature of fraud (including defalcations), a properly designed and executed audit may not detect a material misstatement due to fraud.

5-8 Contributory negligence used in legal liability of auditors is a defense used by the auditor when he or she claims the client or user also had a responsibility in the legal case. An example is the claim by the auditor that management knew of the potential for fraud because of weaknesses in internal control, but refused to correct them. The auditor thereby claims that the client contributed to the fraud by not correcting material weaknesses in internal control.

5-9 An engagement letter from the auditor to the client specifies the responsibilities of both parties and states such matters as fee arrangements and deadlines for completion. The auditor may also use this as an opportunity to inform the client that the responsibility for the prevention of fraud is that of the client. A well-written engagement letter can be useful evidence in the case of a lawsuit, given that the letter spells out the terms of the engagement agreed to by both parties. Without an engagement letter, the terms of the engagement are easily disputed.

5-10 Liability to clients under common law has remained relatively unchanged for many years. If a CPA firm breaches an implied or expressed contract with a client, there is a legal responsibility to pay damages. Traditionally the distinction between privity of contract with clients and lack of privity of contract with third parties was essential in common law. The lack of privity of contract with third parties meant that
third parties would have no rights with respect to auditors except in the case of gross negligence.

That case's precedent was established by the Ultramares case. In recent years some courts have interpreted Ultramares more broadly to allow recovery by third parties if those third parties were known and recognized to be relying upon the work of the professional at the time the professional performed the services (*foreseen users*). Still others have rejected the Ultramares' doctrine entirely and have held the CPAs liable to anyone who relies on the CPAs' work, if that work is performed negligently. The liability of third parties under common law continues in a state of uncertainty. In some jurisdictions the precedence of Ultramares is still recognized whereas in others there is no significant distinction between liability to third parties and to clients for negligence.

5-11 In recent years the auditor's liability to a third party has become affected by whether the party is known or unknown. Now a known third party, under common law, usually has the same rights as the party that is privy to the contract. An unknown third party usually has fewer rights. The approach followed in most states is the *Restatement of Torts* approach to the foreseen users concept. Under the *Restatement of Torts* approach, foreseen users must be members of a reasonably limited and identifiable group of users that have relied on the CPA's work, even though those persons were not specifically known to the CPA at the time the work was done.

5-12 The differences between the auditor's liability under the securities acts of 1933 and 1934 are because the 1933 act imposes a heavier burden on the auditor. Third party rights as presented in the 1933 act are:

1. Any third party who purchases securities described in the registration statement may sue the auditor.
2. Third party users do not have the burden of proof that they relied on the financial statements or that the auditor was negligent or fraudulent in doing the audit. They must only prove that the financial statements were misleading or not fairly stated.

In conjunction with these third party rights, the auditor has a greater burden in that he or she must demonstrate that:

1. The statements are not materially misstated.
2. An adequate audit was conducted.
3. The user did not incur the loss because of misleading financial statements.

The liability of auditors under the 1934 act is not as harsh as under the 1933 act. In this instance, the burden of proof is on third parties to show that they relied on the statements and that the misleading statements were the cause of the loss.

The principal focus of accountants' liability under the 1934 act is on Rule 10b-5. Under Rule 10b-5, accountants *generally* can only be held liable if they intentionally or recklessly misrepresent information intended for third-party use. Many lawsuits involving accountants' liability under Rule 10b-5 have resulted in accountants being liable when they knew all of the relevant facts, but merely made poor judgments. In recent years, however, courts have decided that poor judgment doesn't necessarily prove fraud on the part of the accountant.

5-13 The auditor's *legal liability to the client* can result from the auditor's failure to properly fulfill his or her contract for services. The lawsuit can be for breach of contract, which is a claim that the contract was not performed in the manner agreed upon, or it can be a tort action for negligence. An example would be the client's detection of a misstatement in the financial statements, which would have been discovered if the auditor had performed all audit procedures required in the circumstances (e.g., misstatement of inventory resulting from an inaccurate physical inventory not properly observed by the auditor).

5-13 (Continued)

The auditor's *liability to third parties under common law* results from any loss incurred by the claimant due to reliance upon misleading financial statements. An example would be a bank which has loans outstanding to an audited company. If the audit report did not disclose that the company had contingent liabilities which subsequently became real liabilities and forced the company into bankruptcy, the bank could proceed with legal action against the auditors for the material omission.

Civil liability under the Securities Act of 1933 provides the right of third parties to sue the auditor for damages if a registration statement or a prospectus contains an untrue statement of a material fact or omits to state a material fact that would result in misleading financial statements. The third party does not have to prove reliance upon the statements or even show his or her loss resulted from the misstatement. An example would be stock purchased by an investor in what appears, based upon audited financial statements, to be a sound company. If the investor relied upon the financial statements which are later found to be inaccurate or misleading, and the investment loses value as a result of a situation existing but not disclosed at the date of the financial statements, the investor could file legal proceedings against the auditor for negligence.

Civil liability under the Securities Act of 1934 relates to audited financial statements issued to the public in annual reports or 10-K reports. Rule 10b-5 of the Act prohibits fraudulent activity by direct sellers of securities. Several federal court decisions have extended the application of Rule 10b-5 to accountants, underwriters and others. An example would be an auditor knowingly permitting the issuance of fraudulent financial statements of a publicly-held client.

Criminal liability of the auditor may result from federal or state laws if the auditor defrauds another person through knowingly being involved with false financial statements. An example of an act which could result in criminal liability would be an auditor's certifying financial statements which he or she knows overstate income for the year and the financial position of the company at the audit date.

5-14 The SEC can impose the following sanctions against a CPA firm:

1. Suspend the right to conduct audits of SEC clients.
2. Prohibit a firm from accepting any new clients for a period.
3. Require a review of the firm's practice by another CPA firm.
4. Require firms to participate in continuing education programs.

5-15 Some of the ways in which the profession can positively respond and reduce liability in auditing are:
1. Continued research in auditing.
2. Standards and rules must be revised to meet the changing needs of auditing.
3. The AICPA can establish requirements that the better practitioners always follow in an effort to increase the overall quality of auditing.
4. Establish new peer review requirements.
5. CPA firms should oppose all unfounded lawsuits rather than settling out of court.
6. Users of financial statements need to be better educated regarding the attest function.
7. Improper conduct and performance by members must be sanctioned.
8. Lobby for changes in state and federal laws concerning accountants' liability.

■ Multiple Choice Questions From CPA Examinations

5-16 a. (2)   b. (4)   c. (2)   d. (2)

5-17 a. (1)   b. (2)

5-18 a. (3)   b. (1)   c. (3)

■ Discussion Questions and Problems

5-19 a. Cosden and Co. should use the defenses of meeting generally accepted auditing standards and contributory negligence. The fraud perpetuated by Joslin Supply Company was a reasonably complex one and difficult to uncover except by the procedures suggested by Cosden.

    In most circumstances it would not be necessary to physically count all inventory at different locations on the same day. Furthermore the president of the company contributed to the failure of finding the fraud by refusing to follow Cosden's suggestion. There is evidence of that through his signed statement.

    b. There are two defenses Cosden and Company should use in a suit by East City National Bank. First there is a lack of privity of contract. Even though this was a known third party, it does not necessarily mean that there is any duty to that party in this situation. That defense is unlikely to be successful in most jurisdictions today. The second defense which Cosden is more likely to be successful with is that the firm followed generally accepted auditing standards in the audit of inventory, including the employment of due care. Ordinarily it is unreasonable to expect a CPA firm to find such an unusual problem in the course of an ordinary audit. Because the CPA firm did not uncover the fraud does not mean it has responsibility for it.

    c. She is likely to be successful in her defense against the client because of the contributory negligence. The company has responsibility for instituting adequate internal controls. The president's statement that it was impractical to count all inventory on the same day because of personnel shortages and customer preferences puts considerable burden on the company for its own loss.

    It is also unlikely that East City National Bank will be successful in a suit. The court is likely to conclude that Cosden followed due care in the performance of her work. The fact that there was not a count of all inventory on the same date is unlikely to be sufficient for a successful suit. The success of Cosden's defenses is also heavily dependent upon the jurisdiction's attitude about privity of contract. In this case there is likely to be a claim of extreme negligence. Therefore it would be required for the court to both ignore the privity of contract precedence and find Cosden negligent for the suit to be successful.

    d. The issues and outcomes should be essentially the same under the suit brought under the Securities Exchange Act of 1934. If the suit were brought under Rule 10b-5, it is certainly unlikely that the plaintiff would be successful, inasmuch as there was no intent to deceive. The plaintiff would likely be unsuccessful in such a suit.

5-20 Yes. Normally a CPA firm will not be liable to third parties with whom it has neither dealt nor for whose benefit its work was performed. One notable exception to this rule is fraud. When the financial statements were fraudulently prepared, liability runs to all third parties who relied upon the false information contained in them. Fraud can be either actual or constructive. Here, there was no actual fraud on the part of Small or the firm in that there was no deliberate falsehood made with the requisite intent to deceive. However, it would appear that constructive fraud may be present. Constructive fraud is found where the auditor's performance is found to be grossly negligent. That is, the auditor really had either no basis or so flimsy a basis for his or her opinion that he or she has manifested a reckless disregard for the truth. Small's disregard for standard auditing procedures would seem to indicate such gross negligence and, therefore, the firm is liable to third parties who relied on the financial statements and suffered a loss as a result.

5-21 The answers provided in this section are based on the assumption that the traditional legal relationship exists between the CPA firm and the third party user. That is, there is no privity of contract, the known versus unknown third party user is not a significant issue, and high levels of negligence are required before there is liability.

a. False. There was no privity of contract between Watts and Williams, therefore, ordinary negligence will usually not be sufficient for a recovery.
b. True. If gross negligence is proven, the CPA firm can and probably will be held liable for losses to third parties.
c. True. See a.
d. False. Gross negligence (constructive fraud) is treated as actual fraud in determining who may recover from the CPA.
e. False. Martinson is an unknown third party and will probably be able to recover damages only in the case of gross negligence or fraud.

Assuming a liberal interpretation of the legal relationship between auditors and third parties, the answers to a. and d. would probably both be true. The other answers would remain the same.

5-22 The accounting firm, Spark, Watts, and Wilcox, is potentially liable to its client because of the possible negligence of its agent, the in-charge accountant on the audit, in carrying out duties that were within the scope of his employment. Should there be a finding of negligence, liability would be limited to those losses that would have been avoided had reasonable care been exercised.

There being no evidence of the assumption of a greater responsibility, the in-charge accountant's conduct is governed by the usual standard; i.e., that the accountant perform his duties with the profession's standards of conduct prevailing. The question arises as to whether the duty of reasonable care was breached when the in-charge accountant failed to make further investigation after being apprised by a competent subordinate of exceptions to six percent of the vouchers payable examined. Moreover, a question of causation arises; i.e., whether further actions by the in-charge accountant would have disclosed the fraud. If both lack of due care and causation are established, recovery for negligence will be available.

5-23 a. The legal issues involved in this case revolve around the auditor's compliance with generally accepted auditing standards and contributory negligence. Auditing standards require that accounts receivable be confirmed by the auditor. This procedure was employed in the case, and the legal issue is whether or not the auditor used due care in following up on the confirmation replies received.

As a defense in the lawsuit, the auditor would claim to have followed generally accepted auditing standards by properly confirming accounts receivable. In addition, the auditor may defend him or herself by testifying that the company controller was responsible for investigating the reason for the differences reported on the confirmation replies. The auditor may state that he or she had a right to conclude that the controller had reviewed the explanations provided by the bookkeeper, and concluded they were correct. The auditor might also use the defense that there was contributory negligence. The controller should not have delegated the work to the bookkeeper and should have recognized the potential for intentional wrong-doing by the bookkeeper.

b. The CPA's deficiency in conducting the audit of accounts receivable was his or her failure to investigate and obtain evidence to substantiate the explanations provided by the bookkeeper. The auditor should have investigated each of the timing differences, through which he or she may have discovered that no sales allowance had been granted to the customer, but in fact, the customer had mailed payment for the merchandise which the bookkeeper had stolen.

5-24 a. Yes. Smith was a party to the issuance of false financial statements. The elements necessary to establish an action for common law fraud are present. There was a material misstatement of fact, knowledge of falsity (scienter), intent that the plaintiff bank rely on the false statement, actual reliance, and damage to the bank as a result thereof. If the action is based upon fraud there is no requirement that the bank establish privity of contract with the CPA. Moreover, if the action by the bank is based upon ordinary negligence, which does not require a showing of scienter, the bank may recover as a third-party beneficiary because it is a primary beneficiary. Thus, the bank will be able to recover its loss from Smith under either theory.

b. No. The lessor was a party to the secret agreement. As such, the lessor cannot claim reliance on the financial statements and cannot recover uncollected rents. Even if the lessor was damaged indirectly, his or her own fraudulent actions led to the loss, and the equitable principle of "unclean hands" precludes the lessor from obtaining relief.

c. Yes. Smith had knowledge that the financial statements did not follow generally accepted accounting principles and willingly prepared an unqualified opinion. That is a criminal act because there was an intent to deceive.

5-25 Ward & East's strongest defense would be that they had exercised due care in performing the audit and that they had adhered to generally accepted auditing standards. The fact that Jasper & Co. later found fraud should not significantly affect the case in as much as they were specifically engaged to determine the existence of fraud, not to do an ordinary audit.

5-25 (Continued)

Ward & East are likely to have to demonstrate that the audit was adequately planned and sufficient competent evidence was accumulated and properly evaluated. For example, the case states that the managers who were defrauding the company negotiated lower than normal rents in return for the kickbacks. It is possible that analytical procedures or other audit tests might have revealed that some rents were abnormally low. The auditor may have to prove that such procedures were not necessary in the circumstances or would not have uncovered the fraud. Similarly, the decentralization of lease negotiation may also be cited by the plaintiff as evidence that internal controls were inadequate and additional testing was necessary that could have uncovered the fraud. Ward & East may have to prove that the understanding of internal control they obtained was adequate and the audit evidence they accumulated was appropriate, given the decentralized lease negotiations.

5-26 a. The case should be dismissed. A suit under Section 10(b) and Rule 10b-5 of the Securities Exchange Act of 1934 must establish fraud. Fraud is an intentional tort and as such requires more than a showing of negligent manner; the CPAs neither participated in the fraudulent scheme nor did they know of its existence. The element of scienter or guilty knowledge must be present in order to state a cause of action for fraud under Section 10(b) of the Securities Exchange Act of 1934.

b. The plaintiffs might have stated a common law action for negligence. However, they may not be able to prevail due to the privity requirement. There was no contractual relationship between the defrauded parties and the CPA firm. Although the exact status of the privity rule is unclear, it is doubtful that the simple negligence in this case would extend Gordon & Groton's liability to the customers who transacted business with the bank. However, the facts of the case as presented in court would determine this.

Another possible theory which has been attempted recently in the courts is liability under Section 17 of the Securities Exchange Act of 1934, which requires registered brokers to submit audited financial statements to the SEC. In one such case, the plaintiff claimed that the accountant failed to perform a proper audit and thereby created liability to the customers of the brokerage firm who suffered losses as a result of the financial collapse of the brokerage firm.

5-27 The bank is likely to succeed. Robertson apparently knew that Majestic was "technically bankrupt" at December 31, 1999. Reporting standards require the auditor to add an explanatory paragraph to the audit report when there is substantial doubt about an entity's ability to continue as a going concern. She did not include such a paragraph. To make matters worse, it appears that Robertson was convinced not to issue the report with the going concern paragraph because of the negative impact on Majestic Co., not because of the solvency of the company. That may be interpreted as a lack of independence by Robertson and may indicate a fraudulent act, potentially a criminal charge that could result in a prison term.

5-27 (Continued)

Robertson's most likely defense is that after determining all of the facts, in part through discussion with management, she concluded that the Majestic Co. was not technically bankrupt and did not require an explanatory paragraph in the audit report. She might also argue that even if such a report was appropriate, her failure to do so was negligence or bad judgment, not with the intent to deceive the bank. Such a defense does not seem to be strong given the statement about her knowledge of Majestic's financial condition.

Robertson might also falsely testify that she did not believe that a going concern problem existed. Such statements would be perjury and are unprofessional and not worthy of a professional accountant. Perjury is also a criminal act and could result in further actions by the courts.

■ **Cases**

5-28 PART 1

a. In order for Thaxton to hold Mitchell & Moss liable for his losses under the Securities Exchange Act of 1934, he must rely upon the antifraud provisions of section 10(b) of the act. In order to prevail, Thaxton must establish that:

1. There was an omission or misstatement of a material fact in the financial statements used in connection with his purchase of the Whitlow & Company shares of stock.
2. He sustained a loss as a result of his purchase of the shares of stock.
3. His loss was caused by reliance on the misleading financial statements.
4. Mitchell & Moss acted with scienter (knowledge of the misstatement).

Based on the stated facts, Thaxton can probably prove the first three requirements cited above. To prove the fourth requirement, Thaxton must show that Mitchell & Moss had knowledge of the fraud or recklessly disregarded the truth. The facts clearly indicate that Mitchell & Moss did not have knowledge of the fraud and did not recklessly disregard the truth.

b. The customers and shareholders of Whitlow & Company would attempt to recover on a negligence theory based on Mitchell & Moss' failure to comply with GAAS. Even if Mitchell & Moss were negligent, Whitlow & Company's customers and shareholders must also establish either that:

1. They were third party beneficiaries of Mitchell & Moss' contract to audit Whitlow & Company, or
2. Mitchell & Moss owed the customers and shareholders a legal duty to act without negligence.

5-28 (Continued)

Although many cases have expanded a CPA's legal responsibilities to a third party for negligence, the facts of this case may fall within the traditional rationale limiting a CPA's liability for negligence; that is, the unfairness of imputing an indeterminate amount of liability to unknown or unforeseen parties as a result of mere negligence on the auditor's part. Accordingly, Whitlow & Company's customers and shareholders will prevail only if (1) the courts rule that they are either third-party beneficiaries or are owed a legal duty and (2) they establish that Mitchell & Moss was negligent in failing to comply with generally accepted auditing standards.

PART 2

a. The basis of Jackson's claim will be that she sustained a loss based upon misleading financial statements. Specifically, she will rely upon section 11(a) of the Securities Act of 1933, which provides the following:

> In case any part of the registration statement, when such part became effective, contained an untrue statement of a material fact or omitted to state a material fact requirement to be stated therein or necessary to make the statements therein not misleading, any person acquiring such security (unless it is proved that at the time of such acquisition he knew of such untruth or omission) may, either at law or in equity, in any court of competent jurisdiction, sue . . . every accountant . . . who has with his consent been named as having prepared or certified any part of the registration statement. . . .

To the extent that the relatively minor misstatements resulted in the certification of materially false or misleading financial statements, there is potential liability. Jackson's case is based on the assertion of such an untrue statement or omission coupled with an allegation of damages. Jackson does not have to prove reliance on the statements nor the company's or auditor's negligence in order to recover the damages. The burden is placed on the defendant to provide defenses that will enable it to avoid liability.

b. The first defense that could be asserted is that Jackson knew of the untruth or omission in audited financial statements included in the registration statement. The act provides that the plaintiff may not recover if it can be proved that at the time of such acquisition she knew of such "untruth or omission."

Since Jackson was a member of the private placement group and presumably privy to the type of information that would be contained in a registration statement, plus any other information requested by the group, she may have had sufficient knowledge of the facts claimed to be untrue or omitted. If this be the case, then she would not be relying on the certified financial statements but upon her own knowledge.

5-28 (Continued)

The next defense available would be that the untrue statement or omission was not material. The SEC has defined the term as meaning matters about which an average prudent investor ought to be reasonably informed before purchasing the registered security. For section 11 purposes, this has been construed as meaning a fact that, had it been correctly stated or disclosed, would have deterred or tended to deter the average prudent investor from purchasing the security in question.

Allen, Dunn, and Rose would also assert that the loss in question was not due to the false statement or omission; this is, that the false statement was not the cause of the price drop. It would appear that the general decline in the stock market would account for at least a part of the loss. Additionally, if the decline in earnings was not factually connected with the false statement or omission, the defendants have another basis for refuting the causal connection between their wrongdoing and the resultant drop in the stock's price.

Finally, the accountants will claim that their departure from generally accepted auditing standards was too minor to be considered a violation of the standard of due diligence required by the act.

5-29 The purposes of this case are:

- To make students aware of the magnitude and nature of damages that can result from an audit failure.
- To give them some familiarity with the legal process.
- To allow them to consider several possible violations of GAAS.
- To provide the instructor with an opportunity to emphasize the need to exercise due care and to discuss the concept of professional skepticism.
- To have students consider the relative roles of parties in a failure situation.

The students can be told that this case is based on an actual case and that the questions and answers, although abbreviated, are real. In this case, the deposition of the manager lasted about three and one-half days. Because there was clearly an audit failure, the case was settled, rather than being tried in court. Instructors may wish to discuss the relevant factors in deciding when to go to trial and when to settle, the advantages of a jury versus a bench trial, and so forth. The authors' overall experience is that about half the suits they have been exposed to had merit and about half of those were audit failures. Of those with merit, about 80 percent have been settled rather than being tried. Instructors may also wish to role play a deposition, or view a video of a trial, to give students a sense of the pressure of being a defendant. In cases like this one, it is likely the manager's career with the firm will have been abruptly stopped by the event of the litigation.

5-29 (Continued)

The possible violations of GAAS implied by the deposition excerpts are:

- *Lack of independence of mental attitude (professional skepticism) in performing the audit.* The authors' experience is that this is the most common root cause of all audit failures. In almost all cases of failure observed, the evidence of the problem passed before the auditor's eyes, but was not recognized as such. This problem appears in the length of time Raines worked on the audit, the focus on managements' representations about the condition of leases, and failure to challenge the true meaning of the ABC bankruptcy revelation.
- *Inadequate technical training.* There are a number of unique aspects to auditing a financial institution such as a leasing company. The important audit aspects are presented in the *AICPA Industry Audit Guide for Finance Companies*, which Raines does not seem to be particularly familiar with. He has not had special training and does not recognize the uniqueness of the industry.
- *Failure to adequately plan the engagement.* In addition to unique aspects of the industry, Raines does not recognize the requirements of GAAS to determine and respond to risk in various audit areas. This aspect of auditing may not yet be known to the students; however, they should recognize that the adequacy of loss reserves requires a great deal of attention in the audit of a financial institution.
- *Insufficient evidence.* In auditing the loss reserves, the auditors apparently did not determine that the lease card files were complete before taking their sample. In addition, the primary evidence was management's representations, which should have been corroborated.
- *Lack of due care.* In addition to the above, which imply a lack of due care, it appears that Raines may not have considered whether the $.3 million "cushion" was sufficient to cover the many millions of dollars of leases not considered on the delinquency list, again relying primarily on managements' representations. Note that the fact that some of the representations are made in writing does not improve their evidential quality.
- *Inadequate supervision.* Where was the engagement partner while Raines was conducting the audit? It does not appear he or she was supervising Raines.

It is difficult to say how responsibility should be shared in a case like this. Clearly, the responsible parties are Sinclair & Lewis and its partners and employees, Vernon and probably other personnel at WSI, and the Maxwells as directors. Sinclair & Lewis' defense will include contributory negligence and the claim that fraud was perpetuated on them by management. The courts would have to sort it out. Under joint and several liability, if Vernon and others have no resources and if the Maxwells are found to be of no fault, Sinclair & Lewis would suffer the entire damages, even though others are at fault.

Internet Problem Solution: SEC Enforcement

5-1 a. The SEC's Enforcement Division posts Litigation Releases, which are descriptions of SEC civil and selected criminal suits in the federal court proceedings. Look up the case of the "Dream Beam" (Litigation Release #16072: Futrex, Inc., Futrex Medical Instrumentation, Inc., and Robert D. Rosenthal; February 25, 1999), and answer the following questions:

1. What was the "Dream Beam" purported to be?
2. What sections of the federal securities law(s) was Mr. Rosenthal alleged to have violated and why?

The entire text of the Litigation Release is provided below as the solution to questions 1 and 2 of part a.

LITIGATION RELEASE NO. 16072/ February 25, 1999

SECURITIES AND EXCHANGE COMMISSION v. FUTREX, INC., FUTREX MEDICAL INSTRUMENTATION, INC., AND ROBERT D. ROSENTHAL, No. 1: 96CV02192 (RWR)(D.D.C.)

SEC OBTAINS FINAL JUDGMENTS CONCLUDING FUTREX SECURITIES FRAUD CASE

The Securities and Exchange Commission has obtained a final judgment against Futrex, Inc., Futrex Medical Instrumentation, Inc. (jointly referred to as "Futrex"), and Robert D. Rosenthal, Futrex's chairman of the board, chief executive officer, president, and treasurer, in a fraud case arising from Futrex's private placement of securities in 1994 and abortive initial public offering in 1995. Without admitting or denying the Commission's allegations, the defendants consented to entry of the judgment, which enjoins them from violating Section 17(a) of the Securities Act of 1933, Section 10(b) of the Securities Exchange Act of 1934, and Rule 10(b)-5 thereunder, and orders Rosenthal to pay a $50,000 civil penalty.

The Commission's complaint, filed on September 23, 1996, alleged that the defendants, in connection with Futrex's 1994 private placement and 1995 abortive initial public offering, made materially false and misleading statements concerning Futrex's "Dream Beam" product, a hand-held laboratory instrument that purportedly could measure a person's blood glucose level by passing infrared light through his or her finger. Among other things, the complaint alleged that the defendants fraudulently made unsupportable claims about the effectiveness of the Dream Beam, failed to disclose adverse results from studies of the Dream Beam, and staged deceptive demonstrations of the Dream Beam for prospective investors. (See also Litigation Rel. No. 15061 (Sept. 23, 1996)).

5-1 (Continued)

b. In 1998 and 1999 the SEC focused increased attention on auditor independence. On January 14, 1999 the SEC announced a settlement with PricewaterhouseCoopers (PwC), one of the largest public accounting firms in the U.S. and abroad, on charges the firm had violated Rule 2-01 (b) of Regulation S-X of the Securities Exchange Act of 1934 as well as generally accepted auditing standards. The action sent a message to the profession that the SEC takes independence very seriously. The SEC's Enforcement Division posts proceedings of its administrative actions as Accounting and Auditing Enforcement Releases (AAER). The PwC action is recorded in Release No. 1098 dated January 14, 1999. Find the release and answer the following questions:

1. Briefly describe a few of the specific stock ownership violations discussed in the AAER. Do you believe these violations actually resulted in biased or less than objective judgment on the part of the independent auditors?
2. How much money did PwC agree to pay for program(s) towards further awareness and education throughout the profession relating to the independence requirements for public accounting firms? List two other actions the firm agreed to take as part of the settlement.

The entire AAER can be linked via the solution posted on the Companion Website. In summary, Coopers and Lybrand before the July 1998 merger with Price Waterhouse failed 70 times from 1996 through 1998 to detect violations including four instances of auditors in the Tampa, Fla. office of owning shares of public companies they personally audited, and 31 instances of partners investing in firm clients they didn't individually audit. PwC agreed to be censured, to strengthen its independence oversight procedures, to annually review portfolios of randomly selected partners and professionals, and to establish a $2.5 million fund to establish educational programs to enhance the profession's awareness.

Did the violations impair independence in fact? A close read suggests that the violations probably did not impair independence in fact. The instances of direct ownership related to a senior tax associate who had little to do with the audit.

(**Note**: Internet problems address current issues using Internet sources. Because Internet sites are subject to change, Internet problems and solutions may change. Current information on Internet problems is available at www.prenhall.com/arens/.)

Chapter 6

Audit Responsibilities and Objectives

■ Review Questions

6-1 The objective of the ordinary audit of financial statements by the independent auditor is the expression of an opinion on the fairness with which the financial statements present financial position, results of operations, and cash flows in conformity with generally accepted accounting principles.

The auditor meets that objective by accumulating sufficient competent evidence to determine whether the financial statements are fairly stated.

6-2 It is management's responsibility to adopt sound accounting policies, maintain adequate internal control and make fair representations in the financial statements. The auditor's responsibility is to conduct an audit of the financial statements in accordance with generally accepted auditing standards and report the findings of the audit in the auditor's report.

6-3 An error is an unintentional misstatement of the financial statements. Fraud represents intentional misstatements. The auditor is responsible for obtaining reasonable assurance that material misstatements in the financial statements are detected, whether those misstatements are due to errors or fraud.

An audit must be designed to provide reasonable assurance of detecting material misstatements in the financial statements. Further, the audit must be planned and performed with an *attitude of professional skepticism* in all aspects of the engagement. Because there is an attempt at concealment of fraud, material misstatements due to fraud are usually more difficult to uncover than errors. The auditor's best defense when material misstatements (either errors or fraud) are not uncovered in the audit is that the audit was conducted in accordance with generally accepted auditing standards.

6-4 Misappropriation of assets represents the theft of assets by employees. Fraudulent financial reporting is the intentional misstatement of financial information by management or a theft of assets by management, which is covered up by misstating financial statements.

Misappropriation of assets ordinarily occurs either because of inadequate internal controls or a violation of existing controls. The best way to prevent theft of assets is through adequate internal controls that function effectively. Many times theft of assets is relatively small in dollar amounts and will have no effect on the fair presentation of financial statements. There are also the cases of large theft of assets that result in bankruptcy to the company. Fraudulent financial reporting is inherently difficult to uncover because it is possible for one or more members of management to override internal controls. In many cases the amounts are extremely large and may affect the fair presentation of financial statements.

6-5 True, the auditor must rely on management for certain information in the conduct of his or her audit. However, the auditor must not accept management's representations blindly. He or she must, whenever possible, obtain competent evidential matter to support the representations of management. As an example, if management represents that certain inventory is not obsolete, the auditor should be able to examine purchase orders from customers which prove that part of the inventory is being sold at a price which is higher than the company's cost plus selling expenses. If management represents an account receivable as being fully collectible, the auditor should be able to examine subsequent payments by the customer or correspondence from the customer which indicates a willingness and ability to pay.

6-6

CHARACTERISTIC	AUDIT STEPS
1. Management's characteristics and influence over the control environment.	■ Investigate the past history of the firm and its management. ■ Discuss the possibility of fraudulent financial reporting with previous auditor and company legal counsel after obtaining permission to do so from management.
2. Industry conditions.	■ Research current status of industry and compare industry financial ratios to the company's ratios. Investigate any unusual differences. ■ Read AICPA's *Industry Audit Risk Alert* for the company's industry, if available. Consider the impact of specific risks that are identified on the conduct of the audit.
3. Operating characteristics and financial stability.	■ Perform analytical procedures to evaluate the possibility of business failure. ■ Investigate whether material transactions occur close to year-end.

6-7 The cycle approach is a method of dividing the audit such that closely related types of transactions and account balances are included in the same cycle. For example, sales, sales returns, and cash receipts transactions and the accounts receivable balance are all a part of the sales and collection cycle. The advantages of dividing the audit into different cycles are to divide the audit into more manageable parts, to assign tasks to different members of the audit team and to keep closely related parts of the audit together.

6-8

GENERAL LEDGER ACCOUNT	CYCLE
Sales	Sales & Collection
Accounts Payable	Acquisition & Payment
Retained Earnings	Capital Acquisition & Repayment
Accounts Receivable	Sales & Collection
Inventory	Inventory & Warehousing
Repairs & Maintenance	Acquisition & Payment

6-9 There is a close relationship between each of these accounts. Sales, sales returns and allowances, and cash discounts all affect accounts receivable. Allowance for uncollectible accounts is closely tied to accounts receivable and should not be separated. Bad debt expense is closely related to the allowance for uncollectible accounts. To separate these accounts from each other implies that they are not closely related. Including them in the same cycle helps the auditor keep their relationships in mind.

6-10 Management assertions are implied or expressed representations by management about classes of transactions and the related accounts in the financial statements. These assertions are part of the criteria management uses to record and disclose accounting information in financial statements. SAS 31 (AU 326) classifies five broad categories of assertions:

1. Existence or occurrence
2. Completeness
3. Valuation or allocation
4. Rights and obligations
5. Presentation and disclosure

6-11 General audit objectives follow from and are closely related to management assertions. General audit objectives, however, are intended to provide a framework to help the auditor accumulate sufficient competent evidence required by the third standard of field work. Audit objectives are more useful to auditors than assertions because they are more detailed and more closely related to helping the auditor accumulate sufficient competent evidence.

6-12

RECORDING MISSTATEMENT	TRANSACTION-RELATED AUDIT OBJECTIVE VIOLATED
Repair service is recorded on the wrong date.	Timing
Repair is capitalized as a fixed asset instead of an expense.	Classification

6-13 The existence objective deals with whether amounts included in the financial statements should actually be included. Completeness is the opposite of existence. The completeness objective deals with whether all amounts which should be included have actually been included.

In the audit of accounts receivable, a nonexistent account receivable will lead to overstatement of the accounts receivable balance. Failure to include a customer's account receivable balance, which is a violation of completeness, will lead to understatement of the accounts receivable balance.

6-14 Specific audit objectives are the application of the general audit objectives to a given class of transactions or account balance. There must be at least one specific audit objective for each general audit objective and in many cases there should be more. Specific audit objectives for a class of transactions or an account balance should be designed such that, once they have been satisfied, the general audit objective should also have been satisfied for that class of transactions or account.

6-15 For the specific balance-related audit objective, all recorded fixed assets exist at the balance sheet date, the management assertion and the general balance-related audit objective are both "existence."

6-16 Management assertions and general balance-related audit objectives are constant for all asset accounts for every audit. They were developed by the Auditing Standards Board, practitioners, and academics over a period of time. One or more specific balance-related audit objectives are developed for each general balance-related audit objective in an audit area such as accounts receivable. For any given account, a CPA firm may decide on a constant set of specific balance-related audit objectives for accounts receivable, or it may decide to use different objectives for different audits.

6-17 The four phases of the audit are:

1. Plan and design an audit approach.
2. Perform tests of controls and substantive tests of transactions.
3. Perform analytical procedures and tests of details of balances.
4. Complete the audit and issue an audit report.

The auditor uses these four phases to meet the overall objective of the audit, which is to express an opinion on the fairness with which the financial statements present fairly, in all material respects, the financial position, results of operations and cash flows in conformity with GAAP. By accumulating sufficient competent evidence for each audit objective, the overall objective is met. The accumulation of evidence is accomplished by performing the four phases of the audit.

■ **Multiple Choice Questions From CPA Examinations**

6-18   a. (2)   b. (2)   c. (1)

6-19   a. (1)   b. (2)

6-20   a. (3)   b. (4)   c. (4)

Discussion Questions And Problems

6-21 a. The purpose of the report of management is for management to state its responsibilities for the preparation of financial statements in accordance with GAAP, implementing adequate internal controls, and engaging an independent certified public accountant to serve as external auditor. The company is not required to issue such a letter.

The purpose of the auditor's report (report of independent accountant) is to express an opinion on the fairness of the presentation of the financial statements in accordance with GAAP. CPAs are required to issue a report on any engagements in which they are associated with the financial statements. This includes all audits.

b. The report of management emphasizes that it has certain responsibilities and it asserts that management acts in a certain manner. It is a statement of how management purports to conduct its financial and certain business affairs.

c. The audit committee is a subcommittee of the board of directors, primarily responsible for meeting with internal and independent auditors to discuss conflicts with management, weaknesses in internal control, problems in accumulating evidence or other matters of interest to a company's accounting responsibilities.

The phrase, *consisting entirely of outside directors*, means that none of the directors on the audit committee is a member of the company's operating management. That implies that they are more independent than they would be otherwise.

d. It is an unqualified report within an explanatory paragraph. There is an explanatory paragraph stating the change in the application of generally accepted accounting principles with regard to the method of accounting for start-up costs.

e. One month and twelve days, which is the time span between December 31 and February 12.

6-22 a.

1. The function of the auditor in the audit of financial statements is to provide users of the statements with an informed opinion based on reasonable assurance obtained as to the fairness with which the statements portray financial position, results of operations, and cash flows in accordance with generally accepted accounting principles applied on a basis consistent with that of the preceding year.

2. The responsibility of the independent auditor is to express an opinion on the financial statements he or she has audited. Inasmuch as the financial statements are the representation of management, responsibility rests with management for the proper recording of transactions in books of account, for the safeguarding of assets, and for the substantial accuracy and adequacy of the financial statements.

6-22 (Continued)

In developing the basis for his or her opinion, the auditor is responsible for conducting an audit that conforms to generally accepted auditing standards. These standards constitute the measure of the adequacy of the audit. Those standards require the auditor to obtain sufficient, competent evidential matter about material management assertions in the financial statements.

The informed judgment of a qualified professional accountant is required of an independent auditor. The auditor must exercise this judgment in selecting the procedures he or she uses in the audit and in arriving at an opinion.

In presenting himself or herself to the public as an independent auditor, he or she makes himself or herself responsible for having the abilities expected of a qualified person in that profession. Such qualifications do not include those of an appraiser, valuer, expert in materials, expert in styles, insurer, or lawyer. The auditor is entitled to rely upon the judgment of experts in these other areas of knowledge and skill.

b. Auditors are responsible for obtaining reasonable assurance that material misstatements included in the financial statements are detected, whether those misstatements are due to error or fraud. Professional standards acknowledge that it is often more difficult to detect fraud than errors because management or employees perpetrating the fraud attempt to conceal the fraud. That difficulty, however, does not change the auditor's responsibility to properly plan and perform the audit. Auditors are required to specifically assess the risk of material misstatement due to fraud and should consider that assessment in designing the audit procedures to be performed.

In recent years there has been increased emphasis on auditors' responsibility to evaluate factors that may indicate an increased likelihood that fraud may be occurring. For example, assume that management is dominated by a president who makes most of the major operating and business decisions himself. He has a reputation in the business community for making optimistic projections about future earnings and then putting considerable pressure on operating and accounting staff to make sure those projections are met. He has also been associated with other companies in the past that have gone bankrupt. These factors, considered together, may cause the auditor to conclude that the likelihood of fraud is fairly high. In such a circumstance, the auditor should put increased emphasis on searching for material misstatements due to fraud.

SAS No. 82 requires that the auditor specifically assess the risk of material misstatement due to both fraudulent financial reporting and misappropriation of assets. The SAS identifies the following three categories of risk factors for fraudulent financial reporting:

- Management's characteristics and influence over the control environment
- Industry conditions
- Operating characteristics and financial stability

6-22 (Continued)

The auditor may also uncover circumstances during the audit that may cause suspicions of fraudulent financial reporting. For example, the auditor may find that management has lied about the age of certain inventory items. When such circumstances are uncovered, the auditor must evaluate their implications and consider the need to modify audit evidence.

SAS No. 82 identifies two categories of risk factors for misappropriation of assets:

- Susceptibility of assets to misappropriation
- Controls

Adequate internal control should be the principal means of thwarting and detecting misappropriation of assets. To rely entirely on an independent audit for the detection of misappropriation of assets would require expanding the auditor's work to the extent that the cost might be prohibitive.

The auditor normally assesses the likelihood of material misappropriation of assets as a part of understanding the entity's internal control and assessing control risk. Audit evidence should be expanded when the auditor finds an absence of adequate controls or failure to follow prescribed procedures, if he or she believes a material fraud could result.

The independent auditor is not an insurer or guarantor. The auditor's implicit obligation in an engagement is that the audit be made with due professional skill and care in accordance with generally accepted auditing standards. A subsequent discovery of fraud, existent during the period covered by the independent audit, does not of itself indicate negligence on the auditor's part.

c. If an independent auditor uncovers circumstances arousing suspicion as to the existence of fraud, he or she should weigh the effect of the circumstances on the opinion on the financial statements. When the auditor believes that the amount of the possible fraud is material, the matter must be investigated before an opinion can be given. The auditor should consider the implications for other aspects of the audit and discuss the matter with an appropriate level of management that is at least one level above those involved and with senior management. Additionally, the auditor should obtain additional evidential matter to determine whether material fraud has occurred or is likely to have occurred. The auditor may suggest that the client consult with legal counsel. Whenever the auditor has determined that there is evidence that fraud may exist, that matter should be brought to the attention of the audit committee, unless the matter is clearly inconsequential.

6-23 SAS No. 82 (AU 316) requires the auditor to assess the risk of material misstatements of the financial statements due to fraud and to consider that assessment in designing the audit procedures to be performed. In making this assessment, the auditor should consider fraud risk factors that relate to both (a) misstatements arising from fraudulent financial reporting and (b) misstatements arising from misappropriation of assets. SAS No. 82 (AU 316) goes on to note that because of (a) the concealment aspects of fraudulent activity, including the fact that fraud often involves collusion or falsified documentation, and (b) the need to apply professional judgment in the identification and evaluation of fraud risk factors, even a properly planned and performed audit may not detect a material misstatement due to fraud.

6-23 (Continued)

Because the SEC has investigated the case and concluded that GAAS were properly followed, the auditor should not be liable. The potential bearers of the loss are the company, its officers and directors, persons within the organization who were involved in the fraud, and the stockholders who have lost their investment.

The persons within the organization who perpetrated the fraud are the most directly responsible for the occurrence of the company's plight. The officers and directors are indirectly responsible for not controlling the occurrence of the fraud by instituting preventive or detective controls. The stockholders' responsibility for the fraud stems from their election of the directors and their loss is limited to the extent of their investment in the company.

Investors have a responsibility to evaluate the risk in investments including the possibility of information risk as discussed in Chapter 1. Investors who are not in a position to accept risk of loss should not invest material amounts in any given equity investment. For the individuals involved in this situation, their investments should either have been sufficiently diversified to minimize the loss, or alternatively, other investments should have been made that were more secure, such as government funds. Investments inherently carry some risk. In the opinion of the authors, the investors should recognize that there is a possibility of loss even in an apparently well managed business that has an annual audit of its financial statements.

6-24

CLASS OF TRANSACTIONS	a. FINANCIAL STATEMENT BALANCE	b. TITLE OF JOURNAL	c. TRANSACTION CYCLE
PURCHASE RETURNS	Purchase returns & allowances	Acquisitions Journal	Acquisition & Payment
RENTAL REVENUE	Rent revenue	Revenue Journal	Sales & Collection
CHARGE-OFF OF UNCOLLECTIBLE ACCOUNTS	Bad debts	Adjustments Journal	Sales & Collection
ACQUISITION OF GOODS AND SERVICES	Repair and maintenance	Acquisitions Journal	Acquisition & Payment
RENTAL ALLOWANCES	Rental allowances	Adjustments Journal	Sales & Collection
ADJUSTING ENTRIES (FOR PAYROLL)	Accrued payroll	Adjustments Journal	Payroll & Personnel
PAYROLL SERVICE & PAYMENTS	Sales salaries	Payroll Journal	Payroll & Personnel
CASH DISBURSEMENTS	Accounts payable	Cash Disbursements Journal	Acquisition & Payment
CASH RECEIPTS	Accounts receivable	Cash Receipts Journal	Sales & Collection

d. Rental revenue is likely to be recorded in the cash receipts journal at the time the cash is received from renters. It is therefore likely to be recorded as a debit to cash receipts and a credit to rental revenue. The journal will be summarized monthly and posted to the general ledger. There will be required adjusting entries for unearned rent and for rent receivable. A record will be kept of each renter and a determination made whether rent is unpaid or unearned at the end of each accounting period. The entries that are likely to be made in the adjustments journal are posted to the general ledger. Then the financial statements are prepared from the adjusted general ledger. Reversing entries may be used to eliminate the adjusting entries.

6-25 a.

CYCLE	BALANCE SHEET ACCOUNTS	INCOME STATEMENT ACCOUNTS
SALES AND COLLECTION	Accounts receivable Cash Notes receivable--trade Allowance for doubtful accounts Interest receivable	Sales Bad debt expense Interest income
ACQUISITION AND PAYMENT	Income tax payable Accounts payable Unexpired insurance Furniture and equipment Cash Accumulated depreciation of furniture and equipment Inventory Property tax payable	Income tax expense Advertising expense Traveling expense Purchases Property tax expense Depreciation expense--furniture and equipment Telephone and telegraph expense Insurance expense Rent expense
PAYROLL AND PERSONNEL	Cash Accrued sales salaries	Sales salaries expense Salaries, office and general
INVENTORY AND WAREHOUSING	Inventory	Purchases
CAPITAL ACQUISITION AND REPAYMENT	Bonds payable Common stock Cash Notes payable Retained earnings Prepaid interest expense	Interest expense

b. The general ledger accounts are not likely to differ much between a retail and a wholesale company unless there are departments for which there are various categories. There would be large differences for a hospital or governmental unit. A governmental unit would use the fund accounting system and would have entirely different titles. Hospitals are likely to have several different kinds of revenue accounts, rather than sales. They are also likely to have such things as drug expense, laboratory supplies, etc. At the same time, even a governmental unit or a hospital will have certain accounts such as cash, insurance expense, interest income, rent expense, and so forth.

SPECIFIC BALANCE-RELATED AUDIT OBJECTIVE	MANAGEMENT ASSERTION	COMMENTS
a. There are no unrecorded receivables.	2. Completeness	Unrecorded transactions or amounts deal with the completeness objective.
b. Receivables have not been sold or discounted.	4. Rights and obligations	Receivables not being sold or discounted concerns the rights and obligations objective and assertion.
c. Uncollectible accounts have been provided for.	3. Valuation or allocation	Providing for uncollectible accounts concerns whether the allowance for uncollectible accounts is adequate. It is part of the realizable value objective and the valuation or allocation assertion.
d. Receivables that have become uncollectible have been written off.	3. Valuation or allocation	This is part of the realizable value objective and the valuation or allocation assertion. There may also be some argument that this is part of the existence objective and assertion. Accounts that are uncollectible are no longer valid assets.
e. All accounts on the list are expected to be collected within one year.	3. Valuation or allocation	Accounts that are not expected to be collected within a year should be classified as long-term receivables. It is therefore being included as part of the classification objective and consequently under the valuation or allocation assertion. Some people believe that it is also a part of the presentation and disclosure assertion.
f. Any agreement or condition that restricts the nature of trade receivables is known and disclosed.	5. Presentation and disclosure	The nature of trade receivables is a part of the presentation and disclosure objective and therefore the presentation and disclosure assertion.

6-26 (Continued)

SPECIFIC BALANCE-RELATED AUDIT OBJECTIVE	MANAGEMENT ASSERTION	COMMENTS
g. All accounts on the list arose from the normal course of business and are not due from related parties.	3. Valuation or allocation	Concerns the classification of accounts receivable and is therefore a part of the classification objective and the valuation or allocation assertion. Some people believe that like item e., it is a part of presentation and disclosure.
h. Sales cutoff at year-end is proper.	3. Valuation or allocation	Cutoff is a part of the cutoff objective and therefore part of the valuation or allocation assertion.

6-27 a. Management assertions are implied or expressed representations by management about the classes of transactions and related accounts in the financial statements. SAS 31 (AU 326) classifies five broad categories of assertions which are stated in the problem. These assertions are the same for every transaction cycle and account. General transaction-related audit objectives are essentially the same as management assertions, but they are expanded somewhat to help the auditor decide which audit evidence is necessary to satisfy the management assertions. Accuracy, classification, timing, and posting and summarization are a subset of the valuation or allocation assertion. Specific transaction-related audit objectives are determined by the auditor for each general transaction-related audit objective. These are done for each transaction cycle to help the auditor determine the specific amount of evidence needed for that cycle to satisfy the general transaction-related audit objectives.

b. and
c. The easiest way to do this problem is to first identify the general transaction-related audit objectives for each specific transaction-related audit objective. It is then easy to determine the management assertion using **Table 6-4** as a guide.

6-27 (Continued)

SPECIFIC TRANSACTION-RELATED AUDIT OBJECTIVE	b. MANAGEMENT ASSERTION	c. GENERAL TRANSACTION-RELATED AUDIT OBJECTIVE
a. Recorded cash disbursement transactions are for the amount of goods or services received and are correctly recorded.	3. Valuation or allocation	8. Accuracy
b. Cash disbursement transactions are properly included in the accounts payable master file and are correctly summarized.	3. Valuation or allocation	11. Posting and summarization
c. Recorded cash disbursements are for goods and services actually received.	1. Existence or occurrence	6. Existence
d. Cash disbursement transactions are properly classified.	3. Valuation or allocation	9. Classification
e. Existing cash disbursement transactions are recorded.	2. Completeness	7. Completeness
f. Cash disbursement transactions are recorded on the correct dates.	3. Valuation or allocation	10. Timing

6-28　a.　The first objective concerns amounts that should not be included on the list of accounts payable because there are no amounts due to such vendors. This objective concerns only the overstatement of accounts payable. The second objective concerns the possibility of accounts payable that should be included but that have not been included. This objective concerns only the possibility of understated accounts payable.
　　　b.　The first objective deals with existence and the second deals with completeness.
　　　c.　For accounts payable, the auditor is usually most concerned about understatements. An understatement of accounts payable is usually considered more important than overstatements because of potential legal liability. The completeness objective is therefore normally more important in the audit of accounts payable. The auditor is also concerned about overstatements of accounts payable. The existence objective is also therefore important in accounts payable, but usually less so than the completeness objective.

6-29 a. The purposes of the general balance-related audit objectives are to provide a framework that the auditor can use to accumulate audit evidence. Once the nine general balance-related audit objectives have been satisfied, the auditor can conclude that the account balance in question is fairly stated. Specific balance-related audit objectives are applied to each account balance and are used to help the auditor become more specific about the audit evidence to accumulate.

There is at least one specific balance-related audit objective for each general balance-related audit objective and in many cases there are several specific objectives. There are specific balance-related audit objectives for each account balance, and specific balance-related audit objectives for an account such as fixed assets are likely to differ significantly from those used in accounts receivable. In some audits, the auditor may conclude that certain specific balance-related audit objectives are not important. At the end of the audit, the auditor must be satisfied that each specific balance-related audit objective has been satisfied. The general balance-related audit objectives help the auditor determine the appropriate specific balance-related audit objectives.

b.

GENERAL BALANCE-RELATED AUDIT OBJECTIVE	SPECIFIC BALANCE-RELATED AUDIT OBJECTIVE
1. EXISTENCE	d. Fixed assets physically exist and are being used for the purpose intended.
2. COMPLETENESS	a. There are no unrecorded fixed assets in use.
3. ACCURACY	e. Property, plant, and equipment are recorded at the correct amount.
	j. Depreciation is determined in accordance with an acceptable method and is materially correct as computed.
4. CLASSIFICATION	i. Expense accounts do not contain amounts that should have been capitalized.
5. CUTOFF	h. Cash disbursements and/or accrual cutoff for property, plant, and equipment items are proper.
6. DETAIL TIE-IN	c. Details of property, plant, and equipment agree with the general ledger.
7. REALIZABLE VALUE	k. Fixed asset accounts have been properly adjusted for declines in historical cost.
8. RIGHTS AND OBLIGATIONS	b. The company has valid title to the assets owned.
	f. The company has a contractual right for use of assets leased.
9. PRESENTATION AND DISCLOSURE	g. Liens or other encumbrances on property, plant, and equipment items are known and disclosed.

6-30 a. A review provides limited assurance about the fair presentation of financial statements with generally accepted accounting principles but far less assurance than an audit. Presumably, the bank decided that the assurances provided by a review were needed before a loan could be approved, but an audit was not necessary. A review includes a CPA firm performing analytical procedures, making inquiries about the fair presentation of the statements, and examining the information for reasonableness. Because of a CPA firm's expertise in accounting, the accountant from the CPA firm can often identify incorrect presentations in the financial statements that have been overlooked by the accountant for the company. Reviews are common for smaller privately-held companies with relatively small amounts of debt.

The bank probably did not require an audit because the additional cost of an audit was greater than the benefit the bank perceived. In many cases, the decision as to whether to have a review or an audit is negotiated between the company seeking a loan and the bank loan officer. Both the company and the bank have options in negotiating such things as the amount of the loan, the rate of interest, and whether to require an audit or a review. The bank can reject the loan request and the company can go to other banks that want to make loans.

Frequently, banks have a list of CPA firms in which they have considerable confidence due to their reputation in the community or past work they have done for other bank customers.

b. Because the amount of the loans from the bank to Ritter increased, the bank probably wanted additional assurance about the reliability of the financial statements. It is also likely that Rene Ritter negotiated the one percent reduction of the interest rate by offering to have an audit instead of a review. A one percent reduction in the interest rate saves Ritter $30,000 annually compared to the $5,000 additional fee for an audit.

c. Rene referred to the CPA firm as partners in a professional sense, not a business sense. The CPA firm had provided many consulting and tax services, as well as providing review and audit services over the entire business life of the company. Rene recognized that these professional services had contributed to the success of the business and she chose to acknowledge those contributions during her retirement comment. Assuming that the CPA firm retained an attitude of independence throughout all audits and reviews, no violation of professional independence standards occurred. Most well run CPA firms provide consulting, tax, and assurance service for their clients without violating independence requirements.

d. As the external auditor, the firm of Gonzalez & Fineberg provide the stockholders, creditors, and management an independent opinion as to the fair presentation of the financial statements. Given the potential biases present when management prepares the financial statement, the stockholders and creditors must consider the potential for information risk that might be present. The independent audit conducted by Gonzalez & Fineberg helps stockholders and creditors reduce their information risk. Management also benefits by having the external auditors independently assess the financial statements even though those statements are prepared by management. Due to the complexities involved in preparing financial statements in accordance with generally accepted accounting principles, the potential for error on the part of management increases the need for an

6-30 (Continued)

objective examination of those financial statements by a qualified independent party.

e. The auditor is responsible for obtaining reasonable assurance that material misstatements are detected, whether those misstatements are due to errors and fraud. To obtain reasonable assurance, the auditor is required to gather sufficient, competent evidence. The auditor's chief responsibility to stockholders, creditors, and management is to conduct the audit in accordance with generally accepted auditing standards in order to fulfill their responsibilities of the engagement.

■ Internet Problem Solution: Assertions and Evidence Associated with New Assurance Services

6-1 Chapter 1 of the text includes a brief description of the new assurance service known as "ElderCare Plus." The AICPA has developed a business plan for ElderCare Plus, which can be accessed at its Internet site. The business plan indicates that one aspect of this service may be to examine evidence to determine whether care givers are meeting certain performance criteria.

1. Provide two examples of possible performance criteria associated with a client living in a long-term facility. Who would likely determine the performance criteria? In what form and to whom would the CPA's findings be reported?

   Here are some examples of performance criteria associated with providing assurance related to a client living in a long-term care facility:

   - current state or federal licensing
   - the timely delivery of meals, medication, or physical therapy
   - cleanliness of facility, room and bedding
   - types and quality of meals or social activities
   - delivery or availability of beautician services

   The performance criteria would likely be determined by the client (probably the children or family of the elderly person in this instance). The CPA would most likely report to the family in whatever form was agreed upon at the beginning of the engagement.

2. For the two examples you identified in number 1, what "management assertions" would be tested, and how would these assertions be tested? Please be as specific as you can in your description of necessary evidence and assurance procedures.

   Student responses will vary. The AICPA's business plan suggests potential procedures such as "inspecting logs, diaries, or other evidence to determine whether care givers are meeting the performance criteria agreed upon with the customer/client." Some evidence would probably be gathered via inquiry and observation.

(**Note**: Internet problems address current issues using Internet sources. Because Internet sites are subject to change, Internet problems and solutions may change. Current information on Internet problems is available at www.prenhall.com/arens/.)

Chapter 7

Audit Evidence

■ Review Questions

7-1 In both a legal case and in an audit of financial statements, evidence is used by an unbiased person to draw conclusions. In addition, the consequences of an incorrect decision in both situations can be equally undesirable. For example, if a guilty person is set free, society may be in danger if the person repeats his or her illegal act. Similarly, if investors rely on materially misstated financial statements, they could lose significant amounts of money. Finally, the guilt of a defendant in a legal case must be proven beyond a reasonable doubt. This is similar to the concept of sufficient competent evidence in an audit situation. As with a judge or jury, an auditor cannot be completely convinced that his or her opinion is correct, but rather must obtain a high level of assurance.

The nature of evidence in a legal case and in an audit of financial statements differs because a legal case relies heavily on testimony by witnesses and other parties involved. While inquiry is a form of evidence used by auditors, other more reliable types of evidence such as confirmation with third parties, physical examination, and documentation are also used extensively. A legal case also differs from an audit because of the nature of the conclusions made. In a legal case, a judge or jury decides the guilt or innocence of the defendant. In an audit, the auditor issues one of several audit opinions after evaluating the evidence.

7-2 The four major audit evidence decisions that must be made on every audit are:

1. Which audit procedures to use.
2. What sample size to select for a given procedure.
3. Which items to select from the population.
4. When to perform the procedure.

7-3 An audit procedure is the detailed instruction for the collection of a type of audit evidence that is to be obtained. Because audit procedures are the instructions to be followed in accumulating evidence, they must be worded carefully to make sure the instructions are clear.

7-4 An audit program for accounts receivable is a list of audit procedures that will be used to audit accounts receivable for a given client. The audit procedures, sample size, items to select, and timing should be included in the audit program.

7-5 Sufficient competent evidential matter is to be obtained through inspection, observation, inquiries and confirmations to afford a reasonable basis for an opinion regarding the financial statements under audit. There are three major phrases of the standard.

7-5 (Continued)

PHRASE	MEANING OF PHRASE
Sufficient competent evidence	The auditor must obtain evidence that is reliable and there must be a reasonable quantity of that evidence.
Through inspection, observation, inquiries and confirmations	These are the major types of evidence available for the auditor to use.
To afford a reasonable basis for an opinion regarding the financial statements	The auditor cannot expect to be completely certain that the financial statements are fairly presented but there must be persuasive evidence. The collection of evidence gathered by the auditor provides the basis for the auditor's opinion.

7-6 There are two primary reasons why the auditor can only be persuaded with a reasonable level of assurance, rather than be convinced that the financial statements are correct:

1. The cost of accumulating evidence. It would be extremely costly for the auditor to gather enough evidence to be completely convinced.
2. Evidence is normally not sufficiently reliable to enable the auditor to be completely convinced. For example, confirmations from customers may come back with erroneous information, which is the fault of the customer rather than the client.

7-7 The two determinants of the persuasiveness of evidence are competency and sufficiency. Competency refers to the degree to which evidence can be considered believable or worthy of trust. Competency relates to the audit procedures selected, including the timing of when those procedures are performed. Sufficiency refers to the quantity of evidence and it is related to sample size and items to select.

7-8 Following are seven characteristics that determine competence and an example of each.

FACTOR DETERMINING COMPETENCE	EXAMPLE OF COMPETENT EVIDENCE
Relevance	Trace inventory items located in the warehouse to their inclusion in the inventory subsidiary ledger
Independence of provider	Confirmation of a bank balance
Effectiveness of client's internal controls	Use of duplicate sales invoices for a large well-run company
Auditor's direct knowledge	Physical examination of inventory by the auditor
Qualifications of provider	Letter from an attorney dealing with the client's affairs
Degree of objectivity	Count of cash on hand by auditor
Timing	Observe inventory as of the last day of the fiscal year

TYPES OF AUDIT EVIDENCE	EXAMPLES
1. Physical examination	■ Count petty cash on hand ■ Examine fixed asset additions
2. Confirmation	■ Confirm accounts receivable balances of a sample of client customers ■ Confirm client's cash balance with bank
3. Documentation	■ Examine cancelled checks returned with cutoff bank statement ■ Examine vendors' invoices supporting a sample of cash disbursement transactions throughout the year
4. Observation	■ Observe the taking of inventory ■ Observe the preparation of the monthly bank reconciliation
5. Inquiries of the client	■ Inquire of management whether there is obsolete inventory ■ Inquire of management regarding the collectibility of large accounts receivable balances
6. Reperformance	■ Recompute invoice total by multiplying item price times quantity sold ■ Foot the sales journal for a one-month period and compare all totals to the general ledger
7. Analytical procedures	■ Evaluate reasonableness of receivables by calculating and comparing ratios ■ Compare expenses as a percentage of net sales with prior year's percentages

7-10 The four characteristics of the definition of a confirmation are:

1. Receipt
2. Written or oral response
3. From independent third party
4. Requested by the auditor

A confirmation is prepared specifically for the auditor and comes from an external source. External documentation is in the hands of the client at the time of the audit and was prepared for the client's use in the day-to-day operation of the business.

7-11 *Internal documentation* is prepared and used within the client's organization without ever going to an outside party, such as a customer or vendor.

Examples:
- check request form
- receiving report
- payroll time card
- adjusting journal entry

External documentation either originated with an outside party or was an internal document that went to an outside party and is now either in the hands of the client or is readily accessible.

Examples:
- vendor's invoice
- cancelled check
- cancelled note
- validated deposit slip

7-12 Analytical procedures are useful for indicating account balances that may be distorted by unusual or significant transactions and that should be intensively investigated. They are also useful in reviewing accounts or transactions for reasonableness to corroborate tentative conclusions reached on the basis of other evidence.

7-13 The most important reasons for performing analytical procedures are the following:

1. Understanding the client's industry and business
2. Assessment of the entity's ability to continue as a going concern
3. Indication of the presence of possible misstatements in the financial statements
4. Reduction of detailed audit tests

7-14 The decrease of the current ratio indicates a liquidity problem for Harper Company since the ratio has dropped to a level close to the requirements of the bond indenture. Special care should be exercised by the auditor to determine that the 2.05 ratio is proper since management would be motivated to hide any lower ratio. The auditor should expand procedures to test all current assets for proper cutoff and possible overstatement and to test all current liabilities for proper cutoff and possible understatement.

7-15 Attention directing analytical procedures occur when significant, unexpected differences are found between current year's unaudited financial data and other data used in comparisons. If an unusual difference is large, the auditor must determine the reason for it, and satisfy himself or herself that the cause is a valid economic event and not an error or misstatement due to fraud.

When an analytical procedure reveals no unusual fluctuations, the implication is minimized. In that case, the analytical procedure constitutes substantive evidence in support of the fair statement of the related account balances, and it is possible to perform fewer detailed substantive tests in connection with those accounts.

7-15 (Continued)

Frequently, the same analytical procedures can be used for attention directing and for reducing substantive tests, depending on the outcome of the tests. Simple procedures such as comparing the current year account balance to the prior year account balance is more attention directing (and provides less assurance) than more complex analytical procedures; i.e., those which rely on regression analysis. More sophisticated analytical procedures help the auditor examine relationships between several information variables simultaneously. The nature of these tests may provide greater assurance than simple procedures.

7-16 The statement is correct. Except for certain accounts with small dollar balances, analytical procedures are essential to help the auditor identify trends in a client's business and to see the relationship between the client's performance and industry averages. However, the auditor is responsible for gathering sufficient competent evidential matter through inspection, observation and confirmation in addition to the evidence obtained as a result of the analytical procedures.

7-17 Gordon could improve the quality of his analytical tests by:

1. Making internal comparisons to ratios of previous years.
2. In cases where the client has more than one branch in different industries, computing the ratios for each branch and comparing these to the industry ratios.

7-18 Roger Morris performs his ratio and trend analysis at the end of every audit. By that time, the audit procedures are completed. If the analysis was done at an interim date, the scope of the audit could be adjusted to compensate for the findings. SAS 56 (AU 329) requires that analytical procedures be performed in the planning phase of the audit and near the completion of the audit.

The use of ratio and trend analysis appears to give Roger Morris an insight into his client's business and affords him an opportunity to provide excellent business advice to his client.

7-19 The investigation of differences discovered through analytical procedures is affected by:

1. The materiality of the amount. A potential material misstatement will require extensive investigation, whereas an immaterial difference will be dismissed.
2. The auditor's knowledge of the client's business. The auditor may know of events that caused the change in ratios.
3. The results of other auditing procedures. Other information obtained during the audit may substantiate the results of the analytical procedures.
4. The purpose of the analytical procedure. The objective of the tests will also affect the auditor's response to the findings.
5. The level of aggregation of data. If the auditor uses disaggregated data, he or she may be able to isolate specific segments, locations, or time periods which require further investigation.

■ Multiple Choice Questions From CPA Examinations

7-20 a. (2)   b. (1)   c. (4)   d. (1)

7-21 a. (3)   b. (4)   c. (4)   d. (4)

■ Discussion Questions And Problems

7-22 a.

1. External	7. Internal	13. Internal
2. Internal	8. Internal	14. External
3. External	9. External	15. Internal
4. External	10. Internal*	16. External
5. Internal*	11. External	17. External
6. Internal	12. External**	18. External

*   Even though these may be signed or initialed by employees, they are still internal documents.

** Bills of lading are ordinarily signed by the freight company. That signature will be included on the top of the bill of lading, therefore, it is an external document.

b. External evidence is considered more reliable than internal evidence because external evidence has been in the hands of both the client and another party, implying agreement about the information and the conditions stated on the document.

7-23
1. (5) inquiry of client
2. (4) observation
3. (1) physical examination
4. (2) confirmation
5. (6) reperformance
6. (2) confirmation
7. (3) documentation
8. (7) analytical procedures
9. (5) inquiry of client
10. (6) reperformance
11. (4) observation
12. (1) physical examination
13. (7) analytical procedures
14. (3) documentation
15. (5) inquiry of client
16. (7) analytical procedures
17. (3) documentation
18. (6) reperformance
19. (1) physical examination
20. (2) confirmation

7-24 Examples of audit evidence the auditor can use to support each of the functions are:

    a. Examine invoice from vendor
       Direct confirmation with vendor
    b. Physical examination
       Direct confirmation with custodian
    c. Direct confirmation with customer
       Examine cash receipts journal and bank deposits for subsequent cash receipts
    d. Examine title for ownership of asset
       Examine invoice from vendor
    e. Direct confirmation with vendor
       Examine client's copy of vendor's statement
    f. Physical examination
       Examine sales invoice of subsequent sale of goods showing marked down sale price
    g. Count petty cash
       Direct confirmation with custodian

7-25
    a. Confirmations are normally more reliable evidence than inquiries of the client because of the independence of the outside party confirming the information.
    b. Confirmation of bank balances is considered highly reliable whereas confirmation of a department store charge account is often not considered reliable. Banks are accustomed to confirmations from auditors and normally maintain excellent accounting records, whereas most customers of department stores have neither characteristic.
    c. If an auditor is not qualified to distinguish between valuable inventory (e.g., diamonds) and worthless inventory (e.g., glass), the physical examination of inventory would not be considered to be reliable evidence.
    d. Reperformance tests are highly reliable because the auditor is able to gain 100% assurance of the accuracy, but the tests only verify whether the recorded amounts are accurately totalled. These tests do not uncover omissions or fictitious amounts.
    e. Relatively reliable documentation examples include: vendor statements, bank statements, and signed lease agreements. Relatively unreliable documentation examples may be: copies of customer invoices, internal memoranda and other communications, and a listing of fixed asset additions.
        The difference between reliable and unreliable documentation examples above is whether they originate from outside or inside the client's organization. External information is considered more reliable than internal documentation.

7-25 (Continued)

f.
1. Confirmation of accounts receivable - Corporation accustomed to confirmations compared to a member of the general public.
2. Examination of the corporate minutes - Experienced partner compared to a new assistant.
3. Physical observation of inventory - Auditor knowledgeable in the client's inventory compared to one who is not.
4. Attorney's letter - General counsel compared to an attorney involved only with patents.

g. Analytical procedures are evidence of the likelihood of misstatements in the financial statements, but they are rarely sufficient by themselves to conclude that the statements are misstated. Other supportive evidence is needed to determine whether apparent misstatements are actually material.

7-26

a.
1. An auditor should consider the following factors in evaluating oral evidence provided by client officers and employees in response to these questions:
   a) The competence of the questioned individual concerning the topic. For example, the perpetual inventory clerk would be more likely to know about slow-moving inventory items than current market prices.
   b) The logic and reasonableness of the response. As an auditor becomes familiar with his client's operations and personnel, he or she becomes more adept at choosing the right person to question and evaluating the answer. The auditor will also observe a pattern of response forming and determine whether it is internally consistent.
2. The auditor relies heavily upon the responses of client personnel, but he or she must recognize that this information may lack reliability. The reliance placed upon such evidence will vary based on the factors discussed in 1.a., but heavier weight generally is accorded to evidence generated independently of the client. The auditor should seek additional evidence in instances where he or she judges a client's response to be uninformed or unreliable. In crucial matters, the auditor should ask the client to confirm the representation in writing and also obtain additional evidence from independent sources.

b. The evidence provided by ratio analysis usually is classified as circumstantial. As such, it ranks lower in competence than direct evidence such as confirmation, physical examination, and inspection of original documents. However, ratio analysis has an important supplemental role in the audit, especially in larger engagements where the auditor reviews a relatively small portion of the direct evidence. The use of ratio analysis provides a broad overview and enables the auditor to determine unusual areas where additional testing may be necessary.

ACCOUNT NAME	FROM WHOM CONFIRMED	INFORMATION TO BE CONFIRMED
CASH IN BANK	All banks in which Star had deposits during the year including those which may have had an account that was closed out during the year.	■ Name and address of the bank. ■ The amount on deposit for each account as of the balance sheet date plus the name of each account, the account number, whether or not the account is subject to withdrawal by check, and the interest rate if the account is interest bearing. ■ The amount for which Star was directly liable to the bank for loans as of the balance sheet date plus the date of the loan, the due date, the interest rate, the date to which interest is paid, and description of the liability and collateral. ■ If internal controls over cash are weak, the auditor may wish to request that the bank include a list of authorized signatures with the confirmation.
TRADE ACCOUNTS RECEIVABLE	A representative sample of debtors at a selected confirmation date which may be either at the balance sheet or an interim date. Confirmations should also be requested for the following types of accounts: ■ Accounts with large balances; ■ Past-due accounts; ■ Accounts with zero or credit balances; ■ Accounts written off during the current period; ■ Accounts whose collection is considered questionable; ■ Other accounts of an unusual nature.	The confirmation can be either a positive or negative form of request. The positive form requests the debtor to directly notify the auditor whether the information is correct and if not correct, which items are considered incorrect. The negative form requests a reply only if the information is incorrect. In both cases the information should include: ■ Name and address of the debtor ■ Account number (if applicable) ■ The confirmation "as of" date ■ The aged account balance *or* individual invoices included in such balance (with invoice date).

7-27 (Continued)

ACCOUNT NAME	FROM WHOM CONFIRMED	INFORMATION TO BE CONFIRMED
NOTES RECEIVABLE	A selected sample of notes receivable outstanding at the balance sheet date. If a note receivable was written off during the year, the balance written off should be confirmed.	■ Name and address of the debtor. ■ Date of the note. ■ Due date. ■ Unpaid balance at balance sheet date. ■ Payment arrangements. ■ Interest rate. ■ Date of last interest payment. ■ Collateral, if any, to secure the note.
INVENTORIES	Public warehouses or other outside custodians (if any).	■ Name and address of public warehouse or other outside custodian. ■ The inventory date. ■ Detailed lists of inventory stored. Under generally accepted auditing standards, direct confirmation is acceptable provided supplemental inquiries are made that the inventory is the property of the company, unless the amount is a significant percent of current or total assets.
TRADE ACCOUNTS PAYABLE	Suppliers from whom substantial purchases have been made during the year, regardless of the balances of their accounts at the balance sheet date.	■ Name and address of the supplier. ■ The amount due and the amount of any purchase commitments as of the balance sheet date. When internal controls are considered good, the confirmation can be at an interim date; however, a thorough review must then be made of changes in the major accounts during the intervening period between the confirmation date and the year-end. It should also be noted that with interim confirmation, the auditor loses a desirable audit procedure for disclosing unrecorded and contingent liabilities at the balance sheet date. As an alternative to confirmation letters, it is becoming common practice to ask the vendor to send, directly to the independent auditor, a statement of the vendor's account with the client as of the balance sheet date rather than send an accounts payable confirmation.

7-27 (Continued)

ACCOUNT NAME	FROM WHOM CONFIRMED	INFORMATION TO BE CONFIRMED
MORTGAGES PAYABLE	Mortgagee for each mortgage that has a balance at the balance sheet date.	■ Name and address of mortgagee. ■ Original amount. ■ Date of note. ■ Maturity date. ■ Balance due at balance sheet date. ■ Payment arrangements. ■ Interest rate. ■ Interest payment dates. ■ Date of last interest payment. ■ Nature of defaults and if any events of default are known to mortgagee. ■ Location of mortgaged property.
CAPITAL STOCK	If Star uses an outside transfer agent and registrar, confirmations should be sent to both.	■ Name and address of transfer agent and registrar. ■ Number of shares of common stock authorized, issued, outstanding, and held as treasury shares for the company as of the balance sheet date.
LEGAL FEES	All of Star's major attorneys. Letters should also be sent to attorneys that the independent auditor knows the client has used extensively in prior years.	The auditor should request a letter from each attorney as to litigation being handled as of and subsequent to the balance sheet date. For each case, the attorney should give a description, report on its status as of the balance sheet date and as of the date of the letter, and give his or her opinion as to the ultimate liability. The attorney should also state Star's indebtedness to him or her as of the balance sheet date.
SALES AND EXPENSE ACCOUNTS	Occasionally, confirmation may be requested from an outside party for individual transactions contributing to total expenses or sales. This may be true where a major item is based on a formal contract and the auditor wants independent confirmation of agreement on the significant term of the contract and that these terms have been satisfactorily completed.	■ Name and address of outside party. ■ Other specific information would depend on the nature of the item and the reason the auditor feels it is necessary to confirm the item.

7-28

AUDIT PROCEDURE	a. TYPE OF AUDIT EVIDENCE	b. BALANCE-RELATED AUDIT OBJECTIVE
1. Test extend unit prices times quantity on the inventory list, test foot the list and compare the total to the general ledger.	Reperformance	Detail tie-in
2. Trace selected quantities from the inventory list to the physical inventory to make sure that it exists and the quantities are the same.	Physical examination	Existence and Accuracy
3. Question operating personnel about the possibility of obsolete or slow-moving inventory.	Inquiry of the client	Realizable value
4. Select a sample of quantities of inventory in the factory warehouse and trace each item to the inventory count sheets to determine if it has been included and if the quantity and description are correct.	Physical examination	Completeness and Accuracy
5. Compare the quantities on hand and unit prices on this year's inventory count sheets with those in the preceding year as a test for large differences.	Analytical procedures	Accuracy
6. Examine sales invoices and contracts with customers to determine whether any goods are out on consignment with customers. Examine vendors' invoices and contracts with vendors to determine if any goods on the inventory listing are owned by vendors.	Documentation	Rights
7. Send letters directly to third parties who hold the client's inventory and request they respond directly to us.	Confirmation	Existence, Completeness, and Accuracy

7-29 a. An audit procedure is the detailed instruction for the collection of a type of evidence to be obtained during the audit.
  b. Because it is an instruction for the accumulation of audit evidence, the wording should be sufficiently precise so that the person performing the audit procedure will understand what is expected.
  c.

TYPE OF EVIDENCE	AUDIT PROCEDURE
Confirmation	Mail 35 positive accounts receivable confirmations to customers 10 days after the balance sheet date to confirm balances as of year end.
Documentation	For accounts receivable confirmations not returned, examine shipping documents and duplicate sales invoices to determine whether the terms of the sale were valid and billed at the correct time.
Inquiries of the client	Inquire of the credit manager as to reasons why accounts receivable outstanding more than ninety days have not been collected and evaluate the reasonableness of his or her responses.
Reperformance	Foot the total balance column in the accounts receivable trial balance and compare the total to the general ledger.
Analytical procedures	Calculate the ratio of allowance for uncollectible accounts to accounts receivable as of the balance sheet date and compare the percentage to those of previous years.

7-30 a. The seven factors determining the competence of evidence are:

  1. Relevance
  2. Independence of provider
  3. Effectiveness of client's internal controls
  4. Auditor's direct knowledge
  5. Qualifications of individuals providing the information
  6. Degree of objectivity
  7. Timeliness

7-30 (Continued)

b. and c.

SITUATION	TYPE OF EVIDENCE THAT IS MORE RELIABLE	FACTOR AFFECTING COMPETENCE
1	Confirmation with business organizations	Qualifications of provider
2	Physically examine three-inch steel plates	Qualifications of provider (in this case the auditor)
3	Examine documents when several competent people are checking each other's work	Effectiveness of internal controls
4	Examine inventory of parts for the number of units on hand	Degree of objectivity
5	Discuss potential lawsuits with CPA firm's legal counsel	Independence of provider
6	Confirm a bank balance	Degree of objectivity
7	Confirm a bank balance	Independence of provider
8	Physically count the client's inventory	Auditor's direct knowledge
9	Physically count the inventory	Independence of provider and auditor's direct knowledge

7-31

PROCEDURE	a. APPROPRIATE TERM	b. TYPE OF EVIDENCE
1	Observe (j)	Observation
2	Compute (d)	Analytical procedure
3	Foot (f), Trace (g)	Reperformance
4	Scan (b)	Analytical procedure
5	Inquire (k)	Inquiry of client
6	Confirm (l)	Confirmation
7	Count (i)	Physical examination
8	Examine (a), Compare (h)	Documentation
9	Recompute (e)	Reperformance
10	Read (c)	Documentation

7-32 a. The use of analytical procedure in an audit has two general advantages to a CPA: 1) a broad view is obtained of the data under audit, and 2) attention is focused on exceptions or variations in the data.

A broad view of the data under audit is needed by the CPA to draw conclusions about the data as a whole--such conclusions cannot be drawn by merely looking at individual transactions. The application of analytical procedures to obtain this broad view requires a discerning analysis of the data, which results in overall conclusions upon which the CPA's audit satisfaction rests. The CPA is thus able to satisfy himself or herself as to the reasonableness, validity, and consistency of the data in view of the surrounding circumstances.

The focusing of the CPA's attention on exceptions or variations in the data results in a more efficient and economical audit because there is a reduction in the amount of detailed testing which would be required, in the absence of overall checks, to uncover these exceptions or variations. Furthermore, manipulations of accounts may be revealed because the double-entry bookkeeping system extends the effects of manipulations to additional accounts, which will then bear a changed relationship to other accounts.

In addition, managerial problems and trouble spots will be highlighted for the CPA and may lead to the opportunity for the auditor to be of additional service to his client.

b. The ratios that an auditor may compute during an audit as overall checks on balance sheet accounts and related income accounts may include the following:

1. Accruals of individual expenses to related total expenses (accrued interest/interest expense, accrued payroll/salaries and wages)
2. Accounts payable to purchases (days of purchases outstanding)
3. Long-term debt and interest expense thereon
4. Return on equity (relationship of net income to owners' equity)
5. Return on investments (relationship of investment income to investments).

c.

1. The possible reasons for a decrease in the rate of inventory turnover include the following:
   a) Decline in sales
   b) Increase in inventory quantities, intentional or unintentional
   c) Incorrect computation of inventory because of errors in pricing, extensions, or taking of physical inventory
   d) Inclusion in inventory of slow-moving or obsolete items
   e) Erroneous cutoff of purchases
   f) Erroneous cutoff of sales in a perpetual inventory system
   g) Unrecorded purchases
   h) Change in inventory valuation method.

7-32 (Continued)

2. The possible reasons for an increase in the number of days' sales in receivables including the following:
   a) Change in credit terms
   b) Decreasing sales
   c) Change in the sales mix of products with different sales terms
   d) Change in mix of customers
   e) Improper sales cutoff
   f) Unrecorded sales
   g) Lapping
   h) Slower collections caused by tighter economic conditions or lowering of the quality of the receivables.

7-33 a. Gross margin percentage for drug and nondrug sales is as follows:

	DRUGS	NONDRUGS
1999	40.6%	32.0%
1998	42.2%	32.0%
1997	42.1%	31.9%
1996	42.3%	31.8%

The explanation given by Adams is correct in part, but appears to be overstated. The gross margin percentage for nondrugs is approximately consistent. For drugs, the percent dropped significantly in the current year, far more than industry declines. The percent had been extremely stable before 1999. In dollars, the difference is approximately $82,000 (42.2% - 40.6% x $5,126,000) which appears to be significant. Of course, the decline in Jones' prices may be greater than the industry due to exceptional competition.

b. As the auditor, you cannot accept Adams' explanation if $82,000 is material. The decline in gross margin could be due to an understatement of drug inventory, a theft of drug inventory, or understated sales. Further investigation is required to determine if the decline is due to competitive factors or to a misstatement of income.

7-34 a.

1. Commission expense could be overstated during the current year or could have been understated during each of the past several years. Or, sales may have been understated during the current year or could have been overstated in each of the past several years.
2. Obsolete or unsalable inventory may be present and may require markdown to the lower of cost or market.
3. Especially when combined with 2 above, there is a high likelihood that obsolete or unsalable inventory may be present. Inventory appears to be maintained at a higher level than is necessary for the company.
4. Collection of accounts receivable appears to be a problem. Additional provision for uncollectible accounts may be necessary.

7-34 (Continued)

      5. Especially when combined with 4 above, the allowance for uncollectible accounts may be understated.

      6. Depreciation expenses may be understated for the year.

b. **ITEM 1** - Make an estimated calculation of total commission expense by multiplying the standard commission rate times commission sales for each of the last two years. Compare the resulting amount to the commission expense for that year. For whichever year appears to be out of line, select a sample of individual sales and recompute the commission, comparing it to the commission recorded.

ITEMS 2 AND 3 - Select a sample of the larger inventory items (by dollar value) and have the client schedule subsequent transactions affecting these items. Note the ability of the company to sell the items and the selling prices obtained by the client. For any items that the client is selling below cost plus a reasonable markup to cover selling expenses, or for items that the client has been unable to sell, propose that the client mark down the inventory to market value.

ITEMS 4 AND 5 - Select a sample of the larger and older accounts receivable and have the client schedule subsequent payments and credits for each of these accounts. For the larger accounts which show no substantial payments, examine credit reports and recent financial statements to determine the customers' ability to pay. Discuss each account for which substantial payment has not been received with the credit manager and determine the need for additional allowance for uncollectible accounts.

ITEM 6 - Discuss the reason for the reduced depreciation expense with the client personnel responsible for the fixed assets accounts. If they indicate that the change resulted from a preponderance of fully depreciated assets, test the detail records to determine that the explanation is reasonable. If no satisfactory explanation is given, expand the tests of depreciation until satisfied that the provision is reasonable for the year.

7-35

RATIO NUMBER	NEED FOR INVESTIGATION	REASON FOR INVESTIGATION	NATURE OF INVESTIGATION
1.	Yes	Current ratio has decreased from previous year and is significantly lower than the industry averages. This could indicate a shortage of working capital required for competition in this industry.	Obtain explanation for the decrease in current ratio and investigate the effect on the company's ability to operate, obtain needed financing, and meet the requirements of its debt agreements.
2.	Yes	An 11-2/3% increase in the amount of time required to collect receivables provides less cash with which to pay bills. This change could represent a change in the collection policy, which could have a significant effect on the company in the future. It may also indicate that a larger allowance for uncollectible accounts may be needed if accounts receivable are less collectible than in 1998.	Determine the cause of the change in the time to collect and evaluate the long-term effect on the company's ability to collect receivables and pay its bills. The difference between the company's and the industry's days to collect could indicate a more strict credit policy for the company. The investigation of this possibility could indicate that the company is forfeiting a large number of sales and lead to a recommendation for a more lenient credit policy.
3.	Yes	The difference in the company's days to sell and the industry is significant. This could indicate that the company is operating with too low an inventory level causing stock-outs and customer dissatisfaction. In the long term, this could have a significant adverse effect on the company.	Investigate the reasons for the difference in the days to sell between the company and the industry. Determine the effect on the company in terms of customer dissatisfaction and lost customers due to stock-outs or long waits for delivery.
4.	No	N/A	N/A

7-35 (Continued)

RATIO NUMBER	NEED FOR INVESTIGATION	REASON FOR INVESTIGATION	NATURE OF INVESTIGATION
5.	Yes	The industry average increased almost 10% indicating that the industry is building inventories either intentionally to fill an increased demand or unintentionally due to decreased demand and inability to dispose of inventory (as indicated further by significant decrease in the industry gross margin percent - see 8 below).	Investigate the market demand for the company's product to determine if a significant disposal problem may exist. There may be a net realizable value problem due to these conditions.
6.	No	N/A	N/A
7.	No	N/A	N/A
8.	Yes	The company appears to have raised prices during the past year to achieve the gross margin of the industry. However, it appears that the industry's gross margins have been reduced from either increased cost of goods which could not be passed on to customers in price increases or reduction in selling prices from competition, decreased demand for product, or overproduction. The result of these changes could be significant to the company's ability to produce a profit on its operations.	Determine the reason for the change in the industry's gross percent and the effect this might have on the company.
9.	No	N/A	N/A

7-35 (Continued)

    c. Mahogany Products operations differ significantly from the industry. Mahogany has operated in the past with higher turnover of inventory and receivables by selling at a lower gross margin and lower operating earnings. However, the company has changed significantly during the past year. The days to convert inventory to cash have increased 7% (11 days), while the current ratio has decreased by 15%. The company was able to increase its gross margin percent during the year when the industry was experiencing a significant decline in gross margin.

7-36 a. The company's financial position is deteriorating significantly. The company's ability to pay its bills is marginal (quick ratio = 0.97) and its ability to generate cash is weak (days to convert inventory to cash = 280.8 versus 179.9 in 1995). The earnings per share figure is misleading because it appears stable while the ratio of net income to common equity has been halved in two years. The accounts receivable may contain a significant amount of uncollectible accounts (accounts receivable turnover reduced 25% in four years), and the inventory may have a significant amount of unsalable goods included therein (inventory turnover reduced 40% in four years). The company's interest expense has become a significant expense (29% of earnings before taxes) and burden for the company as increased inventory and accounts receivable levels have required additional borrowings. The company may experience problems in paying its operating liabilities and required debt repayments in the near future.

7-36 (Continued)

b.

ADDITIONAL INFORMATION	REASON FOR ADDITIONAL INFORMATION
1. Debt repayment requirements, lease payment requirements, and preferred dividend requirements	To project the cash requirements for the next several years in order to estimate the company's ability to meet its obligations.
2. Debt to equity ratio	To see the company's capital investment and ability of the company to exist on its present investment.
3. Industry average ratios	To compare the company's ratios to those of the average company in its industry to identify possible problem areas in the company.
4. Aging of accounts receivable, bad debt history, and analysis of allowance for uncollectible accounts	To see the collection potential and experience in accounts receivable. To compare the allowance for uncollectible accounts to the collection experience and determine the reasonableness of the allowance.
5. Aging of inventory and history of markdown taken	To compare the age of the inventory to the markdown experience since the turnover has decreased significantly. To evaluate the net realizable value of the inventory.
6. Short- and long-term liquidity trend ratios	To indicate whether the company may have liquidity problems within the next five years.

  c. Based on the ratios shown, the following aspects of the company should receive special emphasis in the audit:

  1. Ability of the company to continue to acquire inventory, replace obsolete or worn-out fixed assets, and meet its debt obligations based on its current cash position.
  2. Reasonableness of the allowance for uncollectible accounts based on the reduction in accounts receivable turnover and increase in days to collect receivables.
  3. Reasonableness of the inventory valuation based on the decreased inventory turnover and increased days to sell inventory.

7-36 (Continued)

4. Computation of the earnings per share figure. It appears inconsistent that earnings per share could remain relatively stable when net earnings divided by common equity has decreased by 50%. This could be due to additional stock offerings during the period, or a stock split.

■ **Case**

7-37 Computer Solution.

When the computer option is assigned, an Excel spreadsheet (Filename P737.XLS) is used to compute a set of ratios as would be done manually (as shown below.) Five specific aspects of using the computer in doing this are discussed below. The first applies to both the manual and the computer approach.

1. Computation of ratios. The selection of ratios is arbitrary and should include a set that gives a good overview of all aspects of the company's financial statements that the user is interested in. And, in computing specific ratios, certain decisions must be made, such as whether to use net sales or gross sales. The formulas for the ratios selected for this solution are shown below. Note: where possible, the solution uses average balances (inventory and accounts receivable, for example) when required by the ratio formulas. Since 1995 balances are not available for computing 1996 average inventory and receivables, the solution does not calculate average inventory and accounts receivable turnover ratios for 1996.

Quick ratio = (cash + accounts receivable - allowance for doubtful accounts) / current liabilities

Gross margin/sales = gross margin / gross sales

Average inventory turnover = (cost of goods sold) / average inventory

Current ratio = Current assets / current liabilities

Average days to collect receivables = (average accounts receivable x 360) / (net sales)

Net income/total assets = (self-explanatory)

Net income/sales = net income / gross sales

Sales/equity = Gross sales / equity

Debt/equity = (total liabilities) / total equity

Net income/equity = (self-explanatory)

7-37 (Continued)

Allowance for doubtful accounts / accounts receivable = (self explanatory)

Bad debts/sales = bad debts / gross sales

Sales returns and allowances/sales = sales returns and allowances/gross sales

2. Set-up. Excel spreadsheets must be *planned* in advance. This can be referred to as "set-up." A useful technique is to use a block diagram to plan the set-up. This helps see the overall shape and content of the spreadsheet and is helpful for guiding its detailed preparation and how outputs will be controlled and formatted. A block diagram for this spreadsheet follows. It shows the spreadsheet divided into three sections: the heading, the input section, where data will be entered, and the results section where the ratios will be calculated. A vertical structure is used to facilitate printouts that will fit in an 8-1/2 x 14 inch format. The structure could just as easily be side-by-side.

7-37 (Continued)

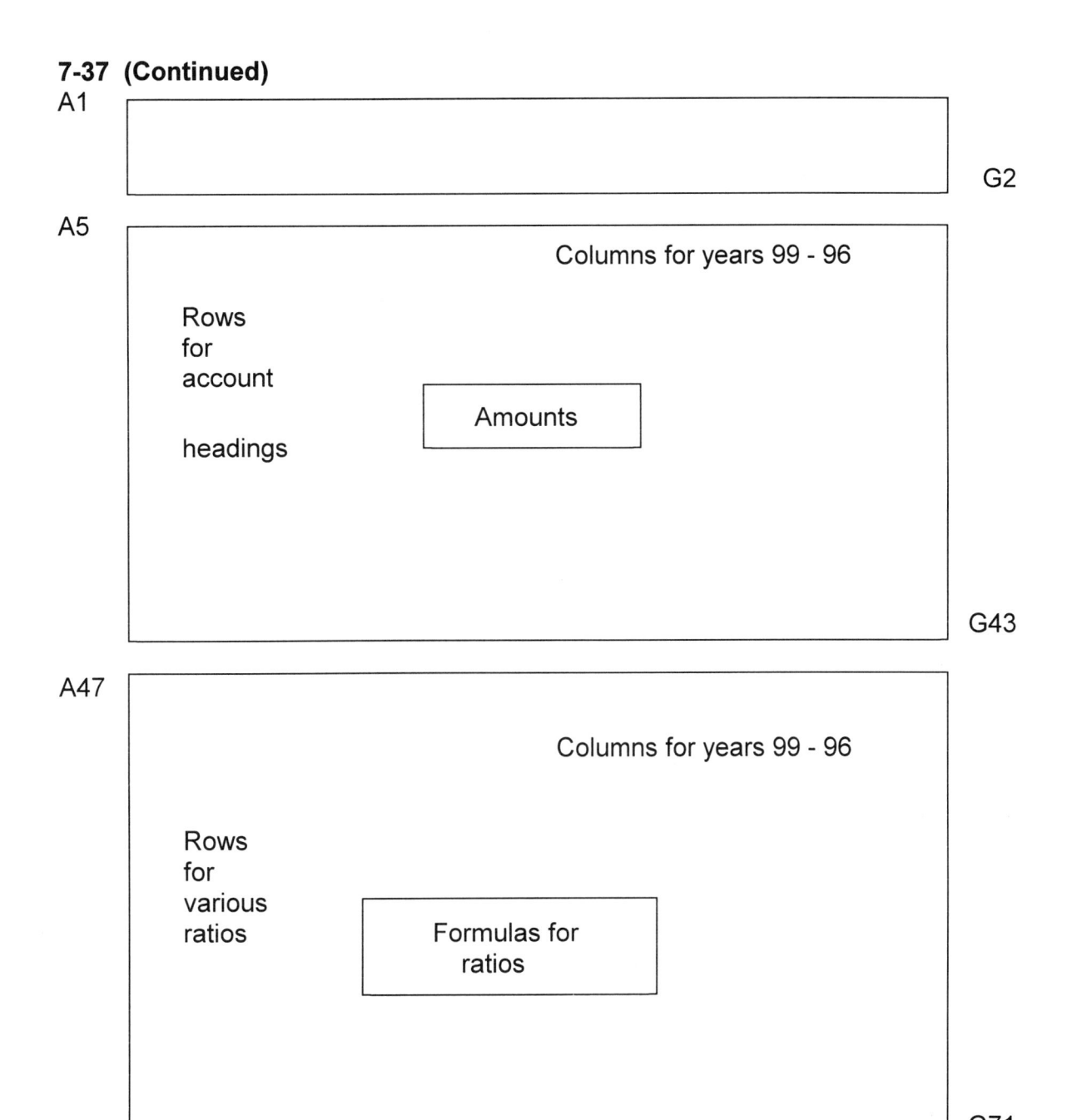

A1
```
                                                                    G2
```

A5
```
                    Columns for years 99 - 96

    Rows
    for
    account
              Amounts
    headings


                                                                   G43
```

A47
```
                    Columns for years 99 - 96

    Rows
    for
    various
    ratios    Formulas for
                 ratios


                                                                   G71
```

3. Check on accuracy of inputs. A major concern is knowing that input data has been entered accurately. This can usually be achieved by two alternative procedures. The first is computing totals and comparing them to check figures. For example, the details of assets can be computed and added to 100. The second procedure is verification of details on a figure-by-figure basis back to the source.

4. Treatment of negative values. Negative values can be entered as negative inputs or positive inputs. It is important to respond properly to the treatment used when the values are included in computations.

5. Check on accuracy of formulas. One of the biggest problems with using spreadsheets is errors in the development of formulas. One use of each formula should be done manually to check its correctness and the formulas should receive a careful second party review. If this second step is impractical, a second party should at least review the results for reasonableness.

7-37 (Continued)

Templates for the computer solutions prepared using Excel are included on the Companion Website and on the diskette accompanying this manual.

Soloman Bros. Manufacturing Co.
Analytical Procedures

Calculated from adjusted year-end balances

KEY RATIOS	1999	1998	1997	1996
Quick	.96	.83	.81	.74
Gross margin/sales	21.0%	22.1%	23.2%	25.0%
Average inventory turnover	1.79	1.82	1.93	NA
Current	2.19	1.96	1.91	1.75
Average days to collect receivables	129.31	122.24	114.47	NA
Net income/total assets	3.9%	3.9%	3.9%	4.3%
Net income/sales	5.0%	5.2%	5.3%	6.1%
Sales/equity	3.89:1	4.37:1	4.88:1	5.27:1
Debt/equity	4.02:1	4.82:1	5.64:1	6.42:1
Net income/equity	.19:1	.23:1	.26:1	.32:1
Allowance for doubtful accounts/accounts receivable	10.6%	11.5%	12.5%	14.8%
Bad debts/sales	3.7%	4.0%	4.1%	4.6%
Sales returns and allowances/gross sales	3.1%	3.0%	3.0%	2.9%

The Solomon brothers are considering going public to expand the business at a time that land and building costs in Boston are at extremely inflated values. Presently gross profit margins are 21% of sales and net income is 5% of sales. Both ratios decreased during the past year. To finance expansion, additional debt is out of the question because long-term debt is presently extremely high (debt to equity ratio is 4.02). Depreciation on new plant and equipment at the inflated prices will cause high depreciation charges which may significantly reduce the profit margins.

7-37 (Continued)

b. The account that is of the greatest concern is allowance for uncollectible accounts.

The following are three key analytical procedures indicating a possible misstatement of allowance for uncollectible accounts:

1. | **Breakdown of the aging in percent** | **1999** | **1998** | **1997** | **1996** |
|---|---|---|---|---|
| 0 - 30 days | 39.8% | 42.1% | 46.0% | 49.9% |
| 31 - 60 days | 33.5% | 33.3% | 32.0% | 30.1% |
| 61 - 120 days | 19.1% | 17.6% | 16.0% | 15.0% |
| over 120 days | 7.6% | 7.0% | 6.0% | 5.0% |
| | 100.0% | 100.0% | 100.0% | 100.0% |

2. Allowance/accounts receivable   10.6%   11.5%   12.5%   14.8%
3. Bad debts/sales   3.7%   4.0%   4.1%   4.6%

It appears that the allowance is understated:

1. If accounts were as collectible as before, allowance/accounts receivable should be about constant.
2. If accounts become less collectible, allowance/accounts receivable should increase.
3. Number 2 seems to be the case.

The aging of accounts receivable shows a deterioration in the overall aging (0-30 decreased significantly in the past several years, while those in all other categories increased), while the allowance for uncollectible accounts as a percentage of accounts receivable has decreased from 14.8% to 10.6% This indicates that the allowance for uncollectible accounts may be understated, especially considering the trend between 1996 and 1998.

Accounts Receivable.
The average days to collect receivables has increased steadily over the four-year period, which indicates that some accounts may not be collectible. This idea is supported by the deterioration in overall aging noted above.

Sales.
Finally, gross margin as a percentage of sales has declined steadily over the four-year period from 25% to 21%. Net Income/Sales has also declined. The auditor should seek an explanation from the client for these trends. It is possible that the decline in these ratios is due to an overstatement of sales.

Internet Problem Solution: Analytical Procedures—Industry Comparisons

7-1 Chapter 7 highlights the use of analytical procedures during the planning phase of the audit by presenting selected key financial statement ratios for a hypothetical clothing retailing company, SmartClothes.

Compare the SmartClothes ratios and seasonal sales with those of The Gap, and write a brief memo outlining your comparisons and conclusions. (Hint: You can find The Gap's financial information at either their website (www.gap.com) or the SEC's EDGAR Database (http://www.sec.gov). EdgarScan is an interface to the EDGAR Database. EdgarScan is developed at the PwC Global Technology Centre. EdgarScan pulls filings from the SEC's servers and parses them automatically to find key financial tables and normalize financials to a common format that is comparable across companies. Using hyperlinks we can go directly to specific sections of the filing, including the financial statements, footnotes, extracted financial data and computed ratios. You can find EdgarScan here (http://bamboo.tc.pw.com/).

> Here is the suggested solution. The SmartClothes' information is based on The Gap's 1997-1998 data. Therefore, students should find that SmartClothes' ratios and seasonal sales appear consistent with The Gap's. Specifically, SmartClothes' current ratio is slightly lower than The Gap's, their average inventory turnover and return on total assets are higher than The Gap's and the seasonal sales are very similar.
>
> (**Note**: Internet problems address current issues using Internet sources. Because Internet sites are subject to change, Internet problems and solutions may change. Current information on Internet problems is available at www.prenhall.com/arens/.)

Chapter 8

Audit Planning and Documentation

■ **Review Questions**

8-1 There are three primary benefits from planning audits: it helps the auditor obtain sufficient competent evidence for the circumstances, helps keep audit costs reasonable, and helps avoid misunderstandings with the client.

8-2 Seven major steps in planning audits are:

1. Preplan
2. Obtain background information
3. Obtain information about client's legal obligations
4. Perform preliminary analytical procedures
5. Set materiality, and assess acceptable audit risk and inherent risk
6. Understand internal control and assess control risk
7. Develop overall audit plan and audit program

8-3 The new auditor (successor) is required by SAS 84 (AU 315) to communicate with the predecessor auditor. This enables the successor to obtain information about the client so that he or she may evaluate whether to accept the engagement. Permission must be obtained from the client before communication can be made because of the confidentiality requirement in the *Code of Professional Conduct*. The predecessor is required to respond to the successor's request for information; however, the response may be limited to stating that no information will be given. The successor auditor should be wary if the predecessor is reluctant to provide information about the client.

8-4 Prior to accepting a client, the auditor should investigate the client. The auditor should evaluate the client's standing in the business community, financial stability, and relations with its previous CPA firm. The primary purpose of new client investigation is to ascertain the integrity of the client and the possibility of fraud. The auditor should be especially concerned with the possibility of fraudulent financial reporting since it is difficult to uncover. The auditor does not want to needlessly expose himself or herself to the possibility of a lawsuit for failure to detect such fraud.

8-5 An engagement letter is an agreement between the CPA firm and the client concerning the conduct of the audit and related services. It should state what services will be provided, whether any restrictions will be imposed on the auditor's work, deadlines for completing the audit, and assistance to be provided by client personnel. The engagement letter may also include the auditor's fees. In addition, the engagement letter informs the client that the auditor cannot guarantee that all acts of fraud will be discovered.

8-6 The four types of information the auditor should obtain or review as part of gaining background information for the audit and an example of how the information will be useful in conducting the audit are:

TYPE OF INFORMATION	EXAMPLE OF HOW INFORMATION USEFUL
1. Obtain knowledge of the client's industry and business.	Determination of obsolete inventory for an apparel manufacturer.
2. Tour the plant and offices.	Review of labor make-up in standard inventory costs will be facilitated by seeing that the manufacturing process is "labor intensive."
3. Identify related parties.	The auditor's knowledge of an affiliated company will help the auditor evaluate the existence of related party transactions.
4. Evaluate need for outside specialists.	Early recognition that the client has material amounts of chemical inventories permits the auditor to engage a specialist to help determine the valuation of the chemicals.

8-7 During the course of the plant tour the CPA will remember that an important aspect of the audit will be an effective analysis of the cost system. Therefore, the auditor will observe the nature of the company's products, the manufacturing facilities and processes, and the flow of materials so that the information obtained can later be related to the functions of the cost system.

The nature of the company's products and the manufacturing facilities and processes will reveal the features of the cost system that will require close audit attention. For example, the audit of a company engaged in the custom-manufacture of costly products such as yachts would require attention to the correct charging of material and labor to specific jobs, whereas the allocation of material and labor charges in the audit of a beverage-bottling plant would not be verified on the same basis. The CPA will note the stages at which finished products emerge and where additional materials must be added. He or she will also be alert for points at which scrap is generated or spoilage occurs. The auditor may find it advisable, after viewing the operations, to refer to auditing literature for problems encountered and solved by other CPAs in similar audits.

The auditor's observation of the manufacturing processes will reveal whether there is idle plant or machinery that may require disclosure in the financial statements. Should the machinery appear to be old or poorly maintained, the CPA might expect to find heavy expenditures in the accounts for repairs and maintenance. On the other hand, if the auditor determines that the company has recently installed new equipment or constructed a new building, he or she will expect to find these new assets on the books.

8-7 (Continued)
In studying the flow of materials, the auditor will be alert for possible problems that may arise in connection with the observation of the physical inventory, and he or she may make preliminary estimates of audit staff requirements. In this regard, the auditor will notice the various storage areas and how the materials are stored. The auditor may also keep in mind for further investigation any apparently obsolete inventory.

The auditor's study of the flow of materials will disclose the points at which various documents such as material requisitions arise. He or she will also meet some of the key manufacturing personnel who may give the auditor an insight into production problems and other matters such as excess or obsolete materials, and scrap and spoilage. The auditor will be alert for the attitude of the manufacturing personnel toward accounting controls. The CPA may make some inquiries about the methods of production scheduling, timekeeping procedures and whether work standards are employed. As a result of these observations, the internal documents that relate to the flow of materials will be more meaningful as accounting evidence.

The CPA's tour of the plant will give him or her an understanding of the plant terminology that will enable the CPA to communicate fluently with the client's personnel. The measures taken by the client to safeguard assets, such as protection of inventory from fire or theft, will be an indication of the client's attention to internal control measures. The location of the receiving and shipping departments and the procedures in effect will bear upon the CPA's evaluation of internal control. The auditor's overall impression of the client's plant will suggest the accuracy and adequacy of the accounting records that will be audited.

8-8 One type of information the auditor obtains in gaining knowledge about the clients' industry is the nature of the client's products, including the likelihood of their technological obsolescence and future salability. This information is essential in helping the auditor evaluate whether the client's inventory may be obsolete or have a market value lower than cost.

8-9 A related party is defined in SAS 45 (AU 334) as an affiliated company, principal owner of the client company, or any other party with which the client deals where one of the parties can influence the management or operating policies of the other.

Material related party transactions must be disclosed in the financial statements by management. Therefore, the auditor must identify related parties and make a reasonable effort to determine that all material related party transactions have been properly disclosed in the financial statements.

8-10 Jennifer Bailey's practice of ignoring prior year working papers and permanent files is improper. Though it is wise not to rely completely on the prior year's audit program and to set the current year's scope independent of the prior year, consideration must be given to problem areas of the previous year and to information contained in the permanent files in order to properly understand the client and wisely set the scope for the current engagement. Failure to examine prior year working papers will probably lead to inefficiencies in the current year's audit. This would prove costly to the CPA firm employing Jennifer.

8-11 In the audit of a client previously audited by a different CPA firm, it would be necessary to obtain a copy of the corporate charter and bylaws for the permanent files and to read these documents and prepare a summary abstract of items to test for compliance. In an ongoing engagement, this work has been performed in the past and is unnecessary each year. The auditor's responsibility is to determine what changes have been made during the current year and to update and review the summary abstract prepared in previous years for compliance.

8-12 The information in a mortgage that is likely to be relevant to the auditor includes the following:

1. The parties to the agreement
2. The effective date of the agreement
3. The amounts included in the agreement
4. The repayment schedule required by the agreement
5. The definition and terms of default
6. Prepayment options and penalties specified in the agreement
7. Assets pledged or encumbered by the agreement
8. Liquidity restrictions imposed by the agreement
9. Purchase restrictions imposed by the agreement
10. Operating restrictions imposed by the agreement
11. Requirements for audit reports or other types of reports on compliance with the agreement
12. The interest rate specified in the agreement
13. Any other requirements, limitations, or agreements specified in the document

8-13 Information in the client's minutes that is likely to be relevant to the auditor includes the following:

1. Declaration of dividends
2. Authorized compensation of officers
3. Acceptance of contracts and agreements
4. Authorization for the acquisition of property
5. Approval of mergers
6. Authorization of long-term loans
7. Approval to pledge securities
8. Authorization of individuals to sign checks
9. Reports on the progress of operations

It is important to read the minutes early in the engagement to identify items that need to be followed up on as a part of conducting the audit. For instance, if a long-term loan is authorized in the minutes, the auditor will want to make certain that the loan is recorded as part of long-term liabilities.

8-14 The purposes of the working papers are as follows:

1. To provide a basis for planning the audit. The auditor may use reference information from the previous year in order to plan this year's audit, such as the evaluation of internal control, the time budget, etc.

8-14 (Continued)
   2. To provide a record of the evidence accumulated and the results of the tests. This is the primary means of documenting that an adequate audit was performed.
   3. To provide data for deciding the proper type of audit report. Data are used in determining the scope of the audit and the fairness with which the financial statements are stated.
   4. To provide a basis for review by supervisors and partners. These individuals use the working papers to evaluate whether sufficient competent evidence was accumulated to justify the audit report.

Working papers are used for several purposes, both during the audit and after the audit is completed. One of the uses is the review by more experienced personnel. A second is for planning the subsequent year audit. A third is to demonstrate that the auditor has accumulated sufficient competent evidence if there's a need to defend the audit at a later date. For these uses, it is important that the working papers provide sufficient information so that the person reviewing the working papers knows the name of the client, contents of the paper, period covered, who prepared the working paper, when it was prepared, and how it ties into the rest of the working papers with an index code.

8-15 Working papers should include the following:

Name of the client Enables the auditor to identify the appropriate file to include the working paper in if it is removed from the file.

Period covered Enables the auditor to identify the appropriate year to which a working paper for a client belongs if it is removed from the file.

Description of the contents A list of the contents enables the reviewer to determine whether all important parts of the paper have been included. The contents description is also used as a means of identifying working papers in the same manner that a table of contents is used.

Initials of the preparer Indicates who prepared the working paper in case there are questions by the reviewer or someone who wants information from the papers at a later date. It also clearly identifies who is responsible for preparing the working papers if the audit must be defended.

Date of preparation Helps the reviewer to determine the sequence of the preparation of the working papers. It is also useful for the subsequent year in planning the sequence of preparing working papers.

Indexing Helps in organizing and filing working papers. Indexing also facilitates in searching between related portions of the working papers.

8-16 The permanent file contains data of an historical and continuing nature pertinent to the current audit. Examples of items included in the file are:

1. Articles of incorporation
2. Bylaws, bond indentures, and contracts
3. Analysis of accounts that have continuing importance to the auditor
4. Information related to the understanding of internal control:
   a. flowcharts
   b. internal control questionnaires
5. Results of previous years' analytical procedures, such as various ratios and percentages compiled by the auditors

By separating this information from the current year's working papers, it becomes easily accessible for the following year's auditors to obtain.

8-17 The purpose of an *analysis* is to show the activity in a general ledger account during the entire period under audit, tying together the beginning and ending balances. The *trial balance* includes the detailed make-up of an ending balance. It differs from an analysis in that it includes only those items comprising the end of the period balance. A *test of reasonableness* schedule contains information that enables the auditor to evaluate whether a certain account balance appears to be misstated. One example of a test of reasonableness schedule is a schedule that compares current year expenses to prior years' amounts. This type of schedule is intended to show which accounts need investigation due to significant variances.

8-18 Unanswered questions and exceptions may indicate the potential for significant errors or fraud in the financial statements. These should be investigated and resolved to make sure that financial statements are fairly presented.

The working papers can also be subpoenaed by courts as legal evidence. Unanswered questions and exceptions may indicate lack of due care by the auditor.

8-19 Tick marks are symbols written adjacent to information in working papers for the purpose of indicating the work performed by the auditor. An explanation of the tick mark must be included at the bottom of the working paper to indicate what was done and who did it.

8-20 Working papers are owned by the auditor. They can be used by the client if the auditor wants to release them after a careful consideration of whether there might be confidential information in them. The working papers can be subpoenaed by a court and thereby become the property of the court. They can be released to another CPA firm without the client's permission if they are being reviewed as a part of a voluntary peer review program under AICPA, state CPA society, or state Board of Accountancy authorization. The working papers can be sold or released to other users *if* the auditor obtains permission from the client.

8-21 It is a violation unless the CPA obtains permission from each client before the working papers for that client are released.

■ Multiple Choice Questions From CPA Examinations

8-22 a. (3)   b. (2)

8-23 a. (4)   b. (4)   c. (2)

8-24 a. (3)   b. (3)   c. (4)

8-25 a. (4)   b. (3)

■ Discussion Questions And Problems

8-26 Generally, the first step in preparing to supervise and plan the field work for an audit is to review and/or study current and background information on the client and industry. The most important sources in this preparatory stage are as follows:

1. Engagement letter
2. Audit permanent file
3. Last year's working papers
4. Client correspondence files
5. Last year's reports, including management letter and/or internal control memorandum
6. Last year's in-charge auditor
7. Industry and governmental publications
8. AICPA industry audit guides or firm audit guides

The purpose of this preparatory review and study is to become familiar with such things as:

1. The client's organizational structure, including key personnel.
2. Business activities and special problems of the client or industry in general.
3. Recent financial data or other important activities such as new security offerings or bond financing.
4. The client's records and procedures especially as they relate to internal control.
5. Reports that are anticipated for this engagement.

After the above review, you should make preliminary plans for the field work. You need to determine what audit tests can be done on an interim basis and what must be done on or after the balance-sheet date, including tests that should be done on a surprise basis. You must plan for what work can be done by the client's accounting and/or internal audit staff. You should also schedule critical dates for such things as cash counts, inventory observations, and confirmations. You should develop a detailed time budget and assign specific areas of the audit to each staff member on the engagement. Additionally, you should consider whether you need special expertise, e.g., a computer specialist.

You should prepare audit programs based on the prior year's assessment of internal control and any related current correspondence, as well as suggestions in last year's working papers. It is often possible to use last year's programs with revisions for changed conditions or desired audit emphasis.

8-26 (Continued)

If possible, visit the client to meet the appropriate officers and employees and discuss arrangements for the engagement.

After completing the preliminary preparation and planning as outlined above, it is wise to schedule a conference with all staff members assigned to the audit. The agenda would include a review of the engagement letter, estimate of the scope of the work, review of reports to be issued, review of the primary business operations of the client, assignment of audit areas to the staff, and review of specific problems or difficulties that are anticipated for this engagement. After this meeting, it is important to assure that each staff member has adequate time to review and prepare for his or her assigned audit area.

A final step is to make sure that the necessary work bags, supplies, permanent files, and prior year's working papers are carefully packed and prepared for transport to the client's office. If there is still time before starting the work at the client's office, you can assign staff to set up working paper analyses and lead schedules.

8-27 a. A related party transaction occurs when one party to a transaction has the ability to impose contract terms that would not have occurred if the parties had been unrelated. FASB 57 concludes that related parties consist of all affiliates of an enterprise, including (1) its management and their immediate families, (2) its principal owners and their immediate families, (3) investments accounted for by the equity method, (4) beneficial employee trusts that are managed by the management of the enterprise, and (5) any party that may, or does, deal with the enterprise and has ownership, control, or significant influence over the management or operating policies of another party to the extent that an arm's-length transaction may not be achieved.

When related party transactions or balances are material, the following disclosures are required:

1. The nature of the relationship or relationships.
2. A description of the transaction for the period reported on, including amounts if any, and such other information deemed necessary to obtain an understanding of the effect on the financial statements.
3. The dollar volume of transactions and the effects of any change in the method of establishing terms from those used in the preceding period.
4. Amounts due from or to related parties, and if not otherwise apparent, the terms and manner of settlement.

b. Financial statements are used by people to make decisions about the future. The presumption is that the nature of the transactions and balances in the financial statement are likely to be repeated in the future unless there is information to the contrary. Related party transactions can be conducted on a basis other than that which would normally happen with independent parties. That may indicate that these transactions may be on more or less favorable terms than can be expected to occur in the future. These transactions may affect users' decisions about a company, and therefore are relevant for their decision making.

8-27 (Continued)

c. The most important related parties that are likely to be involved in related party transactions involving management include relatives of management or management itself, companies in which such related parties have financial interests or dealings, significant suppliers of materials and services, and customers.

d. Related party transactions that could take place in a company include:

1. Lease of property by the company from a corporate officer who owns the property.
2. Acquisition of materials or merchandise by a company from another company which is owned or managed by an officer of the company or in which an officer of the company has a financial interest.
3. A company conducts a seminar at a facility which is owned or managed by the family or friend of an officer or another employee of the company.
4. A company contracts with a food service to run the company's cafeteria. An officer of the company has an investment in the food service.

e. Auditors can determine the existence of material transactions with related parties by performing the following procedures:

1. Obtain background information about the client in the manner discussed in this chapter to enhance understanding of the client's industry and business; i.e., examine corporate charter bylaws, minutes of board meetings, material contracts, etc.
2. Perform analytical procedures of the nature discussed in Chapters 7 and 8 to evaluate the possibility of business failure and assess areas where fraudulent financial reporting is likely.
3. Review and understand the client's legal obligations in the manner discussed in this chapter to become familiar with the legal environment in which the client operates.
4. Review the information available in the audit files, such as permanent files, audit programs, and the preceding year's working papers for the existence of material non-arm's-length transactions. Also discuss with tax and management personnel assigned to the client their knowledge of management involvement in material transactions.
5. Discuss the possibility of fraudulent financial reporting with company counsel after obtaining permission to do so from management.
6. When more than one CPA firm is involved in the audit, exchange information with them about the nature of material transactions and the possibility of fraudulent financial reporting.
7. Investigate whether material transactions occur close to year-end.
8. In all material transactions, evaluate whether the parties are economically independent and have negotiated the transaction on arm's-length basis, and whether each transaction was transacted for a valid business purpose.

8-27 (Continued)

9. Whenever there are material non-arm's-length transactions, each one should be evaluated to determine its nature and the possibility of its being recorded at the improper amount. The evaluation should consider whether the transaction was transacted for a valid business purpose, was not unduly complex, and was presented in conformity with its substance.
10. When management is indebted to the company in a material amount, evaluate whether management has the financial ability to settle the obligation. If collateral for the obligation exists, evaluate its acceptability and value.
11. Inspect entries in public records concerning the proper recording of real property transactions and personal property liens.
12. Make inquiries with related parties to determine the possibility of inconsistencies between the client's and related parties' understanding and recording of transactions that took place between them.
13. Inspect the records of the related party to a material transaction that is recorded by the client in a questionable manner.
14. When an independent party, such as an attorney or bank, is significantly involved in a material transaction, ascertain from them their understanding of the nature and purpose of the transaction.

f. For each of the non-arm's-length transactions in part d. above, the auditor can evaluate whether they are fraudulent, if he or she knows the transactions exist, by:

1. Comparing the terms of the lease to the terms in another comparable situation to determine that the terms are fair to the parties involved.
2. Comparing the price paid or received and other circumstances involved in the transaction to determine whether or not the circumstances are comparable to those available in the market.
3. Receiving a rate quote from a similar facility for similar service and comparing this to the amount paid by the company.
4. Receiving a quote from another company that would be willing to provide a similar service to the company and comparing this to the rate presently being paid by the company.

g. The auditor must first evaluate the significance of inadequate disclosure. Assuming it is material (highly material), the auditor must issue a qualified (adverse) opinion for the failure to follow generally accepted accounting principles. Disclosure of the facts must be made in a separate paragraph.

8-28 a. First the minutes of each meeting refer to the minutes of the previous meeting. The auditor should also obtain the next year's minutes, probably for February 2000, to make sure the previous minutes referred to were those from September 15, 1999.

Additionally, the auditor will request the client to include a statement in the client representation letter stating that all minutes were provided to the auditor.

8-28 (Continued)

b.

INFORMATION RELEVANT TO 1999 AUDIT	AUDIT ACTION REQUIRED
February 16	
1. Approval for increased distribution costs of $50,000	During analytical procedures, an increase of $50,000 should be expected for distribution costs.
2. Unresolved tax dispute.	Evaluate resolution of dispute and adequacy of disclosure in the financial statements if this is a material uncertainty.
3. Computer equipment donated.	Determine that old equipment was correctly treated in 1998 in the statements and that an appropriate deduction was taken for donated equipment.
4. Annual cash dividend.	Calculate total dividends and determine that dividends were correctly recorded.
5. Officers' bonuses.	Determine whether bonuses were accrued at 12-31-98 and were paid in 1999. Consider the tax implications of unpaid bonuses to officers.
September 15	
1. 1999 officers elected.	Inform staff of possibility of related party transactions.
2. Officers' salary information.	Note information in working papers for 2000 audit.
3. Pension/profit sharing plan.	Determine if the pension/profit sharing plan was approved. If so, make sure all assets and liabilities have been correctly recorded.
4. Acquisition of new computer.	Determine that there is appropriate accounting treatment of the disposal of the 1-year-old equipment. Also trace the cash receipts to the journals and evaluate correctness of the recording.
5. Loan.	Examine supporting documentation of loan and make sure all provisions noted in the minutes are appropriately disclosed. Confirm loan information with bank.
6. Auditor selection.	Thank management for selecting your firm for the 1999 audit. If your firm has experience with pension and profit sharing plans, ask management if there is anything they need help with regarding their new proposed plan.

8-28 (Continued)

    c. The auditor should have obtained and read the February minutes, before completing the 12-31-98 audit. Three items were especially relevant and require follow-up for the 12-31-98 audit: unresolved dispute with the IRS, replacement of computer equipment, and approval for the 12-31-98 bonuses.

8-29 a. The president's salary is a significant item this year and therefore should be included in the financial statements as information which should be disclosed to the shareholders.

    b. Management is primarily responsible for financial statement presentation. You have the responsibility of determining whether the president's salary, which is apparently material in amount, is adequately disclosed in the financial statements. The president's salary would be adequately disclosed if it were shown as a separate item in the income statement and if the increase in salary were also readily apparent because of the use of comparative statements. The president's salary could be adequately disclosed also by a footnote which gave the prior year's salary for comparison purposes. Should the client object to the disclosure of the president's salary as a separate item in the income statement or as a footnote, you would be compelled to decide whether to qualify your opinion because the financial statements failed to disclose information of material importance or to render an adverse opinion because the financial statements are not a fair presentation.

    c.

        1. You would be concerned with the fairness of the presentation of the financial statements because of the need for disclosure, as discussed in the preceding paragraph, and the possibility that a portion of the salary of the president, who is a substantial stockholder, may be deemed excessive by the IRS and treated as a dividend instead of as a business expense. Tax authorities may attach great significance to the fact that much of the potential increase in profits was distributed in the form of salary.

            You should have a discussion with the client to consider the possibility of salary expense disallowance by the IRS. If you believe that a disallowance may occur, you should recommend an appropriate increase in the provision for income taxes or footnote disclosure of the potential liability. If the client prefers not to adopt either recommendation, you should decide whether to qualify your opinion by taking exception to the failure to disclose the potential income tax liability or to render an adverse opinion because the financial statements are not a fair presentation.

        2. The consistency of the application of accounting principles has not been disturbed by the use of a different basis for determining the president's salary. The change in the method of computing the president's salary is not grounds for a consistency explanatory paragraph in your report because it is not a change in accounting methods.

8-30 a. The purpose of working papers is to aid the auditor in providing reasonable assurance that an adequate audit was conducted in accordance with generally accepted auditing standards. Specifically, the working papers provide:

1. a basis for planning the audit
2. a record of the evidence accumulated and results of tests
3. data for deciding the proper audit report
4. a basis for review by supervisors and partners

b. Working papers are the CPA's records of the procedures followed, tests performed, and conclusions reached during the audit. Working papers may include audit programs, analyses, memoranda, letters of confirmation and representation, abstracts of company documents, and schedules or commentaries prepared or obtained by the auditor.

c. The factors that affect the CPA's judgment of the type and content of the working papers for an engagement include:

1. The nature of the auditor's report
2. The nature of the client's business
3. The nature of the financial statements, schedules, or other information upon which the CPA is reporting and the materiality of the items included therein
4. The nature and condition of the client's records and internal controls
5. The needs for supervision and review of work performed by assistants

8-31 In general, the working paper is not set up in a logical manner to show what the auditor wants to accomplish. The primary objective of the working paper is to verify the ending balance in notes receivable and interest receivable. A secondary objective is to account for all interest income, cash received and cash disbursed for new notes, collateral as security, and other information about the notes for disclosure purposes.

Specific deficiencies of the working paper presented in the question are:

8-31 (Continued)

a. DEFICIENCY	b. IMPROVEMENT
1. Tick mark explanation "tested" does not indicate specifically what was done.	Should have separate tick marks meaning: - Agreed to confirmation - Footed - Traced to cash receipts journal - Recomputed, etc.
2. Explanation of some tick marks is not given.	Explain all tick marks on the same page of the working paper.
3. Classification of long-term portion indicates no verification.	Recompute portions of notes which are long-term.
4. Paid-to-date row is confusing.	Column should say "date paid to" and this should be confirmed.
5. Due dates are missing for J.J. Co., P. Smith, and Tent Co.	Include due dates on working paper for these notes.

c. **Spreadsheet Solution**

The purpose of using an Excel spreadsheet in this problem is to give the student some experience in preparing a simple working paper using an Excel spreadsheet. It should be explained to students that this type of working paper may or may not be prepared in actual practice, and that often templates are used to prepare more time-consuming working papers. Also, whether or not tick marks are computerized is a matter to be decided. The advantage is that the completed audit work can then be stored and reviewed electronically, a direction many firms are going. On the other hand, it may be more efficient to indicate audit work manually as it is performed, and a contrast in the color of the tick marks through use of a colored pencil may be desirable.

The following solution was prepared with Excel (Filename P831.XLS). The formulas used are self-evident, so no listing is provided, although it is available on the Companion Website and on the diskette accompanying this manual. Two items deserve comment:

1. An advantage of using a spreadsheet program for these types of analyses is that footing and crossfooting are done automatically.
2. When auditor tick marks are done by computer, a problem arises as to how to place them on the worksheet. One could use narrow columns inserted between the scheduled client data, or, as done here, the tick marks are placed in blank rows beneath the related data.

8-14

8-31 (Continued)

VANDERVOORT COMPANY
A/C #110 - NOTES RECEIVABLE
12/31/99

Schedule Prepared by N-1 JD Date 1/21/00
Approved by PP 2/15/00

Account #110 - Notes Receivable

Maker		Date Made/Due	Interest Rate/Date Paid to	Face Amount	Value of Security	Balance 12/31/98	Additions	Payments	Balance 12/31/99	Interest Receivable 12/31/98	Interest Earned	Interest Received	Interest Receivable 12/31/99
Apex Co.	c*	6/15/98 / 6/15/00	5% / None pd.	5000	None	4000 tp	0	1000	3000	104 tp	175	0	279
Ajax, Inc.	c*	11/21/98 / Demand	5% / 12/31/99	3591	None	3591 tp	0	3591 r	0	0 tp	102 ∨	102 r	0
J.J. Co.	c*	11/1/98 / 4/1/04 ($200/Mo.)	5% / 12/31/99	13180	24000	12780 tp	0	2400 r	10380	24 tp	577 ∨	601 r	0
P.Smith	c*	7/26/99 / 8/1/01 ($1000/Mo.)	5% / 9/30/99	25000	50000	0	25000 r	5000 r	20000	0	468 ∨	200 r	268
Martin-Peterson	c*	5/12/98 / Demand	5% / 12/31/99	2100	None	2100 tp	0	2100 r	0	0 tp	105 ∨	105 r	0
Tent Co.	c*	9/3/99 / 2/1/02 ($400/Mo.)	6% / 11/30/99	12000	10000	0	12000 r	1600 r	10400	0	162 ∨	108 r	54
						22471 f tp	37000 f	15691 f	43780 f, cf wtb	128 f tb	1589 f op	1116 f	601 f, cf wtb

Legend of Auditor's Tick Marks

f	Footed
cf	Crossfooted
tp	Traced to prior year working papers
wtb	Traced total to working trial balance
op	Traced total to operations working paper - OP6
*****	Examined note for payee, made and due dates, interest rate, face amount, and value of security. No exceptions noted.
c	Received confirmation, including date interest paid to, interest rate, interest paid during 1999, note balance, and security. No exceptions noted.
r	Traced to cash receipts journal
∨	Recomputed for the year

8-32 This case illustrates the common problem of an audit partner having to allocate his scarcest resource—his time. In this case, Winston Black neglects a new client for an existing one and causes himself several serious problems.

    a. AU 161 incorporates the AICPA's statement of quality control standards governing an audit practice into GAAS. One of the quality control standards requires that firms maintain client acceptance procedures. Henson, Davis has such a policy; however, whatever enforcement mechanism for compliance with it must not be sufficient, as McMullan Resources was accepted without the procedures being completed. More to the point, AU 315 makes the importance of adequate communication by a successor auditor with the predecessor auditor abundantly clear. In this case, Sarah Beale initiated a communication, but then left it incomplete when the predecessor auditor did not return her call. She rationalized this away by accepting representations from the new client. Of course, the predecessor auditor may be able to offer information that conflicts with the new client's best interest. It is not appropriate or in accordance with GAAS to consider management's representations in lieu of a direct communication with the predecessor auditor. The client should not have been accepted until an sufficient communication occurred.

        Can this be remedied? Yes and no. While SAS 84 (AU 315) requires communication with the predecessor auditor before accepting the engagement, a communication with the predecessor auditor should be conducted now, presumably by Black. However, if alarming information is obtained, Henson, Davis would find itself in the awkward position of having accepted a client it might not want. In that case, if it decides to withdraw from the engagement, it may be breaching a contractual obligation. If it continues, it may be taking an unwanted level of business and/or audit risk.

        A related implication is the wisdom of Black's assumption about Beale's competence and how that affects her performance on the engagement. Black relied on Beale extensively, yet Beale's performance on the new client acceptance was deficient. Does this mean that Beale's performance in other areas was deficient as well? Certainly, Black can do a thorough review of Beale's work, but review may or may not reveal all engagement deficiencies.

        Black's handling of this engagement also implies something about his attitude and objectivity. This was an initial engagement, yet he delegated almost all responsibility up to final review to Beale. He got credit for bringing in the new client, which directly benefitted him in terms of his compensation. It would be against his best interest to not accept (withdraw from) this client. If he is unwilling to "do the right thing" here, how will he handle other difficult audit problems?

    b. In the audit of long-term contracts, it is essential to obtain assurance that the contract is enforceable so that income can be recognized on the percentage-of-completion basis. It is also important to consider other aspects of the contract that relate to various accounting aspects, such as price and other terms, cancellation privileges, penalties, and contingencies. In this case, Beale has concluded that the signed contract, written in French, is McMullan's "standard" contract, based on client representation. Of course, GAAS require that management's representations, a weak form of evidence,

8-32 (Continued)

be corroborated with other evidence where possible. Beale might argue that the confirmation obtained constitutes such evidence.

Beale's argument may seem logical with regard to enforcement, however, the confirmation form refers to existing disputes. It says nothing about contractual clauses that may foreshadow enforceability. For that reason the audit program requires the contract to be read. How would an auditor know whether the contract form was that of a standard contract without reading it? Furthermore, it may be unrealistic to assume there is such a thing as a "standard" contract in the first place. Long-term and short-term contracts are the result of negotiation and often contain special clauses and changed language.

In this case, not reading the contract was an insufficiency and the French-language copy should be translated by an independent translator and read by the auditors.

c. Compliance with GAAS is a matter that is always subject to professional judgment. One professional auditor may conclude he or she has complied with GAAS, and another would conclude that GAAS has been violated, so these matters are very seldom clear cut. However, in this case, it appears that Black and Beale may have violated GAAS in the following ways:

Standard of Field Work No. 1 - The work is to be adequately planned and assistants, if any, are to be properly supervised. The requirements of AU 315, discussed above, relate to this standard. More generally, the audit partner should participate in planning, at least with a timely review. This would be more important than otherwise in the situation of a first-time engagement, as we have here. Similarly, some level of on-going partner supervision would seem prudent and logical. Black, apparently, did not really participate at all until final review.

Standard of Field Work No. 3 - Sufficient competent evidential matter is to be obtained through inspection, observation, inquiries, and confirmations to afford a reasonable basis for an opinion regarding the financial statements under audit. As discussed above, the work on the Montreal contract was deficient and further evidence is required.

In addition, whenever the field work standards are violated there are implied violations of other standards. It might be argued that Beale was not proficient as an auditor because of her failures with the new client acceptance procedures and the Montreal contract. Similarly, it might be argued that due professional care was not taken both by Beale and by Black for delegating so much to Beale.

Internet Problem Solution: Industry Research and Client Acceptance

8-1 Chapter 8 highlights the importance of obtaining sufficient knowledge about the industry in which the client operates. This Internet problem asks the students to suppose that they are approached by a prospective client, "AAAA WhirlPools," in the whirlpool tub industry. While AAAA WhirlPool started out several years ago as a small player, they have experienced dramatic growth and are considering going public. The chief executive officer, Terry Tinkow, provided its audit firm with some summary historical financial and operating data. In 1997 and 1998, AAAA WhirlPool reported sales of 225,000 and 450,000 units, respectively.

Are AAAA WhirlPools' 1997 and 1998 unit sales reasonable? Why or why not? (**Hint**: Visit the U.S. Census Bureau's website (http://www.census.gov/). Once at the site, go to the "Business" section and then to the "Manufacturing" section. Look in the most recent Manufacturing Profile under "Building Material," "Plumbing Fixtures.")

The 1997 and 1998 sales do not appear reasonable. The U.S. Census Bureau reports that shipments of whirlpool baths were as follows:

- 1993 – 385,000 units shipped
- 1994 – 426,000 units shipped
- 1995 – 442,000 units shipped
- 1996 – 483,000 units shipped

These statistics suggest that the entire industry probably shipped fewer than 550,000 units in 1998. It seems unlikely that AAAA WhirlPool represents such a large percentage of the industry's sales. Find the U.S. Census Manufacturing Profiles here (http://www.census.gov/econ/www/manumenu.html) or view the 1996 Manufacturing Profile. This file is in PDF format and can be read using the Adobe Acrobat Reader 3.0. If you do not currently have this program, you may download a copy of the Adobe website (http://www.adobe.com).

(**Note**: Internet problems address current issues using Internet sources. Because Internet sites are subject to change, Internet problems and solutions may change. Current information on Internet problems is available at www.prenhall.com/arens/.)

Chapter 9

Materiality and Risk

■ **Review Questions**

9-1 The planning phases are: preplan, obtain background information, obtain information about client's legal obligations, perform preliminary analytical procedures, set materiality and assess acceptable audit risk and inherent risk, understand internal control and assess control risk, and develop overall audit plan and audit program. Evaluation of materiality and risk is therefore part five.

9-2 Materiality is defined as: the magnitude of an omission or misstatement of accounting information that, in light of the surrounding circumstances, makes it probable that the judgment of a reasonable person relying on the information would have been changed or influenced by the omission or misstatement.

"Obtain reasonable assurance," as used in the audit report, means that the auditor does not *guarantee* or insure the fair presentation of the financial statements. There is some risk that the financial statements contain a material misstatement.

9-3 Materiality is important because if financial statements are materially misstated, users' decisions may be affected, and thereby cause financial loss to them. It is difficult to apply because there are often many different users of the financial statements. The auditor must therefore make an assessment of the likely users and the decisions they will make. Materiality is also difficult to apply because it is a relative concept. The professional auditing standards offer little specific guidance regarding the application of materiality. The auditor must, therefore, exercise considerable professional judgment in the application of materiality.

9-4 The preliminary judgment about materiality is the maximum amount by which the auditor believes the financial statements could be misstated and still not affect the decisions of reasonable users. Several factors affect the preliminary judgment about materiality and are as follows:

1. Materiality is a relative rather than an absolute concept.
2. Bases are needed for evaluating materiality.
3. Qualitative factors affect materiality decisions.
4. Expected distribution of the financial statements will affect the preliminary judgment of materiality. If the financial statements are widely distributed to a large number of users, the preliminary judgment of materiality will probably be set lower than if the financial statements are not expected to be widely distributed.
5. The level of acceptable audit risk will also affect the preliminary judgment of materiality.

9-5 Because materiality is relative rather than absolute, it is necessary to have bases for establishing whether misstatements are material. For example, in the audit of a manufacturing company, the auditor might use as bases: net income before taxes, total assets, current assets, and working capital. For a governmental unit, such as a school district, there is no net income before taxes, and therefore that would be an unavailable base. Instead, the primary bases would likely be fund balances, total assets, and perhaps total revenue.

9-6 The following qualitative factors are likely to be considered in evaluating materiality:

   a. Amounts involving fraud are usually considered more important than unintentional errors of equal dollar amounts.
   b. Misstatements that are otherwise minor may be material if there are possible consequences arising from contractual obligations.
   c. Misstatements that are otherwise immaterial may be material if they affect a trend in earnings.

9-7 A preliminary judgment about materiality is set for the financial statements as a whole. Tolerable misstatement is the maximum amount of misstatement that would be considered material for an individual account balance. The amount of tolerable misstatement for any given account is dependent upon the preliminary judgment about materiality. Ordinarily, tolerable misstatement for any given account would have to be lower than the preliminary judgment about materiality. In many cases, it will be considerably lower because of the possibility of misstatements in different accounts which, in total, cannot exceed the preliminary judgment about materiality.

9-8 There are several possible answers to the question. One example is:

Cash	$500	Overstatement
Fixed assets	$3,000	Overstatement
Long-term loans	$1,500	Understatement

Note: Cash and fixed assets are tested for overstatement and long-term loans for understatement because the auditor's objective in this case is to test for overstatements of owner's equity.

The least amount of tolerable misstatement was allocated to cash and long-term loans because they are relatively easy to audit. The majority of the total allocation was to fixed assets because there is a greater likelihood of misstatement of fixed assets in a typical audit.

9-9 An estimate of the total misstatement in a segment is the estimate of the total misstatements based upon the sample results. If only a sample of the population is selected and audited, the auditor must project the total sample misstatements to a total estimate. This is done audit area by audit area. The misstatements in each audit area must be totaled to make an estimate of the total misstatements in the overall financial statements. It is important to make these estimates so that the auditor can evaluate whether the financial statements, taken as a whole, may be materially misstated. The estimate for each segment is compared to tolerable misstatement for that segment

9-9 (Continued)

and the estimate of the overall misstatement on the financial statements is compared to the preliminary judgment about materiality.

9-10 If an audit is being performed on a medium-sized company that is part of a conglomerate, the auditor must make a materiality judgment based upon the conglomerate. Materiality may be larger for a company that is part of a conglomerate because even though the financial statements of the medium-sized company may be misstated, the financial statements of the large conglomerate might still be fairly stated. If, however, the auditor is giving a separate opinion on the medium-sized company, the materiality would be lower than for the audit of a conglomerate.

9-11 The audit risk model is as follows:

$$PDR = \frac{AAR}{IR \times CR}$$

Where PDR = Planned detection risk
 AAR = Acceptable audit risk
 IR = Inherent risk
 CR = Control risk

Planned detection risk A measure of the risk that audit evidence for a segment will fail to detect misstatements exceeding a tolerable amount, should such misstatements exist.

Acceptable audit risk A measure of how willing the auditor is to accept that the financial statements may be materially misstated after the audit is completed and an unqualified opinion has been issued.

Inherent risk A measure of the auditor's assessment of the likelihood that there are material misstatements in a segment before considering the effectiveness of internal control.

Control risk A measure of the auditor's assessment of the likelihood that misstatements exceeding a tolerable amount in a segment will not be prevented or detected by the client's internal controls.

9-12 Planned detection risk is a measure of the risk that the audit evidence for a segment will fail to detect misstatements exceeding a tolerable amount, should such misstatements exist. When planned detection risk is increased from medium to high, the amount of evidence the auditor must accumulate is reduced.

9-13 An increase in planned detection risk may be caused by an increase in acceptable audit risk or a decrease in either control risk or inherent risk.

9-14 Inherent risk is a measure of the auditor's assessment of the likelihood that there are material misstatements in a segment before considering the effectiveness of internal control.

Factors affecting assessment of inherent risk include:

- Nature of the client's business
- Factors related to misstatements arising from fraudulent financial reporting
- Results of previous audits
- Initial vs. repeat engagement
- Related parties
- Nonroutine transactions
- Judgment required to correctly record transactions and balances
- Susceptibility of assets to misappropriation
- Makeup of the population

9-15 Inherent risk is set for segments rather than for the overall audit because misstatements occur in segments. By identifying expectations of misstatements in segments, the auditor is thereby able to modify audit evidence by searching for misstatements in those segments.

When inherent risk is increased from medium to high, the auditor should increase the audit evidence accumulated to determine whether the expected misstatement actually occurs. The audit evidence goes in the opposite direction in Review Question 9-12.

9-16 Extensive misstatements in the prior year's audit would cause inherent risk to be set at a high level (maybe even 100%). An increase in inherent risk would lead to a decrease in planned detection risk, which would require that the auditor increase the level of planned audit evidence.

9-17 Acceptable audit risk is a measure of how willing the auditor is to accept that the financial statements may be materially misstated after the audit is completed and an unqualified opinion has been issued.

Acceptable audit risk has an inverse relationship to evidence. If acceptable audit risk is reduced, planned evidence should increase.

9-18 When the auditor is in a situation where he or she believes that there is a high exposure to legal liability, the acceptable audit risk would be set lower than when there is little exposure to liability. Even when the auditor believes that there is little exposure to legal liability, there is still a minimum acceptable audit risk that should be met.

9-19 The first category of factors that determine acceptable audit risk is the degree to which users rely on the financial statements. The following factors are indicators of this:

- Client's size
- Distribution of ownership
- Nature and amount of liabilities

9-19 (Continued)

The second category of factors is the likelihood that a client will have financial difficulties after the audit report is issued. Factors affecting this are:

- Liquidity position
- Profits (losses) in previous years
- Method of financing growth
- Nature of the client's operations
- Competence of management

The third category of factors is the auditor's evaluation of management's integrity. Factors that may affect this are:

- Relationship with current or previous auditors
- Frequency of turnover of key financial or internal audit personnel
- Relationship with employees and labor unions

9-20 Exact quantification of all components of the audit risk model is not required to use the model in a meaningful way. An understanding of the relationships among model components and the effect that changes in the components have on the amount of evidence needed will allow practitioners to use the audit risk model in a meaningful way.

9-21 The auditor should revise the components of the audit risk model when the evidence accumulated during the audit indicates that the auditor's original assessments of inherent risk or control risk are too low or too high or the original assessment of acceptable audit risk is too low or too high.

The auditor should exercise care in determining the additional amount of evidence which will be required. This should be done without the use of the audit risk model. If the audit risk model is used to determine a revised planned detection risk, there is a danger of not increasing the evidence sufficiently.

■ Multiple Choice Questions From CPA Examinations

9-22 a. (4)   b. (4)

9-23 a. (1)   b. (1)   c. (1)

9-24 a. (2)   b. (3)   c. (1)

■ Discussion Questions And Problems

9-25 a. The justification for a lower preliminary judgment about materiality for overstatements is directly related to legal liability and audit risk. Most auditors believe they have a greater legal and professional responsibility to discover overstatements of owners' equity than understatements because users are likely to be more critical of overstatements. That does not imply there is no responsibility for understatements.

9-25 (Continued)

b. There are two reasons for permitting the sum of tolerable misstatements to exceed overall materiality. First, it is unlikely that all accounts will be misstated by the full amount of tolerable misstatement. Second, some accounts are likely to be overstated while others are likely to be understated, resulting in net misstatement that is likely to be less than overall materiality.

c. This results because of the estimate of sampling error for each account. For example, the likely estimate of accounts receivable is an understatement of $7,500 + or - a sampling error of $11,500. You would be most concerned about understatement for accounts receivable because the estimated understatement of $19,000 exceeds the tolerable misstatement of $18,000 for that account.

d. You would be most concerned about understatement amounts since the total estimated understatement amount ($30,000) exceeds the preliminary judgment about materiality for understatements ($20,000). You would be most concerned about accounts receivable given that the total misstatement for that account exceeds tolerable misstatement for understatement.

e.
1. This may occur because total tolerable misstatement was allowed to exceed the preliminary judgment (see Part b for explanation).
2. The auditor must determine whether the actual total overstatement amount actually exceeds the preliminary judgment by performing expanded audit tests or by requiring the client to make an adjustment for estimated misstatements.

9-26 a. The profession has not established clear-cut guidelines as to the appropriate preliminary estimates of materiality. These are matters of the auditor's professional judgment.

To illustrate, the application of the illustrative materiality guidelines shown in **Figure 9-2** (page 253), are used for the problem. Other guidelines may be equally acceptable.

STATEMENT COMPONENT	PERCENT GUIDELINES	DOLLAR RANGE (IN MILLIONS)
Earnings from continuing operations before taxes	5 - 10%	$20.9 - $ 41.8
Current assets	5 - 10%	$112.7 - $225.4
Current liabilities	5 - 10%	$ 60.7 - $121.5
Total assets	3 - 6%	$115.8 - $231.6

b. The allocation to the individual accounts is not shown. The difficulty of the allocation is far more important than the actual allocation. There are several ways the allocation could be done. The most likely way would be to allocate only on the basis of the balance sheet rather than the income statement. Even then the allocation could vary significantly. One way would be to allocate the same amount to each of the balance sheet accounts on the consolidated statement of financial position. Using a materiality limit of

9-26 (Continued)

$21,000,000 before taxes (because it is the most restrictive) and the same dollar allocation to each account excluding retained earnings, the allocation would be approximately $1,000,000 to each account. There are 21 account summaries included in the statement of financial position which is divided into $21,000,000.

An alternative is to assume an equal percentage misstatement in each of the accounts. Doing it in that manner, total assets should be added to total liabilities and owners' equity, less retained earnings. The allocation would be then done on a percentage basis.

c. Auditors generally use *before* tax net earnings instead of *after* tax net earnings to develop a preliminary judgment about materiality given that transactions and accounts being audited within a segment are presented in the accounting records on a pretax basis. Auditors generally project total misstatements for a segment and accumulate all projected total misstatements across segments on a pretax basis and then compute the tax effect on an aggregate basis to determine the effects on after tax net earnings.

d. By allocating 75% of the preliminary estimate to accounts receivable, inventories, and accounts payable, there is far less materiality to be allocated to all other accounts. Given the total dollar value of those accounts, that may be a reasonable allocation. The effect of such an allocation would be that the auditor may be able to accumulate sufficient competent evidence with less total effort than would be necessary under part b. Under part b, it would likely be necessary to audit, on a 100% basis, accounts receivable, inventories, and accounts payable. On most audits it would be expensive to do that much testing in those three accounts.

It would likely be necessary to audit accounts such as cash and temporary investments on a 100% basis. That would not be costly on most audits because the effort to do so would be small compared to the cost of auditing receivables, inventories, and accounts payable.

e. It is necessary for you to be satisfied that the actual estimate of misstatements is less than the preliminary judgment about materiality for all of the bases. First you would reevaluate the preliminary judgment for earnings. Assuming no change is considered appropriate, you would likely require an adjusting entry or an expansion of certain audit tests.

9-27 a. The following terms are audit planning decisions requiring professional judgment:

- Preliminary judgment about materiality
- Acceptable audit risk
- Tolerable misstatement
- Inherent risk
- Control risk
- Planned detection risk

9-27 (Continued)

    b. The following terms are audit conclusions resulting from application of audit procedures and requiring professional judgment:

- Estimate of the combined misstatements
- Estimated total misstatement in a segment

    c. It is acceptable to change any of the factors affecting audit planning decisions at any time in the audit. The planning process begins before the audit starts and continues throughout the engagement.

9-28 Acceptable audit risk is a measure of how willing the auditor is to accept that the financial statements may be materially misstated after the audit is completed and an unqualified opinion has been issued.

    a. True. A CPA firm should attempt to use reasonable uniformity from audit to audit when circumstances are similar. The only reasons for having a different audit risk in these circumstances are the lack of consistency within the firm, different audit risk preferences for different auditors, and difficulties of measuring audit risk.

    b. True. Users who rely heavily upon the financial statements need more reliable information than those who do not place heavy reliance on the financial statements. To protect those users, the auditor needs to be more sure that the financial statements are fairly stated. That is equivalent to stating that acceptable audit risk is lower. Consistent with that conclusion, the auditor is also likely to face greatest legal exposure in situations where external users rely heavily upon the statements. Therefore, the auditor should be more certain that the financial statements are correctly stated.

    c. True. The reasoning for c is essentially the same as for b.

    d. True. The audit opinion issued by different auditors conveys the same meaning regardless of who signs the report. Users cannot be expected to evaluate whether different auditors take different risk levels. Therefore, for a given set of circumstances, every CPA firm should attempt to obtain approximately the same audit risk.

9-29 a. False. The acceptable audit risk, inherent risk, or control risk may all be different. A change of any of these factors will cause a change in audit evidence accumulated.

    b. False. Inherent risk and control risk may be different. Even if acceptable audit risk is the same, inherent risk and control risk will cause audit evidence accumulation to be different.

    c. True. These are the primary factors determining the evidence that should be accumulated. Even in those circumstances, however, different auditors may choose to approach the evidence accumulation differently. For example, one firm may choose to emphasize analytical procedures, whereas other firms may emphasize tests of controls.

9-30 a.

1. The auditor may set inherent risk at 100% because of lack of prior year information. If the auditor believes there is a reasonable chance of a material misstatement, 100% inherent risk is appropriate. Similarly, because the auditor does not plan to test internal controls due to the ineffectiveness of internal controls, a 100% risk is appropriate for control risk.
2. Acceptable audit risk and planned detection risk will be identical. Using the formula:

    PDR = AAR ÷ (IR x CR), if IR and CR equal 1,
    then PDR = AAR.

3. If planned detection risk is lower, the auditor must accumulate more audit evidence than if planned detection risk is higher. The reason is that the auditor is willing to take only a small risk that substantive audit tests will fail to uncover existing misstatements in the financial statements.

b.

1. The auditor should be conservative in estimates of the likelihood of misstatements in the financial statements, because the costs of being wrong are relatively high. It would be inappropriate for auditors to set low levels of inherent and control risk without doing substantive testing to determine if the financial statements are actually misstated. For example, using the formula of the audit risk model shown in part a, assume inherent and control risk are each set at 20% and acceptable audit risk is 4%. Using the formula, planned detection risk would be equal to 100%. Therefore, no substantive audit testing would be necessary. That is inconsistent with the responsibilities of the auditor. Therefore, relatively high inherent and control risk are used even under the most ideal circumstances. Furthermore, given that internal control effectiveness is often dependent on the performance of procedures performed by employees who may be prone to errors or management override, control risk cannot be set too low.
2. Using the formula in a., planned detection risk is equal to 20% [PDR = .05 / (.5 x .5) = .2].
3. Less evidence accumulation is necessary in b-2 than if planned detection risk were smaller. Comparing b-2 to a-2 for an acceptable audit risk of 5%, considerably less evidence would be required for b-2 than for a-2.

9-30 (Continued)

c.

1. The auditor might set acceptable audit risk high because Redwood City is in relatively good financial condition and there are few users of financial statements. It is common in municipal audits for the only major users of the financial statements to be state agencies who only look at them for reasonableness. Inherent risk might be set low because of good results in prior year audits and no audit areas where there is a high expectation of misstatement. Control risk would normally be set low because of effective internal controls in the past, and continued expectation of good controls in the current year.
2. Using the formula in a-2, PDR = .05 / (.2 x .2) = 1.25. Planned detection risk is equal to more than 100% in this case.
3. No evidence would be necessary in this case, because there is a planned detection risk of more than 100%. The reason for the need for no evidence is likely to be the immateriality of repairs and maintenance, and the effectiveness of internal controls. The auditor would normally still do some analytical procedures, but if those are effective, no additional testing is needed. It is common for auditors to use a 100% planned detection risk for smaller account balances. It would ordinarily be inappropriate to use such a planned detection risk in a material account such as accounts receivable or fixed assets.

9-31 a. *Acceptable audit risk* A measure of how willing the auditor is to accept that the financial statements may be materially misstated after the audit is completed and an unqualified opinion has been issued. This is the risk that the auditor will give an incorrect audit opinion.

Inherent risk A measure of the auditor's assessment of the likelihood that there are material misstatements in a segment before considering the effectiveness of internal control. This risk relates to the auditor's expectation of misstatements in the financial statements, ignoring internal control.

Control risk A measure of the auditor's assessment of the likelihood that misstatements exceeding a tolerable amount in a segment will not be prevented or detected by the client's internal controls. This risk is related to the effectiveness of a client's internal controls.

Planned detection risk A measure of the risk that audit evidence for a segment will fail to detect misstatements exceeding a tolerable amount, should such misstatements exist. In audit planning, this risk is determined by using the other three factors in the risk model using the formula PDR = AAR / (IR x CR).

9-31 (Continued)

b.

	1	2	3	4	5	6
Acceptable Audit Risk	.05	.05	.05	.05	.01	.01
IR x CR	1.00	.24	.24	.06	1.00	.24
PDR = AAR / (IR x CR)	.05	.208	.208	.833	.01	.042
Planned Detection Risk in percent	5%	20.8%	20.8%	83.3%	1%	4.2%

c.

1. Decrease; Compare the change from situation 1 to 5.
2. Increase; Compare the change from situation 1 to 2.
3. Increase; Compare the change from situation 1 to 2.
4. No effect; Compare the change from situation 2 to 3.

d. Situation 5 will require the greatest amount of evidence because the planned detection risk is smallest. Situation 4 will require the least amount of evidence because the planned detection risk is highest. In comparing those two extremes, notice that acceptable audit risk is lower for situation 5, and both control and inherent risk are considerably higher.

9-32

a. Low, medium, and high for the four risks and planned evidence have meaning only in comparison to each other. For example, an acceptable audit risk that is high means the auditor is willing to accept more risk than in a situation where there is medium risk without specifying the precise percentage of risk. The same is true for the other three risk factors and planned evidence.

b.

	1	2	3	4	5	6
Acceptable Audit Risk	H	H	L	L	H	M
IR x CR	L	M	H	M	M	M
PDR = AAR / (IR x CR)	H	M	L	L	M	M
Planned Evidence	L	M	H	H	M	M

L = low, M = medium, H = high

9-32 (Continued)

c.

EFFECT ON PDR	EFFECT ON EVIDENCE
(1) Increase	Decrease
(2) Decrease	Increase
(3) NA	Decrease
(4) Decrease	Increase
(5) No effect	No effect

9-33

	CONTROL RISK	INHERENT RISK	ACCEPTABLE AUDIT RISK	PLANNED EVIDENCE
a	N	N or I	D	I
b	N	N	D	I
c	D	N	N	D
d	N	I	N	I
e	N	N	I	D
f	D	D	N	D
g	N	I	N	I
h	I	I	D	I
i	I	I	N	I
j	D	I	N	C

9-12

MAJOR CONCERNS	REASONS FOR CONCERN	b. INVESTIGATION APPROACH
1. Whirland Chemical Co. is a publicly traded company.	Low acceptable audit risk is associated with public stockholders and governmental regulating agencies.	N/A
2. First-year audit.	Unfamiliarity with the company, its operations, and its previous history.	Thorough research into the previous history of the company, review of the working papers prepared on previous engagements by the predecessor auditors, discussion with the members of the previous audit team, and thorough documentation and analysis of the company's internal controls.
3. Relationship with previous auditors was severed over accounting disputes.	Attempt by management to record transactions improperly (i.e., as they had done in the previous year).	Thorough discussion with previous auditors and client personnel as to the nature of these disputes, the handling of these items, and the effect on the current year.
4. The company has prospered even though its industry as a whole has suffered dramatic setbacks in recent years.	Normally companies follow the trends of their industry. The company's prosperity could indicate misrepresented financial statements or a downturn several years after the industry's experience.	You should be more skeptical than usual and you should be especially alert to signs of a downturn in business or possible fraudulent financial reporting.
5. Executives receive relatively low salaries with a high proportion of income resulting from an unusually generous profit-sharing plan.	Executives have an unusually high motivation to create large profits for the company; in fact, their existence depends on it.	You should be especially alert for the possibility of income generating transactions which are improper. You should develop audit procedures to test revenue transactions in detail.

9-34 (Continued)

MAJOR CONCERNS	REASONS FOR CONCERN	b. INVESTIGATION APPROACH
6. The accounting records for the company are not highly sophisticated.	The audit trail and the support for transactions may be nonexistent or difficult to achieve.	You should be deliberate in your examination of detailed transactions. Lack of support for transactions should not be tolerated.
7. The personnel in the accounting department are being overworked and unpaid relative to other employees.	These employees may not be motivated to achieve accurate recording of transactions or to assure that the proper internal controls are enforced.	You should be deliberate in your examination of detailed transactions. Lack of support for transactions should not be tolerated.
8. The company recently installed a sophisticated computer system.	Part of the audit trail may have disappeared with the use of the computer, and control over the entry of transactions may no longer rest with the accounting department.	You must perform a review of the computer and properly audit the transactions through or around the computer.
9. The first six months' profit decreased by only 10% from the previous year even though the volume was reduced significantly and a segment of the business was disposed of.	The reduction in volume and disposal of the segment normally would have produced a more dramatic drop in profits.	You should investigate the statistics, obtain a reasonable explanation of this situation, and perform proper audit procedures to verify the explanation you receive.

9-34 (Continued)

MAJOR CONCERNS	REASONS FOR CONCERN	b. INVESTIGATION APPROACH
10. Mercury Supply Co., which was purchased from Bert Randolph's brother as an attractive acquisition several years ago, has been an unprofitable segment. Most of the sales of Mercury Supply Co. were to another company which Bert Randolph's brother also owns. After the purchase of Mercury Supply Co., Mercury Corp. discontinued its purchases from Mercury Supply Co.	If transactions were definitely non-arm's-length, there appears to have been potential for a fraud against Whirland Chemical. The profits of Mercury Supply Co. prior to the purchase may have been inflated because most of its sales were to a related company. The sale of Mercury Supply Co. during the year could have been another non-arm's-length transaction with the potential for fraud.	You should investigate the original purchase of Mercury Supply Co. and attempt to establish the reasonableness of the financial statements of Mercury Supply Co. at the time of the original purchase. If possible, you should verify the reasonableness of the transactions between Mercury Supply Co. and Mercury Corp. prior to the purchase of the company by Whirland Chemical. In addition, you should investigate the sale of Mercury Supply Co. during the current year to determine if the sales agreement is reasonable under the circumstances.
11. Mercury Corp. buys a large volume of its products from Whirland Chemical.	Transactions between Mercury Corp. and Whirland Chemical are non-arm's-length and could be tainted with fraud.	You should investigate the terms of the sales between Whirland and Mercury Corp. to determine that they are consistent with terms available in the market.
12. Financial analysts believe that Whirland is severely underfinanced.	Such underfinancing could lead to financial difficulties and possible bankruptcy for the company.	The auditor should consider sources of financing available to the company and determine whether or not disclosure should be made of the difficulties associated with the company's financing problems.

9-15

■ Case

9-35

Computer prepared Excel worksheets (P935A.XLS and P935B.XLS) are contained on the Companion Website and on the diskette accompanying this manual.

a. See Worksheet 9-35A on pages 9-21 and 9-22. It is important to recognize that there is no *one* solution to this requirement. The determination of materiality and allocation to the accounts is *always* arbitrary. In this illustration, the auditor makes estimated adjustments for problems noted in analytical review. This is an important step as the potential adjustments *reduce* income before taxes, and thus materiality. The illustrated solution recognizes that with downward adjustments, actual income may be much closer to the contractual amount required for an additional contribution to the employee's pension plan. This creates a sensitivity that will need to be watched carefully as the audit progresses.

The allocation to the accounts is particularly arbitrary. It is noteworthy that the sum of allocated amounts equals 1.5 times materiality. It is assumed that this is consistent with the audit firm's internal policies.

b. The level of acceptable audit risk is based on an evaluation of three factors:

1. The degree to which external users rely on the statements.
2. The likelihood that the client will have financial difficulties after the audit report is issued.
3. The auditor's evaluation of management's integrity.

Stanton Enterprise is a public company and therefore has a high degree of reliance by external users on its financial statements. The Company's operating results and financial condition indicate that there is very little likelihood of financial difficulty in the immediate future. With regard to management's integrity, although there has been some concern with Leonard Stanton's past bankruptcy, the carefully monitored relationship has been good for the four years Stanton has been a client. On that basis, it appears management integrity is good.

Overall, then, an acceptable audit risk level of medium would seem appropriate.

c. See Worksheet 9-35B on pages 9-23 and 9-24 that shows both horizontal and vertical analysis of the 1998 audited and the 1999 unaudited financial statements, as well as computation of applicable ratios. Following are the key observations to be made:

9-35 (Continued)

Overall Results Stanton Enterprises apparently had an extremely successful year in 1999. Sales increased by 36.4 percent, gross margin increased by 4 absolute percentage points, and income before taxes increased by 138.5 percent. Return on total assets and return on equity increased and are at admirable levels. These results allowed the Company to increase its dividends by 25 percent (recognizing that more shares were outstanding) and total stockholder's equity by 101.9 percent. Furthermore, the Company's current, quick, cash and times interest earned ratios are up, and its debt to equity ratio is down, indicating that the Company is extremely sound from a liquidity standpoint.

Trade Accounts Receivable In the face of such growth, trade accounts receivable increased by 59.3 percent, and at the same time, accounts receivable turnover and days to collect improved. However, the allowance for uncollectible accounts was only .7 percent of gross receivables at the end of 1999, down from 1.7 percent at the end of 1998. This implies that the allowance may be significantly understated for 1999 and must be looked at very carefully during the current audit. This review would include considering whether a liberalization of credit policies was used to help increase sales.

Property, Plant and Equipment The Company made a significant additional investment in property, plant and equipment, increasing them by 30.5 percent. These new assets will need to be verified during the current audit. It is noteworthy that accumulated depreciation increased by only 16.1 percent. This could indicate that depreciation on the new assets was, but may not, depending on dates of acquisition and depreciation method used. Depreciation must be tested considering these facts as determined.

Goodwill Goodwill also increased significantly, by $855,000. This implies that the Company made an acquisition during the year. This could explain the increase in operating assets, and any such transaction must be examined in detail as part of the audit. Also, the goodwill from prior transactions must be considered during each audit as to its amortization and recoverability.

Accounts Payable Accounts payable went *down* from 1998 to 1999. This doesn't seem reasonable at all given an increase in business activity. It is very possible there are unrecorded liabilities at the end of 1999, and this must be an area of major emphasis during the audit.

Bank Loan Payable It seems somewhat strange for the Company to have an outstanding balance on its bank loan payable at the end of 1999 given its admirable results. Its possible this was the result of an acquisition, or they simply haven't paid it off. In any case, verifying this balance is a relatively easy audit procedure.

9-35 (Continued)

Federal Income Taxes Payable and Income Tax Expense The Company's effective tax rate for 1998 was 34 percent. Income tax expense is only 22.5 percent of income before taxes. Federal income taxes payable on the balance sheet is significantly lower at 12-31-99 than would be expected based on 1998. These both indicate that the Company has not made its final tax accrual for 1999, and this area will require careful attention during the audit.

Common Stock Common stock increased by 25 percent. Its possible that this occurred in connection with an acquisition (see Goodwill), or in some other way. The issuance of new shares and surrounding circumstances will need to be understood and examined.

Sales Whenever there is a drastic increase in business activity, there is an increased risk of problems. It is possible that controls will lapse or not be carefully observed. It is possible that transactions will not be carefully accounted for. Therefore, in a situation such as Stanton's it is important to understand the nature of the changes that took place and to do a careful review of controls. It will be especially important to thoroughly test cutoffs if both sales and purchase transactions.

Cost of Goods Sold and Gross Profit Consistent with the comments under sales, the auditors must determine why the gross profit percent has made such a significant improvement. Tests of costs and inventories will be more extensive than in more stable circumstances.

Pension Cost It appears that the Company exceeded the contractual amount for additional pension contribution. Yet, pension cost is a lesser percent of sales in 1999 than in 1998. This may indicate that an accrual for additional pension cost was not made. As pension cost is a complex and important area, it will be verified in detail during the audit.

9-35 (Continued)

	ACCEPTABLE AUDIT RISK	INHERENT RISK	ANALYTICAL PROCEDURES
Detail tie-in	Medium	Medium	See Note 5
Existence	Medium	Medium	See Note 5
Completeness	Medium	Medium	See Note 5
Accuracy	Medium	Medium	See Note 5
Cutoff	Medium	High	High
Realizable value	Medium	High	High
Rights	Medium	Medium	See Note 5
Presentation and disclosure	Medium	Medium	See Note 5

Tolerable misstatement:
- Trade accounts receivable — $80,000
- Allowance for uncollectible accounts — 15,000
- Total — $95,000

RATIONALE

1. Acceptable audit risk is medium for the engagement, therefore, it is medium for accounts receivable and all of its related objectives.

2. Inherent risk for the engagement would be considered medium for the following reasons:
   a. Stanton's background problems.
   b. Stanton's autocratic management style.
   c. Some indication of weakness in the control environment, particularly rejection of recommendation to establish an internal audit function.

3. Inherent risk for cutoff is considered high due to the Company's rapid growth in 1999 and the general frequency of cutoff errors.

4. Inherent risk for realizable value is considered high because of the Company's rapid growth and the amount of judgment involved in establishing the allowance for uncollectible accounts.

9-35 (Continued)
5. The analytical procedures performed are <u>preliminary</u> only, and don't provide substantive evidence. However, they can indicate areas where possible problems exist. In other words, they can't lower risk, but can increase it. In this case, they corroborate the high inherent risk level specified for cutoff and realizable value.

9-35 (Continued)

Stanton Enterprises
Worksheet 9-35A
Determination of Materiality and
Allocation to the Accounts
12/31/99

DETERMINATION OF MATERIALITY:

Income before taxes	$8,004,277	
Possible adjustments - estimated.		
See Worksheet 9-35B:		
Increase allowance for uncollectible accounts	(60,248)	Increase to 1.7% of trade accounts receivable.
Increase accounts payable	(1,069,997)	Reflect same increase as cost of goods sold.
Pension cost	NA	Can't estimate. May or may not be required.
Adjusted net income before taxes	$6,874,032	
5 percent	$343,702	
Round down to	$340,000	

Note: A key consideration is whether the Company will be required to make its additional pension contribution. As more information is obtained, the amount considered material may be reduced to assure any possible misstatements in earnings are considered in light of that contractual obligation.

9-21

9-35 (Continued)

Stanton Enterprises
Worksheet 9-35A, cont.
ALLOCATION TO THE ACCOUNTS:

	Prelim. 12/31/99	Tolerable Misstatement	
Cash	$243,689	10000	Easy to audit at low cost.
Trade accounts receivable	3,544,009	80000	Large tolerable misstatement (TM) because account is large and requires extensive sampling to audit.
Allowance for uncollectible accounts	(120,000)	15000	Fairly tight TM because of inherent risk.
Inventories	4,520,902	100000	Large TM because account is large and requires extensive sampling to audit.
Prepaid expenses	29,500	5000	Easy to audit at low cost.
Total current assets	8,218,100		
Property, plant and equipment, at cost	12,945,255	100000	Small TM as a percent of account balance because most of balance is unchanged from prior year & audit of additions is relatively low cost.
Less: accumulated depreciation	(4,382,990)	50000	Fairly tight TM due to possible risk of misstatement. See 9-35B.
	8,562,265		
Goodwill	1,200,000	20000	Fairly tight TM due to possible risk of misstatement. See 9-35B.
Total assets	$17,980,365		
Accounts payable	$2,141,552	70000	LargeTM because account is large and requires extensive sampling to audit.
Bank loan payable	150,000	0	Easy to audit at low cost.
Accrued liabilities	723,600	20000	Easy to audit at low cost.
Federal income taxes payable	1,200,000	40000	Fairly tight TM due to possible risk of misstatement. See 9-35B.
Current portion of long-term	240,000	0	Easy to audit at low cost.
Total current liabilities	4,455,152		
Long-term debt	960,000	0	Easy to audit at low cost.
Stockholders' equity:			
Common stock	1,250,000	0	Easy to audit at low cost.
Additional paid-in capital	2,469,921	0	Easy to audit at low cost.
Retained earnings	8,845,292	NA	
Total stockholders' equity	12,565,213		
Total liabilities and stockholders' equity	$17,980,365	$510,000	(1.5 x $340,000)

9-35 (Continued)

Stanton Enterprises
Worksheet 9-35B
Analysis of Financial Statements
and Audit Planning Worksheet
12/31/99

BALANCE SHEET

	Preliminary 12/31/99	%	Audited 12/31/98	%	% Change
Cash	$243,689	1.4	$133,981	1.1	81.9
Trade accounts receivable	3,544,009	19.7	2,224,921	17.7	59.3
Allowance for uncollectible accounts	(120,000)	-0.7	(215,000)	-1.7	-44.2
Inventories	4,520,902	25.1	3,888,400	31.0	16.3
Prepaid expenses	29,500	0.2	24,700	0.2	19.4
Total current assets	8,218,100	45.7	6,057,002	48.3	35.7
Property, plant and equipment:					
At cost	12,945,255	72.0	9,922,534	79.1	30.5
Less, accumulated depreciation	(4,382,990)	-24.4	(3,775,911)	-30.1	16.1
	8,562,265	47.6	6,146,623	49.0	39.3
Goodwill	1,200,000	6.7	345,000	2.7	247.8
	$17,980,365	100.0	$12,548,625	100.0	43.3
Accounts payable	$2,141,552	11.9	$2,526,789	20.1	-15.2
Bank loan payable	150,000	0.8	0	0.0	--
Accrued liabilities	723,600	4.0	598,020	4.8	21.0
Federal income taxes payable	1,200,000	6.7	1,759,000	14.0	-31.8
Current portion of long-term debt	240,000	1.3	240,000	1.9	0.0
Total current liabilities	4,455,152	24.8	5,123,809	40.8	-13.0
Long-term debt	960,000	5.3	1,200,000	9.6	-20.0
Stockholder's equity:					
Common stock	1,250,000	7.0	1,000,000	8.0	25.0
Additional paid-in capital	2,469,921	13.7	1,333,801	10.6	85.2
Retained earnings	8,845,292	49.2	3,891,015	31.0	127.3
	12,565,213	69.9	6,224,816	49.6	101.9
	$17,980,365	100.0	$12,548,625	100.0	43.3

9-35 (Continued)

Stanton Enterprises
Worksheet 9-35B, cont.
COMBINED STATEMENT OF INCOME AND RETAINED EARNINGS

	Preliminary 12/31/99	%	Audited 12/31/98	%	% Change
Sales	$43,994,931	100.0	$32,258,015	100.0	36.4
Cost of goods sold	24,197,212	55.0	19,032,229	59.0	27.1
Gross profit	19,797,719	45.0	13,225,786	41.0	49.7
Selling, general and administrative expenses	10,592,221	24.1	8,900,432	27.6	19.0
Pension cost	1,117,845	2.5	865,030	2.7	29.2
Interest cost	83,376	0.2	104,220	0.3	-20.0
	11,793,442	26.8	9,869,682	30.6	19.5
Income before taxes	8,004,277	18.2	3,356,104	10.4	138.5
Income tax expense	1,800,000	4.1	1,141,000	3.5	57.8
Net income	6,204,277	14.1	2,215,104	6.9	180.1
Beginning retained earnings	3,891,015		2,675,911		
	10,095,292		4,891,015		
Dividends declared	(1,250,000)		(1,000,000)		
Ending retained earnings	$8,845,292		$3,891,015		

SIGNIFICANT RATIOS

Current ratio	1.84	1.18
Quick ratio	0.82	0.42
Cash ratio	0.05	0.03
Accounts receivable turnover	12.41	14.50
Days to collect	29.00	24.83
Inventory turnover	5.35	4.89
Days to sell	67.26	73.55
Days to convert to cash	96.26	98.38
Debt to equity ratio	0.43	1.02
Tangible net assets to equity	1.34	1.96
Times interest earned	97.00	33.20
Efficiency ratio	2.62	2.64
Profit margin ratio	0.18	0.11
Profitability ratio	0.48	0.28
Return on total assets	0.45	0.27
Return on equity	0.64	0.54

Note: Some ratios are based on year-end balances, as 12-31-97 balances are not provided.

Internet Problem Solution: Materiality and Tolerable Misstatement

9-1

1. Your firm's materiality guidelines indicate that normally overall materiality will be between 5 and 10 percent of income before taxes. Apply these guidelines to Microsoft's 1998 financial statements. What percentage of net income before taxes would you use and why (i.e., select a number between 5 and 10%)? Using your percentage, what would overall materiality have been for 1998? Considering Microsoft's balance sheet, what asset line item would be allocated the highest amount of tolerable misstatement and why?

    Microsoft's income before taxes in 1998 was $7,117 million. Therefore, materiality could range from $356 million to $712 million. Students recommended percentages will differ, but a higher percentage seems justified given Microsoft's financial condition and market position. The two largest asset line items are "Cash and short-term investments" at $13,927 million and "Equity Investments" at $4,703 million. Other balance-sheet line items are much smaller than these accounts. Cash and short-term investments and Equity Investments would likely receive the largest allocation of tolerable misstatement. A large allocation to Equity Investments appears justified due to valuation issues, accounting complexity, and audit difficulty.

2. View the report, "Recommendations of the Big Five Audit Materiality Task Force." Why was the task force formed, and what were the task force's recommendations? The file above is in PDF format and can be read using the Adobe Reader 3.0. If you do not currently have this program, you may download a copy from the Adobe website (http://www.adobe.com).

    In 1998, the Big 5 firms each appointed a representative to form a task force to examine concerns that have been expressed (mainly by the SEC) about the application of materiality standards and concepts by auditors in a financial statement audit—including the recording or non-recording of audit adjustments. The task force made four specific recommendations:

    (1) Adopting a set of audit requirements aimed at encouraging audit clients to record proposed audit adjustments (see suggested approach in Exhibit A of the report).
    (2) Developing guidance covering the auditor's consideration of qualitative factors when evaluating the materiality of proposed audit adjustments (see draft in Exhibit B of the report).
    (3) Committing each of our firms to a) review the adequacy of its consultation requirements dealing with the auditor's consideration of proposed audit adjustments; and b) issue a communication to its audit personnel discussing the importance of effective evaluation of these proposed adjustments and the consultation process when issues arise in this regard (see example policy in Exhibit C of the report).
    (4) Sponsoring audit research to better understand whether the evaluation of materiality by the auditor needs to be updated for changing investor expectations (see Exhibit D for a description of the research project).

    (**Note**: Internet problems address current issues using Internet sources. Because Internet sites are subject to change, Internet problems and solutions may change. Current information on Internet problems is available at www.prenhall.com/arens/.)

Chapter 10

Internal Control and Control Risk

■ Review Questions

10-1 There are seven parts of the planning phase of audits: preplan, obtain background information, obtain information about the client's legal obligations, perform preliminary analytical procedures, set materiality and assess acceptable audit risk and inherent risk, understand internal control and assess control risk, and develop an overall audit plan and audit program. Understanding internal control and assessing control risk is therefore part six of planning. Only developing an overall audit plan and audit program follow understanding internal control and assessing control risk.

10-2 Management and the auditor are both concerned that internal controls provide reliable data for financial reporting and that they safeguard the company's assets and records. Their concerns differ in that the auditor is primarily interested in the effect of the controls on the financial statements, whereas management is also concerned that internal controls promote operational efficiency and encourage adherence to prescribed policies. For publicly held companies, management should also be concerned about complying with laws and regulations.

10-3 The independent auditor should point out to management that without reliable financial data, many of management's critical business decisions may be based on erroneous information. Such decisions might be improper and could prove costly to the company. In addition, without proper controls over assets, the company's resources may be drained by employee defalcation or theft by outsiders without subsequent detection.

10-4 The six transaction-related audit objectives are:

1. Recorded transactions exist (existence).
2. Existing transactions are recorded (completeness).
3. Recorded transactions are stated at the correct amounts (accuracy).
4. Transactions are properly classified (classification).
5. Transactions are recorded on the correct dates (timing).
6. Recorded transactions are properly included in the master files and correctly summarized (posting and summarization).

10-5 The control environment consists of the actions, policies, and procedures that reflect the overall attitudes of top management, directors, and owners of an entity about internal control and its importance to the entity. The following are the most important subcomponents the control environment:

10-5 (Continued)
- Integrity and ethical values
- Commitment to competence
- Board of directors or audit committee participation
- Management's philosophy and operating style
- Organizational structure
- Assignment of authority and responsibility
- Human resource policies and practices

10-6 Internal control includes five categories of controls that management designs and implements to provide reasonable assurance that its control objectives will be met. These are called the components internal control, and are:

- The control environment
- Risk assessment
- Control activities
- Information and communication
- Monitoring

The control environment is the broadest of the five and deals primarily with the way management implements its attitude about internal controls. The other four components are closely related to the control environment. Risk assessment is management's identification and analysis of risks relevant to the preparation of financial statements in accordance with GAAP. To respond to this risk assessment, management implements control activities and creates the accounting information and communication system to meet its objectives for financial reporting. Finally, management periodically assesses the quality of internal control performance to determine that controls are operating as intended and that they are modified as appropriate for changes in conditions (monitoring).

10-7 The five categories of control activities are:

- Adequate separation of duties
    Example: The following two functions are performed by different people: processing customer orders and billing of customers.
- Proper authorization of transactions and activities
    Example: The granting of credit is authorized before shipment takes place.
- Adequate documents and records
    Example: Recording of sales is supported by authorized shipping documents and approved customer orders.
- Physical control over assets and records
    Example: A password is required before entry into the computerized accounts receivable master file can be made.
- Independent checks on performance
    Example: Accounts receivable master file contents are independently verified.

10-8 Separation of operational responsibility from record keeping is intended to reduce the likelihood of operational personnel biasing the results of their performance by incorrectly recording information.

Separation of the custody of assets from accounting for these assets is intended to prevent misappropriation of assets. When one person performs both functions, the possibility of that person's disposal of the asset for personal gain and adjustment of the records to relieve himself or herself of responsibility for the asset without detection increases.

10-9 General authorizations refer to management-established policies that the organization is to follow. Subordinates are instructed to implement these general authorizations by approving all transactions within the limits set by the policies. Examples of general authorization include the issuance of fixed price lists for the sale of products, credit limits for customers, and fixed automatic reorder points for purchases.

Specific authorization relates to individual transactions for which management is unwilling to establish a general policy of authorization. Instead, they prefer to make authorizations on a case-by-case basis. Examples are the authorization of a sales transaction by a sales manager for a used car dealer or loan approvals over a specific limit in a bank.

10-10 An example of a physical control the client can use to protect each of the following assets or records is:

1. Petty cash should be kept locked in a fireproof safe.
2. Cash received by retail clerks should be entered into a cash register to record all cash received.
3. Accounts receivable records should be stored in a locked, fireproof safe. If the records are computerized, adequate backup copies should be maintained and access to the master files should be restricted via passwords.
4. Raw material inventory should be retained in a locked storeroom with a reliable and competent employee controlling access.
5. Perishable tools should be stored in a locked storeroom under control of a reliable employee.
6. Manufacturing equipment should be kept in an area protected by burglar alarms and fire alarms and kept locked when not in use.
7. Marketable securities should be stored in a safety deposit vault.

10-11 Independent checks on performance are internal control activities designed for the continuous internal verification of other controls. Examples of independent checks include:

- Preparation of the monthly bank reconciliation by an individual with no responsibility for recording transactions or handling cash.
- Recomputing inventory extensions for a listing of inventory by someone who did not originally do the extensions.
- The preparation of the sales journal by one person and the accounts receivable master file by a different person, and a reconciliation of the control account to the master file.
- The counting of inventory by two different count teams.
- The existence of an effective internal audit staff.

10-12 The purpose of obtaining an understanding internal control is to find out how the client believes the internal controls operate. It involves evaluating the design of internal controls and determining whether those controls have been placed in operation. Assessing control risk means to state the degree to which the auditor intends to rely on internal controls to reduce substantive tests. For example, the auditor might assess control risk as low.

The understanding of internal control is done by interviewing client personnel, examining procedures manuals, describing the flow of documents and records by the use of flowcharts and narrative descriptions, and using an internal control questionnaire. Assessing control risk is done judgmentally, based upon the findings in the understanding of internal control and the results of the tests of controls. It is an auditor's decision using professional judgment.

10-13 A control is an existing procedure that aids in the prevention of errors or fraud in the accounting system. A weakness describes a situation where controls are inadequate for a given transaction-related audit objective.

Controls

- Sales invoices are independently checked to customers' orders for prices, quantities, extensions, footings, credit discount, and freight terms.
- The management of the credit department operates independently of the sales department.
- The billing department is segregated from accounts receivable and shipping functions.
- All discounts given other than those in the normal course of the company policy require the approval of a responsible official.
- Detailed customers' ledgers are maintained for all receivable accounts by personnel segregated from all cash functions.
- Cash receipts are entered in the books of original entry by persons independent of the mail opening and cash receipts listing function.

Weaknesses

- The absence of any of these controls, if there were not compensating controls, would constitute a weakness.

10-14 The most important internal control weakness which permitted the defalcation to occur was the failure to adequately segregate the accounting responsibility of recording billings in the sales journal from the custodial responsibility of receiving the cash. Regardless of how trustworthy James appeared, no employee should be given the combined duties of custody of assets and accounting for those assets.

10-15 Maier is correct in her belief that internal controls frequently do not function in the manner they are supposed to. However, regardless of this, her approach ignores the value of beginning the understanding of internal control by preparing or reviewing a rough flowchart. Obtaining an early understanding of the client's internal control will provide Maier with a basis for a decision about the audit procedures and sample sizes based on assessed control risk. By not obtaining an understanding of internal control until later in the engagement, Maier risks performing either too much or too little work, or emphasizing the wrong areas during her audit.

10-16 The flowchart provides an overview of the workings of the client's internal controls, while the internal control questionnaire is a checklist reminder of many different types of controls.

Advantages of flowcharting:

1. Provides concise overview of client's system--useful as a tool to aid in identifying weaknesses.
2. Superior to written description--easier to follow the diagram than to read a description. It is also easier to update a flowchart than a narrative.

Disadvantages of flowcharting:

1. Tendency for confusion if every processing detail is shown.

Advantages of internal control questionnaire:

1. A good questionnaire gives relatively complete and quick coverage of each audit area.
2. Can usually be prepared easily at the beginning of an audit.

Disadvantages of internal control questionnaire:

1. Individual parts of the client's system are examined without providing an overall view.
2. A standard questionnaire is often inapplicable to some audit clients, especially smaller ones.
3. Frequently prepared in a mechanized fashion without carefully interviewing personnel and evaluating the implication of "no" responses.

10-17 Reportable conditions are defined by SAS 60 (as amended by SAS 78, AU 325) as "significant deficiencies in the design or operation of internal control". They should be reported by the auditor to the audit committee. If there is no audit committee, then reportable conditions should be communicated to the person or persons in the organization who have overall responsibility for internal control (board of directors or owner-manager, for example).

10-18 The purpose of the control risk matrix is to assist the auditor in assessing control risk. The control risk matrix helps the auditor identify controls and weaknesses for each of the six transaction-related audit objectives.

If control risk is assessed as low, the auditor believes that the controls are likely to detect and correct misstatements which may occur. If control risk is assessed as moderate, the auditor believes that the controls are less likely to detect and correct misstatements which may occur than if control risk was assessed as low.

10-19 Tests of controls are audit procedures to test the effectiveness of controls in support of a reduced assessed control risk. An examination of documents test of control would be: examine time cards for initials which indicate that hours were recalculated by an independent payroll clerk. A reperformance test of control would be: recalculate the hours on a sample of time cards and compare the totals with the original calculations.

■ **Multiple Choice Questions From CPA Examinations**

10-20 a. (3)   b. (3)   c. (3)   d. (4)

10-21 a. (3)   b. (4)   c. (1)

10-22 a. (3)   b. (4)   c. (4)   d. (2)

■ **Discussion Questions and Problems**

10-23 1. a. Adequate segregation of duties and proper authorization of transactions and activities.
  b. Recorded transactions exist.
  c. An unauthorized or invalid time card turned in by an existing employee. The time card may be for an employee who formerly worked for the company or one who is temporarily laid off.
  d. An employee could be claiming too many hours by having a friend punch him or her in early, or by making manual changes on time cards.
  e. Check to see that all employees that are punched in one day are physically present.

  2. a. Adequate documents and records.
  b. Existing transactions are recorded.
  c. A missing time card number never could be identified before preparation of payroll starts.
  d. An employee would not be paid for a time period. (The employee is almost certain to bring this to management's attention.) The primary benefit of the control would be to prevent misstatements for a short period of time and to prevent employee dissatisfaction from failure to pay them.
  e. Obtain a list of company employees and make sure that each one has received a paycheck for the time period in question.

10-23 (Continued)

3. a. Proper authorization of transactions and activities.
   b. Recorded transactions exist.
   c. A paycheck cannot be processed for an invalid employee number.
   d. A fictitious payroll check could be processed for a fictitious employee if invalid employee numbers are included in the employee master file.
   e. Include test data transactions with invalid employee numbers in the data to be inputted into the payroll accounting system and determine that all invalid transactions are automatically rejected by the software application.

4. a. Adequate separation of duties.
   b. Recorded transactions exist.
   c. A fictitious payroll check that is originated by the person both preparing the payroll checks and distributing the payroll checks.
   d. If one person kept a record of time, prepared the payroll, and distributed the checks, that person could add a nonexistent employee to the payroll, process the information for the employee and deposit the paycheck in his or her own bank account without detection.
   e. Perform a surprise payoff in which the auditor accounts for all paychecks and distributes them to the employees, who must provide identification in order to receive their checks.

5. a. Independent check on performance.
   b. Recorded transactions are stated at the correct amounts.
   c. Mechanical errors of adding up the number of hours, calculating the gross payroll incorrectly, or calculating withholding incorrectly.
   d. Payroll checks incorrectly calculated could be paid to employees.
   e. Recheck the amounts for gross payroll, withholding and net payroll.

6. a. Adequate documents and records.
   b. Existing transactions are recorded.
   c. Preparation of a check for an inappropriate person, the distribution of that check to that person, and the recording of that check in the cash disbursements journal as a voided check.
   d. An employee who is supposed to void a check could record it as voided on the books and cash the check. At month-end the amount of the check could be covered by adjusting the bank reconciliation.
   e. Test month-end bank reconciliations in detail to determine that the account reconciles properly, that all supporting documents are proper, looking especially for a check that cleared and was supposed to be voided, and that no alterations have been made to the bank statement.

7. a. Proper authorization of transactions and activities.
   b. Recorded transactions exist and recorded transactions are stated at the correct amounts.
   c. Both errors and fraud are likely to be prevented if competent trustworthy employees are hired. Hiring honest employees minimizes a likelihood of fraud. Hiring competent employees minimizes the likelihood of unintentional errors.

10-23 (Continued)

    d. Several types of intentional misstatements could occur if a dishonest person is hired. Similarly, several types of unintentional errors could occur if an incompetent person is hired.

    e. An examination of cancelled checks and supporting documents, including time cards and personnel records, is a test of the possibility of fraud. A test of the calculation of payroll is a test for an unintentional error caused by employees who are not competent.

8. a. Proper authorization of transactions and activities, and adequate documents and records.

    b. Recorded transactions exist.

    c. The preparation of an inappropriate payroll check for a former employee is prevented.

    d. A terminated employee could be continued on the payroll with someone else obtaining the paycheck.

    e. Perform a surprise payoff in which the auditor accounts for all paychecks and distributes them to the employees, who must provide identification to receive their checks.

9. a. Physical control over assets and records, and adequate segregation of duties.

    b. Recorded transactions exist.

    c. Checks prepared for nonexistent employees or employees on vacation, or absent for other reasons are controlled and safeguarded.

    d. Checks could be lost which are intended for absent employees or a check could be taken by the person responsible for distributing the checks.

    e. Examine cancelled checks to make certain that each check is properly endorsed, supported by a time card, and the person for whom the check is made out is still working for the company.

10. a. Proper authorization of transactions and activities and adequate separation of duties.

    b. Recorded transactions exist and recorded transactions are stated at the correct amounts.

    c. Preparation of a check for a fictitious employee or preparation of checks using an unapproved pay rate are prevented.

    d. A fictitious payroll check could be processed for a fictitious employee if those with record keeping responsibilities are allowed to enter new employee numbers into the master file. Also, paychecks to valid employees could be overstated if unauthorized personnel have the ability to make changes to the pay rates in the master files.

    e. Attempt to access the on-line payroll master file using a password that is not allowed access to that master file.

10-24
1. a. Adequate documents and records and independent checks on performance.
   b. Transactions are stated at the correct amounts.
   c. (1) Make sure that the billing clerk receives the current price list.
      (2) Internal verification by someone who has the current price list.

2. a. Adequate documents and records.
   b. Recorded transactions exist.
   c. 1) Require that payments only be made on original invoices.
      2) Require a receiving report be attached to the vendor's invoice before a payment is made.

3. a. Adequate documents and records, physical control over assets and records, and independent checks on performance.
   b. Recorded transactions exist.
   c. 1) Fence in the physical facilities and prohibit employees from parking inside the fencing.
      2) Require the accounting department to maintain perpetual inventory records and take physical counts of actual sides of beef periodically.

4. a. Independent checks on performance.
   b. Recorded transactions are stated at the correct amounts.
   c. Counts by qualified personnel and independent checks on performance.

5. a. Proper authorization of transactions and activities.
   b. Transactions are stated at the correct amounts.
   c. 1) Make sure that the salesman has a current price list.
      2) Require independent approval of all transactions, including the price, before shipment is made.

6. a. Adequate documents and records, and independent checks on performance.
   b. Transactions are recorded on the correct dates.
   c. Carefully coordinate the physical count of inventory on the last day of the year with the recording of sales to make certain counted inventory has not been billed and billed inventory has not been counted.

7. a. Proper authorization of transactions and adequate documents and records.
   b. Recorded transactions exist.
   c. Include a control in the accounts payable software that requires the input of a valid receiving report number before the software will process a payment on an accounts receivable.

8. a. Adequate separation of duties.
   b. Recorded transactions exist.
   c. Restrict the accounts payable clerk from being able to make changes to the approved vendor master file. Only allow purchasing personnel to input changes to that master file.

10-25 The criteria for dividing duties is to keep all asset custody duties with one person (Cooper). Document preparation and recording is done by the other person (Smith). Miller will perform independent verification. The two most important independent verification duties are the bank reconciliation and reconciling the accounts receivable master file with the control account, therefore they are assigned to Miller. The duties should be divided among the three as follows:

Robert Smith:	†1	†3	†7	9	†10	†12	14	16	17
James Cooper:	†2	†4	5	†6	†8	†11	†13		
Bill Miller:	15	18							

10-26 a. Three controls are established by this procedure:

1. The adding machine operator, who records the sale, is not the same individual who takes the money. In this way he is prevented from not recording the sale of a certain item and keeping the money.
2. By recording on the tape the number of people in the party, the cashier is able to check to see that additional people are not leaving with another party and avoiding paying their bill.
3. By stapling the second tape to the first tape, the customer is prevented from merely presenting the smaller tape as payment and leaving without paying the larger amount.

b. The manager can make an evaluation of these control procedures by comparing the totals on the cash register to those on the adding machine tapes, and comparing that to the cash received. Also, he or she can compare this amount to the amount of food used to see if the cash total is appropriate.

c. The usual cafeteria setup has a cashier at the end of the line. This prevents a customer from leaving without paying since the customer can't leave in any direction but past the cashier. However, there may be an insufficient check on the cashier to assure he or she is not keeping the cash and failing to record the sale. A control to help prevent this type of fraud is a visual display on the cash register showing the amount of the sale and a cash register receipt given to the customer.

d. The benefit of this system is a prevention of the theft of cash by the cashier, a prevention of customers from leaving without paying and a faster handling of customers on the cafeteria line. The cost of this system is the salary of the extra employee.

10-27 a. The size of a company has a significant effect on the nature of the controls likely to exist. A small company has difficulty establishing adequate separation of duties and justifying an internal audit staff. However, a major type of control available in a small company is the knowledge and concern of the top operating person, who is frequently an owner-manager. His or her ability to understand and oversee the entire operation of the company is potentially a significant compensating control. The owner-manager's interest in the organization and close relationship with the personnel enable him or her to evaluate the competence of the employees and the effectiveness of internal controls.

10-27 (Continued)

While some of the five control activities are unavailable in a small company, especially adequate segregation of duties, it is still possible for a small company to have proper authorization of transactions and activities, adequate documents and records, physical controls over assets and records, and, to a limited degree, independent checks on performance.

b. Phersen and Collier take opposite and extreme views as to the credence to be given internal control in a small firm. Phersen seems to treat a small firm in the same manner as he would a large firm, which is inefficient. Because many types of controls are usually lacking in a small firm, assessed control risk should be increased and more extensive substantive tests must be used. Because assessed control risk is higher, less emphasis is needed to identify the internal controls.

Collier is not meeting the standards of the profession (SAS 55—as amended by SAS 78—AU 319) in that she completely ignores the possibility of a severe weakness in the system. She must obtain an understanding of internal control to determine whether it is possible to conduct an audit at all.

Auditing standards require, at a minimum, an understanding of internal control (SAS 55—as amended by SAS 78—AU 319). The auditor must understand the control environment and the flow of transactions. It is not necessary, however, for the auditor to prepare flowcharts or internal control questionnaires. The auditor is not required to identify weaknesses if he or she does not plan to reduce control risk below maximum, which would be common on many small audit clients.

10-28 1. a.
- Supplying the receiving department with the purchase order is regarded as a weakness in that the department may be less careful in checking goods than they would be if they were working without a record of the quantities that should be received.
- The failure to have the storekeeper receipt for the materials when they are sent to him or her from the receiving department or to tie in the items placed in stores with the acquisition constitutes a weakness in control in that responsibility for shortages cannot be conclusively placed on either receiving or stores. The receiving department might, in collusion with a vendor, report receipts of materials which were never received. Also, either the receiving department or the stores department might fraudulently convert some of the materials and because of the lack of a record of responsibility, the company would be unable to determine which department was responsible.

b.
- This weakness increases the likelihood of obsolete inventory and the possibility of theft of shipments larger than the amount ordered.
- The failure to isolate responsibility for shortages also increases the likelihood of obsolescence in that employees are likely to be less concerned when they are not held accountable. Because the company cannot isolate responsibility, it might also encourage receiving or stores to take goods.

10-28 (Continued)

    c. Use of a "blind" copy of the purchase order or a separate receiving report without a copy of the purchase order. Use of perpetual inventory records to hold the storekeeper accountable. The storekeeper should also initial the receiving report or purchase order when he or she receives the goods.

2.   a.
   - The payroll checks should not be returned to the computer department supervisor but should be distributed by persons independent of those having a part in generating the payroll data.
   - There is a lack of internal verification of the hours, rates, extensions or employees by above.

    b.
   - Padding of payroll with fictitious names and extracting the checks made out to such names when they are returned after they have been signed.
   - There may be misstatements in hours, rates, extensions, and the existence of nonworking employees.

    c.
   - Have the checks handed out by an independent person and not returned to Strode.
   - Internal verification of that information by Webber or someone else.

3.   a. The bank statement and cancelled checks should not be reconciled by the manager, but should be sent by the bank directly to the home office, where the reconciliations should be made against the manager's report of cash disbursements.

    b. The manager may draw checks to herself or others for personal purposes and omit them from her list of cash disbursements or inflate other reported disbursement amounts.

    c. Have all bank statements sent directly to the home office and have Cooper report directly to the home office by use of a list of cash disbursements and all supporting documentation.

WEAKNESS	RECOMMENDATION
1. There is no basis for establishing the documentation of the number of paying patrons.	Prenumbered admission tickets should be issued upon payment of the admission fee.
2. There is no segregation of duties between persons responsible for collecting admission fees and persons responsible for authorizing admission.	One clerk (hereafter referred to as the cash receipts clerk) should collect admission fees and issue prenumbered tickets. The other clerk (hereafter referred to as the admission clerk) should authorize admission upon receipt of the ticket or proof of membership.
3. An independent count of paying patrons is not made.	The admission clerk should retain a portion of the prenumbered admission ticket (admission ticket stub).
4. There is no proof of accuracy of amounts collected by the clerks.	Admission ticket stubs should be reconciled with cash collected by the treasurer each day.
5. Cash receipts records are not promptly prepared.	The cash receipts should be recorded by the cash receipts clerk daily on a permanent record that will serve as the first record of accountability.
6. Cash receipts are not promptly deposited. Cash should not be left undeposited for a week.	Cash should be deposited at least once each day.
7. There is no proof of the accuracy of amounts deposited.	Authenticated deposit slips should be compared with daily cash receipts records. Discrepancies should be promptly investigated and resolved. In addition, the treasurer should establish policy that includes a review of cash receipts.
8. There is no record of the internal accountability for cash.	The treasurer should issue a signed receipt for all proceeds received from the cash receipts clerk. These receipts should be maintained and should be periodically checked against cash receipts and deposit records.

10-30 The following are weaknesses of internal control, by transaction-related audit objective.

Existence

- The receiving report is not sent to the stores department. A copy of the receiving report should be sent from the receiving room directly to the stores department with the materials received. The stores department, after verifying the accuracy of the receiving report, should indicate approval on that copy and send it to the accounts payable department. The copy sent to accounts payable will serve as proof that the materials ordered were received by the company and are in the user department.
- The controller should not be responsible for cash disbursements. The cash disbursement function should be the responsibility of the treasurer, not the controller, so as to provide proper segregation of duties between the custody of assets and the recording of transactions.
- The purchase requisition is not approved. The purchase requisition should be approved by a responsible person in the stores department. The approval should be indicated on the purchase requisition after the approver is satisfied that it was properly prepared based on a need to replace stores or the proper request from a user department.
- Preliminary review should be made before preparing purchase orders. Prior to preparation of the purchase order, the purchase office should review the company's need for the specific materials requisitioned and approve the request.

Completeness

- Purchase orders and purchase requisitions should not be combined and filed with the unmatched purchase requisitions, in the stores department. A separate file should be maintained for the combined and matched documents. The unmatched purchase requisitions file can serve as a control over merchandise requisitioned but not yet ordered.
- There is no indication of control over vouchers in the accounts payable department. A record of all vouchers submitted to the cashier should be maintained in the accounts payable department, and a copy of the vouchers should be filed in an alphabetical vendor reference file.
- There is no indication of any control over prenumbered documents. All prenumbered documents should be accounted for.

Accuracy

- Purchase requisitions and purchase orders are not compared in the stores department. Although purchase orders are attached to purchase requisitions in the stores department, there is no indication that any comparison is made of the two documents. Prior to attaching the purchase order to the purchase requisition the requisitioner's functions should include a check that:

10-30 (Continued)

      a. Prices are reasonable;
      b. The quality of the materials ordered is acceptable;
      c. Delivery dates are in accordance with company needs;
      d. All pertinent data on the purchase order and purchase requisition (e.g., quantities, specifications, delivery dates, etc.) are in agreement.

Because the requisitioner will be charged for the materials ordered, the requisitioner is the logical person to perform these steps.

- The purchase office does not review the invoice prior to processing approval. The purchase office should review the vendor's invoice for overall accuracy and completeness, verifying quantity, prices, specifications, terms, dates, etc., and if the invoice is in agreement with the purchase order, receiving report, and purchase requisition, the purchase office should clearly indicate on the invoice that it is approved for payment processing. The approved invoice should be sent to the accounts payable department.
- The copy of the purchase order sent to the receiving room generally should not show quantities ordered, thus forcing the department to count goods received. In addition to counting the merchandise received from the vendor, the receiving department personnel should examine the condition and quality of the merchandise upon receipt.
- There is no indication of control over dollar amounts on vouchers. Accounts payable personnel should prepare and maintain control sheets on the dollar amounts of vouchers. Such sheets should be sent to departments posting transactions to the general ledger and master files.

Note: Classification, timing, and posting and summarization are not applicable. Recording in journals is not included in the flowcharts.

10-31 a. Sales

TRANSACTION-RELATED AUDIT OBJECTIVE	CONTROL
Existence	■ Supervisor approves all invoices. ■ Accounts receivable clerk has no access to cash. ■ Monthly statements are sent to customers. ■ Supervisor approves all credit.
Completeness	■ Cash register is at the front of the store. ■ Sales clerks handle no cash. ■ Sales clerks summarize daily sales, which determine their commission. This summary is compared daily to total sales. ■ Sales transactions are used to update perpetuals and monthly physical inventory is taken.
Accuracy	■ Owner sets all prices. ■ Supervisor rechecks all calculations. ■ Accountant reconciles all computer totals to sales staff summary totals and supervisor's sales summary. ■ Monthly statements are sent to customers.
Classification	None
Timing	■ Sales transactions are recorded daily.
Posting and summarization	■ Computer is used to update records. ■ Monthly statements are sent. ■ The aged trial balance is compared to the general ledger.

10-31 (Continued)

b. **Cash Receipts**

TRANSACTION-RELATED AUDIT OBJECTIVE	CONTROL
Existence	■ Monthly bank reconciliation is prepared. ■ Accounts receivable clerk compares duplicate deposit slip from bank to sales and cash receipts journal.
Completeness	■ Cash register is used for cash sales. ■ Cash collected on receivables is prelisted. ■ Supervisor deposits money in a locked box.
Accuracy	■ Supervisor recaps cash sales and compares totals to the cash receipts tapes. ■ Monthly bank reconciliation prepared. ■ Accounts receivable clerk compares duplicate deposit slip from bank to cash sales and cash receipts journal. ■ Monthly statements are sent to customers.
Classification	None
Timing	■ Cash is deposited daily.
Posting and summarization	■ Computer is used to update records. ■ Monthly statements are sent. ■ The aged trial balance is compared to the general ledger.

c. **Sales and Cash Receipts**

Weaknesses of:

- Supervisor enters all sales in the cash register, recaps sales and cash, and compares the totals to the tapes. She also receives all invoices from sales clerks. (This weakness is offset by the daily summary form prepared by sales clerks and used to calculate sales clerks' commissions.)
- Lack of accounting for a numerical sequence of sales invoices. (Partially offset by control totals used by comparing sales clerks' and supervisor's control totals.)
- No internal verification of key entry for customer name, date, and sales classifications on either cash receipts or sales.

10-31 (Continued)

- There is no internal verification of general totals, posting to accounts receivable master file, or posting to the general ledger.
- There is a lack of internal verification of all of the accounting work done by the accounts receivable clerk.

■ **Case**

10-32

PINNACLE MANUFACTURING

The purpose of this four-part case study is to help students integrate the major parts of the audit process so as to give them an appreciation for the whole as well as the integration of the parts. The case is divided among four chapters, as follows:

Chapter 10- Part I - Understand internal control and assess control risk for the acquisition and payment cycle: Case 10-32.

Chapter 13 - Part II - Design of tests of controls and substantive tests of transactions: Case 13-34.

Chapter 14 - Part III - Determine sample sizes using audit sampling and evaluate results: Case 14-34.

Chapter 15 - Part IV - Design, perform, and evaluate results for tests of details of balances: Case 15-33.

The case can be assigned a part at a time with each chapter, or the entire case can be assigned during or after Chapter 15. Notice that the case concerns accounts payable, not accounts receivable. This will require students to apply the concepts of Chapters 10 through 15 to accounts payable. It is also appropriate to assign the case after the study of the acquisition and payment cycle in Chapter 18. The important thing is that the parts be viewed as part of a broader case to achieve the full learning objectives.

Following are control risk matrices and related notes which are used to direct a discussion of the requirements of the case. It should be understood that judgment is a critical element in this case, and accordingly, there often is no single right answer.

Computer-prepared matrices using Excel (P1032.XLS) are contained on the Companion Website and on the diskette accompanying this manual. They are essentially the same as the following matrices.

10-32 (Continued)

PINNACLE MANUFACTURING - Part I
Control Risk Matrix - Acquisitions

Internal Controls \ Transaction-Related Audit Objective	Recorded acquisitions are for goods and services received (existence).	Existing acquisition transactions are recorded (completeness).	Recorded acquisition transactions are stated at the correct amounts (accuracy).	Acquisition transactions are properly classified (classification).	Acquisition transactions are recorded on the correct dates (timing).	Recorded acquisition transactions are properly included in the master files, and are properly summarized (posting and summarization).
1. Required use of P.O. and receiving report with check of completeness	C					
2. Proper approval	C		C			
3. Segregation of functions	C					
4. Cancellation of documents	C					
5. Prenumbering of documents with accounting for sequence		C				
6. Internal verification of documents/records	C		C	C	C	
7. Use of chart of accounts				C		
8. Procedures requiring prompt processing					C	
9. Monthly reconciliation of A/P master file with general ledger						C
Assessed control risk	Low	Low	Low	Low	Low	Low

10-32 (Continued)

PINNACLE MANUFACTURING - Part I
Control Matrix - Cash Disbursements

Internal Controls \ Transaction-Related Audit Objectives	Recorded cash disbursements are for goods and services actually received (existence).	Existing cash disbursement transactions are recorded (completeness).	Recorded cash disbursement transactions are stated at the correct amounts (accuracy).	Cash disbursement transactions are properly classified (classification).	Cash disbursement transactions are recorded on the correct dates (timing).	Recorded cash disbursement transactions are properly included in the master file and are properly summarized (posting and summarization).
1. Segregation of functions	C					
2. Review of support, signing of checks by authorized person	C					
3. Internal verification	C		C	C	C	C
4. Prenumbered checks; accounted for		C				
5. Monthly bank account reconciliation by an independent person		C	C			
6. Use of chart of accounts				C		
7. Procedures for prompt recording					C	
8. Monthly reconciliation of A/P master file with general ledger						C
Assessed control risk	Low	Low	Low	Low	Low	Low

10-20

10-32 (Continued)

Notes to 10-32, Part I

1. The purpose of Part I is to:
   (a) have the students develop specific transaction-related audit objectives for a cycle,
   (b) obtain controls from a flowchart description,
   (c) relate controls to objectives,
   (d) evaluate a set of controls as a system.
2. Control is quite good. If misstatements occur, they will result from the incorrect application of controls, not their absence. This demonstrates the inherent weaknesses in any control system. It explains the reasons why some misstatements were found last year. However, they were not material in amount. It also indicates the need for tests of controls and substantive tests of details of balances and/or transactions.
3. It is appropriate to use the matrix to consider whether all controls shown are important both to the client and to the auditor. Is it necessary to have all controls (e.g., prenumbering of requisitions)? Are the controls costly (e.g., internal verification of *all* acquisitions)? Should all controls be tested (e.g., cancellation of documents)?
4. Because there is no specific weakness, the last aspect of internal control can be discussed on a "what if" basis.

■ Internet Problem Solution: Corporate Governance

10-1 Visit The Business Roundtable's website and answer the following questions:

1. What is The Business Roundtable?

   The Business Roundtable is an association of chief executive officers of leading U.S. corporations with a combined workforce of more than 10 million employees in the United States. The chief executives are committed to advocating public policies that foster vigorous economic growth; a dynamic global economy; and a well-trained and productive U.S. workforce essential for future competitiveness. Established in 1972, the Roundtable was founded in the belief that chief executives of major corporations should take an increased role in the continuing debates about public policy.

   The Roundtable believes that the basic interests of business closely parallel the interests of the American people, who are directly involved as consumers, employees, shareholders, and suppliers. Thus, chief executives, although they speak as individuals, have responsibilities which relate to many factors—including jobs, products, services, and return on investment—that affect the economic well-being of all Americans.

10-1 (Continued)

2. Within The Business Roundtable site, find the "STATEMENT ON CORPORATE GOVERNANCE," and answer the following questions related to that statement:

   a. What are the 5 major functions of the board of directors?

   (1) Select, regularly evaluate and, if necessary, replace the chief executive officer; determine management compensation; and review succession planning; (2) Review, and, where appropriate, approve the major strategies and other financial objectives and plans of the corporation; (3) Advise management on significant issues facing the corporation; (4) Oversee processes for evaluating the adequacy of internal controls, risk management, financial reporting and compliance, and satisfy itself as to the adequacy of such processes; and (5) Nominate directors and ensure that the structure and practices of the board provide for sound corporate governance.

   The full report is available in Adobe Acrobat format—see the link on the Companion Website for STATEMENT ON CORPORATE GOVERNANCE. If you do not currently have Adobe Acrobat Reader 3.0 you may download a copy from the Adobe website (http://www.adobe.com).

   b. What is the board of directors' function with respect to "Risk Management, Controls, and Compliance"? (Your answer to this question should be more detailed than your answer to 2a. above.)

   "The Board must assure that an effective system of controls is in place for safeguarding the corporation's assets, managing the major risk faced by the corporation, reporting accurately the corporation's financial condition and results of operations, adhering to key internal policies and authorizations, and complying with significant laws and regulations that are applicable to it.

   In performing these functions, the board generally relies on the advice and reports of management, internal and external counsel, and internal and external auditors. The board's role should be to review reports from such experts, to provide them with guidance and to assure that management takes appropriate corrective actions when significant control problems are reported."

(**Note**: Internet problems address current issues using Internet sources. Because Internet sites are subject to change, Internet problems and solutions may change. Current information on Internet problems is available at www.prenhall.com/arens/.)

Chapter 11

The Impact of Technology on the Audit Process

■ Review Questions

11-1 The proper installation of IT can lead to internal control enhancements by replacing manually-performed controls with computer-performed controls. IT-based accounting systems have the ability to handle tremendous volumes of complex business transactions cost effectively. Computer-performed controls can reduce the potential for human error by replacing manual controls with programmed controls that apply checks and balances to each transaction processed. The systematic nature of IT offers greater potential to reduce the risk of material misstatements resulting from random, human errors in processing.

The use of IT based accounting systems also offers the potential for improved management decisions by providing more and higher quality information on a more timely basis than traditional manual systems. IT-based systems are usually administered effectively because the complexity requires effective organization, procedures, and documentation. That in turn enhances internal control.

11-2 When entities rely heavily on IT systems to process financial information, there are new risks specific to IT environments that must be considered. Key risks include the following:

- *Reliance on the functioning capabilities of hardware and software.* The risk of system crashes due to hardware or software failures must be evaluated when entities rely on IT to produce financial statement information.
- *Visibility of audit trail.* The use of IT often converts the traditional paper trail to an electronic audit trail, eliminating source documents and paper-based journals and records.
- *Reduced human involvement.* The replacement of traditional manual processes with computer-performed processes reduces opportunities for employees to recognize misstatements resulting from transactions that might have appeared unusual to experienced employees.
- *Systematic versus random errors.* Due to the uniformity of processing performed by IT based systems, errors in computer software can result in incorrect processing for all transactions processed. This increases the risk of many significant misstatements.
- *Unauthorized access.* The centralized storage of key records and files in electronic form increases the potential for unauthorized on-line access from remote locations.
- *Loss of data.* The centralized storage of data in electronic form increases the risk of data loss in the event the data file is altered or destroyed.
- *Reduced segregation of duties.* The installation of IT-based accounting systems centralizes many of the traditionally segregated manual tasks into one IT function.

11-2 (Continued)
- *Lack of traditional authorization.* IT-based systems can be programmed to initiate certain types of transactions automatically without obtaining traditional manual approvals.
- *Need for IT experience.* As companies rely to a greater extent on IT-based systems, the need for personnel trained in IT systems increases in order to install, maintain, and use systems.

11-3 The audit trail represents the accumulation of source documents and records maintained by the client to serve as support for the transactions occurring during the accounting period. The integration of IT can change the audit trail by converting many of the traditionally paper-based source documents and records into electronic files that cannot be visually observed. Because many of the transactions are entered directly into the computer as they occur, some of the documents and records are even eliminated.

11-4 Random error represents errors that occur in an inconsistent pattern. Manual accounting systems are especially prone to random errors that result from honest mistakes that occur as employees perform day-to-day tasks. When those mistakes do not consistently occur while performing a particular task, errors are distributed randomly into the accounting records. An example of a random error is when an employee accidentally pulls the wrong unit price off the approved price list when preparing a sales invoice for a particular customer.

Systematic error represents errors that occur consistently across all similar transactions. Because IT-based systems perform tasks uniformly for all transactions submitted, any mistake in software programming results in the occurrence of the same error for every transaction processed by the system. An example of a systematic error occurs when a program that is supposed to post sales amounts to the accounts receivable subsidiary ledger actually posts the sales amount twice to customers' accounts.

11-5 In most traditional accounting systems, the duties related to authorization of transactions, recordkeeping of transactions, and custody of assets are segregated across three or more individuals. As accounting systems make greater use of IT, many of the traditionally manually performed tasks are now performed by the computer. As a result, some of the traditionally segregated duties, particularly authorization and recordkeeping, fall under the responsibility of IT personnel. To compensate for the collapsing of duties under the IT function, key IT tasks related to programming, operation of hardware and software, and data control are segregated. Separation of those IT functions restricts an IT employee's ability to inappropriately access software and data files in order to misappropriate assets.

11-6 *General controls* relate to all aspects of the IT function. They have a global impact on all software applications. Examples of general controls include controls related to the administration of the IT function; software acquisition and maintenance; physical and on-line security over access to hardware, software, and related backup; back-up planning in the event of unexpected emergencies; and hardware controls. *Application controls* apply to the processing of individual transactions. An example of an application control is a programmed control that verifies that all time cards submitted are for valid employee id numbers included in the employee master file.

11-7 The typical duties often segregated within an IT function include systems development, computer operations, and data control. Systems development involves the acquisition or programming of application software. Systems development personnel work with test copies of programs and data files to develop new or improved application software programs. Computer operations personnel are responsible for executing live production jobs in accordance with a job schedule and for monitoring consoles for messages about computer efficiency and malfunctions. Data control personnel are responsible for data input and output control. They often independently verify the quality of input and the reasonableness of output. By separating these functions, no one IT employee can make changes to application software or underlying master files and then operate computer equipment to use those changed programs or data files to process transactions.

11-8 If general controls are ineffective, there is a potential for material misstatement in each computer-based accounting application, regardless of the quality of application controls. If, for example, the systems development process is not properly controlled, there is a greater risk that unauthorized and untested modifications to accounting applications software have occurred. If general controls are strong, there is a greater likelihood of placing greater reliance on application controls. Stronger general controls should lead to greater likelihood that underlying applications operate effectively and data files contain accurate, authorized, and complete information.

11-9 Application controls apply to the processing of specific individual transactions within a transaction cycle, such as a computer performed credit approval process for sales on account. Due to the nature of these types of controls, application controls generally link directly to one or more specific transaction objectives. For example, the credit approval application control directly links to the existence objective for sales. Auditors typically identify both manual and computer-performed application controls for each transaction-related objective using a control risk matrix similar to the one discussed in Chapter 10.

11-10 "Auditing around the computer" represents an audit approach whereby the auditor does not use computer controls to reduce control risk. Instead, the auditor uses non-IT controls to support a reduced control risk assessment. In these situations, the use of IT does not significantly impact the audit trail. Typically, the auditor obtains an understanding of internal control and performs tests of controls, substantive tests of transactions, and account balance verification procedures in the same manner as if the accounting system were entirely manual. The auditor is still responsible for gaining an understanding of general and application computer controls because such knowledge is useful in identifying risks that may affect the financial statements.

11-11 The test data approach involves processing the auditor's test data using the client's computer system and the client's application software program to determine whether the computer-performed controls correctly process the test data. Because the auditor designs the test data, the auditor is able to identify which test items should be accepted or rejected by the computer. When using this approach the auditor should assess the following:

11-11 (Continued)
- How effectively does the test data represent all relevant conditions that the auditor wants to test?
- How certain is the auditor that the application programs being tested by the auditor's test data are the same programs as those used by the client throughout the year to process actual transactions?
- How certain is the auditor that test data is effectively eliminated from the client's records once testing is completed?

Parallel simulation with audit software involves the auditor's use of an auditor-controlled software program to perform parallel operations to the client's software by using the same data files. Because the auditor's software is designed to parallel an operation performed by the client's software, this strategy is referred to as parallel simulation testing. Parallel simulation could be used in the audit of payroll by writing a program that calculates the accrued vacation pay liability for each employee using information contained in the employee master file. The total liability calculated by the auditor's software program would then be compared to the client's calculation to determine if the liability for accrued vacation pay is fairly stated at year-end.

11-12 Often companies that purchase and install vendor developed software applications on microcomputer hard drives rely on IT consultants to assist in the installation and maintenance of that software because those companies do not have dedicated IT personnel. Also, assignment of responsibility may reside with user departments. Companies can reduce these risks related to not having IT personnel by performing sufficient reference and background checks about software vendor and IT consultant reputations. In addition, companies can load software programs onto hard drives in a format that does not permit changes by client personnel, particularly non-IT user department personnel who may have primary responsibility for the system. Companies should also consider segregating key duties related to access to master files and responsibilities for processing transactions.

11-13 Because many companies that operate in a network environment decentralize their network servers across the organization, there is an increased risk for a lack of security and lack of overall management of the network operations. The decentralization may lead to a lack of standardized equipment and procedures. In many instances responsibility for purchasing equipment and software, maintenance, administration, and physical security, often resides with key user groups rather than with a centralized IT function. Also, network-related software often lacks the security features, including segregation of duties, typically available in traditionally centralized environments because of the ready access to software and data by multiple users.

11-14 In database management systems, many applications share the same data files. This increases risks in some cases given that multiple users, including individuals outside accounting, access and update data files. Without proper database administration and access controls, risks of unauthorized, inaccurate, and incomplete data files increase. The centralization of data also increases the need to properly back-up data information on a regular basis.

11-15 It is unacceptable for an auditor to assume an independent computer service center is providing reliable accounting information to an audit client because the auditor has no firsthand knowledge as to the adequacy of the service center's controls. If the client's service center application is involved in processing significant financial data, the auditor must consider the need to obtain an understanding of internal control and test the service center's controls.

The auditor can test the service center's system by use of the test data and other tests of controls. Or, he or she may request that the service center auditor obtain an understanding and test controls of the service center, which are summarized in a special report issued by the service center auditor for use by the customer's auditor.

■ Multiple Choice Questions From CPA Examinations

11-16 a. (1)   b. (1)   c. (3)   d. (3)

11-17 a. (1)   b. (3)   c. (2)   d. (3)

■ Discussion Questions and Problems

11-18 A schedule showing the pertinent transaction-related audit objectives and application controls for each type of misstatement is as follows:

MISSTATEMENT	TRANSACTION-RELATED AUDIT OBJECTIVE	COMPUTER-BASED CONTROLS
1. A customer order was filled and shipped to a former customer that had already filed bankruptcy.	■ Recorded transactions exist	■ Preprocessing authorization ■ Preprocessing review ■ Programmed controls (e.g., comparison to customer file)
2. The sales manager approved the price of goods ordered by a customer, but he wrote down the wrong price.	■ Transactions are stated at the correct amounts	■ Preprocessing review ■ Programmed controls (e.g., comparison to the on-line authorized price list)
3. Several remittance advices were batched together for inputting. The cash receipts clerk stopped for coffee, set them on a box, and failed to deliver them to the data input personnel.	■ Existing transactions are recorded ■ Transactions are recorded on the correct dates	■ Control totals reconciled to manual totals of all batches ■ Computer accounts for numerical sequence of batches submitted

11-18 (Continued)

MISSTATEMENT	TRANSACTION-RELATED AUDIT OBJECTIVE	COMPUTER-BASED CONTROLS
4. A customer number on a sales invoice was transposed and, as a result, charged to the wrong customer. By the time the error was found, the original customer was no longer in business.	■ Recorded transactions exist ■ Transactions are properly posted and summarized	■ Key verification ■ Check digit ■ Reconciliation to customer number on purchase order and bill of lading
5. A former computer operator, who is now a programmer, entered information for a fictitious sales return and ran it through the computer system at night. When the money came in, he took it and deposited it in his own account.	■ Recorded transactions exist	■ Input security controls over cash receipts records ■ Scheduling of computer processing ■ Controls over access to equipment ■ Controls over access to live application programs
6. A computer operator picked up a computer-based data file for sales of the wrong week and processed them through the system a second time.	■ Recorded transactions exist ■ Transactions are recorded on the correct dates	■ Correct file controls ■ Cutoff procedures ■ Programmed controls (e.g., check for sequence of dates)
7. For a sale, a data entry operator erroneously failed to enter the information for the salesman's department. As a result, the salesman received no commission for that sale.	■ Existing transactions are recorded	■ Conversion verification (e.g., key verification) ■ Programmed controls (e.g., check field for completeness)
8. A nonexistent part number was included in the description of goods on a shipping document. Therefore, no charge was made for those goods.	■ Existing transactions are recorded	■ Preprocessing review ■ Programmed controls (e.g., compare part no. to parts list master file)

11-19

	PERSON 1	PERSON 2	PERSON 3	PERSON 4
a)	• Systems analyst • Programmer	• Computer operator	• Librarian	• Data control
b)	• Systems analyst • Programmer	• Computer operator	• Librarian • Data control	N/A
c)	• Systems analyst • Programmer • Data control*	• Computer operator • Librarian*	N/A	N/A

* This solution assumes the data control procedures will serve as a check on the computer operator and will allocate work across both persons.

d) If all five functions were performed by one person, internal control would certainly be weakened. However, the company need not be unauditable, for two reasons: First, there may be controls outside the IT function which accomplish good control. For example, users may reconcile all input and output data on a regular basis. Second, the auditor is not required to rely on internal control. He or she may take a substantive approach to the audit assuming adequate evidence is available in support of transactions and balances.

11-20 a. The important controls and related sales transaction-related audit objectives are:

CONTROL	SALES TRANSACTION-RELATED AUDIT OBJECTIVE
1. Use of prenumbered sales orders	■ Existing sales transactions are recorded
2. Segregated approval of sales by credit department; customer purchase orders are attached to sales orders; approval is noted on form	■ Recorded sales are for shipments made to existing customers
3. Segregated entry of approved sales orders	■ Recorded sales are for shipments made to existing customers ■ Recorded sales are posted to correct customer account
Prices are entered using an approved price list	■ Recorded sales are at the correct price
Sales invoices are prepared from the data file created from sales order entry; hash totals are generated and used; sales invoices are prenumbered; control totals are reconciled by an independent person	■ Recorded sales are for shipments made to existing customers ■ Existing sales transactions are recorded ■ Recorded sales are at the correct amount ■ Sales transactions are properly included in the master files
4 & 5. Bills of lading are produced with sales invoices and eventually filed with the sales invoice in numerical order; differences in quantities are corrected and transaction amounts are adjusted	■ Existing sales transactions are recorded ■ Recorded sales are for the correct quantity of goods shipped
6. Hash totals of daily processing matched to hash and control totals generated by independent person	■ Existing sales transactions are recorded. ■ Recorded transactions are for shipments made to existing customers

b. Among the audit procedures to be applied to a sample of the invoices and source documents are the following:

1. Account for the sequence of prenumbered sales order forms.
2. Review the sales order forms for agreement with purchase orders from customers.

11-20 (Continued)

3. Determine that evidence of approval by the credit department appears on all sales order forms.
4. Account for the sequence of prenumbered sales invoices.
5. Ascertain that bills of lading have been prepared for all invoices and are in agreement therewith.
6. Determine that the price list used by the billing clerk has been properly authorized. Trace prices on the list to invoices, and test the extensions and additions on the invoices.
7. Ascertain that the sales invoices are in agreement with the data on the sales order forms.

Among the audit procedures to be applied to the data file are the following:

1. Verify the company's predetermined "hash" totals and control amounts by computing similar totals on selected batches of invoices and items from the data file.
2. Compare totals and see that they reconcile.
3. Arrange for a tabulating run to be made of selected test transactions. Compare the items in this printout with the totals previously compiled from the test transactions.

11-21 a. The classification of each procedure by type of test is as follows:

PROCEDURE	TYPE OF TEST
1	Test of details of balances
2	Test of details of balances
3	Test of details of balances (i.e., cutoff of inventory and accounts payable balances)
4	Test of control
5	Test of details of balances
6	Substantive test of transactions

b. Generalized audit software could be used for each test as shown on the next page:

11-21 (Continued)

PROCEDURE	DATA FILE OR FILES NEEDED	KIND OF TEST OR TESTS THE AUDITOR CAN PERFORM USING GAS	PROCEDURE FOR WHICH GAS IS LIKELY TO BE INAPPROPRIATE
1. Foot listing and trace to G/L	Accounts payable master file	■ Verifying footings	■ Tracing total to general ledger
2. Confirm balances with vendors	Same as 1; and, purchases transaction file	■ Selecting items for confirmation ■ Printing confirmation requests	■ Reconciling differences between balances and replies
3. Cutoff tests	Purchases transaction file	■ Selecting items for testing	■ Verifying receiving dates with respect to dates recorded
4. Test of authorization and cash discount	Purchases transaction file; and cash disbursements file	■ Match payment and purchase files to test whether discount taken	■ Verifying proper authorization (approval)
5. Review of changes in accounts payable listing	Accounts payable master file at beginning and end of year	■ Match items on two files to identify those that changed in excess of $500	■ Examination of vendor's statements
6. Test of unit costs	Purchase transaction file	■ Selecting items for testing	■ Comparison to price lists and catalogs

11-22 a. The major problems the auditor faces in verifying sales and accounts receivable include:

1. Determining that both cash and credit sales are valid, and that all were recorded in the proper amount.
2. Determining that accounts receivable balances are proper and that transactions were recorded in the proper amount and to the proper customer.
3. Determining whether the internal controls are adequate, so that he or she may rely on the system to provide correct information.

In this case, meeting some of these objectives is complicated by the fact that much of the pertinent information is in machine-readable form only.

b. The concept of test data can be employed in this audit by having the auditor make test purchases in different departments of the store and observing whether the sales are recorded properly in the appropriate records. The auditor may also wish to enter invalid data to be sure that the programmed controls reject the transactions. Some of the difficulties the auditor would have to overcome in using test data are:

1. The test data must comprise all relevant conditions that the auditor desires to test so as to test every conceivable weakness of consequence in the system.
2. The program tested by the auditor's test data must be the same program that is used throughout the year by the client to ensure the validity of results.
3. The test data will probably have to be eliminated from most of the client's records since the auditor's purchases would not be part of the company's regular business.

c. Generalized audit software can be employed in this audit by following these steps:

1. Decide the objectives of the test--e.g., to select and analyze a random sample of sales invoices or to compare the totals of master files to the entries into the general ledger.
2. Begin to design the application by identifying and selecting pertinent data from the client's files.
3. Design the most useful format and contents of the auditor's generalized audit software reports.
4. Complete the application design by developing the logical and programmed approach to extract and manipulate the data to produce reports.
5. Process the program and information to produce the reports.

Several tests that can be conducted using a generalized audit program are:

1. Select accounts according to certain selection criteria for accounts receivable confirmation and print the confirmations.
2. Prepare an analysis of sales and cost of sales.

11-22 (Continued)

      3. Test the year-end cutoff of sales.
      4. Review all intercompany sales transactions.
      5. Foot the various files and select unusual or large transactions according to certain criteria.
      6. Age accounts receivable.
      7. Test the recording of sales transactions by parallel simulation.

  d. Several ways to reduce the information entered into the cash register are:

      1. By setting the date in the register for the day, there will be no need to enter the date.
      2. Same as 1 for store code number and sales clerk number.
      3. There is no need to enter cash sale or credit sale since entering the customer account number implies a credit sale.
      4. Install optical scanning point of sale equipment.
      5. Have the computer pull unit prices based on product number from price list master file.

11-23 a. The nature of generalized audit software is to provide computer programs that can process a variety of file media and record formats to perform a number of functions using computer technology.

    There are several types of generalized audit software packages. Usually, generalized audit software is a purchased audit software program that is Windows-based and easily operated on the auditor's desktop or laptop computer. Other generalized audit software exist that contain programs that create or generate other programs, programs that modify themselves to perform requested functions, or skeletal frameworks of programs that must be completed by the user.

    A package can be used to perform or verify mathematical calculations; to include, exclude, or summarize items having specified characteristics; to provide subtotals and final totals; to compute, select, and evaluate statistical samples for audit tests; to print results or sequence that will facilitate an audit step; to compare, merge, or match the contents of two or more files, and to produce machine-readable files in a format specified by the auditor.

  b. Ways in which a generalized audit software package can be used to assist in the audit of inventory of Boos & Baumkirchner, Inc., include the following:

      1. Compare data on the CPA's set of preprinted inventory count cards to data on the disk inventory master file and list all differences. This will assure that the set of count cards furnished to the CPA is complete.
      2. Determine which items and parts are to be test-counted by making a random selection of a sample from the audit deck of count cards or the disk inventory master file. Exclude from the population items with a high unit cost or total value that have already been selected for test counting.
      3. Read the client's disk inventory master file and list all items or parts for which the date of last sale or usage indicates a lack of recent transactions. This list provides data for determining possible obsolescence.

11-23 (Continued)

4. Read the client's disk inventory master file and list all items or parts of which the quantity on hand seems excessive in relation to quantity used or sold during the year. This list provides data for determining overstocked or slow-moving items or parts.
5. Read the client's disk inventory master file and list all items or parts of which the quantity on hand seems excessive in relation to economic order quantity. This list should be reviewed for possible slow-moving or obsolete items.
6. Enter the audit test-count quantities onto the cards. Match these cards against the client's adjusted disk inventory master file, comparing the quantities on the cards to the quantities on the disk file and list any differences. This will indicate whether the client's year-end inventory counts and the master file are substantially in agreement.
7. Use the adjusted disk inventory master file and independently extend and total the year-end inventory and print the grand total on an output report. When compared to the balance determined by the client, this will verify the calculations performed by the client.
8. Use the client's disk inventory master file and list all items with a significant cost per unit. The list should show cost per unit and both major and secondary vendor codes. This list can be used to verify the cost per unit.
9. Use the costs per unit on the client's disk inventory master file, and extend and total the dollar value of the counts on the audit test count cards. When compared to the total dollar value of the inventory, this will permit evaluation of audit coverage.

11-24 a. Strengths of current systems development and program change processes at Granger Container:

- Eric Winecoff's extensive knowledge of the software being used helps lead to effective program changes and new application software developments.
- The small size of the IT staff and its team oriented approach allows the IT team to respond quickly to meet Granger's needs for system change.
- The IT programming staff tests applications using test copies of data files before implementation of the new system.
- Original data files are locked in the file storage room, which can only be accessed by Eric.
- Some documentation is maintained for each program change.

b. Weaknesses in current systems development and program change processes:

- Most program change requests are generated by IT personnel, with few program change requests generated by user department personnel who rely on the system to perform day-to-day tasks.
- No user personnel are involved in the program design and testing processes. Users have less ability to make suggestions of useful programmed controls to be performed automatically by the computer.

11-24 (Continued)

- Over reliance on Eric and the software package purchased from Eric's former employer may not always lead to the most effective and efficient system.
- No written requests for program changes are maintained. Thus, there is no audit trail of program changes that occur over time.
- No documented approval of program changes is maintained. Eric merely extends verbal approval. Again, the lack of documented approval increases the difficulty in determining that only authorized program changes occur.
- Periodic progress reports and approvals are not documented. This lack of documentation increases the potential for mismanaged program development. The lack of documentation makes future changes of those programs more difficult and time-consuming.
- The current review process is dependent on a programmer's willingness to bring issues to Eric's attention. Eric only becomes involved if a programmer approaches him for input. Too much reliance and trust is placed on programmers.
- There is no standardized format for designing programs. Rather, each programmer is able to employ his or her own programming style. Thus, it is more difficult to review current programs under development to determine that only authorized changes are being made. And, future changes involving those programs will be more difficult than if a standardized programming format was employed.
- Programmers have access to the computer room to load programs for testing. That access may allow a programmer to load a live copy of a program for processing. That could lead to inappropriate processing and manipulation of data, which in turn may lead to misstatements in the financial statements due to unauthorized or inaccurate processing.
- Programmers make changes directly into the live copies of actual programs that are currently in use. That could result in inaccurate processing of transactions when operators use that program to process actual data before all program changes have been thoroughly tested and debugged.
- Only Eric reviews test results. Users, internal auditors, and quality assurance personnel should also participate in designing test data and reviewing test results. Users are particularly most knowledgeable of the types of transaction data that the system should be capable of handling.
- Only Eric generates a limited amount of program change documentation. User and operation manuals and systems flowcharts and narratives are not updated for the change.
- There is no formal conversion plan developed that includes pilot testing and parallel testing before and during conversion.
- No user or operator training occurs.

11-24 (Continued)

c. Recommendations to improve processes:

- Encourage user personnel to submit written requests for change on a pre-printed program change request form. Change requests should contain the written approval of user department supervisors before submission to IT.
- Log all program change request forms by assigning a numerical sequence to all program change forms. Maintain a log of all approved and denied program change requests to generate an audit trail of the program change process.
- Develop a team approach to systems development and program changes. Require teams of programmers, user department personnel, internal audit, and a systems analyst to work on the program change from start to finish.
- Institute an IT Steering Committee that approves all significant program change requests. Eric should be required to formally report to this committee on a regular basis. For all other program changes, documented approvals should be obtained from Eric and the user department supervisory personnel for the department affected by the application program subject to change.
- Develop a formal Systems Development Methodology (SDM) that is to be used for all program development projects. When designing the SDM, build in required checkpoints for review and approval for each stage of development.
- Develop standardized programming formats and style to ensure consistent and accurate programming across programmers.
- Only provide test copies of application programs and data files for use by programmers. Never give the programming staff the actual application program currently in use.
- Prohibit programming staff from entering the computer operating room or secondary storage. Require programmers to submit test copies of programs and master files to the operations staff for testing.
- Only accept newly developed software programs into live production if accompanied by all required authorizations and documentation.
- Develop extensive documentation of the entire development process.
- Ensure that all user and operations manuals and systems flowcharts and narratives are updated to reflect recent changes.
- Develop a formal conversion plan that outlines the planned approach to implementing the new program. The plan should include extensive pilot and parallel testing, if possible.
- Train operators and users on the new system features before relying on the new system to process transactions.

INTERNAL CONTROL	TYPE OF CONTROL	TRANSACTION-RELATED AUDIT OBJECTIVE
1	AC	Recorded payroll transactions exist for valid employees
2	AC	Recorded payroll transactions are at the correct amounts
3	AC	Recorded payroll transactions are summarized and posted to the correct general ledger account at the correct amounts
4	MC	Recorded payroll transactions exist; existing payroll transactions are recorded
5	AC	Recorded payroll transactions exist (i.e., are for time actually worked)
6	MC	Recorded payroll transactions exist (i.e., are for time actually worked)
7	AC	Recorded payroll transactions exist (i.e., are for currently employed personnel)
8	MC	Recorded payroll transactions are at the correct amounts
9	AC	Recorded payroll transactions are classified into the correct accounts
10	AC	Recorded payroll transactions exist (i.e., for valid work performed); recorded payroll transactions are at the correct amounts

11-26 Recommendations to improve Hardwood Lumber Company's Information Systems function:

- The Vice President of Information Systems (VP of IS) should report on a day-to-day basis to senior management (i.e, the president) and should not be under the authority of user personnel. This ensures that the IS function is not subordinate to a user function, which might inappropriately allocate IS resources to that user function's projects.

11-26 (Continued)

- The VP of IS should have access to the board of directors and should be responsible for periodically updating the board on significant IS projects. Perhaps, the board should create an IS Steering Committee to oversee IS activities (like the Audit Committee oversees the financial reporting process).
- Operations staff should not have responsibility for maintaining the operating software security features. This responsibility should be assigned to a more senior, trusted IS individual, such as the VP of IS.
- Video monitors should be examined continually. The actual monitors could be viewed on an ongoing basis by building security guards. Hardwood should consider taping what the cameras are viewing for subsequent retrieval in the event of a security breach.
- Consider requiring the use of card-keys and passwords to grant entrance to the computer room to enhance security surrounding unauthorized access to the computer room.
- Hardwood may consider purchasing a vendor developed access security software package to strengthen on-line security beyond the features currently provided by the operation software's security features.
- Restrict programmer access to test copies of software programs for only those programs that have been authorized for program change. Access to copies of other programs may not be necessary when those programs have not been authorized for change.
- Grant systems programmers access only to approved test copies of systems software, and grant application programmers access only to approved copies of application software.
- Consider hiring a systems analyst to coordinate all program development projects. Systems analysts can strengthen communications between user and programming personnel, and they can increase the likelihood that a strong systems development process is followed.
- Develop a weekly Job Schedule that outlines the order in which operators should process jobs. The VP of IS should review computer output to determine that it reconciles to the approved Job Schedule. This will increase the likelihood that only approved jobs are processed and that they are processed in the correct sequence.
- Relocate the secondary storage to a physically secure room separate from the computer room. Only grant the librarian access to this room. This will prevent the unauthorized removal of program and data files.
- Remove the librarian's CHANGE rights to program and data files. The librarian should not be able to make changes to those files. The librarian should only be able to copy the contents of those files.
- Develop regular procedures for preparing backup copies of programs and data files and ensure those copies are sent to off-site storage.
- Use internal header and trailer labels on program tapes to ensure that the proper tapes are mounted for processing.
- Consider purchasing a vendor-developed librarian software package to assist the librarian in maintaining complete and accurate records of secondary storage programs and data files.
- Make sure only user department personnel have the ability to authorization additions or changes to data files.

CASE

11-27

1. Strengths in lines of reporting from IS to senior management at Jacobsons:

    - Melinda Cullen (IS Manager) and the chief operating officer (COO) work closely on identifying hardware and software needs.
    - Melinda's boss, the COO, has access to the board of directors and provides periodic updates about IS issues, if needed.

    Weaknesses in lines of reporting from IS to senior management:

    - The chief IS person (Melinda) is relegated to a manager level and is not considered a part of the senior executive team. This signals a potential lack of adequate support extended by top management to the IS function.
    - The IS Manager reports to a key user, the COO. The COO may place undue pressure on IS to work on IS related projects that affect the COO's areas of responsibility. Thus, other areas, such as those under the chief financial officer's control (i.e., the accounting system), may not receive adequate IS resources.
    - Melinda and the COO make all major hardware and software decisions without input from other user personnel and the board of directors.
    - There does not appear to be a written IS strategic plan that sets direction for the IS function.

    Recommendations related to the lines of reporting from IS to senior management:

    - The IS Manager should report directly to the president and be considered a part of senior management (i.e, on equal footing relative to the COO, CFO, etc.).
    - The board of directors should receive regular input from the IS Manager about the status of IS projects.
    - A written strategic plan should be developed and reviewed annually by the board.
    - Significant hardware and software changes should be approved by the board or its IS Steering Committee. Other changes to application software should also be approved by affected user departments.

2. Assessment of Melinda's fulfillment of IS Manager responsibilities, including her strengths:

    - Melinda is actively involved in the IS function and closely monitors day-to-day IS activities.
    - Melinda is experienced in Jacobson's IS function, having been employed by the company for 12 years. She has served in several IS roles at Jacobsons. Thus, she offers stability for the IS function.
    - Melinda performs extensive background checks before offering candidates employment in IS functions.

11-27 (Continued)
- Melinda has successfully maintained a fairly stable IS staff.
- Melinda conducts weekly IS departmental meetings to discuss issues affecting the performance of the department.
- Apparently the IS department is functioning well, given that few IS-related problems must be reported by the COO to the board.

Concerns about current management of the IS function:

- Melinda may be over delegating tasks to IS personnel without maintaining close accountability for employee actions. For example, programmers are given extensive leeway in programming changes to software and operators check each others' work to ensure that Melinda's job schedule was properly followed.
- Melinda spends too much of her time in the systems analyst role, which leaves little time for her to adequately monitor all IS tasks.

Recommendations for change related to the management of the IS department:

- Consider assigning systems analyst responsibilities to a senior programmer.
- Establish standardized programming procedures and have Melinda review changed programs for compliance with those procedures.
- Melinda should reconcile the Job Processed Log to the job schedule developed by her.
- Melinda should assign or at least approve the assignment of programmer staff responsibilities.

3. Assessment of the strengths of the programming function at Jacobsons:
   - The programming staff is experienced with both systems software and Jacobsons' application software.
   - The assignment of projects based on time availability of programmers ensures that each programmer stays familiar with all types of software in use at Jacobsons.
   - Programmers regular attend continued professional education courses.
   - Extensive logs of tape use and of changes made to programs are maintained.

   Concerns about the programming function:

   - Programmers work with both systems and application software program changes. Thus, a programmer is more likely to be able to implement an unauthorized change to an application program that also requires an unauthorized change to systems software.
   - Programmers are responsible for maintaining secondary storage of live programs and data files. Thus, programmers are able to make unauthorized changes to live production copies of programs and data files.

11-27 (Continued)

Recommendations for change related to the programming function at Jacobsons:

- Divide programmers into systems programmers and application programmers. Only assign system software changes to systems programmers and application software changes to application programmers.
- Reassign responsibility for maintaining secondary storage to either the computer operators or to data control personnel.

4. Assessment of the strengths of the IS operations function at Jacobsons:

- Melinda prepares a job schedule which operators follow to process transactions. Day-shift operators reconcile Job Processed Logs generated during the night shift to the job schedule, and night shift operators do the same type of reconciliation for jobs processed during the day.
- Operators perform routine monthly backup procedures.
- Input batch controls are generated to verify the accuracy and completeness of processing.

Concerns about the IS operations function:

- Backup procedures only occur monthly, which increases the risk of data loss.
- No one, other than operators, verifies that only jobs included on the job schedule are processed. Melinda depends totally on the completeness of the operators' identification of exceptions noted by operators.
- Jobs Processed Logs are generally discarded, unless the output does not reconcile to the job schedule.
- Operators have the authority to make small changes to application programs.
- Comparison of batch input control totals to computer processing is not performed by someone independent of the operator responsible for the processing.

Recommendations for change related to the management of the IS operations function:

- Update key data files and program tapes on a more periodic basis (perhaps daily). Store backup copies offsite.
- Prohibit operators from performing any programming tasks. Restrict access to program files to a READ/USE only capability.

5. Assessment of the strengths of the IS data control function at Jacobsons:

- Data control personnel review exception listings and submit requests for correction on a timely basis.
- Data control clerks monitor the distribution of output.

11-27 (Continued)

Concerns about the IS data control function:

- Data control personnel have the authority to approve changes to master files. Thus, they could add a fictitious employee to the employee master file to generate a payroll check for a non-existent employee.

Recommendations for change related to the management of the IS data control function:

- Restrict data control personnel from being able to authorize changes to master files. Only allow the respective user department to authorize changes to master files. Data control clerks should be held accountable for only inputting user department authorized changes to master files.

6. Users should be responsible for approving changes to master files. They should actively compare authorized input to output to ensure the accuracy, completeness, and authorization of output. Users should also be an active participant in the program systems development process. They should participate in program development design, testing, and implementation. In addition, users should have a voice in establishing the job schedule, given that users understand their processing needs best.

■ Internet Problem Solution: COBIT

11-1 The second edition of COBIT, released by the COBIT Steering Committee and the ISACA, is available at the ISACA website (http://www.isaca.org/). The ISACA website also contains several articles related to COBIT. Based on the information available at the ISACA website, answer the following questions:

1. What does COBIT stand for and what is it?

   COBIT stands Control Objectives for Information and Related Technology (COBIT). This product, following four years of intensive research by a team of international experts, was the largest project ever undertaken by ISACA. The question most frequently asked of auditors is "what are the minimum controls that should be in place for you to say it's well controlled?" COBIT answers this question by defining the control objectives that should be in place for all of the activities within an information systems function. COBIT outlines four domains, 32 processes and 280 detailed control objectives that make up a well controlled IT environment. In addition, COBIT provides, for the information systems auditor, audit guidelines corresponding to each of the 32 processes and addresses each of the 280 detailed control objectives. COBIT is so all-inclusive that "and Related Technology" was added to the name of the product to allow for future technology not yet even defined. COBIT is intended to be the breakthrough IT governance tool that helps in understanding and managing the risks associated with information and IT.

2. COBIT is divided into four parts. Please list and describe what these parts are (Hint: the first part is The Executive Summary, which explains for management why IT needs controlling and that there is a method to do this regardless of configuration, size, industry, or location).

   First, the Executive Summary explains for management why IT needs controlling and that there is a method to do this regardless of configuration, size, industry, or location. Second, the Framework explains this methodology and defines the key functions within all IS organizations for senior management's understanding. Third, Control Objectives define the controls that should be in place within the various processes—answering management's question of "what are the minimum controls?" Fourth, Audit Guidelines explain how to test those controls that should be in place -- from a process owner and auditor perspective.

3. The COBIT executive summary can be found at the ISACA website. Within The Executive Summary is a discussion of the "framework's principles." Identify and briefly describe the four high-level domain classifications. (**Hint**: If you go to the on-line version of The Executive Summary please be aware that it is comprised of several linked pages and contains the following sections "Executive Overview | Background | Framework | Framework's Principles | Summary Table COBIT | Home on-line").

11-1 (Continued)

The COBIT Executive Summary is contains four high-level domain classifications, which include the following.

Planning and Organization: This domain covers strategy and tactics, and concerns the identification of the way IT can best contribute to the achievement of the business objectives. Furthermore, the realization of the strategic vision needs to be planned, communicated and managed for different perspectives. Finally, a proper organization as well as technological infrastructure must be put in place.

Acquisition and Implementation: To realize the IT strategy, IT solutions need to be identified, developed or acquired, as well as implemented and integrated into the business process. In addition, changes in and maintenance of existing systems are covered by this domain to make sure that the life cycle is continued for these systems.

Delivery and Support: This domain is concerned with the actual delivery of required services, which range from traditional operations over security and continuity aspects to training. In order to deliver services, the necessary support processes must be set up. This domain includes the actual processing of data by application systems, often classified under application controls.

Monitoring: All IT processes need to be regularly assessed over time for their quality and compliance with control requirements. This domain thus addresses management's oversight of the organization's control process and independent assurance provided by internal and external audit or obtained from alternative sources.

(**Note**: Internet problems address current issues using Internet sources. Because Internet sites are subject to change, Internet problems and solutions may change. Current information on Internet problems is available at www.prenhall.com/arens/.)

Chapter 12

Overall Audit Plan and Audit Program

■ **Review Questions**

12-1 The five types of tests auditors use to determine whether financial statements are fairly stated include the following:

- Procedures to gain an understanding of internal control
- Tests of controls
- Substantive tests of transactions
- Analytical procedures
- Tests of details of balances

While procedures to gain an understanding of internal control help the auditor obtain information to make an initial assessment of control risk, tests of controls must be performed as support of an assessment of control risk that is below maximum. The purpose of tests of controls is to obtain evidence regarding the effectiveness of controls which may allow the auditor to assess control risk below maximum. If controls are found to be effective and functioning, the substantive evidence may be reduced. Substantive evidence is obtained to reduce detection risk. Substantive evidence includes evidence from substantive tests of transactions, analytical procedures, and tests of details of balances.

12-2 Tests of controls are audit procedures to test the operating effectiveness of control policies and procedures in support of a reduced assessed control risk. Specific accounts affected by performing tests of controls for the acquisition and payment cycle include: cash, accounts payable, purchases, purchase returns and allowances, purchase discounts, manufacturing expenses, selling expenses, prepaid insurance, leasehold improvements, and various administrative expenses.

12-3 Tests of controls are audit procedures to test the operating effectiveness of control policies and procedures in support of a reduced assessed control risk. Examples include:

1. The examination of vendor invoices for indication that they have been clerically tested, compared to a receiving report and purchase order, and approved for payment.
2. Examination of employee time cards for approval of overtime hours worked.
3. Examination of journal entries for proper approval.
4. Examination of approvals for the write-off of bad debts.

Substantive tests of transactions are audit procedures testing for monetary misstatements to determine whether the six transaction-related audit objectives have been satisfied for each class of transactions. Examples are:

12-3 (Continued)
1. Recalculation of amounts (quantity times unit selling price) on selected sales invoices and tracing of amounts to the sales journal.
2. Examination of vendor invoices in support of amounts recorded in the acquisitions journal for purchases of inventories.
3. Recalculation of gross pay for selected entries in the payroll journal.
4. Tracing of selected customer cash receipts to the accounts receivable master file, agreeing customer names and amounts.

12-4 A test of control audit procedure to test that approved wage rates are used to calculate employees' earnings would be to examine rate authorization forms to determine the existence of authorized signatures.

A substantive test of transactions audit procedure would be to compare a sample of rates actually paid, as indicated in the earnings record, to authorized pay rates on rate authorization forms.

12-5 The auditor resolves the problem by making assumptions about the results of the tests of controls and performing both the tests of controls and substantive tests of transactions on the basis of these assumptions. Ordinarily the auditor assumes an effective system of internal control with few or no exceptions planned. If the results of the tests of controls are as good as or better than the assumptions that were originally made, the auditor can be satisfied with the substantive tests of transactions, unless the substantive tests of transactions themselves indicate the existence of misstatements. If the tests of controls results were not as good as the auditor assumed in designing the original tests, expanded substantive tests must be performed.

12-6 The primary purpose of testing sales and cash receipts transactions is to evaluate the internal controls so that the scope of the substantive tests of the account balances may be set. If the auditor performs the tests of details of balances prior to testing internal controls, no benefit will be derived from the tests of controls. The auditor should attempt to understand the client's business and internal controls as early as practical through the analysis of the accounting system, tests of controls, and substantive tests of transactions.

12-7 When the results of analytical procedures are different from the auditor's expectations and thereby indicate that there may be a misstatement in the balance in accounts receivable or sales, the auditor should extend the tests until determining why the ratios are different from expectations. Confirmation of accounts receivable and cutoff tests for sales are two procedures that can be used to do this. On the other hand, if the ratios are approximately what the auditor expects, the other tests can be reduced. This means that the auditor can satisfy the evidence requirements in different ways and that analytical procedures and confirmation are complementary when the results of the tests are both good.

12-8 Substantive tests of transactions are performed to verify the accuracy of a client's accounting system. This is accomplished by determining whether individual transactions are correctly recorded and summarized in the journals, master files, and general ledger. Substantive tests of transactions are also concerned with *classes* of transactions, such as payroll, acquisitions, or cash receipts. Tracing amounts from a file of vouchers to the acquisitions journal is an example of a substantive test of transactions for the acquisition and payment cycle. Tests of details of balances verify the ending balance in an *individual* account (such as inventory, accounts receivable, or depreciation expense) on the financial statements. An example of a test of details of balances for the acquisition and payment cycle is to physically examine a sample of the client's fixed assets.

12-9 The audit of fixed asset additions normally involves the examination of invoices in support of the additions and possibly the physical examination of the additions. These procedures are normally performed on a test basis with a concentration on the more significant additions. If the individual responsible for recording new acquisitions is known to have inadequate training and limited experience in accounting, the sample size for the audit procedures should be expanded to include a larger sample of the additions for the year. In addition, inquiry as to what additions were made during the year may be made by the auditor of plant managers, the controller, or other operating personnel. The auditor should then search the financial records to determine that these additions were recorded as fixed assets.

Care should also be taken when the repairs and maintenance expense account is analyzed since lack of training may cause some depreciable assets to be expensed at the time of acquisition.

12-10 The following shows which types of evidence are applicable for the five types of tests.

TYPE OF EVIDENCE	TYPES OF TESTS
Physical examination	Tests of details of balances
Confirmation	Tests of details of balances
Documentation	All except analytical procedures
Observation	Procedures to obtain an understanding of internal control and tests of controls
Inquiries of the client	All five types
Reperformance	Tests of controls, substantive tests of transactions, and tests of details of balances
Analytical procedures	Analytical procedures

12-11 Going from most to least costly, the types of tests are:

- Tests of details of balances
- Substantive tests of transactions
- Tests of controls
- Analytical procedures
- Procedures to obtain an understanding of internal controls

12-12 C represents the auditor's assessment of the effectiveness of internal control. C_3 represents the idea that the auditor chooses not to perform any tests of controls. Since no tests of controls are performed, no assurance can be obtained from controls and all assurance must come from substantive testing.

Tests of controls at the C_1 level would provide minimum control risk. This would require more testing of the controls than would be required at either C_2 or C_3. Testing controls at the C_1 level allows the auditor to obtain assurance from the controls, thereby allowing for a reduction in the amount of substantive testing which must be performed to meet the level of acceptable audit assurance.

It would be a good decision to obtain assurance from tests of controls at point C_1 if the cost of substantive testing is considerably greater than tests of controls. However, if the cost of testing controls is high, it may be a good decision to obtain assurance at point C_3.

At point C_2, the auditor performs some tests of controls and is able to reduce control risk below maximum. Point C_2 would be appropriate if it is cost beneficial for the auditor to obtain assurance at a level between the two extremes mentioned above (C_1 and C_3).

12-13 Before reduced substantive testing is permitted, internal controls must be effective and the auditor must have found the results of the tests of controls satisfactory. Cost effectiveness of reduced assessed control risk should be considered in making the decisions as to whether to test controls. The cost effectiveness of reduced control risk is an audit *efficiency* issue.

12-14 By identifying the best mix of tests the auditor can accumulate sufficient competent evidence at minimum cost. The auditor can thereby meet the standards of the profession and still be cost effective and competitive.

12-15 The four-step approach to designing tests of controls and substantive tests of transactions is as follows:

1. Apply the transaction-related audit objectives to the class of transactions being tested.
2. Identify specific control policies and procedures that should reduce control risk for each transaction-related audit objective.
3. Develop appropriate tests of controls for each key control.
4. Design appropriate substantive tests of transactions considering weaknesses in internal control and expected results from 3 above.

12-16 The approach to designing tests of controls and substantive tests of transactions (**Figure 12-8**) emphasizes satisfying the transaction-related audit objectives developed in Chapters 6 and 10. Recall that these objectives focus on the proper functioning of the accounting system.

The methodology of designing tests of details of balances (**Figure 12-10**) emphasizes satisfying the balance-related audit objectives developed in Chapter 6. The primary focus of these objectives is on the fair presentation of account balances in the financial statements.

12-17 It is desirable to design tests of details of balances before performing tests of controls and substantive tests of transactions to enable the auditor to determine if the overall planned evidence is the most efficient and effective in the circumstances. In order to do this, the auditor must make assumptions about the results of the tests of controls and substantive tests of transactions. Ordinarily the auditor will assume no significant misstatements or control problems in tests of controls and substantive tests of transactions unless there is reason to believe otherwise. If the auditor determines that the tests of controls and substantive tests of transactions results are different from those expected, the amount of testing of details of balances must be altered.

12-18 If tolerable misstatement is low, and inherent risk and control risk are high, planned tests of details of balances which the auditor must perform will be high. An increase in tolerable misstatement or a reduction of either inherent risk or control risk will lead to a reduction in the planned tests of details of balances.

12-19 The nine balance-related audit objectives and related procedures are as follows:

GENERAL BALANCE-RELATED AUDIT OBJECTIVE	SPECIFIC OBJECTIVE	AUDIT PROCEDURE
Detail tie-in	Inventory on the inventory summary agrees with the physical count, the extensions are correct, and the total is correctly added and agrees with the general ledger.	Check extensions of price times quantity on a sample basis, foot the detailed inventory summary, and trace the balance to the general ledger and financial statements.
Existence	Inventory as stated in financial statements actually exists.	Trace inventory from final inventory summary to actual inventory and physically count selected items.
Completeness	Existing inventory items have been counted and included in the financial statements.	Select items from the physical inventory and trace to the client's final summary to make sure that all items are included.

12-19 (Continued)

GENERAL BALANCE-RELATED AUDIT OBJECTIVE	SPECIFIC OBJECTIVE	AUDIT PROCEDURE
Accuracy	Inventory items included in the financial statements are stated at the correct amounts.	Perform price tests of inventory by examining supporting vendors' invoices for selected inventory items and reverify price times quantity.
Classification	Inventory as included in the financial statements is properly classified.	Compare the classification of inventory into raw materials, work in process, and finished goods by comparing the description on physical inventory count tags with the client's final inventory listing.
Cutoff	Inventory cutoff is properly recorded at the balance sheet date.	Trace selected receiving reports several days before and after the balance sheet date to determine whether inventory purchases are recorded in the proper period and related physical inventory counts are included or excluded from inventory.
Realizable value	Inventory on the financial statements excludes unusable items.	Inquire of factory employees and management regarding obsolescence of inventory, and examine storeroom for evidence of damaged or obsolete inventory.
Rights and obligations	Inventory items in the financial statements are owned by the client.	Review contracts with suppliers and customers for the possibility of the inclusion of consigned or other non-owned inventory.
Presentation and disclosure	Inventory and related accounts in the inventory and warehousing cycle are properly presented and disclosed.	Examine financial statements for proper presentation and disclosure including proper description of pledged inventory and inclusion of significant sales and purchase commitments.

12-20 Auditors frequently consider it desirable to perform audit tests throughout the year rather than waiting until year-end because of the CPA firm's difficulty of scheduling personnel. Due to the uneven distribution of the year-end dates of their clients, there is a shortage of personnel during certain periods of the year and excess available time at other periods. The procedures that are performed at a date prior to year-end are often dependent upon adequate internal controls and when the client will have the information available.

Procedures which may be performed prior to the end of the year are:

1. Update fixed asset schedules.
2. Examine new loan agreements and other legal records.
3. Vouch certain transactions.
4. Analyze changes in the client's accounting systems.
5. Review minutes of board of directors' meetings.
6. If the client has strong internal control, the following procedures may be performed with minor review and updating at year-end:
    (a) Observation of physical inventories;
    (b) Confirmation of accounts receivable balances;
    (c) Confirmation and reconciliation of accounts payable balances.

■ **Multiple Choice Questions From CPA Examinations**

12-21 a. (2) b. (2) c. (3) d. (1)

12-22 a. (2) b. (4) c. (1) d. (3)

12-23 a. (4) b. (3)

■ **Discussion Questions and Problems**

12-24

	a.	b.
1.	TD of B	Reperformance
2.	TD of B	Documentation
3.	AP	Analytical procedures
4.	T of C	Inquiry and observation
5.	TD of B	Confirmation
6.	T of C	Documentation
7.	T of C	Documentation
8.	S T of T	Documentation
9.	AP	Analytical procedures
10.	TD of B	Documentation
11.	T of C	Documentation

12-25

	a.	b.	c.	d.	e.	f.
1.	Acquisition and Payment	Reperformance	Substantive	S T of T	Posting and summarization	N/A
2.	Acquisition and Payment	Documentation	Test of control or Substantive	S T of T	Existence	N/A
3.	Inventory and Warehousing	Analytical procedure	Substantive	A P	N/A	Realizable value
4.	Capital Acquisition and Repayment	Confirmation	Substantive	T D of B	N/A	Existence Accuracy Presentation and disclosure
5.	Acquisition and Payment	Reperformance	Substantive	T D of B	N/A	Detail tie-in
6.	Acquisition and Payment	Documentation	Substantive	T D of B	N/A	Cutoff
7.	Sales and Collection	Inquiry	Substantive	T D of B	N/A	Realizable value

12-8

12-26

	AUDIT TRAIL	TEST OF CONTROL
a.	Yes	Account for numbers included in the sequence to determine that all documents are there.
b.	Yes	Examine a sample of bank reconciliation for indication that the controller prepared each one.
c.	No	Observe whether the supervisor is present and performing his responsibilities at the time employees check in.
d.	Yes	Examine invoices for controller's approval.
e.	No*	Observe the cashier preparing the deposit slip and delivering the deposit to the bank.
f.	Yes	Examine sales invoice for initials.
g.	No*	Observe president's secretary opening mail and prelisting cash receipts. Also examine existence of prelisting.

* The primary concern in these two items is the separation of duties rather than the existence of the deposit slip and prelisting. The primary test of control procedure must therefore be observation.

12-27

a. TRANSACTION-RELATED AUDIT OBJECTIVE	b. TEST OF CONTROL PROCEDURE	c. SUBSTANTIVE TEST
1. Existing acquisition transactions are recorded. (Completeness)	Account for numerical sequence of receiving reports and trace to acquisitions journal entry.	Reconcile vendor statements to accounts payable listing.
2. Existing cash disbursement transactions are recorded, recorded transactions exist, and recorded transactions are stated at the correct amounts. (Completeness, Existence, and Accuracy).	Observe cash handling procedures and examine bank reconciliation to determine if was prepared by an independent person.	Prepare a bank reconciliation as of the balance sheet date.
3. Recorded transactions exist, recorded transactions are stated at the correct amounts, and transactions are properly classified. (Existence, Accuracy, and Classification)	Examine invoice packages for initials indicating that review has been performed.	Examine supporting invoices and recheck items checked by the clerk.
4. Recorded transactions exist. (Existence)*	Examine invoices for the controller's initials.	Examine supporting invoices for same information examined by the controller.
5. Recorded transactions exist. (Existence)	Examine invoices for indication of check number and date.	Examine supporting invoices, purchase orders, and receiving reports containing the proper check number and date for each cash disbursement.

* The objectives satisfied depend upon what she examines. She might for example examine supporting documents for accuracy and even for account classification. In that event, those two objectives would be added.

12-28

(a) INTERNAL CONTROL PROCEDURE	(b) TRANSACTION-RELATED AUDIT OBJECTIVE(S)	(c) TEST OF CONTROL	(d) POSSIBLE MISSTATEMENT	(e) SUBSTANTIVE AUDIT PROCEDURE
1. Independent checks on performance	Accuracy	Examine vendors' invoices for indication of recalculation	A misstatement in calculation of a vendor's invoice	Recalculation of vendors' invoices
2. Proper authorization	Accuracy	Determine existence of approved price lists for acquisitions	Unauthorized prices could be paid for acquisitions	Obtain prices from purchasing department and compare to vendors' invoices
3. Adequate documents or records	Existence Completeness	Account for a numerical sequence of receiving reports	Unrecorded acquisitions exist	Confirm accounts payable, especially vendors with small or zero balances
4. Independent checks on performance	Timing	Examine vendors' invoices for indication of comparison	Cutoff misstatements	Perform search for unrecorded liabilities
5. Independent checks on performance	Posting and summarization	Examine indication of reconciliation of the master file and control account	Misstatements in master file or control account	Foot subsidiary records and compare to control account
6. Independent checks on performance	Classification	Examine vendors' invoices for indication of internal verification	Account classification misstatements	Compare vendors' invoices to acquisitions journal for reasonableness of account classification
7. Proper authorization	Existence	Examine cancelled checks for signature	Invalid or unauthorized payment	Examine supporting documents for appropriateness of expenditures
8. Independent checks on performance	Existence Accuracy	Examine vendors' invoices for indication of comparison	Invalid or unauthorized payment	Examine supporting documents for appropriateness of expenditures
9. Adequate documents or records	Existence	Examine supporting documents for indication of cancellation	Duplicate payment for an acquisition	Examine supporting documents for every payment to selected vendors
10. Separation of duties	Existence	Observe check mailing procedures and inquire about normal procedures	Bookkeeper takes signed check and changes payee name	Compare payee name on cancelled check to supporting documents

12-29 a. The performance of interim tests of controls and substantive tests of transactions is an effective means of keeping overtime to a minimum where many clients have the same year-end date. However, this approach requires additional start-up time each time the auditor enters the field to perform additional tests during different times of the year. In the case of a small client, start up costs and training time may require more total time than waiting until after December 31.

b. Schaefer may find that it is acceptable to perform no additional tests of controls and substantive tests of transactions work as a part of the year-end audit tests under the following circumstances:

1. The results of the tests of the interim period indicate the accounting system is reliable.
2. Inquiries concerning the remaining period may indicate there were no significant changes in internal control and accounting procedures.
3. The transactions occurring between the completion of the tests of controls and substantive tests of transactions and the end of the year are not unusual compared to the transactions previously tested and to the normal operations of the company.
4. Other tests performed at the end of the year do not indicate that the internal controls are less effective than the auditor has currently assessed.
5. The remaining period is not too long in the circumstances. (Some consensus exists in the profession requiring the remaining period to be three months or less, depending upon the circumstances.)
6. Other matters of concern to the auditor indicate that the limitation of interim testing is appropriate (i.e., risk of exposure to legal sanction is not too great; the auditor will probably be familiar with the client's operations and will determine that a reduced control risk is justified; the auditor has appropriate confidence in the competence of personnel and the integrity of management).

c. If Schaefer decides to perform no additional tests of controls and substantive tests of transactions, depending upon the circumstances, she may wish to perform analytical procedures, such as reviewing interim transactions for reasonableness or tracing them to their source, comparing balances to previous periods, or other such procedures, for the remaining period to year-end.

12-30 a. The sequence the auditor should follow is:

3. Assess control risk.
1. Determine whether it is cost effective to perform tests of controls.
4. Perform tests of controls.
2. Perform substantive tests of details of balances.

12-30 (Continued)

The only logical sequences for parts b through e are shown as follows:

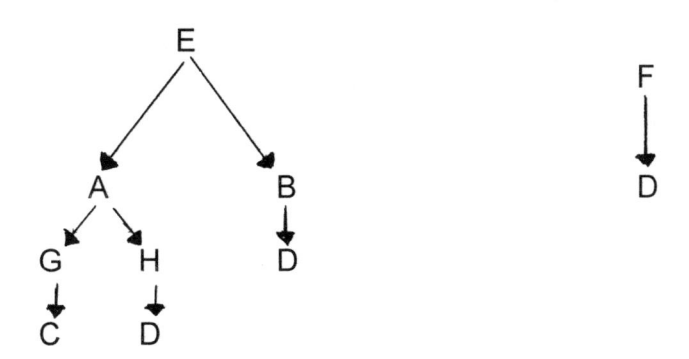

```
        E
       / \
      A   B
     / \  |
    G   H D
    |   |
    C   D


    F
    |
    ↓
    D
```

Any other sequence is not cost effective or incorrect. For example: E, A, G, C would be the sequence when there is planned reduced assessed control risk and effective results of tests of controls.

b. The sequence is E, A, H, D. The logic was reasonable.
   The auditor believed the internal controls would be effective and it would be cost effective to perform tests of controls. In performing the tests of controls the auditor concluded the controls were not effective. Therefore, expanded substantive tests of details of balances were needed.

c. The sequence is E, B, G, C. The auditor concluded the internal controls may be effective, but it was not cost effective to reduce assessed control risk. The auditor should not have performed tests of controls. It would have been more cost effective to skip performing tests and instead follow the sequence E, B, D.

d. The sequence is F, A, G, C. The logic is not reasonable. When the auditor concluded the controls were not effective he or she should have gone immediately to D and performed expanded substantive tests of details of balances.

e. The sequence is F, D. The logic was reasonable. The auditor concluded that internal controls were not effective, therefore the auditor went directly to substantive tests of details of balances and performed expanded tests.

12-31

AUDIT	PROCEDURES TO OBTAIN AN UNDERSTANDING OF INTERNAL CONTROL	TESTS OF CONTROLS	SUBSTANTIVE TESTS OF TRANSACTIONS	ANALYTICAL PROCEDURES	TESTS OF DETAILS OF BALANCES
1	E	E	S	E	S
2	M	N	S	M	E
3	E	E	M	E	S, E*

E = Extensive amount of testing.
M = Medium amount of testing.
S = Small amount of testing.
N = No testing.
S,E* = Small amount of testing for the gross balance in accounts receivable; extensive testing done for the collectibility of the accounts.

a. For audit 1 the recommended strategy is to maximize the testing of internal controls and minimize the testing of the details of all ending balances in inventory. The most important objective would be to minimize the number of locations that need to be visited. The justification for doing this is the quality of the internal controls and the results of prior years' audits. Assuming that some of the locations have a larger portion of the ending inventory balance than other locations, the auditor can likely completely eliminate tests of physical counts of some locations and emphasize the locations with larger dollar balances. The entire strategy is oriented to minimizing the need to visit locations.

b. Audit risk for this audit should be low because of the plans to sell the business, severe under-financing and a first year audit. The lack of controls over accounts payable and the large number of adjusting entries in accounts payable indicate the auditor cannot consider the internal controls effective. Therefore the plan should be to do extensive tests of details of balances, probably through accounts payable confirmation and other end of year procedures. No tests of controls are recommended because of the impracticality of reduced assessed control risk. Some substantive tests of transactions and analytical procedures are recommended to verify the correctness of acquisitions and to obtain information about the reasonableness of the balances.

c. The most serious concern in this audit is the evaluation of the allowance for uncollectible accounts. Given the adverse economic conditions, significant increase of loans receivable, the auditor must be greatly concerned about the adequacy of allowance for uncollectible accounts and the possibility of uncollectible accounts being included in loans receivable. Given the internal controls, the auditor is not likely to be greatly concerned about the gross accounts receivable balance, except for accounts that need to be written off. Therefore, for the audit of gross accounts receivable there will be a greatly

12-31 (Continued)

reduced assessed control risk and relatively minor confirmation of accounts receivable. In evaluating the allowance for uncollectible accounts, the auditor should test the controls over granting loans and following up on collections. However, given the changes in the economy, it will be necessary to do significant additional testing of the allowance for uncollectible accounts. Therefore an "S" is included for tests of details of balances for gross accounts receivable and an "E" for the tests of net realizable value.

12-32 a. The balances in the accounts included in the income statement and statement of cash flows result from the transactions during the period which affect the asset and liability accounts. If the beginning balances are not audited, the auditor cannot be sure that the intervening transactions are correct. A qualified opinion on the income statement and statement of cash flows will be required, though an unqualified opinion for the balance sheet is possible.

b. To verify the beginning balance in accounts receivable, Jackson could:

- Confirm the balance directly with customers (although most customers may not have sufficient records to reply).
- Examine supporting documents for the beginning balances. These would include verifying shipments by examining bills of lading and payments by tracing to the cash receipts journal and bank statement showing deposits.

c. Beginning balances on continuing audit engagements have been verified as ending balances during the previous audit.

12-33 a. Factors which could explain the difference in the amount of evidence accumulated in different parts as well as the total time spent on the engagement are:

1. Internal control;
2. Materiality of the account balance;
3. Size of the populations;
4. Makeup of populations;
5. Initial vs. repeat engagement;
6. Results of the current and previous audits;
7. Existence of unusual transactions;
8. Motivation of the client to misstate the financial statements;
9. Degree of client integrity;
10. Reliance by third parties on the audited financial statements.

12-33 (Continued)

For an example, in the first audit, the partner has apparently made the decision to emphasize tests of controls and substantive tests of transactions and minimize tests of details of balances. That implies effective internal controls and a low expectation of misstatement (low inherent and control risk.) In the third audit, the partner apparently has a high expectation of misstatements, and therefore believes it is necessary to do extensive tests of controls and substantive tests of transactions, as well as extensive tests of details of balances. Audit two is somewhere between audit one and three.

b. The audit partners could have spent time discussing the audit approach and scope with Bryan prior to the beginning of the field work.

c. The nature of these three engagements and the different circumstances appear to be excellent examples of the tailoring of audit procedures to appropriate levels considering the circumstances. Bryan's judgment could have been improved on each engagement if the audit partner discussed the audit approach with her during the engagement.

12-34
a. The following is a time line for the audit procedures, showing the sequence of the parts of a typical audit.

```
                          July                        Audit Report
                          31                             Date
─────────────────────────────────────────────────────────────────
    5, 9, 7, 2                        8    1    3      4    6
```

Parts 5, 9, and 7 are all a part of planning and are therefore done early. These are in the sequence shown in Chapter 8. As part of planning the audit, the auditor obtains an understanding of internal control and initially assesses control risk. The auditor then performs tests of controls and substantive tests of transactions and reassesses control risk.

Ideally, most analytical procedures are performed after the client has prepared financial statements, but before tests of details of balances are performed. Therefore, they should be done before confirmation of accounts payable to provide information about the expectation of misstatement.

Confirmation of accounts payable should be done as early as possible after the balance sheet date to facilitate getting responses back, performing alternative procedures for nonresponses, and reconciling differences before the audit is completed.

Tests for review of subsequent events are normally the last procedures done on the engagement before the audit report date. The audit report is issued after the audit report date.

b. The time line shows that 5, 9, 7 and 2 are frequently done before the balance sheet date.

12-35 a. The major deficiencies in the audit and the reasons for their occurrence are:

1. The change in the accounting system to computerize the inventory, a change in accounting personnel, and the existence of a few more errors in the tests of controls should have alerted the auditors to expand the scope of the work. It was questionable to conclude that the internal controls were effective.
2. Reduction in the scope of the inventory work based on the lack of errors last year was improper since new internal controls were in use with new personnel this year and the inventory balance was higher.
3. The new division should have been audited more thoroughly. It came to Merkle through merger and was likely to have different operating characteristics and internal controls.
4. The determination that the errors in the sample were immaterial was improper. The errors should have been projected from the sample to the population, and the projected error should have been compared to tolerable misstatement, after considering risk. The obsolescence problem uncovered in the audit should have been evaluated carefully to consider the implications on potential obsolescence of inventory.
5. Given the new personnel on the engagement, Brewer apparently failed to adequately supervise and review the work of assistants.
6. There was an apparent lack of the use of analytical procedures. A decline in sales should have warned the auditor to a potential decline in profits and obsolete inventory.

b. Brewer should have been aware that the inventory internal controls and the personnel in that department were new, that the interim tests revealed more errors than normal, and that the inventory tests revealed more errors than normal despite the reduction in scope. In this situation, the scope of the inventory work should have been increased to reveal the magnitude of the problems encountered. In addition, because of the staff turnover on this engagement, Brewer should have devoted more of his time to supervising the work of the staff on this engagement.

c. The likelihood of Brewer losing the suit is high. The auditors appear not to have followed general standards 1 and 3 and standards of field work 1, 2, and 3 in the performance of the engagement. Although the misstatements result from fraud, the auditors may be held responsible because apparently the audit was not conducted in accordance with GAAS.

■ **Case**

12-36 Part I

a. (1) *Assess acceptable audit risk.* This would be done under both audit approaches.

   (2) *Assess inherent risk.* This would be done under both approaches.

   (3) *Obtain an understanding of internal control.* This would be done under both approaches, however, it may be more extensive where control risk is reduced below the maximum due to the knowledge gained through testing.

   (4) *Assess control risk at less than 100%.* This would be done only under the "reducing control risk" approach.

   (5) *Perform analytical procedures.* This would be done under both approaches, although such procedures may be more extensive where control risk is reduced below the maximum.

   (6) *Assess planned detection risk.* This would be done under both approaches.

b. The "reducing control risk" approach has several advantages:

   1. It should result in lower overall audit cost. This will occur where the client's business activity is complex and its volume of transactions is large. In this type of situation, internal controls can provide a great deal of assurance that many of the financial statement assertions are correct, and the audit effort to test those controls can be significantly less than full-scale substantive tests of balances would require.

   2. For very large audits, it would be impossible to complete the audit on-time and at an acceptable cost without relying on controls. Large clients are usually publicly held and must file their Form 10-K with the SEC within 90 days of their fiscal year end. These large companies generally have many locations, including worldwide operations. Controls must be relied upon to do these audits.

   3. The more detailed investigation of controls that is required to reduce control risk, including testing, provides a better understanding of the system. This not only may provide a more concrete basis for conducting substantive tests, it creates more opportunities to make useful recommendations to the client.

   4. Performance of detailed tests of transactions documents creates the opportunity to reveal employee defalcations that would otherwise not be discovered. In addition, employee knowledge that transactions will be examined serves as a deterrent to defalcation in the first place.

12-36 (Continued)

c. The primary advantage of the "substantive" approach is one of efficiency. Where clients are smaller and less complicated, it is generally less costly to *not* test controls, but to focus the audit work on the balance sheet as of the end of the client's fiscal year. Furthermore, by going into the client's office at one point in time and doing the entire audit, auditor scheduling problems are reduced and there is less disruption to the client.

Part II

a. .17 is the level of detection risk for tests of the inventory balance that will provide an overall audit risk of .05 assuming tests of controls and analytical procedures are conducted as planned and achieve the expected results (i.e., don't indicate any misstatements exceeding a tolerable amount). Thus, as individual tests of details of inventory are planned, their design would be based on that level of risk of failing to reveal a greater-than-tolerable misstatement.

b.
$$TDR = \frac{.05}{1.0 \times 1.0 \times .6}$$

$$TDR = .08$$

c. The reduction of risk that can be taken for detailed tests of the inventory balance means that more reliance must be placed on those detailed tests. In this case, the degree of allowable risk is cut in half. In terms of sample size, this will result in a significant increase (the exact impact will depend on the sampling method used). It is also possible the auditor may feel less comfortable relying on analytical procedures to the extent otherwise planned, and may believe some other detailed tests are appropriate.

Part III

It is not appropriate to "rework" the Audit Risk Model as proposed by the staff person. The Audit Risk Model is a planning model that is based on testing the hypothesis that the financial statements do not contain a material misstatement. If an indication of a possible misstatement is revealed by applying the model at *any stage*, the hypothesis must be rejected and the audit plan revised to assume there is a material misstatement that must be subjected to measurement. Stated differently, the Audit Risk Model does not provide for contingent probabilities, which occur as the model is reworked based on findings as it is applied.

Chapter 13

Audit of the Sales and Collection Cycle: Tests of Controls and Substantive Tests of Transactions

■ Review Questions

13-1 a. The *bill of lading* is a document prepared at the time of shipment of goods to a customer indicating the description of the merchandise, the quantity shipped, and other relevant data. Formally, it is a written contract of the shipment and receipt of goods between the seller and carrier. It is also used as a signal to bill the client. The original is sent to the customer and one or more copies are retained.

b. A *sales invoice* is a document indicating the description and quantity of goods sold, the price including freight, insurance, terms, and other relevant data. It is the method of indicating to the customer the amount owed for the sale and the due date of the payments. The original is sent to the customer and one or more copies are retained. The sales invoice is the document for recording sales in the accounting records.

c. The *credit memo* is a document indicating a reduction in the amount due from a customer because of returned goods or an allowance granted. It often takes the same general form as a sales invoice, but it reduces the customer's accounts receivable balance rather than increasing it.

d. The *remittance advice* is a document that accompanies the sales invoice mailed to the customer and can be returned to the seller with the cash payment. It is used to indicate the customer name, sales invoice number, and the amount of the invoice when the payment is received. A remittance advice is used to permit the immediate deposit of cash as a means of improving control over the custody of assets.

e. The *monthly statement to customers* is the document prepared monthly and sent to each customer indicating the beginning balance of that customer's accounts receivable, the amount and date of each sale, cash payment received, credit memos issued, and the ending balance due. It is, in essence, a copy of the customer's portion of the accounts receivable master file.

13-2 Proper credit approval for sales helps minimize the amount of bad debts and the collection effort for accounts receivable by requiring that each sale be evaluated for collection potential.

Adequate controls in the credit function enable the auditor to place more reliance on the client's estimate of uncollectible accounts. Without these controls, the auditor would have to make his or her own credit checks on the customers in order to be convinced that the allowance for uncollectible accounts is reasonable.

13-3 The charge-off of uncollectible accounts receivable is a process whereby the company writes off receivables already in existence that it decides will not be collected. This usually occurs after a customer files for bankruptcy or when the account is turned over to a collection agency. The bad debt expense is a provision for sales that the company will be unable to collect in the future. It is an estimate used because of the matching concept in accounting. Bad debt expense is audited by examining past trends in uncollectibility, as it is a projection of future uncollectibles.

The uncollectible accounts write-off must be carefully audited to assure that accounts that have been paid are not written off to cover up a defalcation. This is done by examining the authorization for the write-off and the correspondence in the files concerning that account, and possibly by confirming accounts receivable.

13-4

TRANSACTION-RELATED AUDIT OBJECTIVE	KEY INTERNAL CONTROLS
1. Recorded sales are for shipments actually made to existing customers (existence).	■ Recording of sales is supported by authorized shipping documents and approved customer orders. ■ Credit is authorized before shipment takes place. ■ Sales invoices are prenumbered and properly accounted for. ■ Only customer numbers existing in the computer data files are accepted when they are entered. ■ Monthly statements are sent to customers; complaints receive independent follow-up.
2. Existing sales transactions are recorded (completeness).	■ Shipping documents are prenumbered and accounted for. ■ Sales invoices are prenumbered and accounted for.
3. Recorded sales are for the amount of goods shipped and are correctly billed and recorded (accuracy).	■ Determination of prices, terms, freight, and discounts is properly authorized. ■ Internal verification of invoice preparation. ■ Approved unit selling prices are entered into the computer and used for sales. ■ Batch totals are compared with computer summary reports.
4. Sales transactions are properly classified (classification).	■ Use of adequate chart of accounts. ■ Internal review and verification.

13-4 (Continued)

TRANSACTION-RELATED AUDIT OBJECTIVE	KEY INTERNAL CONTROLS
5. Sales are recorded on the correct dates (timing).	■ Procedures requiring billing and recording of sales on a daily basis as close to the time of occurrence as possible. ■ Internal verification.
6. Sales transactions are properly included in the accounts receivable master file and are correctly summarized (posting and summarization).	■ Regular monthly statements to customers. ■ Internal verification of accounts receivable master file contents. ■ Comparison of accounts receivable master file or trial balance with general ledger balance.

13-5

Tests of controls:

1. On a sample of sales invoices, examine proper authorization and indication of internal verification of sales amounts.
2. Examine approved computer printout of unit selling prices.
3. Examine file of batch totals for initials of data control clerk; compare totals to summary reports.

Substantive tests of transactions:

1. Recompute information on sales invoices.
2. Trace entries in sales journal to related sales invoices.
3. Trace detail on sales invoices to shipping documents, approved price lists, and customers' orders.

13-6 The most important duties that should be segregated in the sales and collection cycle are:

1. Receiving orders for sales
2. Shipping goods
3. Billing customers and recording sales
4. Maintaining inventory records
5. Maintaining general accounting records
6. Maintaining detailed accounts receivable records
7. Processing cash receipts
8. Granting credit and pursuing unpaid accounts

13-6 (Continued)

Segregation of duties should be used extensively in the sales and collection cycle for two reasons. First, cash receipts are subject to easy manipulation. Second, the large number and nature of transactions within the cycle make the procedure of cross-checking, where one employee's duties automatically serve to verify the accuracy of another's, highly desirable.

If the asset-handling activities (shipping goods and processing cash receipts) are combined with their respective accountability activities (maintaining inventory, accounts receivable, and general accounting records), a serious weakness with respect to safeguarding those assets exists. It would be easy for an employee, by either omitting or adding an entry, to use the company's assets for his or her own purpose. If the credit granting function is combined with the sales function, there may be a tendency of sales staff to optimize volume even at the expense of high bad debt write-offs.

13-7 The use of prenumbered documents is meant to prevent the failure to bill or record sales as well as to prevent duplicate billings and recordings. An example of a useful control to provide reasonable assurance that all shipments are billed, is for the billing clerk to file a copy of all shipping documents in sequential order after a shipment has been billed. Periodically, someone can account for all numbers in the sequence and investigate the reason for missing documents. The same type of a useful test in this area is to account for the sequence of duplicate sales invoices in the sales journal, watching for omitted numbers, duplicate numbers, or invoices outside the normal sequence. This test simultaneously provides evidence of both the "existence" and "completeness" objectives.

13-8 1. Credit is authorized before a sale takes place.

   Test: Analyze the allowance for uncollectible accounts and write-offs of accounts receivable during the period to determine the effectiveness of the credit approval system.

2. Goods are shipped only after proper authorization.

   Test: Review physical inventory shortages to determine the effectiveness of inventory control.

3. Prices, including payment terms, freight, and discounts, are properly authorized.

   Test: Compare actual price charged for different products, including freight and terms, to the price list authorized by management.

13-9 The purpose of footing and crossfooting the sales journal and tracing the totals to the general ledger is to determine that sales transactions are properly included in the accounts receivable master file and are correctly summarized. The auditor will make a sample selection from the sales journal to perform tests of controls and substantive tests of transactions, so he or she must determine that the general ledger agrees with the sales journal.

13-10 The verification of sales returns and allowances is quite different from the verification of sales for three primary reasons:

1. Sales returns and allowances are normally an insignificant portion of operations and therefore receive little attention from the auditor.
2. The primary emphasis the auditor places on sales returns and allowances is to determine that returns and allowances are properly authorized and that sales are not overstated at year-end and subsequently reversed by the issuance of returns.
3. The completeness objective cannot be ignored because unrecorded sales returns and allowances can materially overstate net income.

13-11 Cash is the most liquid asset that a company owns and thus it is the most likely target of misappropriation. The emphasis the auditor places on the possibility of misappropriation of cash is not inconsistent with his or her responsibility, which is to determine the fairness of the presentation of the financial statements. If material fraud has occurred, and it is not fully disclosed in the financial statements, those statements are not fairly presented.

TRANSACTION-RELATED AUDIT OBJECTIVE	KEY INTERNAL CONTROLS
1. Recorded cash receipts are for funds actually received by the company (existence).	■ Separation of duties between handling cash and record keeping. ■ Independent reconciliation of bank accounts.
2. Cash received is recorded in the cash receipts journal (completeness).	■ Separation of duties between handling cash and record keeping. ■ Use of remittance advices or a prelisting of cash. ■ Immediate endorsement of incoming checks. ■ Internal verification of the recording of cash receipts. ■ Regular monthly statements to customers.
3. Cash receipts are deposited and recorded at the amounts received (accuracy).	■ Same as 2 above. ■ Approval of cash discounts. ■ Regular reconciliation of bank accounts. ■ Batch totals are compared with computer summary reports.
4. Cash receipts transactions are properly classified (classification).	■ Use of adequate chart of accounts. ■ Internal review and verification.
5. Cash receipts are recorded on the correct dates (timing).	■ Procedure requiring recording of cash receipts on a daily basis. ■ Internal verification.
6. Cash receipts are properly included in the accounts receivable master file and are correctly summarized (posting and summarization).	■ Regular monthly statements to customers. ■ Internal verification of accounts receivable master file contents. ■ Comparison of accounts receivable master file or trial balance totals with general ledger balance.

13-13 Audit procedures that the auditor can use to determine whether all cash receipts were recorded are:

- Discussion with personnel and observation of the separation of duties between handling cash and record keeping.
- Account for numerical sequence of remittance advices or examine prelisting of cash receipts.
- Observe immediate endorsement of incoming checks.

13-13 (Continued)

- Examine indication of internal verification of the recording of cash receipts.
- Observe whether monthly statements are being sent to customers.
- Trace from remittance advices or prelisting to cash receipts journal.

13-14 Proof of cash receipts is a procedure to test whether all recorded cash receipts have been deposited in the bank account. In this test, the total cash receipts recorded in the cash receipts journal for a period of time, such as a month, are reconciled to the actual deposits made to the bank during the same time period. The procedure is not useful to discover cash receipts that have not been recorded in the journals or time lags in making deposits, but it is useful to discover recorded cash receipts that have not been deposited, unrecorded deposits, unrecorded loans, bank loans deposited directly into the bank account, and similar misstatements.

13-15 Lapping is the postponement of entries for the collection of receivables to conceal an existing cash shortage. The fraud is perpetrated by someone who records cash in the cash receipts journal and then enters them into the computer system. The person defers recording the cash receipts from one customer and covers the shortage with receipts from another customer. These in turn are covered by the receipts from a third customer a few days later. The employee must either continue to cover the shortage through lapping, replace the stolen money, or find another way to conceal the shortage.

This fraud can be detected by comparing the name, amount and dates shown on remittance advices to cash receipts journal entries and related duplicate deposit slips. Since the procedure is relatively time-consuming, auditors ordinarily perform the procedure only where there is a specific concern with fraud because of internal control weaknesses discovered.

13-16 The audit procedures most likely to be used to verify accounts receivable charged off as uncollectible and the purpose of each procedure are as follows:

- Examine approvals by the appropriate persons of individual accounts charged off. The purpose is to determine that charge-offs are approved.
- Examine correspondence in client's files that indicates the uncollectibility of the accounts for a selected number of charge-offs. The purpose is to determine that the account appears to be uncollectible.
- Examine Dun and Bradstreet credit records as an indication of the uncollectibility of an account. The purpose is the same as the previous procedure.
- Consider the reason for the charge-off compared to the company policy for writing off uncollectible accounts. The purpose is to determine whether or not company policy is being followed.

13-17 The primary objective of the tests of controls and substantive tests of transactions for sales and cash receipts is to determine whether or not the auditor may rely on internal controls to produce accurate information. If it is determined through tests of controls and substantive tests of transactions that the system provides reliable information as to accounts receivable balances, the auditor may reduce the sample size for the confirmation of accounts receivable and adjust the type of confirmation and timing of the tests. If the system is not considered effective because of weaknesses in internal control, the sample size must be increased, positive confirmations will probably be necessary, and the confirmations will most likely be as of the balance sheet date.

13-18 It is always acceptable to perform tests of controls and substantive tests of transactions at an interim date. The auditor may decide it is necessary to test the untested period at year-end. It is acceptable to perform tests of controls and substantive tests of transactions for sales and cash receipts at an interim date and not perform additional tests of the system at year-end under the following circumstances:

- The auditor feels that internal controls are effective.
- The auditor does not anticipate significant changes in the internal controls during the remaining period.
- The transactions normally occurring between the completion of the tests of controls and substantive tests of transactions and the end of the year are similar to the transactions prior to the test date.
- The remaining period is not too long.

13-19 Generally, successful tests of controls and substantive tests of transactions allow for a reduction of tests of details of balance at year-end. However, Diane Smith chose the month of March, which only represents one-twelfth of the year, as her test period. With such a short test period, Diane cannot conclude that she has selected a representative sample from the total population; therefore, without testing additional months (consensus of several CPA firms requires at least nine months coverage), Diane should not change the scope of her tests of details of balances at year-end.

■ **Multiple Choice Questions From CPA Examinations**

13-20 a. (4)   b. (4)   c. (1)   d. (3)

13-21 a. (4)   b. (2)   c. (1)   d. (1)

13-22 a. (2)   b. (4)   c. (4)

■ **Discussion Questions and Problems**

13-23

1.
   a. Recorded sales are for the amount of goods ordered and are correctly billed and recorded. (Accuracy)
   b. Examine indication of internal verification on sales documents.
   c. Incorrect prices may be charged, the customer may be billed for the wrong quantity, or the total amount may be computed incorrectly.
   d. Recompute information on the sales invoices. Trace details on sales invoices to shipping records, price lists, and customers' orders.

13-23 (Continued)

2. a. Recorded sales and credit transactions are for shipments actually made and existing sales transactions are recorded. (Existence and Completeness)
   b. Account for the numerical sequences of sales orders, invoices, and credit memoranda.
   c. Shipments or returns are not recorded. Orders from customers are misplaced and not filled.
   d. Examine correspondence concerning credit memoranda to assure that they were properly issued. Trace sample of shipping documents to related sales invoices and entries into the sales journal and accounts receivable master file. Confirm accounts receivable.

3. a. Existing transactions are recorded; recorded transactions exist. (Completeness and Existence)
   b. The auditor should observe the employees and discuss the procedures with personnel.
   c. Sales could be made and not recorded, with the employee keeping the proceeds of the sale.
   d. Trace selected shipping documents to related duplicate sales invoices, the sales journal, and accounts receivable master file.

4. a. Existing transactions are recorded. (Completeness)
   b. The auditor should observe the activities of those employees and discuss the procedures with personnel.
   c. These unusual sales could be made but not recorded and the proceeds kept from the company.
   d. Examine sales documents for these sales and trace the entries into the cash receipts journal.

5. a. Existing transactions are recorded and recorded sales are for the amount of goods ordered and are correctly billed. (Completeness and Accuracy)
   b. The auditor should observe the activities of employees and discuss the procedures with personnel.
   c. A receivable might intentionally not be recorded, allowing the cash to be kept from the company.
   d. Trace from the shipping records to the sales invoice, to the accounts receivable master file, and to the cash receipts journal.

6. a. Sales and cash receipts transactions are properly included in the accounts receivable master file and are correctly summarized. (Posting and summarization)
   b. Observation of procedures and examination of indication of internal verification.
   c. Unintentional errors could be posted in the control accounts and left undetected for long periods of time.
   d. Perform tests of clerical accuracy--foot journals and trace postings from journal to general ledger and accounts receivable master file.

7. a. Existing cash receipts transactions are recorded. (Completeness)
   b. Observation and discussion of procedures with employees.
   c. Cash could be received, not recorded, and kept from the company by an employee or lost prior to deposit.
   d. Trace receipts recorded on a list—such as from a prelisting of cash—to the books of original entry. Confirm accounts receivable.

13-23 (Continued)

8. a. Transactions are recorded on the correct dates. (Timing)
   b. Compare date per books to the date that the deposit appears on the bank statement.
   c. Cash receipts might be recorded in the wrong accounting period, lost, or stolen.
   d. Trace cash recorded on a list, such as a prelisting of cash, to the cash receipts journal and to the bank statement.

13-24

1. a. Error
   b. Internal verification of invoice preparation and posting by an independent person.
   c. Test clerical accuracy of sales invoices.
2. a. Error
   b. Sales invoices are prenumbered, properly accounted for in the sales journal, and a notation on the invoice is made of entry into the sales journal.
   c. Account for numerical sequence of invoices recorded in the sales journal, watching for duplicates. Confirm accounts receivable at year-end.
3. a. Fraud.
   b. All payments from customers should be in the form of a check payable to the company. Monthly statements should be sent to all customers.
   c. Trace from recorded sales transactions to cash receipts for those sales; confirm accounts receivable balances at year-end.
4. a. Fraud.
   b. The prelisting of cash receipts should be compared to the postings in the accounts receivable master file and to the validated bank deposit slip.
   c. Trace cash received from prelisting to cash receipts journal. Confirm accounts receivable.
5. a. Error.
   b. Use of prenumbered bills of lading that are periodically accounted for.
   c. Trace a *sequence* of prenumbered bills of lading to recorded sales transactions. Confirm accounts receivable at year-end.
6. a. Error.
   b. No merchandise may leave the plant without the preparation of a prenumbered bill of lading.
   c. Trace credit entries in the perpetual inventory records to bills of lading and the sales journal. Confirm accounts receivable at year-end.
7. a. Error.
   b. Internal review and verification by an independent person.
   c. Test accuracy of invoice classification.

13-25

1. a. Test of control
   b. Recorded sales returns are for returns from existing customers. (Existence)
   c. Documentation
2. a. Test of control
   b. Existing sales transactions are recorded. (Completeness)
   c. Documentation
3. a. Test of control
   b. Recorded sales are for shipments actually made to existing customers. (Existence)
   c. Documentation
4. a. Substantive test of transactions
   b. Recorded sales are for the amount of goods shipped. (Accuracy)
   c. Documentation
5. a. Substantive test of transactions
   b. Sales transactions are properly included in the accounts receivable master file and are correctly summarized. (Posting and summarization)
   c. Reperformance
6. a. Test of control
   b. (1) Cash received is recorded in the cash receipts journal. (Completeness)
      (2) Cash receipts are recorded on the correct dates. (Timing)
   c. Observation or documentation
7. a. Substantive test of transactions
   b. (1) Recorded receipts are for funds actually received by the company. (Existence)
      (2) Cash received is recorded in the cash receipts journal. (Completeness)
      (3) Cash receipts are deposited at the amount received. (Accuracy)
      (4) Cash receipts are recorded on the correct dates. (Timing)
   c. Documentation

13-26 a. *Objective 1* A given sale is recorded more than once, or a sale is recorded for which a shipment was not made.
   Objective 2 A shipment took place for which no sale was recorded.
   Objective 3 A sales journal was incorrectly footed, or a sales transaction was posted to the incorrect customer account.
   b. The first objective deals with overstatement of sales resulting from recording sales for which no shipment had occurred. The second objective concerns understatement of sales. It results from a shipment that has not been recorded.
   c. Procedures 2, 3, and 4 are tests of controls. Procedures 1, 5, and 6 are substantive tests of transactions.

13-26 (Continued)

d.

	(1) EXISTENCE	(2) COMPLETENESS	(3) POSTING AND SUMMARIZATION
SUBSTANTIVE TEST OF TRANSACTIONS	Procedure 6	Procedure 1	Procedure 5
TEST OF CONTROL	Procedure 2	Procedure 4	Procedure 3

e.

PROCEDURE	CONTROL BEING TESTED	NATURE OF MISSTATEMENT TRYING TO PREVENT
2	A shipping document is attached to each duplicate sales invoice.	To prevent billing to a customer or recording a sale for which no shipment has been made.
3	An independent person traces from the sales journal to the accounts receivable master file. A tick mark is shown in the margin of the sales journal after a transaction is traced.	Preventing misstatements in failure to post to the accounts receivable master file, posting to the wrong customer, at the wrong amount, or at the wrong date.
4	At the time of billing, the duplicate sales invoice number is written on the bottom left-hand corner of each shipping document. Periodically, the entire sequence of shipping documents is accounted for and each is examined to make certain there is an invoice number which indicates that a given shipment has been billed.	The failure to bill customers for shipments actually made.

13-27 a. (4) b. (2) c. (3)

13-28

TEST OF CONTROL OR SUBSTANTIVE TEST OF TRANSACTIONS	TRANSACTION-RELATED AUDIT OBJECTIVE(S)	SUBSTANTIVE TEST
1 S T of T	Accuracy	Not applicable
2 S T of T	Posting and summarization	Not applicable
3 T of C	Accuracy	Compare unit selling prices on duplicate sales invoices to the approved price list.
4 T of C	Classification	Examine a sample of sales transactions to determine if each one is correctly classified in the sales journal.
5 S T of T	Classification	Not applicable
6 S T of T	Completeness Accuracy Timing Posting and summarization	Not applicable
7 S T of T	Existence Completeness Accuracy Timing	Not applicable
8 T of C	Accuracy	Recalculate the cash discounts for a sample of remittances and determine whether each one was consistent with company policy.
9 T of C	Completeness	Trace from a sample of remittance advices to the cash receipts journal to determine if the related cash is recorded.

13-29 a. The lack of separation of duties was the major deficiency that permitted the fraud for Appliance Repair and Service Company. Gyders has responsibility for opening mail, prelisting cash, updating accounts receivable, and authorizing sales allowances and write-offs for uncollectible accounts. It is easy for Gyders to take the cash before it is prelisted and to charge off an accounts receivable as a sales allowance or as a bad debt.

b. The benefit of prelisting cash is to immediately document cash receipts at the time that they are received by the company. Assuming all cash is included on the prelisting, it is then easy for someone to trace from the prelisting to the cash receipts journal and deposits. Furthermore, if a dispute arises with a customer, it is easy to trace to the prelisting and determine when the cash was actually received. The prelisting should be prepared by a competent person who has no significant responsibilities for accounting functions. The person should not be in a position to withhold the recording of sales, adjust accounts receivable or sales for credits, or adjust accounts receivable for sales returns and allowances or bad debts.

c. Subsequent to the prelisting of cash, it is desirable for an independent person to trace from the prelisting to the bank statement. This can be done by anyone independent of whoever does the prelisting, or prepares or makes the deposit.

d. A general rule that should be followed for depositing cash is that it should be deposited as quickly as possible after it is received, and handled by as few people as possible. It is, ideally, the person receiving the cash that should prepare the prelisting and prepare the deposit immediately afterward. That person should then deposit the cash in the bank. Any unintentional errors in the preparation of the bank statement should be discovered by the bank. The authenticated duplicate deposit slip should be given to the accounting department who would subsequently compare the total to the prelisting. When an independent person prepares the bank reconciliation, there should also be a comparison of the prelisting to the totals deposited in the bank.

Any money taken before the prelisting should be uncovered by the accounting department when they send out monthly statements to customers. Customers are likely to complain if they are billed for sales for which they have already paid.

13-30 a. A proof of cash receipts is the reconciliation of the cash receipts recorded in the cash receipts journal to the cash receipts included as deposits in the bank statement. The purpose of the proof of cash is to identify cash receipts recorded in the cash receipts journal that were not deposited, deposits that have not been included in the cash receipts journal, or amounts that are different.

b. 1. (i)
    2. (iii)
    3. (iv) It may actually not be a misstatement. The cash was not deposited, and the company should be able to obtain a second check. It may, however, indicate the possibility of a bad debt because of the inability to collect a second time. The auditor is likely to uncover the problem by a confirmation of accounts receivable. If the check and remittance advice had been thrown away for some time, the problem is likely to show up in evaluating the aging schedule for accounts receivable.

13-30 (Continued)

4. (iii) Misstatement 4 can be found by performing substantive test of transactions for cash receipts, including tracing from the prelisting to the cash receipts journal and accounts receivable master file. The confirmation of accounts receivable is also likely to find such a misstatement.
5. (iv)
6. (ii)

c. In both 3 and 5, the most effective way to uncover the misstatement is through confirmation of customer account balances.

13-31 a.

WEAKNESS	RECOMMENDED IMPROVEMENT
1. Financial secretary exercises too much control over collections.	To extent possible, financial secretary's responsibilities should be confined to record keeping.
2. Finance committee is not exercising its assigned responsibility for collection.	Finance committee should assume a more active supervisory role.
3. The auditing function has been assigned to the finance committee, which also has responsibility for the administration of the cash function. Moreover, the finance committee has not performed the auditing functions.	An audit committee should be appointed to perform periodic auditing procedures or engage outside auditors.
4. The head usher has sole access to cash during the period of the count. One person should not be left alone with the cash until the amount has been recorded or control established in some other way.	The number of counters should be increased to at least two, and cash should remain under joint surveillance until counted and recorded so that any discrepancies will be brought to attention.
5. The collection is vulnerable to robbery while it is being counted and from the church safe prior to its deposit in the bank.	The collection should be deposited in the bank's night depository immediately after the count. Physical safeguards, such as locking and bolting the door during the period of the count, should be instituted. Vulnerability to robbery will also be reduced by increasing the number of counters.

13-31 (Continued)

WEAKNESS	RECOMMENDED IMPROVEMENT
6. The head usher's count lacks usefulness from a control standpoint because he surrenders custody of both the cash and the record of the count.	The financial secretary should receive a copy of the collection report for posting to the financial records. The head usher should maintain a copy of the report for use by the audit committee.
7. Contributions are not deposited intact. There is no assurance that amounts withheld by the financial secretary for expenditures will be properly accounted for.	Contributions should be deposited intact. If it is considered necessary for the financial secretary to make cash expenditures, he should be provided with a petty cash fund. The fund should be replenished by a check based upon a properly approved reimbursement request and satisfactory support.
8. Members are asked to draw checks to "cash," thus making the checks completely negotiable and vulnerable to misappropriation.	Members should be asked to make checks payable to the church. At the time of the count, ushers should stamp the church's restrictive endorsement (For Deposit Only) on the back of the check.
9. No mention is made of bonding.	Key employees and members involved in receiving and disbursing cash should be bonded.
10. Written instructions for handling cash collections apparently have not been prepared.	Especially because much of the work involved in cash collections is performed by unpaid, untrained church members, often on a short-term basis, detailed written instructions should be prepared.
11. The envelope system has not been encouraged. Control features which it could provide have been ignored.	The envelope system should be encouraged. Ushers should indicate on the outside of each envelope the amount contributed. Envelope contributions should be reported separately and supported by the empty collection envelopes. Prenumbered envelopes will permit ready identification of the donor by authorized persons without general loss of confidentiality.

13-32 a. The internal control weakness in the Robinson Company's procedures for customer billings and remittances include the following:

a. WEAKNESS	b. LIKELY ERROR OR FRAUD	c. SUBSTANTIVE AUDIT PROCEDURE
1. No evaluation is made of the customer's credit rating.	Substantial bad debts may be incurred by selling an open account to existing customer's delinquent in their remittances or to new customers in weak financial position.	Examine existing delinquent accounts and determine whether the Robinson Company has continued to ship to those customers.
2. The functions of authorizing shipment (preparation of the sales invoices with copies to the shipping department) and of billing should be separated.	Possibility of an individual initiating shipment to a personal account and later, after shipment, destroying the shipping notice (copy #3) and invoicing copies (#1 and #2).	Trace copy #5 of the sales invoice to the sales journal.
3. The sales invoices are not prenumbered and their numerical sequence is not accounted for.	Invoices prepared are not included in the totals posted to the general ledger control accounts and in the details posted to the accounts receivable master file. Such prenumbering and accountability would also serve to thwart the potential fraudulent practice outlined in #2.	Trace copy #5 of the sales invoice to the sales journal.
4. Invoices are not checked for accuracy of quantities, prices, or discounts.	Mechanical errors in quantities, prices, or discounts are more likely.	Recompute information on sales invoices and compare prices on sales invoices to authorized price lists.
5. There is no follow-up of unprocessed sales invoices held by the accounts receivable clerk.	Increases the likelihood of unrecorded sales, through the failure of the clerk to bill customers or record amounts in the journals.	Examine dates on sales invoices held by accounts receivable and determine if any have been unduly delayed.

13-32 (Continued)

a. WEAKNESS	b. LIKELY ERROR OR FRAUD	c. SUBSTANTIVE AUDIT PROCEDURE
6. Collections on accounts are not restrictively endorsed at the earliest possible time upon receipt by the company.	The accounts receivable clerk or someone else could endorse the check and assign it to themselves. The use of the restriction, "Deposit to the account of Robinson Company only," prevents that.	Trace from correspondence accompanying receipts to cash receipts book and the accounts receivable records and compare to bank statement.
7. The accounts receivable clerk performs the billings, posts to the accounts receivable master file, and receives the remittances prior to endorsement.	This mingling of the functions of billing and posting of billings and cash receipts permits the clerk to not record a sale to a customer and later divert the cash receipt.	Trace copy #5 of the sales invoice to the sales journal.
8. Responsibility of approval of customer deductions for discounts, freight and advertising allowances, returns, etc., should not be vested in the accounts receivable clerk.	Combining this authority with responsibility for recording and handling cash leaves open the opportunity for diverting a cash receipt and subsequently authorizing a credit of the same amount for an allowance or returned goods.	Trace credit entries in accounts receivable master file to valid source.
9. The preparation of the monthly trial balance of open accounts receivable and comparison of the total with the general ledger control account	Misstatements may be concealed by the accounts receivable clerk who may be attempting to avoid personal criticism. Although the posting misstatements are likely to lead to no direct material benefit to the accounts receivable clerk, the	Perform tests of clerical accuracy, e.g., footing journals and tracing postings to total general ledger and accounts receivable master file.

13-32 (Continued)

a. WEAKNESS	b. LIKELY ERROR OR FRAUD	c. SUBSTANTIVE AUDIT PROCEDURE
for accounts receivable is done by the accounts receivable clerk.	misstatements can result in losses for the company when an individual account balance is understated and the customer remits the lesser amount appearing on the monthly statement. On the other hand, if posting misstatements results in an overstatement of this account, the customer is unlikely to pay the amount.	

13-33 a.

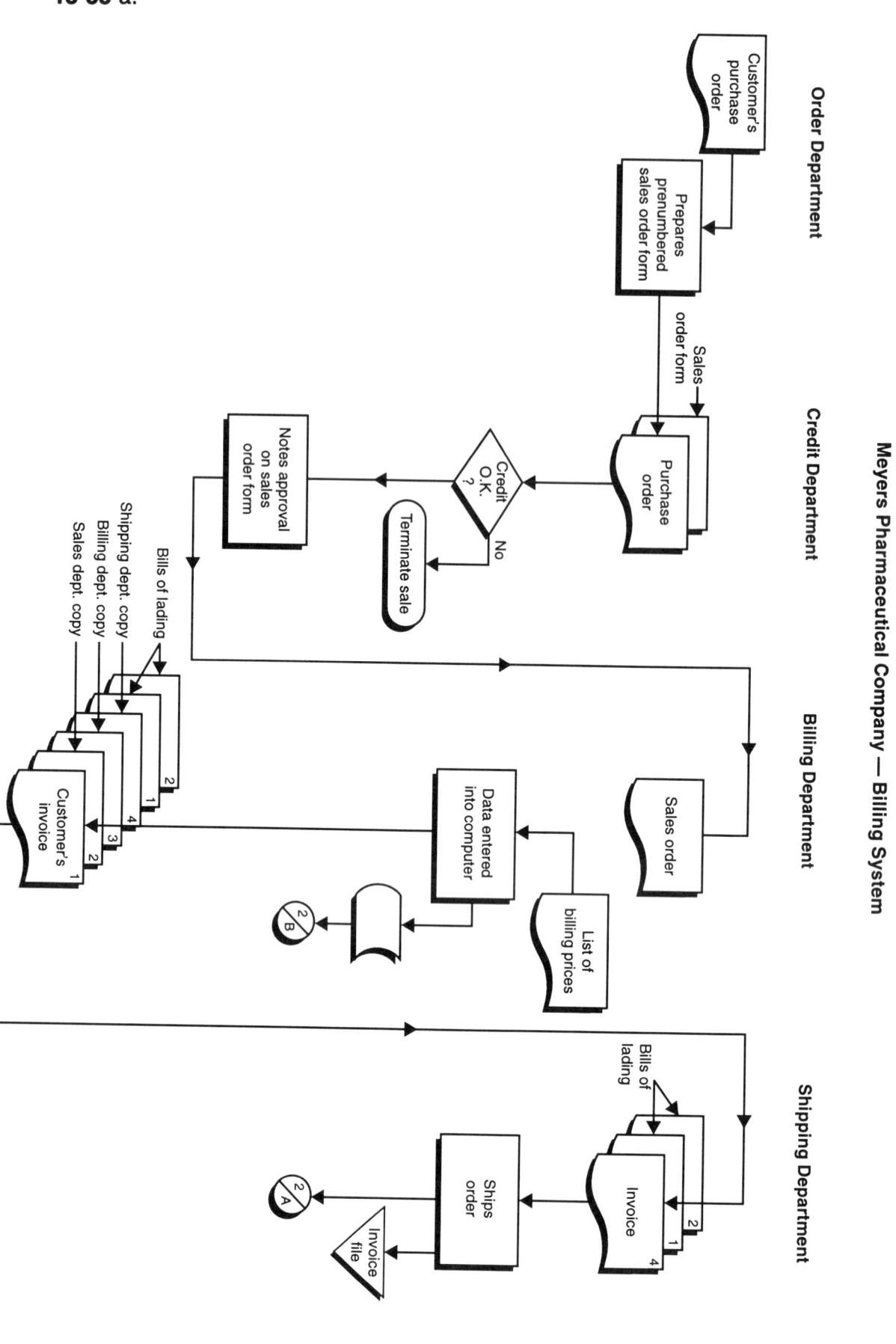

Meyers Pharmaceutical Company — Billing System

Order Department
- Customer's purchase order → Prepares prenumbered sales order form → Sales order form

Credit Department
- Purchase order → Credit O.K.? → No: Terminate sale; Yes: Notes approval on sales order form

Billing Department
- Sales order → Data entered into computer (with List of billing prices) → Customer's invoice (copies 1–4: Sales dept. copy, Billing dept. copy, Shipping dept. copy, Bills of lading) → to 2/B

Shipping Department
- Bills of lading, Invoice (copies 1, 2, 4) → Ships order → Invoice file → to 2/A

13-33 (Continued)

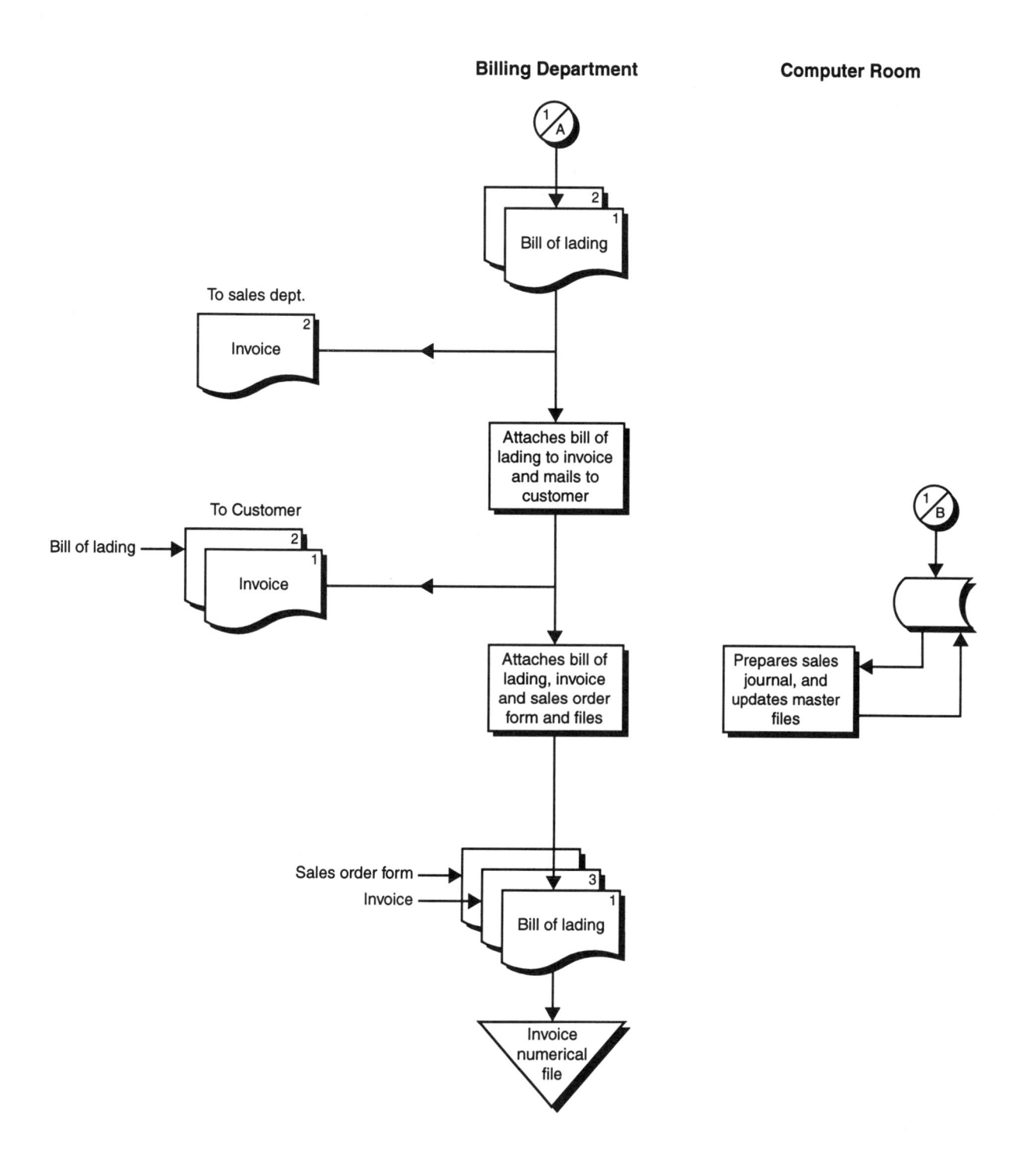

Billing Department

(1/A)

Bill of lading (2, 1)

→ Invoice (2) To sales dept.

Attaches bill of lading to invoice and mails to customer

Bill of lading → Invoice (2, 1) To Customer

Attaches bill of lading, invoice and sales order form and files

Sales order form →
Invoice →
Bill of lading (3, 1)

▽ Invoice numerical file

Computer Room

(1/B)

Prepares sales journal, and updates master files

13-21

13-33 (Continued)

b. and c.

TRANSACTION-RELATED AUDIT OBJECTIVE	INTERNAL CONTROLS	TEST OF CONTROL
1. Recorded sales exist.	Bill of lading and sales order form are attached to invoice. Sales are initiated by sales order form from customer.	Examine invoice package for presence of bill of lading and sales order form.
	Credit department investigates customer credit and approves sales before shipment of merchandise is authorized.	Examine sales order form for indication of credit approval. Review client's credit approval system for effectiveness.
2. Existing sales transactions are recorded.	Bill of lading and invoices are prenumbered (numerical sequence is not accounted for) and must be prepared before merchandise is shipped.	Account for numerical sequences of bills of lading and sales invoices and determine that all have been recorded.
3. Recorded sales are at the correct amounts.	Control totals are prepared and checked by computer. (No verification of the sales price is performed.)	Examine computer edit reports for indication of errors and disposition thereof.
4. Recorded sales are properly classified.	None.	Not applicable.
5. Sales are recorded on the correct dates.	None.	Not applicable.
6. Sales transactions are properly included in the accounts receivable master file and are correctly summarized.	Sales transactions are simultaneously recorded in sales, accounts receivable, cost of sales, and relieved from the perpetual inventory.	Trace sales transactions to sales journal.

13-22

13-33 (Continued)

d.

TRANSACTION-RELATED AUDIT OBJECTIVE	SUBSTANTIVE TEST OF TRANSACTIONS AUDIT PROCEDURES
1. Recorded sales exist.	Select a sample of sales from sales journal and examine customer's purchase order, sales order form, and bill of lading to determine that the goods were ordered and shipped.
2. Existing sales transactions are recorded.	Perform analytical tests, including comparisons of operating statistics to prior years and month to month at year-end.
3. Recorded sales transactions are stated at the correct amounts.	Compare sales prices to price lists. Examine customer correspondence indicating pricing disputes. Test clerical accuracy of a sample of sales invoices.
4. Recorded sales are properly classified.	Examine sales documents to determine that sales transactions are properly classified.
5. Sales are recorded on the correct dates.	Compare dates on bills of lading to the sales journal to determine that sales are recorded on a timely basis. Compare sales month to month and investigate any significant fluctuations, especially near year-end.
6. Sales transactions are properly included in the accounts receivable master file and are correctly summarized.	Foot the sales journal and trace the balance to the general ledger.

e. An audit program for conducting the audit of sales is as follows:

1. Obtain the sales journal for the year and perform the following procedures:
    (a) Foot the journal for one month and reconcile to the general ledger balance.
    (b) From the journal, select a sample of invoices and perform the following:
        (1) See that the customer's purchase order, sales order form, and bill of lading are available. Compare quantity, sales price, customer name, and date of shipment to sales journal. Obtain explanation of any differences.
        (2) Examine sales order form for indication of credit approved.
        (3) Compare sales price to price list.
        (4) Test clerical accuracy of sales invoices.
        (5) Determine propriety of classification of sales transactions.

13-33 (Continued)
2. Select a sample of bill of lading numbers. Locate the corresponding bills of lading and trace them to the sales journal to determine that the shipments were recorded. Compare the date per the bill of lading to the date per the sales journal to determine the promptness of recording.
3. Examine customer correspondence during the year for disputes on pricing of invoices.
4. Prepare a schedule of sales, cost of sales, and gross margin percentage, showing comparison between recent years and month to month. Obtain explanation of any significant fluctuations.

■ **Case**

13-34

When the computer is used, references to relevant procedures should be added to the matrices started in Part I (Case 10-32). Copies of these matrices with the references added are on the Companion Website and on the diskette accompanying this manual. The matrices have been prepared using Excel (Filenames P1334A.XLS and P1334B.XLS). The following solution for parts a and b is organized in the same manner as **Tables 13-4** and **13-5** on pages 420 through 422. The solution for part c is organized like **Figure 13-9** on page 423.

13-34 (Continued)
a. and b.

PINNACLE MANUFACTURING
INSTRUCTOR'S EXHIBIT - PART II a
Acquisitions

TRANSACTION-RELATED AUDIT OBJECTIVE	KEY INTERNAL CONTROL	TEST OF CONTROL (a)	SUBSTANTIVE TESTS OF TRANSACTIONS (b)
Recorded acquisitions are for goods and services actually received (existence).	■ Segregation of the purchasing, receiving, and cash disbursement functions. ■ Internal verification of document package prior to preparation of checks.	■ Discuss segregation with personnel and observe activities. (1a) ■ Examine document package for indication of internal verification. (6g)	■ Trace entries in the acquisitions journal to related vendors' invoices, receiving reports, and purchase orders. (6) ■ Examine supporting documents for propriety. (6b) ■ Compare prices on vendor invoices with approved price limits established by management. (6c)
Existing acquisition transactions are recorded (completeness)	■ Use of prenumbered purchase order and document packages, properly accounted for.	■ Account for a sequence of purchase orders and document packages. (7)	■ Trace a sample of receiving reports to the acquisitions journal. (8)
Recorded acquisition transactions are stated at the correct amounts (accuracy).	■ Internal verification of document package prior to preparation of checks.	■ Examine indication of internal verification of unit costs, extensions, footings and recording in the journal. (6a)	■ Trace entries in acquisitions journal to related vendors' invoices, purchase orders and receiving reports. (6) ■ Recompute

13-25

13-34 (Continued)
a. and b.

TRANSACTION-RELATED AUDIT OBJECTIVE	KEY INTERNAL CONTROL	TEST OF CONTROL (a)	SUBSTANTIVE TESTS OF TRANSACTIONS (b)
(accuracy) (cont.)			■ information on vendor invoices. (6d)
Acquisitions are properly classified (classification).	■ Internal verification of document package. ■ Use of adequate chart of accounts.	■ Examine indication of internal verification of account classification. (6a) ■ Inquire of client as to the use of a chart of accounts. (1b)	■ Examine vendors' invoices for proper classification. (6e)
Acquisition transactions are recorded on the correct dates (timing)	■ Internal verification of document package.	■ Examine indication of internal verification of dates. (6a)	■ Compare dates of recorded acquisitions with dates on receiving reports. (6f)
Acquisition transactions are properly included in the master files, and are properly summarized (posting and summarization).	■ Internal verification of document package. ■ A/P master file and general ledger are reconciled monthly.	■ Examine indication of internal verification of posting and summarization. (6a) ■ Inquire of client about monthly reconciliation procedures. (1c)	■ Foot acquisitions journal and trace postings to the general ledger and accounts payable master file. (2)

13-34 (Continued)
a. and b.

PINNACLE MANUFACTURING
INSTRUCTOR'S EXHIBIT - PART II a
Cash Disbursements

TRANSACTION-RELATED AUDIT OBJECTIVE	EXISTING CONTROL	TEST OF CONTROL (a)	SUBSTANTIVE TESTS OF TRANSACTIONS (b)
Recorded cash disbursements are for goods and services actually received (existence).	■ Segregation of purchasing, receiving, and cash disbursement functions. ■ Review of supporting documents and signing of checks by an independent, authorized person. ■ Internal verification of document package prior to preparation of checks.	■ Discuss segregation of duties with personnel and observe activities. (1a) ■ Examine checks for signature. (9b) ■ Examine indication of internal verification. (6a)	■ Trace cancelled check to the related cash disbursements journal entry and examine for payee, name, and amount. (9a) ■ Examine cancelled check for authorized signature, proper endorsement, and cancellation by the bank. (9b)
Existing cash disbursement transactions are recorded (completeness).	■ Use of prenumbered checks, properly accounted for. ■ Independent monthly reconciliation of bank statement.	■ Account for a sequence of checks. (4) ■ Examine file of completed bank reconciliations. (3)	■ Reconcile recorded cash disbursements with the cash disbursements on the bank statement (proof of cash disbursements). (5)

13-34 (Continued)
a. and b.

TRANSACTION-RELATED AUDIT OBJECTIVE	EXISTING CONTROL	TEST OF CONTROL (a)	SUBSTANTIVE TESTS OF TRANSACTIONS (b)
Recorded cash disbursement transactions are stated at the correct amounts (accuracy).	■ Internal verification of document package prior to preparation of checks. ■ Independent monthly reconciliation of bank statement.	■ Examine indication of internal verification of document package. (6a) ■ Examine file of completed reconciliations. (3)	■ Compare cancelled checks with the related cash disbursements journal entries. (9a) ■ Reconcile recorded cash disbursements with cash disbursements on the bank statement. (5) ■ Recompute cash discounts. (9d)
Cash disbursement transactions are properly classified (classification).	■ Internal verification of document package prior to preparation of checks. ■ Use of adequate chart of accounts.	■ Examine indication of internal verification of document package for classification. (6a) ■ Inquire of client as to the use of a chart of accounts. (1b)	■ Compare classification with chart of accounts by reference to vendors' invoices and acquisitions journal. (6e)
Cash disbursement transactions are recorded on the correct dates (timing).	■ Internal verification of document package prior to preparation of checks.	■ Examine indication of internal verification of document package for dates. (6a)	■ Compare dates on cancelled checks with the cash disbursements journal. (9a) ■ Compare dates on cancelled checks with the bank cancellation date. (9c)

13-34 (Continued)
a. and b.

TRANSACTION-RELATED AUDIT OBJECTIVE	EXISTING CONTROL	TEST OF CONTROL (a)	SUBSTANTIVE TESTS OF TRANSACTIONS (b)
Cash disbursement transactions are properly included in the master file, and are properly summarized (posting and summarization).	■ Internal verification of documents package prior to preparation of checks. ■ A/P master file and general ledger are reconciled monthly.	■ Examine indication of internal verification of posting and summarization. (6a) ■ Inquire of client about monthly reconciliation procedures. (1c)	■ Foot cash disbursements journal and trace postings to general ledger and accounts payable master file. (2)

c.

General

1. Discuss the following items with client personnel and observe activities:
   a. Segregation of duties
   b. Use of an adequate chart of accounts
   c. Monthly reconciliation of accounts payable master file with the general ledger

2. Foot acquisitions and cash disbursements journals and trace postings to the general ledger.

3. Examine file of completed bank reconciliations.

4. Account for a sequence of cancelled checks.

5. Reconcile recorded cash disbursements with cash disbursements on the bank statement.

Acquisitions

6. Trace entries in the acquisitions journal to related vendors' invoices, receiving reports, and purchase orders.
   a. Examine indication of internal verification of dates, unit costs, prices, extensions and footings, account classification, recording in the journal, and posting and summarization.
   b. Examine supporting documents for propriety.

13-34 (Continued)

    c. Compare prices on vendors' invoices with approved price limits established by management.
    d. Recompute information on vendors' invoices.
    e. Examine vendors' invoices for proper classification.
    f. Compare dates of recorded acquisitions with dates on receiving reports.
    g. Examine voucher package for indication of internal verification.

7. Account for a sequence of purchase orders and document packages.

8. Trace a sample of receiving reports to the acquisitions journal.

Cash Disbursements

9. Select a sample of cancelled checks and:
    a. Trace cancelled check to the related cash disbursements journal entry and examine for payee, name, amount, and date.
    b. Examine check for signature, proper endorsement, and cancellation by the bank.
    c. Compare date on cancelled check with bank cancellation date.
    d. Recompute cash discounts.

■ Internet Problem Solution: Electronic Funds Transfer

13-1 On the Federal Electronic Commerce Program Office's (FECPO) site (http://www.ec.fed.gov/), the FECPO provides a "List of Best Practices." Within that list locate the section on "Electronic Fund Transfer," and then open the link to the description of the "Social Security Administration Electronic Invoicing of Telephone Bills." In a short memo, briefly address the following questions:

a. What was the problem with respect to telephone bills?
b. What was the solution?
c. What are the benefits of the solution?
d. What new risks does the solution present?
e. What controls are in place to mitigate these risks?

The complete description of the "Social Security Administration Electronic Invoicing of Telephone Bills" case is provided below. The answers to questions a - c can be easily determined from the case description. The description suggests a new risk (question d) to the SSA office would be various forms of overpayment (e.g., billing errors, double billings, phantom billings, etc.) as the billings are paid automatically via EFT. One control, if observed, that would mitigate this risk (question e) is that the local offices are provided a paper copy of the statement and should be verifying the accuracy of the billing.

13-1 (Continued)

Description of Problem: The SSA Office of Financial Policy and Operations determined that paying local telephone bills was a high volume, paper and resource intensive process. Research revealed that the telephone industry is known for being advanced in its use of Electronic Data Interchange (EDI) documents under the ANSI X12 standards. SSA initiated a project to streamline the current process of paying local telephone bills by third party draft in each field office and manually coding transactions to record the expenditures in the accounting system. The object of the new process is for the Office of Finance to receive an electronic bill for all locations serviced by a telephone company and automatically process it for payment while simultaneously posting it to the accounting system.

Reason for Development: The Office of Financial Policy and Operations has significantly reduced its staff under the streamlining initiatives set forth by SSA. This project has the potential to save the manual resources needed to receive, process and pay local telephone bills. In addition, this project works in concert with the mandatory electronic funds transfer (EFT) legislation.

How it works: The local telephone company submits an electronic bill to the SSA Office of Finance that contains the same charges as a paper memo bill provided to the field office. The bill is recorded in the Financial Accounting System (FACTS) and paid automatically by EFT. The bill is a net total of all charges and adjustments for the billing period. The recording of telephone expenditures in FACTS occurs when the electronic bill is received from the telephone company. The local telephone company continues to provide the SSA field office with a paper copy memo of the monthly charges. The field office is still responsible for verifying the bill and dealing with the local telephone company to resolve differences and to make adjustments to the bill. Under this approach, all adjustments are reflected on the next month's bill.

Benefits: The goals of the electronic telephone billing process were established to provide the major benefits of distributing automatically the telephone charges to the appropriate field office, accounting classification codes for the timely recording of expenditure, eliminating the use of third party drafts for local telephone bills, and preparing an automated EFT payment to Treasury for the net amount of the total bill.

> (**Note**: Internet problems address current issues using Internet sources. Because Internet sites are subject to change, Internet problems and solutions are subject to change. Current information on Internet problems is available at www.prenhall.com/arens/).

Chapter 14

Audit Sampling for Tests of Control and Substantive Tests of Transactions

■ **Review Questions**

14-1 A representative sample is one in which the characteristics of interest for the sample are approximately the same as for the population (that is, the sample accurately represents the total population). If the population contains significant misstatements, but the sample is practically free of misstatements, the sample is nonrepresentative, which is likely to result in an improper audit decision. The auditor can never know for sure whether he or she has a representative sample because the entire population is ordinarily not tested, but certain things, such as the use of random selection, can increase the likelihood of a representative sample.

14-2 Statistical sampling is the use of mathematical measurement techniques to calculate formal statistical results. The auditor therefore quantifies sampling risk when statistical sampling is used. In nonstatistical sampling, the auditor does not quantify sampling risk. Instead, conclusions are reached about populations on a more judgmental basis.
   For both statistical and nonstatistical methods, the three main parts are:

1. Plan the sample
2. Select the sample and perform the tests
3. Evaluate the results

14-3 In replacement sampling, an element in the population can be included in the sample more than once if the random number corresponding to that element is selected more than once. In nonreplacement sampling, an element can be included only once. If the random number corresponding to an element is selected more than once, it is simply treated as a discard the second time. Although both selection approaches are consistent with sound statistical theory, auditors rarely use replacement sampling; it seems more intuitively satisfying to auditors to include an item only once.

14-4 A simple random sample is one in which every possible combination of elements in the population has an equal chance of selection. Two methods of simple random selection are use of a random number table, and use of the computer to generate random numbers. Auditors most often use the computer to generate random numbers because it saves time, reduces the likelihood of error, and provides automatic documentation of the sample selected.

14-5 In systematic sampling, the auditor calculates an interval and then methodically selects the items for the sample based on the size of the interval. The interval is set by dividing the population size by the number of sample items desired.

To select 35 numbers from a population of 1,750, the auditor divides 35 into 1,750 and gets an interval of 50. He or she then selects a random number between 0 and 49. Assume the auditor chooses 17. The first item is the number 17. The next is 67, then 117, 167, and so on.

The advantage of systematic sampling is its ease of use. In most populations a systematic sample can be drawn quickly, the approach automatically puts the numbers in sequential order and documentation is easy.

A major problem with the use of systematic sampling is the possibility of bias. Because of the way in which systematic samples are selected, once the first item in the sample is selected, all other items are chosen automatically. This causes no problems if the characteristics of interest, such as control deviations, are distributed randomly throughout the population; however, in many cases they are not. If all items of a certain type are processed at a certain time of the month or with the use of certain document numbers, a systematically drawn sample has a higher likelihood of failing to obtain a representative sample. This shortcoming is sufficiently serious that some CPA firms do not permit the use of systematic sampling.

14-6 The purpose of using nonstatistical sampling for tests of controls and substantive tests of transactions is to estimate the proportion of items in a population containing a characteristic or attribute of interest. The auditor is ordinarily interested in determining internal control deviations or monetary misstatements for tests of controls and substantive tests of transactions.

14-7 A block sample is the selection of several items in sequence. Once the first item in the block is selected, the remainder of the block is chosen automatically. Thus, to select 5 blocks of 20 sales invoices, one would select one invoice and the block would be that invoice plus the next 19 entries. This procedure would be repeated 4 other times.

14-8 The terms below are defined as follows:

TERM	DEFINITION
a. Acceptable risk of assessing control risk too low (ARACR)	The risk the auditor is willing to take of accepting a control as effective or a rate of monetary misstatements as tolerable, when the true population exception rate is greater than the tolerable exception rate.
b. Computed upper exception rate (CUER)	The highest estimated exception rate in the population at a given ARACR.
c. Estimated population exception rate (EPER)	The exception rate that the auditor expects to find in the population before testing begins. It is necessary to plan the appropriate sample size.
d. Sample exception rate (SER)	The actual rate of exception discovered in the sample. It is calculated by dividing the actual number of exceptions in the sample by the sample size.
e. Tolerable exception rate (TER)	The exception rate that the auditor will permit in the population and still be willing to use the assessed control risk and/or the amount of monetary misstatements in the transactions established during planning.

14-9 The sampling unit is the population item from which the auditor selects sample items. The major consideration in defining the sampling unit is making it consistent with the objectives of the audit tests. Thus, the definition of the population and the planned audit procedures usually dictate the appropriate sampling unit.

The sampling unit for verifying the existence of recorded sales would be the entries in the sales journal since this is the document the auditor wishes to validate. The sampling unit for testing the possibility of omitted sales is the shipping document from which sales are recorded because the failure to bill a shipment is the exception condition of interest to the auditor.

14-10 The tolerable exception rate (TER) represents the exception rate that the auditor will permit in the population and still be willing to use the assessed control risk and/or the amount of monetary misstatements in the transactions established during planning. TER is determined by choice of the auditor on the basis of his or her professional judgment.

The computed upper exception rate (CUER) is the highest estimated exception rate in the population, at a given ARACR. For nonstatistical sampling, CUER is determined by adding an estimate of sampling error to the SER (sample exception rate). For statistical sampling, CUER is determined by using a statistical sampling table after the auditor has completed the audit testing and therefore knows the number of exceptions in the sample.

14-11 Sampling error is an inherent part of sampling that results from testing less than the entire population. Sampling error simply means that the sample is not perfectly representative of the entire population.

Nonsampling error occurs when audit tests do not uncover errors which exist in the sample. Nonsampling error can result from:

1. The auditor's failure to recognize exceptions, or
2. Inappropriate or ineffective audit procedures.

There are two ways to reduce sampling risk:

1. Increase sample size.
2. Use an appropriate method of selecting sample items from the population.

Careful design of audit procedures and proper supervision and review are ways to reduce nonsampling risk.

14-12 An attribute is the definition of the characteristic being tested and the exception conditions whenever audit sampling is used. The attributes of interest are determined directly from the audit program.

14-13 An attribute is the characteristic being tested for in a population. An exception occurs when the attribute being tested for is absent. The exception for the audit procedure, the duplicate sales invoice has been initialed indicating the performance of internal verification, is the lack of initials on duplicate sales invoices.

14-14 Tolerable exception rate is the result of an auditor's judgment. The suitable TER is a question of materiality and is therefore affected by both the definition and the importance of the attribute in the audit plan.

The sample size for a TER of 6% would be smaller than that for a TER of 3%, all other factors being equal.

14-15 The appropriate ARACR is a decision the auditor must make using professional judgment. The degree to which the auditor wishes to reduce assessed control risk below the maximum is the major factor determining the auditor's ARACR.

The auditor will choose a smaller sample size for an ARACR of 10% than would be used if the risk were 5%, all other factors being equal.

14-16 The relationship between sample size and the four factors determining sample size are as follows:

a. As the ARACR increases, the required sample size decreases.
b. As the population size increases, the required sample size is normally unchanged, or may increase slightly.
c. As the TER increases, the sample size decreases.
d. As the EPER increases, the required sample size increases.

14-17 In this situation, the SER is 3%, the sample size is 100 and the ARACR is 5%. From the 5% ARACR table (**Table 14-8**) then, the CUER is 7.6%. This means that the auditor can state with a 5% risk of being wrong that the true population exception rate does not exceed 7.6%.

14-18 Analysis of exceptions is the investigation of individual exceptions to determine the cause of the breakdown in internal control. Such analysis is important because by discovering the nature and causes of individual exceptions, the auditor can more effectively evaluate the effectiveness of internal control. The analysis attempts to tell the "why" and "how" of the exceptions after the auditor already knows how many and what types of exceptions have occurred.

14-19 When the CUER exceeds the TER, the auditor may do one or more of the following:

1. Revise the TER or the ARACR. This alternative should be followed only when the auditor has concluded that the original specifications were too conservative, and when he or she is willing to accept the risk associated with the higher specifications.
2. Expand the sample size. This alternative should be followed when the auditor expects the additional benefits to exceed the additional costs, that is, the auditor believes that the sample tested was not representative of the population.
3. Revise assessed control risk upward. This is likely to increase substantive procedures. Revising assessed control risk may be done if 1 or 2 is not practical and additional substantive procedures are possible.
4. Write a letter to management. This action should be done in conjunction with each of the three alternatives above. Management should always be informed when its internal controls are not operating effectively. If a weakness in internal control is considered to be a reportable condition, a significant deficiency in the design or operation of internal control, SAS 60 (AU 325) requires the auditor to communicate the reportable condition to the audit committee or its equivalent.

14-20 Random (probabilistic) selection is a part of statistical sampling, but it is not, by itself, statistical measurement. To have statistical measurement, it is necessary to mathematically generalize from the sample to the population.
   Probabilistic selection must be used if the sample is to be evaluated statistically, although it is also acceptable to use probabilistic selection with a nonstatistical evaluation. If nonprobabilistic selection is used, nonstatistical evaluation must be used.

14-21 The decisions the auditor must make in using attributes sampling are:

- What are the objectives of the audit test?
- Does audit sampling apply?
- What attributes are to be tested and what exception conditions are identified?
- What is the population?
- What is the sampling unit?
- What should the TER be?
- What should the ARACR be?
- What is the EPER?
- What generalizations can be made from the sample to the population?
- What are the causes of the individual exceptions?
- Is the population acceptable?

In making the above decisions, the following should be considered:

- The individual situation.
- Time and budget constraints.
- The availability of additional substantive procedures.
- The professional judgment of the auditor.

■ **Multiple Choice Questions From CPA Examinations**

14-22 a. (1)   b. (3)   c. (2)   d. (4)

14-23 a. (1)   b. (3)   c. (4)

14-24 a. (4)   b. (2)   c. (3)

■ **Discussion Questions and Problems**

14-25 See next page

14-25

a.

SAMPLING UNIT	NUMBERING SYSTEM FOR THE POPULATION	EXCEL SELECTION FORMULA
1. Sales invoice	All invoices numbered 0001 to 6211	=RANDBETWEEN(1,6211)
2. Bill of lading	All bills of lading numbered 21926 through 28511 (if a random number table is used, the left-most digit "2" can be dropped)	=RANDBETWEEN(21926, 28511)
3. Customer	A pair of random numbers, where the first random number is the page number (1-10), and the second random number is the line number on the page (1-60)	=RANDBETWEEN(1,10) and =RANDBETWEEN(1,60)
4. Line numbers on the sales journal that have a sales invoice recorded on them	A pair of random numbers, where the first random number is the page number (1-185), and the second random number is the invoice as counted down from the top of the page (1-75)	=RANDBETWEEN(1,185) and =RANDBETWEEN(1,75)

An example random sampling plan prepared in Excel (P1425.XLS) is available on the Companion Website and on the diskette accompanying this manual. The command for selecting the random number can be entered directly onto the spreadsheet, or can be selected from the function menu (math & trig) functions. It may be necessary to add the analysis tool pack to access the RANDBETWEEN function. Once the formula is entered, it can be copied down to select additional random numbers. When a pair of random numbers is required, the formula for the first random number can be entered in the first column, and the formula for the second random number can be entered in the second column.

14-25 (Continued)

b. First five numbers using systematic selection:

SAMPLING UNIT	INTERVAL	RANDOM STARTING POINT	FIRST 5 SAMPLE ITEMS
1. Sales invoice	124 (6211/50)	67	67 191 315 439 563
2. Bill of lading	132 [(28511-21926) = 6585/50]	22011	22011 22143 22275 22407 22539
3. Customer	11 (576 lines/50)	Page 1, line #8	**Page** **Line** 1 8 1 19 1 30 1 43 1 54

Using systematic selection, the definition of the sampling unit for determining the selection interval for population 3 is the total number of lines in the population. The length of the interval is rounded down to ensure that all line numbers selected are within the defined population.

14-26 a. To test whether shipments have been billed, a sample of warehouse removal slips should be selected and examined to see if they have the proper sales invoice attached. The sampling unit will therefore be the warehouse removal slip.

b. *Attributes sampling method*: Assuming the auditor is willing to accept a TER of 3% at a 10% ARACR, expecting no exceptions in the sample, the appropriate sample size would be 76, determined from **Table 14-7**.
Nonstatistical sampling method: There is no one right answer to this question because the sample size is determined using professional judgment. Due to the relatively small TER (3%), the sample size should not be small. It will most likely be similar in size to the sample chosen by the statistical method.

c. Systematic sample selection:

- 22839 = Population size of warehouse removal slips (37521-14682).
- 76 = Sample size using statistical sampling (students' answers will vary if nonstatistical sampling was used in part b.
- 300 = Interval (22839/76) if statistical sampling is used (students' answers will vary if nonstatistical sampling was used in part b).
- 14825 = Random starting point.

Select warehouse removal slip 14825 and every 300th warehouse removal slip after (15125, 15425, etc.)

Computer generation of random numbers using Excel (P1426.XLS):

=RANDBETWEEN(14682,37521)

The command for selecting the random number can be entered directly onto the spreadsheet, or can be selected from the function menu (math & trig) functions. It may be necessary to add the analysis tool pack to access the RANDBETWEEN function. Once the formula is entered, it can be copied down to select additional random numbers.

d. Other audit procedures that could be performed are:

1. Test extensions on attached sales invoices for clerical accuracy. (Accuracy)
2. Test time delay between warehouse removal slip date and billing date for timeliness of billing. (Timing)
3. Trace entries into perpetual inventory records to determine that inventory is properly relieved for shipments. (Posting and summarization)

e. The test performed in part c cannot be used to test the existence of sales because the auditor already knows that inventory was shipped for these sales. To test the existence of sales, the sales invoice entry in the sales journal is the sampling unit. Since the sales invoice numbers are not identical to the warehouse removal slips it would be improper to use the same sample.

14-27 a. It would be appropriate to use attributes sampling for all audit procedures except audit procedure 1. Procedure 1 is an analytical procedure for which the auditor is doing a 100% review of the entire cash receipts journal.
b. The appropriate sampling unit for audit procedures 2-5 is a line item, or the date the prelisting of cash receipts is prepared. The primary emphasis in the test is the completeness objective and audit procedure 2 indicates there is a prelisting of cash receipts. All other procedures can be performed efficiently and effectively by using the prelisting.
c. The attributes for testing are as follows:

AUDIT PROCEDURE	ATTRIBUTE
2	Cash receipts in the prelisting are recorded in the cash receipts journal.
3	Customer name, date, and amount are equal on the prelisting and cash receipts journal.
4	Cash discounts were approved on the related remittance advice.
5	Cash included in the prelisting has been included on the deposit slip.

d. The sample sizes for each attribute are as follows:

AUDIT PROCEDURE	TEST OF CONTROL OR SUBSTANTIVE TEST OF TRANSACTIONS	ARACR	TER	EPER	SAMPLE SIZE
2	S T of T	5%	6%	1%	78
3	S T of T	5%	6%	1%	78
4	T of C	5%	8%	2%	77
5	S T of T	5%	6%	1%	78

14-28 a. Because the sample sizes under nonstatistical sampling are determined using auditor judgment, students' answers to this question will vary. They will most likely be similar to the sample sizes chosen using attributes sampling in part b. The important point to remember is that the sample sizes chosen should reflect the changes in the four factors (ARACR, TER, EPER, and population size). The sample sizes should have fairly predictable relationships, given the changes in the four factors. The following reflects some of the relationships that should exist in student's sample size decisions:

	SAMPLE SIZE	EXPLANATION
1.	90	Given
2.	> Column 1	Decrease in ARACR
3.	> Column 2	Decrease in TER
4.	> Column 1	Decrease in ARACR (column 4 is the same as column 2, with a smaller population size)
5.	< Column 1	Increase in TER-EPER
6.	< Column 5	Decrease in EPER
7.	> Column 3	Decrease in TER-EPER

b. Using the attributes sampling table in **Table 14-7**, the sample sizes for columns 1-7 are:

1. 88
2. 127
3. 181
4. 127
5. 25
6. 18
7. 149

c.

	CHANGE IN FACTORS	EFFECT ON SAMPLE SIZE	ILLUSTRATION IN PART a or b
1	Increase in ARACR.	Decrease	Compare columns 4 and 1
2	Increase in TER.	Decrease	Compare columns 3 and 2 (population sizes are not consistent, but this has little effect on sample size)
3	Increase in EPER.	Increase	Compare columns 6 and 5
4	Increase in population size.	No effect or slight increase	Compare columns 4 and 2

14-28 (Continued)

d. The difference in the sample size for columns 3 and 6 result from the larger ARACR and larger TER in column 6. The extremely large TER is the major factor causing the difference.

e. *The greatest effect on the sample size is the difference between TER and EPER.* For columns 3 and 7, the differences between the TER and EPER were 3% and 2% respectively. Those two also had the highest sample size. Where the difference between TER and EPER was great, such as columns 5 and 6, the required sample size was extremely small.

Population size had a relatively small effect on sample size. The difference in population size in columns 2 and 4 was 99,000 items, but the increase in sample size for the larger population was marginal (actually the sample sizes were the same using the attributes sampling table).

f. The sample size is referred to as the initial sample size because it is based on an estimate of the SER. The actual sample must be evaluated before it is possible to know whether the sample is sufficiently large to achieve the objectives of the test.

14-29 a.

	SER	TER-SER	ALLOWANCE FOR SAMPLING ERROR SUFFICIENT?
1.	2%	3%	Yes
2.	2%	3%	Probably*
3.	2%	3%	No (due to small sampling size)
4.	2%	3%	Probably*
5.	2%	3%	No (due to smaller sample size)*
6.	10%	NA	No (SER exceeds TER)
7.	0%	5%	Yes
8.	0%	5%	No due to small sample size

* Students' answers as to whether the allowance for sampling error risk is sufficient will vary, depending on their judgment. However, they should recognize the effect that lower sample sizes have on the allowance for sampling risk in situations 3, 5 and 8.

14-29 (Continued)

b. Using the attributes sampling table in **Table 14-8**, the CUERs for columns 1-8 are:

1. 4.0%
2. 4.5%
3. 9.1%
4. 4.5%
5. 6.2%
6. 16.4%
7. 3.0%
8. 11.3%

c.

	CHANGE IN FACTORS	EFFECT ON CUER	ILLUSTRATIONS IN PART a or b
1	Decrease in ARACR	Increase	Compare columns 1 and 2
2	Decrease in population size	No effect or minor decrease	Compare columns 4 and 2
3	Decrease in sample size	Increase	Compare columns 2 and 3 (both sample exception rates are 2%)
4	Decrease in the number of exceptions in the sample	Decrease	Compare columns 6 and 7

d. The factor that appears to have the greatest effect is the number of exceptions found in the sample compared to sample size. For example, in columns 5 and 6, the increase from 2% to 10% SER dramatically increased the CUER. Population size appears to have the least effect. For example, in columns 2 and 4, the CUER was the same using the attributes sampling table even though the population in column 4 was 10 times larger.

e. The CUER represents the results of the actual sample whereas the TER represents what the auditor will allow. They must be compared to determine whether or not the population is acceptable.

14-30 a. and b. The sample sizes and CUERs are shown in the following table:

	ACTUAL SAMPLE SIZE	INITIAL SAMPLE SIZE FROM TABLE 14-7	SER	CUER FROM TABLE 14-8
1	100	127	2.0%	6.2%
2	100	99	0.0	3.0
3	60	65	1.7	6.3
4	100	93	4.0	8.9
5	20	18	5.0	18.1
6	60	60	13.3	>20.0

a. The auditor selected a sample size smaller than that determined from the tables in populations 1 and 3. The effect of selecting a smaller sample size than the initial sample size required from the table is the increased likelihood of having the CUER exceed the TER. If a larger sample size is selected, the result may be a sample size larger than needed to satisfy TER. That results in excess audit cost. Ultimately, however, the comparison of CUER to TER determines whether the sample size was too large or too small.

b. The SER and CUER are shown in columns 4 and 5 in the preceding table.

c. The population results are unacceptable for populations 1, 4, and 6. In each of those cases, the CUER exceeds TER.

The auditor's options are to change TER or ARACR, increase the sample size, or perform other substantive tests to determine whether there are actually material misstatements in the population. An increase in sample size may be worthwhile in population 1 because the CUER exceeds TER by only a small amount. Increasing sample size would not likely result in improved results for either population 4 or 6 because the CUER exceeds TER by a large amount.

d. Analysis of exceptions is necessary even when the population is acceptable because the auditor wants to determine the nature and cause of all exceptions. If, for example, the auditor determines that a misstatement was intentional, additional action would be required even if the CUER was less than TER.

14-30 (Continued)

e.

TERM	NATURE OF TERM
1. Estimated population exception rate	Nonstatistical estimate made by auditor.
2. Tolerable exception rate	Audit decision.
3. Acceptable risk of assessing control risk too low	Audit decision.
4. Actual sample size	Audit decision (determined by other audit decisions).
5. Actual number of exceptions in the sample	Sample result.
6. Sample exception rate	Sample result.
7. Computed upper exception rate	Statistical conclusion about the population.

14-31 a. The following shows which are exceptions and why:

INVOICE NUMBER	EXCEPTION ?	TYPE OF EXCEPTION
5028	No	Error was detected and corrected by client.
6791	No	Sales invoice was voided.
6810	Yes	Proof of shipment not presented.
7364	No	Credit collection problem; should be noted for review of allowance for doubtful accounts.
7625	Yes	Duplicate sales invoice not properly filed.
8431	Yes	Invoices not recorded by proper date; represents potential cutoff problem.
8528	Yes	Customer orders not included in invoice package to verify compliance with the order.
8566	Yes	Error in pricing. No internal verification.
8780	Yes	Duplicate sales invoice not properly filed.
9169	Yes	Credit not authorized.
9974	Yes	Internal verification of price extensions and postings of sales invoices was not included.

14-31 (Continued)

b. It is inappropriate to set a single acceptable tolerable exception rate and estimated population exception rate for the combined exceptions because each attribute has a different significance to the auditor and should be considered separately in analyzing the results of the test.

c. The CUER assuming a 5% ARACR for each attribute and a sample size of 150 is as follows:

INVOICE NUMBER	DESCRIPTION OF ATTRIBUTE	NUMBER OF EXCEPTIONS	SER
6810	Shipping document not located	1	.67%
7625 8780 8528	Duplicate sales invoice/customer order not located	3	2.00%
8431	Invoice date improper	1	.67%
8566	Price extensions postings incorrect	1	.67%
8566 9974	Price extensions and postings not internally verified	2	1.33%
9169	Credit not authorized	1	.67%

d.

INVOICE NUMBER	TER-SER	SAMPLING ERROR SUFFICIENT?
6810	5.33%	Yes
7625 8780 8528	4.0%	Probably*
8431	5.33%	Yes
8566	5.33%	Yes
8566 9974	4.67%	Probably*
9169	5.33%	Yes

*Students' answers will most likely vary for this attribute.

14-31 (Continued)

e. For each exception, the auditor should check with the controller to determine an explanation for the cause. In addition, the appropriate analysis for each type of exception is as follows:

INVOICE NUMBER	EXCEPTION ANALYSIS
6810	Confirm the account balances to the customers; examine the reduction in the perpetual inventory records.
7625	Trace the amount to the sales journal and accounts receivable master file; examine the shipping document and recompute the sale amount.
8431	Determine who recorded the invoice and check several others prepared by him or her to determine if the problem consistently occurs.
8528	Examine the accounts receivable master file for subsequent cash receipt; examine sales invoices for other invoices to the same customer to determine if customer orders were attached.
8566	Check the price on other invoices to the same customer. Check the price on other invoices that have the same product.
8780	See 7625
9169	Check credit history of customer and evaluate collectibility of the customer's account.
9974	Recheck actual price, extensions and postings; determine who the clerk was and check several other invoices for proper indication of performance.

14-32 a. *Attributes sampling approach:* The test of control attribute had a 6% SER and a CUER of 12.9%. The substantive test of transactions attribute has SER of 0% and a CUER of 4.5%.

Nonstatistical sampling approach: As in the attributes sampling approach, the SERs for the test of control and the substantive test of transactions are 6% and 0%, respectively. Students' estimates of the CUERs for the two tests will vary, but will probably be similar to the CUERs calculated under the attributes sampling approach.

14-32 (Continued)

b. *Attributes sampling approach:* TER is 5%. CUERs are 12.9% and 4.5%. Therefore, only the substantive test of transactions results are satisfactory. *Nonstatistical sampling approach:* Because the SER for the test of control is greater than the TER of 5%, the results are clearly not acceptable. Students' estimates for CUER for the test of control should be greater than the SER of 6%. For the substantive test of transactions, the SER is 0%. It is unlikely that students will estimate CUER for this test greater than 5%, so the results are acceptable for the substantive test of transactions.

c. If the CUER exceeds the TER, the auditor may:

1. Revise the TER if he or she thinks the original specifications were too conservative.
2. Expand the sample size if cost permits.
3. Alter the substantive procedures if possible.
4. Write a letter to management in conjunction with each of the above to inform management of a weakness in their internal controls.

In this case, the auditor has evidence that the test of control procedures are not effective, but no exceptions in the *sample* resulted because of the breakdown. An expansion of the attributes test does not seem advisable and therefore, the auditor should probably expand confirmation of accounts receivable tests. In addition, he or she should write a letter to management to inform them of the control breakdown.

d. In this case, we want to find out why some invoices are not internally verified. Possible reasons are incompetence, carelessness, regular clerk on vacation, etc. It is desirable to isolate the exceptions to certain clerks, time periods or types of invoices.

■ Cases

14-33 a. Audit sampling could be conveniently used for procedures 3 and 4 since each is to be performed on a sample of the population.

b. The most appropriate sampling unit for conducting *most* of the audit sampling tests is the shipping document because most of the tests are related to procedure 4. Following the instructions of the audit program, however, the auditor would use sales journal entries as the sampling unit for step 3 and shipping document *numbers* for step 4. Using shipping document numbers, rather than the documents themselves, allows the auditor to test the numerical control over shipping documents, as well as to test for unrecorded sales. The selection of numbers will lead to a sample of actual shipping documents upon which tests will be performed.

14-33 (Continued)

c. *Note: The sampling data sheet that follows assumes an attributes sampling approach. The only difference between the sampling data sheet for attributes sampling and for nonstatistical sampling is the actual determination of sample size. For nonstatistical sampling, students' answers will vary, but will most likely be comparable to the sample sizes determined under attributes sampling.*

DESCRIPTION OF ATTRIBUTES	EPER	TER	ARACR	INITIAL SAMPLE SIZE*
A duplicate sales invoice exists for the shipping document selected.	1.0	5.0	10	77
Shipping document agrees with related duplicate sales invoice.	0.0	4.0	10	57
The duplicate sales invoice has attached a copy of the shipping document, shipping order, and customer order.	1.0	5.0	10	77
The shipping order has proper credit approval.	1.0	5.0	10	77
The duplicate sales invoice has internal verification of computations.	1.0	5.0	10	77
The duplicate sales invoice has the same price and quantity as approved price list and shipping document.	0.0	4.0	10	57
Customer name, amount and date agrees between duplicate sales invoice and sales journal and subsidiary ledger.	0.0	4.0	10	57

* assumes the shipping document is the sampling unit.

14-34 a. and c. *Note: The sampling data sheet shown in this solution assumes an attributes sampling approach. Under a nonstatistical sampling approach, the planned sample sizes and estimated CUERs will vary among the students' solutions.*

Client: PINNACLE MANUFACTURING

Audit Area: Tests of Controls and Substantive Tests of Transactions—Acquisitions and Cash Disbursements

Define the Objective(s): Examine cancelled checks and related documents to determine if the system has functioned as intended and as described in the audit program.

Define the population precisely (including stratification, if any): Cancelled checks for the period 1/1/99 to 12/31/99. First check number = 6240; last check number = 9875.

Define the sampling unit, organization of population items, and random selection procedures: Check number, recorded sequentially in the cash disbursements journal; random number function in electronic spreadsheet.

14-34 (Continued)

Description of Attributes	Planned Audit					Actual Results			
	EPER	TER	ARACR	Initial Sample Size	Sample Size	Number of Exceptions	SER	CUER
1. Evidence of internal verification of document package including propriety of purchase, dates, unit costs, prices, extensions, footings, account classification, recording in journal, and posting and summarization. (6a, b)	0	6	5	49	50	1	2	9.1
2. Prices on vendor invoices conform to approved price limits established by management. (6c)	0	6	5	49	50	0	0	5.8
3. Dates of entries in purchases journal agree with dates on receiving reports. (6f)	1	7	5	66	65	1	1.5	7.1
4. Evidence of authorization of each purchase voucher. (6g)	2	7	5	88	90	0	0	3.3
5. Amount and other data in the purchases journal agrees with the related vendor invoice. (6d)	1	6	5	78	80	1	1.3	5.8
6. Amount and other data in the purchases journal agrees with related receiving reports. (6d)	1	6	5	78	80	0	0	3.7
7. Amount and other data in the purchases journal agrees with related purchase order. (6d)	1	6	5	78	80	0	0	3.7
8. Payee, name, amount and date on cancelled check agrees with related purchases journal and cash disbursements entry. (9a)	1	5	5	93	90	0	0	3.3
9. Evidence of signature, proper endorsement and cancellation of each check. (9b)	0	4	5	74	75	0	0	3.9

(Number in parentheses is audit program step from performance audit program from Problem 13-34.)

Note: Answers will depend on students' judgment in setting TER and ARACR.

14-34 (Continued)

b.

Population = Check numbers 6240 to 9875

Sample size = 90

Random Selection:

If random selection is performed using Excel, the command to select numbers randomly from the population is:

=RANDBETWEEN(6240,9875)

The command for selecting the random number can be entered directly onto the spreadsheet, or can be selected from the function menu (math & trig) functions. It may be necessary to add the analysis tool pack to access the RANDBETWEEN function. Once the formula is entered, it can be copied down to select additional random numbers. The first 10 random numbers using this approach will vary for each student.

Systematic Selection:

Answers will depend upon students' sample size decisions. If a sample size of 90 is used, the interval is 40 (3635/90). The first 10 random numbers selected will depend on the interval, and the random starting point chosen.

d. A sampling data sheet can be developed using electronic spreadsheet software. It can be a simple working paper layout, or it can be made more sophisticated by adding the attributes sampling tables, accessed using a table look-up function. Such a template is provided using Excel on the Companion Website and on the diskette that accompanies this text, under Filename P1434.XLS.

Chapter 15

Completing the Tests in the Sales and Collection Cycle: Accounts Receivable

■ Review Questions

15-1 Tests of details of balances are designed to determine the reasonableness of the balances in sales, accounts receivable, and other account balances that are affected by the sales and collection cycle. Such tests include confirmation of accounts receivable, and examining documents supporting the balance in these accounts.

Tests of controls and substantive tests of transactions for the sales and collection cycle are intended to determine the effectiveness of internal controls and to test the substance of the transactions which are produced by this cycle. Such tests consist of activities such as examining sales invoices in support of entries in the sales journal, reconciling cash receipts, or reviewing the approval of credit.

The results of the tests of controls and substantive tests of transactions affect the procedures, sample size, timing and items selected for the tests of details of balances (i.e., effective internal controls will result in reduced testing when compared to the tests of details required in the case of inadequate internal controls).

15-2 SAS 67 (AU 330.20) discusses the use of negative accounts receivable confirmations as follows:

> The negative form requests the recipient to respond only if he or she disagrees with the information stated on the request. Negative confirmation requests may be used to reduce audit risk to an acceptable level when (a) the combined assessed level of inherent and control risk is low, (b) a large number of small balances is involved, and (c) the auditor has no reason to believe that the recipients of the requests are unlikely to give them consideration. For example, in the examination of demand deposit accounts in a financial institution, it may be appropriate for an auditor to include negative confirmation requests with the customers' regular statements when the combined assessed level of inherent and control risk is low and the auditor has no reason to believe that the recipients will not consider the requests. The auditor should consider performing other substantive procedures to supplement the use of negative confirmations.

The above requirement that negative confirmations are considered appropriate where the internal controls of the sales and collection cycle are effective is violated by Cynthia Roberts' approach. Not only is her approach questionable from the standpoint that nonresponses have not necessarily proved the existence of the receivable, but her confirmation at an interim date requires her to assume an assessed control risk less than maximum, but she has not tested the related internal controls for the period from the confirmation date until year-end.

15-3 The following are analytical procedures for the sales and collection cycle, and potential misstatements uncovered by each test. Each ratio should be compared to previous years.

ANALYTICAL PROCEDURE	POTENTIAL MISSTATEMENT
1. Gross margin by product line	Including in the physical inventory items for which the corresponding liability had not yet been recorded.
2. Sales returns and allowances as a percentage of gross sales by product line or segment	All returns were not recorded, or shipments to customers were not in accordance with specifications and were returned (this could result in significant operating problems).
3. Trade discounts taken as a percentage of net sales	Discounts that were taken by customers and allowed by the company were not recorded.
4. Bad debts as a percentage of gross sales	Misstatement in determining the allowance for uncollectible accounts.
5. Days sales in receivables outstanding	A problem with collections, an understatement of bad debts and allowance for uncollectible accounts.
6. Aging categories as a percentage of accounts receivables	Collection problems and understatement of allowance for uncollectible accounts.
7. Allowance for uncollectible accounts as a percentage of accounts receivable	Misstatement in determining the allowance for uncollectible accounts.
8. Comparison of the balances in individual customers' accounts over a stated amount with their balances in the previous year	A problem with collections and therefore a misstatement of the allowance for uncollectible accounts.

15-4 The following are balance-related audit objectives and related audit procedures for the audit of accounts receivable.

BALANCE-RELATED AUDIT OBJECTIVE	AUDIT PROCEDURE
Accounts receivable in the aged trial balance agree with related master file amounts; the total is correctly added and agrees with the general ledger.	■ Trace twenty accounts from the trial balance to the related accounts in the master file. ■ Foot two pages of the trial and balance, total all pages, and trace to the general ledger.
The accounts receivable in the aged trial balance exist.	Confirm accounts receivable using positive confirmations. Confirm all amounts over $5,000 and a nonstatistical sample of the remainder.
Existing accounts receivable are included in the aged trial balance.	Trace ten accounts from the accounts receivable master file to the aged trial balance.
Accounts receivable in the trial balance are accurately recorded.	Confirm accounts receivable using positive confirmations. Confirm all amounts over $5,000 and a nonstatistical sample of the remainder.
Accounts receivable in the aged trial balance are properly classified.	Review the receivables listed on the aged trial balance for notes and related party receivables.
Transactions in the sales and collection cycle are recorded in the proper period.	Select the last 10 sales transactions from the current year's sales journal and the first 10 from the subsequent year's and trace each one to the related shipping documents, checking for the date of actual shipment and the correct recording.
Accounts receivable in the trial balance are owned.	Review the minutes of the board of directors for any indication of pledged or factored accounts receivable.
Accounts receivable in the trial balance are stated at realizable value.	Discuss with the credit manager the likelihood of collecting older accounts. Examine subsequent cash receipts and the credit file on older accounts to evaluate whether receivables are collectible.
Accounts in the sales and collection cycle are properly presented and disclosed.	Review the minutes of the board of directors meetings for any indication of pledged or factored accounts receivable.

15-5 The most important objectives satisfied by confirmations are existence, rights, and accuracy. In extreme cases, confirmations are also useful tests for cutoff. Sometimes confirmations may also help the auditor satisfy the completeness objective.

15-6 A necessary audit procedure is to test the information on the client's trial balance for detail tie-in. The footing in the total column and the columns depicting the aging must be checked and the total on the trial balance reconciled to the general ledger to determine that all accounts are included in the listing.

The master file records are the tie-in between tests of controls, substantive tests of transactions, and tests of details of balances. The aged trial balance is the listing of the master file. Since the auditor uses the aged trial balance in tests of details, he or she must be sure that information is the same as that tested in tests of controls and substantive tests of transactions. In addition, a sample of individual balances is traced to the master file to determine that the trial balance has been properly summarized from the master file. In most cases, it will not be necessary to trace each amount to the master file unless a significant number of misstatements is noted and it is determined that reliance cannot be place upon the trial balance with less than 100% testing. Normally a sample of entries on the trial balance could be traced to the master file and would be sufficient to draw a conclusion as to the overall accuracy of the trial balance.

15-7 The purpose of the accuracy tests of gross accounts receivable is to determine the correctness of the total amounts receivable from customers. These tests normally consist of confirmation of accounts receivable or examination of shipping documents in support of the shipment of goods to customers.

The purpose of the test of the realizable value of receivables is to estimate the amount of the accounts receivable balance that will not be collected. To estimate this amount, the auditor normally reviews aging of the accounts receivable, analyzes subsequent cash payments by customers, discusses the collectibility of individual accounts with client personnel, and examines correspondence and financial statements of significant customers.

15-8 In most audits it is more important to carefully test the cutoff for sales than for cash receipts because sales cutoff misstatements are more likely to affect net earnings than are cash receipt cutoff misstatements. Cash receipt cutoff misstatements generally lead to a misclassification of accounts receivable and cash and, therefore, do not affect income.

To perform a cutoff test for sales, the auditor should obtain the number of the last shipping document issued before year-end and examine shipping documents representing shipments before and after year-end and the related sales invoices to determine that the shipments were recorded as sales in the appropriate period.

The propriety of the cash receipts cutoff is determined through tests of the year-end bank reconciliation. Deposits in transit at year-end should be traced to the subsequent bank statement. Any delays in crediting deposits by the bank should be investigated to determine whether the cash receipts books were held open.

15-9 The value of accounts receivable confirmation as evidence can be visualized more clearly by relating it to tests of controls and substantive tests of transactions. If the beginning balance in accounts receivable can be assumed to be correct and careful tests of the controls have been performed, the auditor should be in an excellent position to evaluate the fairness of the ending balance in accounts receivable.

15-9 (Continued)

Confirmations are typically more effective than tests of controls and substantive tests of transactions for discovering certain types of misstatements. These include invalid accounts, disputed amounts, and uncollectible accounts resulting from the inability to locate the customer. Although confirmations cannot guarantee the discovery of any of these types of misstatements, they are more reliable than tests of controls and substantive tests of transactions, because tests of controls and substantive tests of transactions rely upon internally created documents, whereas confirmations are obtained from independent sources.

There are two instances in which confirmations are less likely to uncover omitted transactions and amounts than tests of controls and substantive tests of transactions. First, in order to send a confirmation, it is necessary to have a list of accounts receivable from which to select. Naturally, an omitted account will not be included in the population from which the auditor is selecting the sample. Second, if an account with an omitted transaction is confirmed, customers are less likely to respond to the confirmation, or, alternatively, will state that it is correct. Tracing shipping documents or sales orders to the related duplicate sales invoice and the accounts receivable master file is an effective method of discovering omitted transactions.

Clerical errors in billing customers and recording the amounts in the accounts can be effectively discovered by confirmation, tests of controls, or substantive tests of transactions. Confirmations are typically more effective in uncovering overstatement of accounts receivable than understatements, whereas tests of controls and substantive tests of transactions are effective for discovering both types. The important concept in this discussion is the existence of both a complementary and a substitute relationship between tests of controls and substantive tests of transactions, and confirmations. They are complementary in that both types of evidence, when combined, provide a higher level of overall assurance of the fair presentation of sales, sales returns and allowances, and accounts receivable than can result from either type considered separately. The strengths of tests of controls and substantive tests of transactions combined with the strengths of confirmation result in a highly useful combination. The two types of evidence are substitutes in the sense that the auditor can obtain a given level of assurance by decreasing the tests of controls and substantive tests of transactions if there is an offsetting increase in the confirmation of accounts receivable. The extent to which the auditor should rely upon the tests of controls and substantive tests of transactions is dependent upon his or her evaluation of the effectiveness of internal controls. If the auditor has carefully evaluated internal control, tested internal controls for effectiveness, and concluded that the internal controls are likely to provide correct results, it is appropriate to reduce the confirmation of accounts receivable. On the other hand, it would be inappropriate to bypass confirmation altogether.

In the situation being addressed in this problem, the auditor will want to put more emphasis on tests of controls and substantive tests of transactions than confirmations because of the nature of the customers and the strengths in internal control. Nevertheless, both should be used, regardless of the requirements of the AICPA.

15-10 There are two common types of confirmations used for confirming accounts receivable: "positive" confirmations and "negative" confirmations. A positive confirmation is a letter, addressed to the debtor, requesting that the recipient indicate directly on the letter whether the stated account balance is correct or incorrect and, if incorrect, by what amount. A negative confirmation is also a letter, addressed to the debtor, but it requests a response only if the recipient disagrees with the amount of the stated account balance. A positive confirmation is more reliable evidence because the auditor can perform follow-up procedures if a response is not received from the debtor. With a negative confirmation, failure to reply must be regarded as a correct response, even though the debtor may have ignored the confirmation request.

Offsetting the reliability disadvantage, negative confirmations are less expensive to send than positive confirmations, and thus more of them can be distributed for the same total cost. The determination of which type of confirmation to be sent is an auditor's decision, and it should be based on the facts in the audit. SAS 67 (AU 330) states that it is acceptable to use negative confirmations only when all of the following circumstances are present:

- Accounts receivable is made up of a large number of small accounts.
- Combined assessed control risk and inherent risk is low.
- There is no reason to believe that the recipients of the confirmations are unlikely to give them consideration.

Typically, when negative confirmations are used, the auditor is using a reduced control risk assessment in the audit of accounts receivable. It is also common to use negative confirmations for audits of hospitals, retail stores, and other industries where the receivables are due from the general public. In these cases, far more assurance is obtained from tests of controls and substantive tests of transactions than from confirmations.

It is also common to use a combination of negative and positive confirmations by sending the positives to accounts with large balances and negatives to those with small balances. This allows the auditor to focus the confirmation testing on large account balances, while still testing a representative sample from the rest of the population at minimal cost.

15-11 It is acceptable to confirm accounts receivable prior to the balance sheet date if the internal controls are adequate and can provide reasonable assurance that sales, cash receipts, and other credits are properly recorded between the date of the confirmation and the end of the accounting period. Other factors the auditor is likely to consider in making the decision are the materiality of accounts receivable and the auditor's exposure to lawsuits because of the possibility of client bankruptcy and similar risks. If the decision is made to confirm accounts receivable prior to year-end, it is necessary to test the transactions occurring between the confirmation date and the balance sheet date by examining internal documents and performing analytical procedures at year-end.

15-12 The most important factors affecting the sample size in confirmations of accounts receivable are:

- Tolerable misstatement
- Inherent risk (relative size of total accounts receivable, number of accounts, prior year results, and expected misstatements)
- Control risk
- Achieved detection risk from other substantive tests (extent and results of substantive tests of transactions, analytical procedures, and other tests of details)
- Type of confirmation (negatives normally require a larger sample size)

15-13 In most confirmations of accounts receivable, some type of stratification is desirable. A typical approach to stratification is to consider both the size of the outstanding balance and the length of time an account has been outstanding as a basis for selecting the balances for confirmation, since these are the accounts that are more likely to include a significant misstatement. It is also important to sample some items from every material stratum of the population. Using this approach, the auditor will pay careful attention to the accounts in which misstatements are most likely to occur and will follow the guidelines set forth in Chapter 14 regarding the need to obtain a representative sample of the population.

15-14 Alternative procedures are procedures performed on a positive confirmation not returned by the debtor using documentation evidence to determine whether the recorded receivable exists and is collectible. It is common to send second requests for confirmations and sometimes even third requests. Even with these efforts, some customers do not return the confirmations, so it is necessary to follow up with alternative procedures. The objective of the alternative procedures is to determine, by a means other than confirmation, whether the unconfirmed account existed and was properly stated at the confirmation date. For any confirmation not returned, the following documentation can be examined to verify the existence and accuracy of individual sales transactions making up the ending balance in accounts receivable:

1. *Subsequent cash receipts* Evidence of the receipt of cash subsequent to the confirmation date includes examining remittance advice, entries in the cash receipts records, or perhaps even subsequent credits in the accounts receivable master file. The examination of evidence of subsequent cash receipts is usually the most useful alternative procedure because it is reasonable to assume that a customer would not make a payment unless it was a valid receivable. On the other hand, the fact of payment does not establish whether there was an obligation on the date of the confirmation. In addition, care should be used to match each unpaid sales transaction with evidence of its payment as a test for disputes or disagreements over individual outstanding invoices.
2. *Duplicate sales invoices* These are useful to verify the actual issuance of a sales invoice and the actual date of the billing.
3. *Shipping documents* These are important to establish whether the shipment was actually made and as a test of cutoff.

15-14 (Continued)
   4. *Correspondence with the client* Usually it is unnecessary to review correspondence as a part of alternative procedures, but it can be used to disclose disputed and questionable receivables not uncovered by other means.

The extent and nature of the alternative procedures depends primarily upon the materiality of the unconfirmed accounts, the nature and extent of the misstatements discovered in the confirmed responses, the subsequent cash receipts of the unconfirmed accounts, and the auditor's evaluation of the effectiveness of internal controls. It is normally desirable to account for all unconfirmed balances with alternative procedures, even if the amounts are small, as a means of properly generalizing from the sample to the population.

15-15 Confirmation of accounts receivable is normally performed on only a sample of the total population. The purpose of the confirmation is to obtain outside verification of the balance of the account and to obtain an indication of the rate of occurrence of misstatements in the accounts. Most misstatements which are indicated by the differences on the confirmation replies will not be material; however, each difference must be analyzed to determine its effect and all others considered together on the total accounts receivable balance. Though the individual differences may not be material, they may indicate a material problem when extended to the entire population, and with regard to the internal controls over the accounts receivable.

15-16 Three differences that may be observed on the confirmation of accounts receivable that do not constitute misstatements, and an audit procedure that would verify each difference are as follows:

1. Payment has been made by the customer, but not received by the client at the confirmation date. The subsequent payment should be examined as to the date deposited.
2. Merchandise shipped by the client has not been received by the customer. The shipping documents should be examined to verify that the goods were shipped prior to confirmation date.
3. Merchandise has been returned, but has not been received by the client at the confirmation date. Receiving documents and the credit memo should be examined.

15-17 With regard to the sales and collection cycle, the auditor uses flowcharts, assessing control risk for the accounting cycle, tests of controls, and tests of details of balances in the determination of the likelihood of a material misstatement in the accounts affected by the sales and collection cycle. The flowcharts provide a means for the auditor to document and analyze the accounting systems as represented by the client. The auditor would then make an initial assessment of control risk based on the controls which are present in the accounting cycle as documented in the flowcharts, and would plan the tests of controls based upon the selection of the significant controls. The auditor would then perform the tests of the significant controls to determine the effectiveness of the controls and to plan the substantive tests which are necessary based upon the revised assessment of control risk for this accounting cycle. Finally, after considering the results of tests of controls and substantive tests of transactions,

15-17 (Continued)
the auditor would perform tests of details of balances to determine the occurrences of material misstatements in the account balances.

15-18 GAAP requires that sales returns and allowances be matched with the related sales if the amounts are material. However, most companies record sales returns and allowances in the period in which they occur, under the assumption of approximately equal, offsetting amounts at the beginning and end of each accounting period. This approach is acceptable, if the amounts are not significant.

■ **Multiple Choice Questions From CPA Examinations**

15-19 a. (4)   b. (4)   c. (2)

15-20 a. (2)   b. (4)   c. (2)   d. (2)

15-21 a. (2)   b. (1)

■ **Discussion Questions and Problems**

15-22
1. Detail tie-in
2. Detail tie-in
3. a. Existence
   b. Accuracy
   c. Realizable value (if cash receipts relate to older accounts)
4. a. Existence
   b. Accuracy
5. a. Existence
   b. Accuracy
   c. Realizable value (if cash receipts relate to older accounts)
6. Cutoff
7. a. Rights
   b. Presentation and disclosure
8. Classification

15-23

a. BALANCE-RELATED AUDIT OBJECTIVE	b. PREVENTIVE INTERNAL CONTROL	c. TESTS OF DETAILS OF BALANCES AUDIT PROCEDURES
1. Transactions are recorded in the proper period (cutoff).	Company policy should state that the cash cutoff at end of a month should be achieved by only recording the amounts received prior to month-end in the current month.	The auditor should be present at the client's facility at the end of the last working day of the year, should obtain the amount of the last deposit to be made from current year receipts, and should determine in the audit procedures that this was, indeed, the last deposit recorded during the current year. The auditor should compare the deposits in transit shown on the bank reconciliation to the date that deposits reached the bank to determine that the time lag is reasonable.
2. Accounts receivable are stated at realizable value (realizable value)	The client should perform an analysis of the collectibility of accounts receivable at the end of the year and should communicate with its customers to determine the likelihood of the collectibility of individual accounts.	The auditor should keep informed of current economic conditions and consider their effect on collectibility of accounts receivable for the client. The auditor may compare cash receipts after year-end to the cash receipts of the similar period of the previous year and consider any changes as to their effect on the collectibility of the accounts receivable.
3. Accounts receivable are stated at the correct amounts (accuracy).	The client should record claims for defective merchandise as soon as possible after the claim is received to keep accounts receivable balances as accurate as possible.	The auditor should review the client's correspondence files from customers. The auditor should note any replies to the confirmation of accounts receivable which indicate disputes between a customer and client.

15-23 (Continued)

a. BALANCE-RELATED AUDIT OBJECTIVE	b. PREVENTIVE INTERNAL CONTROL	c. TESTS OF DETAILS OF BALANCES AUDIT PROCEDURES
4. Accounts receivable presentation and disclosures are proper (presentation and disclosure).	The controller should maintain a schedule containing all required disclosure information. This schedule should be updated each time an event occurs which affects this information.	The auditor's standard bank confirmation should contain an inquiry as to assets pledged for loans from that institution. When loan confirmations are sent by the auditor, they should contain an inquiry as to any assets pledged for the indebtedness.
5. Transactions are recorded in the proper period (cutoff).	The client should follow a policy of holding open the books to record any returns in the subsequent period which apply to goods shipped and sales recorded in the current period.	The auditor should review returns recorded in the subsequent period to determine if they apply to goods shipped and sales recorded prior to year-end. The auditor should perform an analytical test to determine whether or not returns in the first month of the next year are similar in magnitude to those experienced in the same period of previous years.
6. Existing accounts receivable are included in the aged trial balance (completeness).	The accounts receivable master file should be reconciled to the control account periodically by an independent person.	Foot the aged trial balance and compare the total to the general ledger. Trace a sample of accounts from master file to the aged trial balance to determine if all are included.
7. Accounts receivable exist (existence).	The accounts receivable master file should be reconciled to the control account periodically by an independent person.	Foot the aged trial balance and compare the total to the general ledger. Trace from the aged trial balance to the master file, looking for duplicates.

15-23 (Continued)

a. BALANCE-RELATED AUDIT OBJECTIVE	b. PREVENTIVE INTERNAL CONTROL	c. TESTS OF DETAILS OF BALANCES AUDIT PROCEDURES
8. Accounts receivable are properly classified (classification).	The client should maintain separate accounts for the recording of receivables due from affiliated companies.	The auditor should review the trial balance of accounts receivable to determine whether or not accounts from affiliated companies are included in the customer accounts. The auditor should be aware of affiliated companies and the transactions between them and the client, and should inquire and follow up to determine that accounts receivable from affiliates are not included in the accounts receivable from customers.
9. Accounts receivable in the aged trial balance agree with related master file amounts, and the total is correctly added and agrees with the general ledger (detail tie-in).	The client should foot the trial balance and reconcile the total to the balance in the general ledger.	The auditor should foot the trial balance of accounts receivable and reconcile it to the balance per the general ledger.

15-24

a. TYPE OF EVIDENCE	b. TYPE OF TEST	c. and d. OBJECTIVE(S)
1. Documentation	(1) Test of control	Completeness
2. Inquiry	(4) Test of details of balances	Cutoff
3. Reperformance	(4) Test of details of balances	Detail tie-in
4. Observation	(1) Test of control	Detail tie-in
5. Documentation	(2) Substantive test of transactions	Timeliness
6. Documentation	(1) Test of control	Existence
7. Documentation	(4) Test of details of balances	Cutoff
8. Analytical procedure	(3) Analytical procedure	N/A
9. Documentation	(1) Test of control	Existence

15-25

PROCEDURE	a. TYPE OF TEST	b. BALANCE-RELATED AUDIT OBJECTIVE
1	Test of details	Existence and accuracy
2	Test of details	Cutoff
3	S T of T	Cutoff
4	Test of details	Accuracy and existence (may also include realizable value if cash receipts examined are for older accounts)
5	S T of T	Classification
6	S T of T	Rights
7	Test of details	Completeness
8	Test of control	Existence
9	Test of details	Presentation and disclosure
		Classification (related party receivables and notes should be segregated from trade receivables)
10	Test of control	Accuracy
11	S T of T	Completeness
12	Test of details	Detail tie-in
13	S T of T	Detail tie-in
14	Test of details	Classification

15-26 a. A shipment should be recorded as a sale on the date of shipment or the passing of title, whichever occurs first. Ordinarily, a shipment is considered a sale when it is shipped, picked up, or delivered by a common carrier.

b. The sales invoice number can be ignored, except to determine the shipping document number.

INVOICE NO.	SHIPPING DOCUMENT NO.	MISSTATEMENT IN SALES CUTOFF	OVERSTATEMENT OR UNDERSTATEMENT OF AUG. 31 SALES
August sales			
4326	2164	none	
4329	2169	1,914.30	overstatement
4327	2165	none	
4328	2168	620.22	overstatement
4330	2166	none	
		2,534.52	
September sales			
4332	2163	4,641.31	understatement
4331	2167	106.39	understatement
4333	2170	none	
4335	2171	none	
4334	2172	none	
		4,747.70	
Net understatement		2213.18	

Adjusting entry

Accounts receivable		2213.18	
Sales			2213.18

c. After making the type of cutoff adjustments shown in part b, current year sales would be overstated by:

	Amount of sale
2168	620.22
2169	1,914.30
2170	852.06
2171	1,250.50
2172	646.58
	5,283.66

15-26 (Continued)

        The best way to discover the misstatement is to be on hand on the balance sheet date and record in the audit working papers the last shipping document issued in the current period. Later, the auditors can examine shipping documents before and after the balance sheet date to determine if they were correctly dated.

        An alternative, if there are perpetual records, is to follow up differences between physical inventory counts and perpetual record balances to determine if the cause was end of the period cutoff misstatements. Assume, for example, that there were 626 units of part X263 on hand August 31, but the perpetual records showed a total of 526, and a shipment of 100 units included on the perpetual August 31, that is a likely indication of a September shipment that had been dated August 31.

d. The following procedures are usually desirable to test for sales cutoff.

1. Be present during the physical count on the last day of the accounting period to determine the shipping document number for the last shipment made in the current year. Record that number in the working papers.
2. During year-end field work, select a sample of shipping documents preceding and succeeding those selected in procedure 1. Shipping documents with the same or with a smaller number than the one determined in procedure 1 should be included in current sales. Those with document numbers larger than that number should have been excluded from current sales.
3. During year-end field work, select a sample of sales from the sales journal recorded in the last few days of the current period, and a sample of those recorded for the first few days in the subsequent period. Trace sales recorded in the current period to related shipping documents to make sure that each one has a number equal to or smaller than the one in procedure 1. Similarly, trace sales recorded in the subsequent period to make sure each sale has a related shipping document number greater than the one in procedure 1.

e. The following are effective controls and related tests of controls to help prevent cutoff misstatements.

15-26 (Continued)

CONTROL	TEST OF CONTROL
(1) Policy requiring the use of prenumbered shipping documents.	Examine several documents for prenumbering.
(2) Policy requiring the issuance of shipping documents sequentially.	Observe issuance of documents, examine document numbers and inquiry.
(3) Policy requiring recording sales invoices in the same sequence as shipping documents are issued.	Observe recording of documents, examine document numbers and inquiry.
(4) Policy requiring dating of shipping documents, immediate recording of sales, and dating sales on the same date as the shipment.	Observe dating of shipping documents and sales invoices, and timing of recording.
(5) Use of perpetual inventory records and reconciliation of differences between physical and perpetual records.	Examine worksheets reconciling physical counts and perpetual records.

15-27 a. The two types of confirmations used for confirming accounts receivable are "positive" and "negative" confirmations. A positive confirmation is a letter, addressed to the debtor, requesting that the recipient indicate directly on the letter whether the stated account balance is correct or incorrect and, if incorrect, by what amount. A negative confirmation requests a response from the debtor only when the debtor disagrees with the stated amount.

When deciding which type of confirmation to use, the auditor should consider the assessed control risk in the sales and collection cycle, the make-up of the population, cost/benefit relationship, and any information about the existence of the accounts. Positive confirmations are more reliable but more expensive than negatives confirmations. Positive confirmations should be used when the population is comprised of a small number of large accounts, and when there are suspected conditions of dispute or inaccuracy. When negative confirmations are used, the auditor has normally assessed control risk below maximum and tested the internal controls for effectiveness. Negative confirmations are often used when accounts receivable are comprised of a large number of small accounts receivable from the general public.

15-27 (Continued)

    b. When evaluating the collectibility of accounts receivable, the auditor may review the aging of accounts receivable, analyze subsequent cash receipts from customers, discuss the collectibility of individual accounts with client personnel, and examine correspondence and financial statements of significant customers. Changes in the aging of receivables should be analyzed in view of any changes in the client's credit policy and in the current economic conditions.

    c. When customers fail to respond to positive confirmation requests, the CPA may not assume with confidence that these customers checked the request, found no disagreement, and therefore did not reply. Some busy customers will not take the time to check confirmation requests and will not respond, hence obvious exceptions may exist without being reported to the CPA. In the case of fraud or embezzlement, the perpetrators could perhaps prevent exceptions from being reported and prevent letters addressed to nonexistent customers from being returned from the post office as undeliverable. Confirmations returned as undeliverable by the post office will require appropriate action to obtain better addresses.

        Follow-up is necessary when customers do not reply because the CPA has selected the positive confirmation route for certain receivables, and the most logical step to follow first is to mail second requests.

    d. When no response is received to the second request for positive confirmation, the auditor should use alternative procedures. These normally include examination of the customer's remittance advice and related cash receipt. This is often a simple and effective check where cash receipts were received subsequent to the balance sheet date. Correspondence in the client's files will also sometimes offer satisfactory evidence. The auditor should also examine shipping documents, sales invoices, contracts, or other documents to substantiate that the charges were proper.

        In unusual cases, the CPA should mail a third request and possibly make telephone calls in an effort to get a reply directly from the customer. The CPA may find it necessary, where significant amounts are involved and circumstances are not clear, to investigate the existence and/or financial status of a customer.

15-28 a. Yes, it is acceptable for the controller to review the list of accounts the auditor intends to confirm. The confirmations will be sent to the company's customers, and the auditor must be sensitive to the client's concern with the treatment of their customers. At the same time, if the client refuses permission to confirm receivables, the auditor must consider the effect on the audit opinion. If the restriction is material, a qualified or disclaimer of opinion may be needed.

    b. The auditor should be willing to perform special procedures which the client requests if the client is in agreement that these procedures may not necessarily be considered within the scope of the auditor's engagement. In the case of the 20 additional confirmations which the controller requested that the auditor send, the auditor should be willing to send the confirmations; however, these confirmations should not be considered in the evaluation of the results of the accounts receivable confirmation sent by the auditor.

15-28 (Continued)

    c. If the auditor complies with the controller's request to eliminate six of the accounts from the confirmation, the auditor must perform alternative procedures on the six accounts and decide whether or not this omission is significant to the scope of the audit. If the auditor believes that the impact of not confirming these accounts is material, he or she must qualify the scope and opinion paragraphs of the auditor's report to indicate the restriction of scope imposed by the client. If the auditor believes that the impact of omitting the six accounts from testing is highly material, a disclaimer of opinion is appropriate.

15-29 For all of the exceptions, the auditor is concerned about four principal things.

  (a) Whether there is a client error. Many times the confirmation response differences are due to timing differences for deposits in the mail and inventory in transit to the customer. Sometimes customers misunderstand the confirmation or the information requested. The auditor must distinguish between those and client errors.

  (b) The amount of the client error if any.

  (c) The cause of the exception. It could be intentional, a misunderstanding of the proper way to record a transaction, or a breakdown of internal control.

  (d) Potential misstatements in the sample not tested. The auditor must estimate the misstatement in the untested population, based on the results of the tests of the sample.

Suggested steps to clear each of the comments satisfactorily are:

1. (a) Examine supporting documents, including the sales invoices and applicable sales and shipping orders, for propriety and accuracy of the sales.

    (b) Review the cash receipts books for the period after December 31, 1999, and note any cash receipts from the PDQ Company. The degree of internal control over cash receipts should be an important consideration in determining the reliance that can be placed on the cash receipts entries. In addition, because there is no assurance that cash receipts after December 31 represent the payment of invoices supporting the December 31 trial balance, consideration should be given to requesting a confirmation from the PDQ Company of the invoices paid by their checks.

2. (a) The cause should be investigated thoroughly. If the credit was posted to the wrong account, it may indicate merely a clerical error. On the other hand, posting to the wrong account may indicate lapping.

    (b) Such a comment may also indicate a delay in posting and depositing of receipts. If this is the case, the company should be informed immediately so that it can take corrective steps.

3. This is a confirmation of the balance with an additional comment about a subsequent payment. Since the customer has given us the data, it is preferable to check to see that the information agrees with the company's records.

15-29 (Continued)

4. This incomplete comment should raise an immediate question: does the customer mean paid before or paid after December 31? Because the customer's intent is unknown, this account should be reconfirmed and the customer asked to state the exact date of payment. Upon receipt of the second confirmation, the information thereon should be traced to the cash receipts journal.

5. The auditor should first evaluate how long it takes to ship goods to the customer in question. If it ordinarily takes more than five days, there is no indication of misstatement.

    A comment of this type may indicate that the company may be recording sales before an actual sale has taken place. The auditor should examine the invoice and review with the appropriate officials the company's policy on shipment terms and determine if sales, cost of sales, inventories and accounts receivable need to be adjusted.

6. (a) Determine if such advance payment has been received and that it has been properly recorded. A review should be made of other advance payments to ascertain that charges against such advances have been properly handled.

    (b) If the advance payment was to cover these invoices, the auditor should propose a reclassification of the $1,350, debiting the advance payment account and crediting accounts receivable--trade.

7. (a) Examine the shipping order for indications that the goods were shipped and, if available, carrier's invoice and/or bill of lading for receipt of the goods.

    (b) If it appears that goods were shipped, ask the client to send all available information to the customer and ask the customer to reconfirm. If the customer still insists that goods were never received, all data should be presented to an appropriate company official for a complete explanation. This may indicate that accounting for shipments is inadequate and consideration should be given to reviewing the procedures to determine if improvements can be made.

    (c) If the goods were not shipped, the auditor should recommend an adjustment reducing sales, cost of sales, and accounts receivable, and increasing inventories.

8. This should be discussed with the appropriate officials and correspondence with the customer should be reviewed to allow determination whether an adjustment should be made in the amount receivable or if an allowance for uncollectible accounts should be set up.

9. As title on any goods shipped on consignment does not pass until those goods are sold, the sales entry should be reversed, inventory charged, and cost of sales credited if it is actually a consignment sale. Other so-called sales should be reviewed and company officials queried to determine if other sales actually represent consignment shipments; if so, a similar adjustment should be made for all consignment shipments.

10. This is a noncurrent asset and should be reclassified to either deposit or prepaid rent. A review of other accounts, especially those with round numbers, may disclose other accounts that should also be reclassified.

11. This may indicate a misposting of the credit or a delay in posting the credit. Comments under 2 above would also apply to credits.

15-30 Additional audit procedures necessary for testing the balances in the sales and collection cycle from August 31 to year-end are as follows:

1. Compare sales and accounts receivable balances at year-end to the balances at August 31 and obtain and verify an explanation for any significant unexpected differences. If either balance appears to be significantly out of line at year-end, consider performing unexpected confirmation procedures again at year-end.
2. Obtain reconciliations of the sales and accounts receivable accounts from August 31 to year-end. Trace reconciling items to supporting journals produced by the system. Obtain explanation and verify the explanation for any unusual transactions.
3. Examine the trial balance of accounts receivable at year-end. Consider confirmation of any accounts which have large balances and were not confirmed as of August 31.
4. Compute the gross margin percent on a monthly basis for the year and determine if the ratios for the months after August 31 are significantly different than before.
5. Compute the ratio of sales returns and allowances to sales on a monthly basis as in 4.
6. Internal controls should be tested for the period August 31 to December 31. The extent of testing should depend on the results of procedures 1 through 5.

15-31 a. If called upon to evaluate the adequacy of the sample size, the type of confirmation used, and the percentage of accounts confirmed, the following additional information would be required:

- The number of accounts that had positive balances at 12/31/99
- The materiality of total accounts receivable
- The distribution and size of the accounts receivable
- The assessment of control risk based on the understanding obtained of internal control and tests of controls
- The results of the confirmation tests in previous years
- The risk of exposure to bankruptcy and similar risks (audit risk)
- Expected misstatements

b. If the amounts are material, it is necessary to perform follow-up procedures for positive confirmations not returned by the debtor. It is common to send second requests for confirmations and sometimes even third requests. Even with these efforts, some customers do not return the confirmation, so it is necessary to follow up on all nonresponses with a method referred to as "alternative procedures."

15-31 (Continued)

    c.   The alternative procedures used for verifying the two nonresponses do not appear to be adequate. In scheduling the subsequent cash receipts, for confirmation request no. 9, the auditor should have indicated which invoices the payments applied to and whether or not the invoices were included in the balance at 12/31/99. In addition, the auditor should have examined copies of checks if they were available or traced the amounts to the bank deposit slip and into the bank statement. The cash receipts listed for confirmation request no. 9 total in excess of the balance due at 12/31/99; the auditor should have indicated what portion of this balance applies to the balance at 12/31/99.

        The alternative procedures for confirmation request no. 26 show a small payment for which no indication of the invoice to which it applies is given. The auditor examined a duplicate sales invoice which may or may not support the balance at 12/31/99. The auditor must determine which sales invoices are represented by the $2,500 balance at 12/31/99 and then examine a shipping document to support the shipment of goods to the customer. The even amount of the balance and periodic payments also raise a question about the possibility of a note outstanding rather than an account receivable.

■ Cases

15-32 a. There are four major factors affecting acceptable audit risk for the audit of Smalltown Regional Hospital.

1. There are several large loans to two local banks, both which have said they are reluctant to extend more credit.
2. A modern hospital is being built in a nearby city, which affects the competitive environment, and therefore the likelihood of financial failure.
3. The hospital has been incurring significant deficits in the past.
4. County taxes may not be able to make up the deficits, as they have in the past.

Considering the combined affect of these factors, the auditor should set a low acceptable audit risk.

    b.   The following are major inherent risks:

1. In the audit of accounts receivable and property, plant and equipment, the amounts are highly material.
2. Misstatements are common in billings, cash receipts, accounts receivable balances, and bad debts.
3. Due to the high unemployment rate, there is a significant risk of increased bad debts.

15-32 (Continued)

    c.   The major difficulty the auditor faces is the ineffective controls over sales and the unreliability of confirmations because of the nature of the customers. The auditor should therefore plan to emphasize substantive tests of transactions for sales and alternative procedures, especially subsequent cash receipts. The controls over cash receipts are such that it is practical to reduce assessed control risk after a proper understanding is obtained of internal control and tests of controls are performed. A likely approach is the following:

1. Test internal controls over cash receipts using tests of controls to make sure that the controls are effective to prevent fraud.
2. Do substantive tests of transactions for revenues, with emphasis on tests for unrecorded revenues, billing misstatements, and recording misstatements. The sample for sales should be traced to subsequent cash receipts to test whether each receipt has been correctly recorded. One important test is to select a sample of patient charts and trace transactions through to the revenue journal. The patient chart is a reliable indicator of services provided to patients.
3. The accounts receivable aged trial balance should be tested for detail tie-in. Minimal confirmations should be sent, with emphasis on large or unusual balances. The emphasis should be on subsequent cash receipts.
4. A careful evaluation of all older, outstanding accounts is essential due to the likelihood of bad debts. The high unemployment rate in the community increases the likelihood of a material misstatement of the allowance for uncollectible accounts.

15-32 (Continued)

d. The following emphasis is appropriate for each type of test:

TYPE OF TEST	EMPHASIS	REASON
1. Test of controls	None, except control of cash receipts.	Controls are weak in all areas except cash receipts.
2. Substantive test of transactions	Extensive	Tests of details of balances evidence (confirmation) is not reliable, therefore substantive tests of transactions are the most important evidence. Substantive tests of transactions are even more important because of potential for misstatement for the completeness objective. Tests of details of balances are unlikely to uncover any existing misstatements for this objective.
3. Analytical procedure	Extensive	An indication of misstatements may result from these tests.
4. Tests of details of balances	Reasonably extensive, except confirmations which should be minimal.	Confirmations are not emphasized because of the lack of reliability in the situation. Tests of details of balances are used most extensively for bad debts and the allowance for uncollectible accounts.

15-33

PINNACLE MANUFACTURING - PART IV
EVALUATION OF THE RESULTS OF ANALYTICAL PROCEDURES
AND TESTS OF DETAILS OF BALANCES

Computer versions in Excel of the worksheet and analysis below are contained on the Companion Website and on the diskette accompanying this manual (Filename P1533.XLS).

a. Relationships, ratios, and trends:

1. Comparison of current listing of accounts payable with that of the previous audit date, noting significant changes in amounts and makeup, e.g., changes in major suppliers.

2. Ratios:

    - Accounts payable ÷ purchases
    - Gross profit ratio
    - Overhead ÷ materials cost
    - Material ÷ total product cost: total dollar basis and unit cost basis
    - Overhead ÷ direct labor
    - Units purchased ÷ units sold
    - Specific expense items ÷ sales

3. Trends

    - Purchases by month
    - Gross profit by month
    - Other recurring expenses by month

15-33 (Continued)
   b.

BALANCE-RELATED AUDIT OBJECTIVE	TESTS OF DETAILS OF BALANCES PROCEDURES
Accounts payable in the list agree with the related master file; the total is correctly added and agrees with the general ledger (detail tie-in).	Foot the accounts payable list and trace the total to the general ledger. (1)
Accounts payable in the accounts payable list exist (existence).	Request from a sample of 25 vendors that they send a copy of their year-end statement directly to you. Reconcile these to the accounts payable list. (2)
Existing accounts payable are in the accounts payable list (completeness).	Examine subsequent cash disbursements > $3,000 and examine related documentation to determine if such disbursements were properly recorded as liabilities as of balance sheet date.(3) Trace receiving reports issued before year-end to related vendors' invoices.(4)
Accounts payable in the accounts payable list are correctly stated (accuracy).	Same procedures as for existence and completeness.
Accounts payable in the accounts payable list are properly classified (classification).	Review the master file for related party transactions/balances, debit balances, and long-term or other payables.(5)
Transactions in the acquisition and payment cycle are recorded in the proper period (cutoff).	Trace receiving reports issued just before and after year-end to the appropriate journal and vendor invoice.(4)
The company has an obligation to pay the liabilities included in accounts payable (obligations).	Examine vendors' statements and determine that the company has an obligation to pay the corresponding amounts in the accounts payable listing.(2)
Accounts in the acquisition and payment cycle are properly presented and disclosed (presentation and disclosure).	Review statements to make sure that material related party transaction/balances and long-term liabilities are properly disclosed.(6)

15-33 (Continued)

b. Evidence Planning Worksheet to Decide Tests of Details of Balances for Pinnacle Manufacturing—Accounts Payable

	Detail tie-in	Existence	Completeness	Accuracy	Classification	Cutoff	Obligations	Presentation and disclosure
Acceptable audit risk	high	high	high	high	high	high	high	high
Inherent risk	low	low	high	medium	low	high	low	low
Control risk - Acquisitions	low	low	low	low	low	low	low	low
Control risk - Cash disbursements	low	low	low	low	low	low	low	low
Control risk - Additional controls	low	low	low	low	low	low	low	low
Substantive tests of transactions - Acquisitions	good results	good results	good results	good results	good results	good results	good results	good results
Substantive tests of transactions - Cash disbursements	good results	good results	good results	good results	good results	good results	good results	good results
Analytical procedures	good results	good results	good results	good results	good results	good results	good results	good results
Planned detection risk for tests of details of balances	high	high	medium	high	high	medium	high	high
Planned audit evidence for tests of details of balances	low	low	medium	low	low	medium	low	low

Tolerable misstatement $7,500

15-27

15-33 (Continued)

c.

PERFORMANCE FORMAT AUDIT PROGRAM

1. Foot the accounts payable list and trace the total to the general ledger.

2. Request from a sample of 25 vendors that they send a copy of their year-end statement directly to you. Reconcile these to the accounts payable listing. Per review of the statements, determine that the company has an obligation to pay the corresponding amounts included in the accounts payable listing.

3. Examine cash disbursements > $3,000 subsequent to year-end and examine related documentation to determine if such items were properly included or excluded from accounts payable at year-end.

4. Trace receiving reports issued just before and after year-end to the appropriate journal and vendor invoice.

5. Review the master file for related party transactions/balances, debit balances, and long-term or other payables.

6. Review statements to make sure that material related party transactions/balances and long-term liabilities are properly disclosed.

d.

	Planned Sample Sizes
Effect of high control risk	larger
Effect of high inherent risk	larger
Analytical procedures indicate potential misstatement	larger

Combined effect—considerably more procedures and/or larger sample sizes.

15-33 (Continued)

e.

PINNACLE MANUFACTURING - PART III
ANALYSIS OF TRADE ACCOUNTS PAYABLE DECEMBER 31, 1999

Vendor	Balance Per Books	Amount Confirmed By Vendor	Difference: Books Over (Under) Amount Confirmed	Reconcilable Difference: No Misstatement	Misstatement in Accounts Payable Dr (Cr)	Balance Sheet Misstatement Dr (Cr)	Income Statement Misstatement Dr (Cr)	Brief Explanation
Fiberchem	6,315.80	8,719.22	(2,403.42)		(2,403.42)		2,403.42	Unrecorded A/P: Dr Purchases* Cr A/P
Mobil Oil	11,480.00	14,350.00	(2,870.00)	2,870.00				Goods in transit
Norris Industries	9,120.00	13,420.00	(4,300.00)		(4,300.00)	4,300.00		Unrecorded A/P: Dr Inventory** Cr A/P
Remington Supply	9,842.10	15,533.90	(5,691.80)	1,984.80	(3,707.00)	3,707.00		Payment in transit; Unrecorded A/P: Dr Inventory** Cr A/P
Advent Sign	2,500.00	4,000.00	(1,500.00)		(1,500.00)	1,500.00		Unrecorded A/P: Dr Fixed Assets*** Cr A/P
Fuller Travel	943.00	1,326.00	(383.00)	383.00				Credit in process
Others Confirmed	91,914.39	91,914.39						
Total Tested	132,115.29	149,263.51	(17,148.22)	5237.80	11,910.42	9,507.00	2403.42	

* Assumes that the items were included in the physical inventory count on 12-31.
** Assumes that the items were excluded from the physical inventory count on 12-31.
*** Assumes that the purchase is for a depreciable asset (sign).

15-33 (Continued)

Summary of misstatements in Pinnacle Manufacturing's records:

Known misstatements:	11,910.42	
Projected misstatements: Assumed to affect income before taxes[1]	5,406.00[1]	
Factor to allow for sampling error (10% of projected misstatements)	541.00	
Total possible misstatement	17,857.42	

[1]Computation:

$$\text{Projected misstatement} = \frac{\text{known misstatements}}{\text{tested accounts}} \times \text{untested accounts}$$

$$= \frac{11,910.42}{132,115.29} \times 59,970.24$$

$$= 5,406$$

Conclusion:

Accounts payable is understated by more than a material amount. An adjustment should be proposed to increase accounts payable by $17,857. Should an adjustment be made for the known misstatements only, accounts payable will no longer be materially misstated, however.

15-30

Internet Problem Solution: Revenue Recognition

15-1 In recent years several high-profile incidents of improper revenue recognition attracted the attention of the business media and led to unflattering coverage. Recently, the SEC expressed concerns about improper revenue recognition. The SEC requested the AICPA put together a "tool kit" summarizing audit guidance in the revenue recognition area. Please download the publication "Audit Issues in Revenue Recognition" here (http://www.aicpa.org/members/div/auditstd/pubaud.htm), and address the following questions: (This file is in PDF format and can be read using the Adobe Acrobat Reader 3.0. If you do not currently have this program, you may download a copy from the Adobe website, http://www.adobe.com).

1. What does the report list as the four deterrents to improper revenue recognition?

    The report references the recommendations of The National Commission on Fraudulent Financial Reporting (Treadway Commission). The four Treadway Commission recommendations discussed in the report are (1) Tone at the Top—it is the most important factor contributing to the integrity of the financial reporting process, (2) Audit Committee of the Board of Directors—the importance of corporate governance has also been discussed by several other reports (e.g., 1993 and 1994 Public Oversight Board reports), (3) Internal Audit Function, and (4) Internal Control. These recommendations should not be too surprising to students.

2. What is a "Bill and Hold" sale?

    In a bill and hold transaction, a customer agrees to purchase the goods but the seller retains physical possession until the customer requests shipment to designated locations. Normally, such an arrangement does not qualify as a sale because delivery has not occurred. Under certain conditions, however, when a buyer has made an absolute purchase commitment and has assumed the risks and rewards of the purchased product but is unable to accept delivery because of a compelling business reason, bill and hold sales may qualify for revenue recognition.

3. Customer of your audit client, ABC Co., made a formal written request to establish a bill and hold arrangement in November 1998. Such storage arrangements are typical in the industry. The customer's written request outlines a delivery schedule that will commence in February 1999. As of November 1998, the product that will be shipped is complete and ready for shipment. Because the sale was completed in 1998, your audit client would like to record the bill and hold transaction described as a sale in 1998. You do not recall noticing any inventory held in a separate area of the client's warehouse during the December 31, 1998 inventory observation. In making your determination regarding the timing of the revenue recognition, what questions do you have for management of ABC Co.?

15-1 (Continued)

Students' answers will vary but they should, at least, address the following issues:

- Does the client have any specific performance obligations such that the earnings process is not complete? (if yes then cannot record a sale)
- Has the risk of loss passed to the buyer? (if no then cannot record a sale)
- Were the ordered goods segregated from the client's inventory? (if no then cannot record a sale)
- Were the ordered goods subject to being used to fill other orders? (if yes then cannot record a sale)

4. Assume that in your review of the written request from the customer the customer had the right to cancel the order up through January 15, 1999. The customer did not exercise that right, and the first February shipment has already been made. Your client, ABC Co., is arguing that the cancellation clause was simply a formality and that there was never any intention of canceling the order—as evidenced by the fact that shipments have already commenced. Would the cancellation clause have any impact on your decision to allow ABC to recognize the related revenue in 1998?

The revenue cannot be recorded in 1998. The cancellation clause was an open option at December 31, 1998 so the sale was not complete and risk of loss remained with ABC. It doesn't matter that the cancellation clause was not exercised. The critical issue is the state of affairs at December 31, 1998.

(**Note**: Internet problems address current issues using Internet sources. Because Internet sites are subject to change, Internet problems and solutions are subject to change. Current information on Internet problems is available at www.prenhall.com/arens/).

Chapter 16

Audit Sampling for Tests of Details of Balances

■ **Review Questions**

16-1 The most important difference between (a) tests of controls and substantive tests of transactions and (b) tests of details of balances is in what the auditor wants to measure. In tests of controls and substantive tests of transactions, the primary concern is testing the effectiveness of internal controls and the rate of monetary misstatements. When an auditor performs tests of controls and substantive tests of transactions, the purpose is to determine if the exception rate in the population is sufficiently low to justify reducing assessed control risk to reduce substantive tests. When statistical sampling is used for tests of controls and substantive tests of transactions, attributes sampling is ideal because it measures the frequency of occurrence (exception rate). In tests of details of balances, the concern is determining whether the monetary amount of an account balance is materially misstated. Attributes sampling, therefore, is seldom useful for tests of details of balances.

16-2 Stratified sampling is a method of sampling in which all the elements in the total population are divided into two or more subpopulations. Each subpopulation is then independently sampled, tested and statistically measured in the same way as variables. After the results of the individual parts have been computed, they are combined into one overall population measurement. Stratified sampling is important in auditing in situations where the misstatements are likely to be either large or small.

In order for an auditor to obtain a stratified sample of 30 items from each of three strata in the confirmation of accounts receivable, he or she must first divide the population into three mutually exclusive strata. A random sample of 30 items is then selected independently for each stratum.

16-3 The point estimate is an estimate of the total amount of misstatement in the population as projected from the known misstatements found in the sample. The projection is based on either the average misstatement in the sample times the population size, or the net percent of misstatement in the sample times the population book value.

The true value of misstatements in the population is the net sum of all misstatements in the population and can only be determined by a 100% audit.

16-4 The statement illustrates how the misuse of statistical estimation can impair the use of an otherwise valuable audit tool. The auditor's mistake is that he or she treats the point estimate as if it is the true population value, instead of but one possible value in a statistical distribution. Rather than judge whether the point estimate is material, the auditor should construct a statistical confidence interval around the point estimate, and consider whether the interval indicates a material misstatement. Among other factors, the interval will reflect appropriate levels of risk and sample size.

16-5 Monetary unit sampling is a method whereby the population is defined as the individual dollars (or other currency) making up the account balance. A random sample is drawn of these individual monetary units and the physical audit units containing them are identified and audited. The results of auditing the physical audit units are applied, pro rata, to the random monetary units, and a statistical conclusion about all population monetary units is derived.

Monetary unit sampling is now the most commonly used method of statistical sampling for tests of details of balances. This is because it uses the simplicity of attributes sampling yet still provides a statistical result expressed in dollars. It does this by using attribute tables to estimate the total proportion of population dollars misstated, based on the number of sample dollars misstated, and then modifies this amount by the amounts of misstatements found. This latter aspect gives monetary unit sampling its "variables" dimension, although normal distribution theory is not used; rather an arbitrary rule of thumb is applied to make the adjustment.

16-6 Sampling risk is the risk that the characteristics in the sample are not representative of those in the population. The two types of sampling risk faced by the auditor testing an account balance are:

a. The risk of incorrect acceptance (ARIA)—this is the risk that the sample supports the conclusion that the recorded account balance is not materially misstated when it is materially misstated.
b. The risk of incorrect rejection (ARIR)—this the risk that the sample supports the conclusion that the recorded account balance is materially misstated when it is not materially misstated.

Sampling risk occurs whenever a sample is taken from a population and therefore applies to all sampling methods. While ARIA applies to all sampling methods, ARIR is only used in variables sampling and difference estimation.

16-7 The steps in nonstatistical sampling for tests of details of balances and for tests of controls are almost identical, as illustrated in the text. The major differences are that sampling for tests of controls deals with exceptions and sampling for tests of details of balances concerns dollar amounts. This results in differences in the application of the two methods, but not the steps.

16-8 The two methods of selecting a monetary unit sample are random sampling and systematic sampling. Under random sampling, in this situation, 57 random numbers would be obtained (the sample size in 16-14) between 1 and 12,625,000. These would be sorted into ascending sequence. The physical audit units in the inventory listing containing the random monetary units would then be identified by cumulating amounts with an adding machine. As the cumulative total exceeds a successive random number, the item causing this event is identified as containing the random dollar unit.

When systematic sampling is used, the population total amount is divided by the sample size to obtain the sampling interval. A random number is chosen between 1 and the amount of the sampling interval to determine the starting point. The dollars to be selected are the starting point and then the starting point plus the interval amount applied successively to the population total. The items on the inventory listing containing the dollar units are identified using the cumulative method described above.

16-8 (Continued)
In applying the cumulative method under both random sampling and systematic sampling, the page totals can be used in lieu of adding the detailed items if the page totals are considered to be reliable.

16-9 A unique aspect of monetary unit sampling is the use of the preliminary judgment about materiality, as discussed in Chapter 9, to directly determine the tolerable misstatement amount for the audit of each account. Most sampling techniques require the auditor to determine tolerable misstatement for each account by allocating the preliminary judgment about materiality. This is not required when monetary unit sampling is used. The preliminary judgment about materiality is used.

16-10 Acceptable risk of incorrect acceptance (ARIA) is the risk the auditor is willing to take of accepting a balance as correct when the true misstatement in the balance is greater than tolerable misstatement. ARIA is the equivalent term to acceptable risk of assessing control risk too low for audit sampling for tests of controls and substantive tests of transactions.

The primary factor affecting the auditor's decision about ARIA is control risk in the audit risk model, which is the extent to which the auditor relies on internal controls. When internal controls are effective, control risk can be reduced, which permits the auditor to increase ARIA, which in turn reduces the required sample size. Besides control risk, ARIA is also affected directly by acceptable audit risk and inversely by inherent risk and other substantive tests already performed on the account balance, assuming effective results. For example, if acceptable audit risk is reduced, ARIA must also be reduced. If analytical procedures were performed and there is no indication of problem areas, there is a lower likelihood of misstatements in the account being tested, and ARIA can be increased.

16-11 The statement reflects a misunderstanding of the statistical inference process. The process is based on the long-run probability that the process will produce correct results in a predictable proportion of the times it is applied. Thus, a random sampling process which produces a 90% confidence interval will produce intervals which do, in fact, contain the true population value 90% of the time. However, the confidence limits of each interval will not all be the same.

16-12 ARIA for tests of details of balances is the equivalent of ARACR for tests of controls and substantive tests of transactions. If internal controls are considered to be effective, control risk can be reduced. A lower control risk requires a lower ARACR, which requires a larger sample size for testing. If controls are determined to be effective after testing, control risk can remain low, which permits the auditor to increase ARIA. An increased ARIA allows the auditor to reduce sample sizes for tests of details of balances.

16-13 In using the binomial distribution, monetary unit sampling estimates the proportion of all population dollars misstated *by some amount*. For the sample items actually misstated, the amounts of those misstatements are used. However, many items in the population have a statistical probability of being misstated by some other amount. An assumption must be made as to what this amount is in order to compute the monetary unit sampling results. This is called the "percent of misstatement assumption."

16-13 (Continued)

Since the purpose of monetary unit sampling is to estimate the most the misstatements in the population are likely to be, there is an inherent need for conservatism in the MUS process. Since account balance details if they are overstated, are unlikely to be overstated by more than their recorded value, a 100% assumption is a conservative choice. On this basis it is easier to justify the 100% misstatement assumption than a less conservative amount, and thus it is commonly used.

16-14 The preliminary sample size is calculated as follows:

Tolerable misstatement	500,000
÷ Average misstatement percent assumption	÷ 1.00
	500,000
÷ Recorded population value	12,625,000
= Tolerable exception rate	4%

Using the table for a 10% ARACR with an expected population exception rate of zero and a tolerable exception rate of 4%, the preliminary sample size is 57.

16-15 Misstatement bounds using the attributes tables

MISSTATE-MENT	RECORDED VALUE	AUDITED VALUE	MISSTATE-MENT	MISSTATEMENT/ RECORDED AMOUNT
1	897.16	609.16	288.00	.321
2	47.02	0	47.02	1.000
3	1,621.68	1,522.68	99.00	.061

Using the attributes sampling table for a sample size of 100, and an ARIA of 10%, the CUER is:

NO. OF MISSTATEMENTS	CUER	INCREASE IN BOUND RESULTING FROM AN ADDITIONAL MISSTATEMENT
0	.023	
1	.038	.015
2	.052	.014
3	.066	.014

In order to calculate the upper and lower misstatement bounds, it will be assumed that for a zero misstatement rate the percent of misstatement is 100%.

16-15 (Continued)

The upper misstatement bound:

NO. OF MISSTATE-MENTS	RECORDED VALUE	x	CUER PORTION	x	UNIT MISSTATE-MENT	=	MIS-STATE-MENT BOUND PORTION
0	12,625,000		.023		1.000		290,375
1	12,625,000		.015		1.000		189,375
2	12,625,000		.014		.321		56,737
3	12,625,000		.014		.061		10,782
					Upper Misstatement Bound		547,269

The lower misstatement bound:

Before adjustment:

NO. OF MISSTATE-MENTS	RECORDED VALUE	x	CUER PORTION	x	UNIT MISSTATE-MENT	=	MIS-STATE-MENT BOUND PORTION
0	12,625,000		.023		1.000		290,375

Adjustment:

Point estimate for overstatements = sum of misstatement percents x recorded value / sample size

= (.321 + 1.000 + .061) x (12,625,000 / 100)

= 1.382 x 126,250

= 174,478

Adjusted lower misstatement bound = initial bound - point estimate for overstatements

= 290,375 - 174,478

= 115,897

Based on this calculation method, the population is not acceptable as stated since the upper misstatement bound exceeds the $500,000 materiality limit.

16-16 The difficulty in determining sample size lies in estimating the number and amount of misstatements that may be found in the sample. The upper bound of a monetary unit sample is sensitive to these factors. Thus, sample size varies a great deal with differing assumptions about them.

Generally, the auditor will determine sample size by making reasonable but conservative assumptions about the sample exception rate and average misstatement amount. In the absence of information about misstatement amount, which is most difficult to anticipate, a 100% assumption is often used.

16-17 The decision rule for difference estimation is:

If the two-sided confidence interval for the misstatements is completely within plus or minus tolerable misstatements, accept the hypothesis that the book value is not misstated by a material amount. Otherwise, accept the hypothesis that the book value is misstated by a material amount. For example, assume the LCL is -10,000, the UCL is 40,000 and tolerable misstatement is $45,000. The following illustrates the decision rule:

```
     -TM                                    +TM
   -45,000 _____0_____ + 45,000


   - 10,000 _____ + 40,000
     LCL                                    UCL
```

The auditor can conclude that the population is not materially misstated since both LCL and UCL are within the tolerable misstatement limits.

16-18 When a population is not considered acceptable, there are several possible courses of action:

1. Perform expanded audit tests in specific areas. If an analysis of the misstatements indicates that most of the misstatements are of a specific type, it may be desirable to restrict the additional audit effort to the problem area.
2. Increase the sample size. When the auditor increases the sample size, sampling error is reduced if the rate of misstatements in the expanded sample, their dollar amount, and their direction are similar to those in the original sample. Increasing the sample size, therefore, may satisfy the auditor's tolerable misstatement requirements.

    Increasing the sample size enough to satisfy the auditor's tolerable misstatement standards is often costly, especially when the difference between tolerable misstatement and projected misstatement is small.
3. Adjust the account balance. When the auditor concludes that an account balance is materially misstated, the client may be willing to adjust the book value.
4. Request the client to correct the population. In some cases the client's records are so inadequate that a correction of the entire population is required before the audit can be completed.

16-18 (Continued)
    5. Refuse to give an unqualified opinion. If the auditor believes the recorded amount in accounts receivable or any other account is not fairly stated, it is necessary to follow at least one of the above alternatives or to qualify the audit opinion in an appropriate manner.

16-19 The population standard deviation is a measure of the difference between the individual values and the mean of the population. It is calculated for all variables sampling methods but not for monetary unit sampling. For the auditor, it is usually estimated before determining the required sample size, based on the previous year's results or on a preliminary sample.

    The population standard deviation is needed to calculate the sample size necessary for an acceptable precision interval when variable sampling methods are used. After the sample is selected and audited, the population standard deviation is estimated from the standard deviation calculated from the values in the sample.

    The required sample size is directly proportional to the square of the population standard deviation.

16-20 This practice is improper for a number of reasons:

1. No determination was made as to whether a random sample of 100 inventory items would be sufficient to generate an acceptable precision interval for a given confidence level. In fact, a confidence limit was not even calculated.
2. The combined net amount of the sample misstatement may be immaterial because large overstatement amounts may be offsetting large understatement amounts resulting in a relatively small combined net amount.
3. Although no misstatement by itself may be material, other material misstatements might not have exhibited themselves if too small of a sample was taken.
4. Regardless of the size of individual or net amounts of misstatements in a sample, the effect on the overall population cannot be determined unless the results are evaluated using a statistically valid method.

16-21 Difference estimation is a method for estimating the total misstatement in a population by multiplying the average misstatement (the audited value minus the recorded value) in a random sample by the number of items in the entire population.

    Ratio estimation is quite similar to difference estimation. However, instead of basing the estimate of total misstatement on the difference between audited and recorded values, it uses the ratio of misstatement amounts to recorded amounts. This ratio for the sample is multiplied times the total population recorded amount to estimate total misstatement. Mean-per-unit estimation is a method of estimating the total audited value of the population by multiplying the arithmetic average, or mean, audited value of the sample times the number of items in the population.

    Stratified mean-per-unit estimation is similar to mean-per-unit estimation except that the population is divided into groups of homogeneous items, called strata, for purposes of sample design. A separate random sample is selected from each stratum and the estimate of the total population audited amount is computed by determining an estimate for each stratum and adding the results.

16-21 (Continued)

The following are examples where each method could be used:

a. Difference estimation can be used in computing the balance in accounts receivable by using the misstatements discovered during the confirmation process, where a significant number of misstatements are found.
b. Ratio estimation can be used to determine the amount of the LIFO reserve where internal inventory records are maintained on a FIFO basis but reporting is on LIFO.
c. Mean-per-unit estimation can be used to determine total inventory value where the periodic inventory method is employed.
d. Stratified mean-per-unit estimation can be used to determine total inventory value where there are several locations and each is sampled separately.

Monetary unit sampling would generally be preferable to any of these where few or no misstatements are expected. Difference and ratio estimation are not reliable where the exception rate is low, and mean-per-unit is generally not as efficient. However, in item "c" above, mean-per-unit must be used because there is only one value per sample item.

16-22 Tolerable misstatement (Chapter 9) represents the portion of overall materiality allocated to each individual account. It is the amount of misstatement the auditor believes can be present in an account and the account balance still be acceptable for audit purposes.

Since hypothesis testing requires a decision rule based on materiality, that amount should be tolerable misstatement for an individual account balance. If test results provide a confidence limit greater than tolerable misstatement, the auditor would conclude the account is misstated. This would result in one or more of several actions:

1. Perform expanded audit tests in specific areas.
2. Increase the sample size.
3. Adjust the account balance.
4. Request the client to correct the population.
5. Refuse to give an unqualified opinion.

In addition, it may be possible to adjust tolerable misstatement (upward) and remake the decision. The basis for this would be a reconsideration of the original judgment concerning determining overall materiality and allocation to the accounts. For example, audit work completed on another account may indicate that a much lower tolerable misstatement exists for that account then originally planned. This would allow a reallocation providing a larger tolerable misstatement to the subject account.

16-23 Difference estimation can be very effective and very efficient where (1) an audited value and a book value is available for each population item, (2) a relatively high frequency of misstatements is expected, and (3) a result in the form of a confidence interval is desired. In those circumstances, difference estimation far outperforms both MUS and mean-per-unit estimation. It may or may not outperform ratio estimation, depending on the relationship of misstatement amounts to recorded amounts, but it does require less computational effort than ratio estimation in any case. If focus on large dollar value items is required, difference estimation can be used with stratification.

16-24 Examples of audit conclusions resulting from the use of attributes, monetary unit, and variables sampling are as follows:

Use of attributes sampling in a test of sales transactions for internal verification:

We have examined a random sample of 100 sales invoices for indication of internal verification; two exceptions were noted. Based on our sample, we conclude, with a 5% risk, that the proportion of sales invoices to which internal verification has not been applied does not exceed 6.2%.

Use of monetary unit sampling in a test of sales transactions for existence:

We have examined a random sample of 100 dollar units of sales transactions for existence. All were supported by properly prepared sales orders and shipping documents. Based on our sample, we conclude, with a 20% risk, that invalid sales do not exceed $40,000.

Use of variables sampling in confirmation of accounts receivable (in the form of an interval estimate and a hypothesis test):

We have confirmed a random sample of 100 accounts receivable. We obtained replies or examined satisfactory other evidence for all sample items. A listing of exceptions is attached. Based on our sample, we estimate, with 10% risk, that the true population misstatement is between $20,000 understatement and $40,000 overstatement. Since tolerable misstatement for accounts receivable is judged to be $50,000, we conclude, with a risk of 5%, that accounts receivable are not materially misstated.

■ **Multiple Choice Questions from CPA Examinations**

16-25 a. (4) b. (3) c. (3)

16-26 a. (4) b. (2) c. (1)

■ **Discussion Questions and Problems**

16-27 a. 92 (Book value/tolerable misstatement) x assurance factor =
  (6,900,000/150,000) x 2
  b. If poor results were obtained for tests of controls and substantive tests of transactions for sales, sales returns and allowances, and cash receipts, the required sample size for tests of details of balances would need to be increased. Using the formula in the problem, the auditor would increase sample size by increasing the assurance factor. This has the same effect has specifying a lower acceptable risk of incorrect acceptance (ARIA).

16-27 (Continued)

c. A systematic sample can be selected based on the number of accounts, or the dollar value of the population. To select a systematic sample based on the number of accounts, the total number of accounts in the population is divided by the required sample size to determine the interval. A random number is then selected between one and the interval as the starting point. Because each account has an equal likelihood of selection, this method is appropriate if all the accounts are similar in size, or if the population is stratified into two or more samples.

To select a systematic sample based on the dollar value of the population, the population value is divided by the required sample size to obtain the appropriate interval. A random number is then selected between one and the interval as the starting point. The interval is added to the starting point to determine the dollar units selected. Accounts are selected for testing where the cumulative total of accounts receivable includes the random number. This method of selection is similar to monetary unit selection, and accounts greater than the amount of the interval are automatically selected using this method.

d. The direct projection of error for the sample can be computed as follows:

(Errors in sample/sample book value) x population book value =

(1,500/230,000) x 6,900,000 = $45,000 overstatement

The projected error of $45,000 is well below tolerable misstatement of $150,000 and provides an allowance for sampling risk of $105,000. Accordingly, the population is deemed to be fairly stated.

16-28 a. If random selection is performed using Excel (P1628.XLS), the command to select numbers randomly from the population is:

=RANDBETWEEN(1,207295)

The 10 random numbers selected using this approach will vary for each student.

The command for selecting the random numbers can be entered directly onto the spreadsheet, or can be selected from the function menu (math & trig) functions. It may be necessary to add the analysis tool pack to access the RANDBETWEEN function. Once the formula is entered, it can be copied down to select additional random numbers.

NOTE: Random dollar items are matched with population item numbers where the cumulative book value of the population includes the random dollar selected.

16-28 (Continued)

b.

$$\text{Interval} = \frac{\text{Population total}}{\text{Number of items selected}}$$

$$= \frac{207{,}295}{10}$$

$$= \underline{20{,}729} \text{ Interval}$$

Using 1857 as a starting point, we have:

	SYSTEMATIC DOLLAR	POPULATION ITEM NO.
1	1,857	2
2	22,586	6
3	43,315	8
4	64,044	8
5	84,773	15
6	105,502	20
7	126,231	26
8	146,960	30
9	167,689	30
10	188,481	35

NOTE: Systematic dollar items are related to population item numbers in the same manner as for part a above.

c. All items larger than the interval will be automatically included. If the interval is 20,729 item 30 will be included at least once, and item 8 at least twice.
   The same is not necessarily true for random number selection, but the probability is high. Note that for item 8, there is a probability of approximately 22% (44,110/207,295) of its being included in a given sample draw. It was included twice in a sample of 10.
d. There is no significant difference in ease of selection between computer generation of random numbers and systematic selection. Some auditors prefer the use of random numbers because they believe this helps ensure an unbiased sample.
e. Monetary unit sampling would be used because (1) it is efficient and (2) it focuses on large dollar items.

16-29 a. The differences that were uncovered include only five misstatements rather than seven. Items 2 and 7 are not misstatements, but only timing differences. Therefore, only the five misstatements are summarized in order to compute the upper and lower misstatement bounds. These misstatements are summarized below.

ITEM	RECORDED VALUE	AUDITED VALUE	MISSTATE-MENT	MISSTATEMENT/ RECORDED VALUE
1	$2,728.00	$2,498.00	$ 230.00	.084
3	3,890.00	1,190.00	2,700.00	.694
4	791.00	815.00	(24.00)	(.030)
5	548.00	1,037.00	(489.00)	(.892)
6	3,115.00	3,190.00	(75.00)	(.024)

Upper misstatement bound before adjustment:

NO. OF MISSTATE-MENTS	RECORDED VALUE	x	CUER PORTION	x	MISSTATE-MENT % ASSUMPTION	=	MIS-STATE-MENT BOUND
0	$1,975,000		.023		1.000		$45,425
1	1,975,000		.015		.694		20,560
2	1,975,000		.014		.084		2,323
			.052				$68,308

Lower misstatement bound before adjustment:

NO. OF MISSTATE-MENTS	RECORDED VALUE	x	CUER PORTION	x	MISSTATE-MENT % ASSUMPTION	=	MIS-STATE-MENT BOUND
0	$1,975,000		.023		1.000		$45,425
1	1,975,000		.015		.892		26,426
2	1,975,000		.014		.030		830
3	1,975,000		.014		.024		664
			.066				$73,345

16-29 (Continued)

Adjustment of upper misstatement bound:

Point estimate for understatement amounts = sum of misstatement percents x recorded value / sample size

= (.892 + .030 + .024) x (1,975,000 / 100)

= .946 x 19,750

= 18,684

Adjusted bound = initial bound - point estimate for understatement amounts

= 68,308 - 18,684

= <u>49,624</u>

Adjustment of lower misstatement bound:

Point estimate for overstatement amounts = Sum of misstatement percents x recorded value/sample size

= (.694 + .084) x (1,975,000 / 100)

= .778 x 19,750

= 15,366

Adjusted bound = initial bound - point estimate for overstatements

= 73,345 - 15,366

= <u>57,979</u>

    b. The population is not acceptable as stated because the lower misstatement bound exceeds materiality. (Note that although the upper misstatement bound does not exceed materiality, it is quite close.)
In this situation, the auditor has the following options:

1. Segregate a specific type of misstatement and test it separately (for the entire population). The sample would then not include the specified type of misstatement since it is being tested separately.
2. Increase the sample size.
3. Adjust the account balance (i.e., propose an adjustment).
4. Request the client to review and correct the population.
5. Consider qualifying the opinion is the client refuses to correct the problem.

16-29 (Continued)

6. Consider the criteria used in the test, possibly in connection with additional audit work in areas outside of accounts receivable.

Of these options, segregating a specific type of misstatement may prove to be the most beneficial. In this problem, items 3 and 5 are cutoff misstatements. Segregating these items, testing cutoff more extensively, and eliminating them from the sample would result in the following bounds:

Upper misstatement bound:

NO. OF MISSTATE-MENTS	RECORDED VALUE	x	CUER PORTION	x	MISSTATE-MENT % ASSUMPTION	=	MIS-STATE-MENT BOUND
0	$1,975,000		.023		1.000		$45,425
1	1,975,000		.015		.084		2,489
			.038				$47,914

Less adjustment [(.030 + .024) (19,750)]   (1,067)
                                           $46,847

Lower misstatement bound:

NO. OF MISSTATE-MENTS	RECORDED VALUE	x	CUER PORTION	x	MISSTATE-MENT % ASSUMPTION	=	MIS-STATE-MENT BOUND
0	$1,975,000		.023		1.000		$45,425
1	1,975,000		.015		.030		889
2	1,975,000		.014		.024		664
			.052				$46,978

Less adjustment [(.084) (19,750)]   (1,659)
                                    $45,319

It can be seen that both misstatement bounds are now within materiality after cutoff misstatements were segregated. These misstatements were significant in two ways. Their existence increased the overall estimated population exception rate, and their magnitude contributed to the amount of estimated misstatements in the portion of the population represented by the misstatements in the sample.

16-30 a. The audit approach of testing all three account balances is acceptable. This approach is also desirable when the following conditions are present:

1. The auditor can obtain valid, reliable information to perform the required tests in all of the areas.
2. The internal controls for each of the three areas are comparable.
3. Misstatements are expected to occur evenly over the entire population. For instance, the auditor does not expect a large number of misstatements in accounts receivable and few, if any, in inventory.

b. The required sample size for all three accounts is:

$$\frac{\text{Tolerable misstatement}}{\text{Recorded population value}} \quad \frac{100,000}{10,000,000} = .01$$

From the attributes table sample size n cannot be determined, but using interpolation it is approximately 114 + (114 - 76)=152. (This is not an appropriate method to determine sample size in practice.)

c. The required sample sizes if each account is tested separately are:

ACCOUNT	FACTOR	APPROXIMATE SAMPLE SIZE
Accounts receivable	$n = \frac{100,000}{3,600,000} = .028$	76
Inventory	$n = \frac{100,000}{4,800,000} = .02$	114
Marketable securities	$n = \frac{100,000}{1,600,000} = .06$	38

The important point is that sample size under b is much smaller than for the combined samples in c.

d. The population would be arranged so that all accounts receivable would be first, followed by inventory and marketable securities. The items would be identified by the cumulative totals. In the example, the number 4,627,871 would relate to an inventory item since it is between the cumulative totals of $3,600,000 and $8,400,000. Accordingly, for this number the inventory audit procedures would be performed.

16-30 (Continued)

e. The misstatement data are as follows:

RECORDED AMOUNT	AUDITED AMOUNT	DIFFERENCE	MISSTATEMENT/ RECORDED AMOUNT
$987.12	$887.12	$100.00	10.1%

Assuming a 100% average misstatement in the population when there are no misstatements found and an ARIA of 10%, the misstatement bounds are:

Upper misstatement bound:

$$\$10,000,000 \times .011 \times 1.0 = \$110,000$$

$$\$10,000,000 \times .008 \times .101 = \underline{8,080}$$
$$\$118,080$$

Lower misstatement bound:

Before adjustment:

$$\$10,000,000 \times .011 \times 1.0 = \$110,000$$

Adjustment:

$$.101 \times \frac{\$10,000,000}{200} = \underline{(5,050)}$$
$$\$104,950$$

Based on the sample results and the stated combined acceptable misstatement of $100,000, the population (i.e., accounts receivable, inventory, and marketable securities *combined*) should not be accepted as stated without further testing.

16-31 1. (a)   2. (c)   3. (a)   4. (d)   5. (d)

16-32

Computer Solution. This is an excellent problem to demonstrate the use of the computer in auditing, as it requires a great deal of computational work. A solution prepared using Excel is included on the Companion Website and on the diskette accompanying this manual (Filename P1632.XLS). Important points to stress are:

1. The spreadsheet program is set up in two sections: one for data entry and one for computations.
2. Cells are set up for variables by name, and the values for the variables are then entered in those cells (e.g., sample size = ____). Computations are then done by reference to the cells rather than by entering values in the formulas. This allows the worksheet to be used as a general program for similar problems.
3. Although the program assures computational accuracy, the formulas *must be correct*. They should always be reviewed and double checked, and test data should be processed to assure accuracy.

    a. Calculating the point estimate:

$$\hat{E} = N \cdot \sum \frac{e_j}{n}$$

$$\hat{E} = 1840 \cdot \frac{173.69}{80}$$

$$\hat{E} = 3994.87$$

Before computing the computed precision interval, we must compute the standard deviation:

e_j	$(e_j)^2$
$(72.00)	5,184.00
65.70	4,316.49
41.10	1,689.21
36.10	1,303.31
51.80	2,683.24
(.12)	.01
30.00	900.00
21.11	445.63
173.69	16,521.79

$$SD = \sqrt{\frac{\sum (e_j)^2 - n(\bar{e})^2}{n - 1}}$$

$$= \sqrt{\frac{16{,}521.79 - 80\left(\frac{173.69}{80}\right)^2}{80 - 1}}$$

$$= 14.30$$

16-32 (Continued)

Computed precision interval:

$$CPI = NZ_A \cdot \frac{SD}{\sqrt{n}} \cdot \sqrt{\frac{N-n}{N}}$$

$$CPI = 1{,}840 \cdot 1.64 \cdot \frac{14.30}{\sqrt{80}} \cdot \sqrt{\frac{1{,}840 - 80}{1{,}840}}$$

$$CPI = \$4{,}718.46$$

The confidence interval is expressed as $3{,}994.87 \pm 4{,}718.46$.

To compute the confidence limits,

$$UCL = \hat{E} + CPI = 3{,}994.87 + 4{,}718.46 = 8{,}713.33$$

$$LCL = \hat{E} - CPI = 3{,}994.87 - 4{,}718.46 = -723.59$$

b. The auditor should not accept the book value of the population since the maximum misstatement in the population that she was willing to accept, $6,000, at a risk level of 5%, is less than the possible amount of true misstatement indicated by the UCL of $8,713.33.

c. The options available to the auditor at this point are:

1. Perform expanded audit tests in specific areas.
2. Increase the sample size.
3. Adjust the account balance.
4. Request the client to correct the population.
5. Refuse to give an unqualified opinion.

16-33 a. It would be desirable to use unstratified difference estimation when the auditor believes that there is not a small number of misstatements in the population that are in total material, and the population has a large number of small misstatements that in total could be material.

Unstratified difference estimation would not be appropriate when either of the above characteristics is not present. For example, if the auditor believes that certain large accounts payable may contain large misstatements which are material, they should be tested separately.

A significant consideration in this situation is whether the auditor can identify the entire population. This consideration applies whether using stratified or unstratified difference estimation. The auditor in this instance is identifying the population based upon an accounts payable list. If this list includes only those accounts with an outstanding balance, the sample is ignoring those accounts that have a recorded balance of zero.

Thus, many accounts could be understated but not considered in the sample or the statistical inferences drawn from the sample.

16-33 (Continued)

b. Ignoring the ARIR, the required sample size may be computed as follows:

$$n = \left[\frac{SD^* \cdot Z_A \cdot N}{TM - E^*} \right]^2$$

where

$TM - E^* = 45{,}000 - 20{,}000 = \$25{,}000$

$$n = \left[\frac{280 \cdot 1.28 \cdot 610}{25{,}000} \right]^2 = 76$$

c. In order to determine whether the population is fairly stated, the computed precision interval must be calculated.

$$CPI = N \cdot Z_A \cdot \frac{SD}{\sqrt{n}} \cdot \sqrt{\frac{N-n}{N}}$$

$$CPI = 610 \cdot 1.28 \cdot \frac{267}{\sqrt{76}} \cdot \sqrt{\frac{610 - 76}{610}} = 22{,}374.33$$

$CI = \hat{E} \pm CPI$

$CI = 21{,}000 \pm 22{,}374$

$UCL = 43{,}374$

$LCL = 1{,}374$

Since both UCL and LCL are less than tolerable misstatement, the auditor can conclude that the population is fairly stated.

The primary reasons the population is acceptable is that (1) the actual point estimate is reasonably close to the expected misstatement, and (2) the actual sample standard deviation is less than the estimated standard deviation.

d. Considering the ARIA, the sample size may be computed from the following formula:

16-33 (Continued)

$$n = \left[\frac{SD^* (Z_A + Z_R) N}{TM - E^*} \right]^2$$

$$n = \left[\frac{280 (1.28 + 1.28) 610}{45{,}000 - 20{,}000} \right]^2 = 306$$

e. The sample size increases significantly with the inclusion of the ARIR because by including it the auditor is establishing the risk he or she will take of rejecting an acceptable population, as well as considering the risk of accepting an unacceptable population. It takes more effort (sample items) to control two risks, rather than just one. The effect can be seen from reviewing the formula for calculating the sample size.

f. The approach described will only result in an appropriate sample size by chance. This would occur when the 25% increment is equal to the increase in the sample size required when the ARIR is considered. This is not a likely occurrence. This approach is not desirable because it is inefficient in terms of time and cost. Unless by chance the sample size is approximately equal to the sample size required by considering ARIR, the sample size will be either too small or too large. Too small a sample will require the sample to be increased. This may be both time consuming and expensive, if it is even possible. Conversely, too large a sample results in the auditor performing more work than is required.

■ **Cases**

16-34

a. *Determination of ARIA* - Note that there are many ways to estimate ARIA. One method is as follows:

    ARIA = AAR / (IR x CR x APR)
         = .05 / (.8 x .5 x 1.0)
         = .05 / .4
         = .13 rounded to .10 (to be conservative)

Tolerable misstatement as a percent:

    TER = TM / Population
        = 800,000 / 12,000,000
        = .067 rounded to .06 (to be conservative)

Sample size determined using **Table 14-7** (assumes an expected misstatement of zero and a misstatement percent of 100%):

    n = 38

16-34 (Continued)

b. *Determination of ARIA* - Note that there are many ways to estimate ARIA. One method is as follows:

$$\begin{aligned} ARIA &= AAR / (IR \times CR \times APR) \\ &= .05 / [1.0 \times .8 \times (1 - .6)] \\ &= .05 / .32 \\ &= .16 \text{ rounded to } .15 \end{aligned}$$

Tolerable misstatement as a percent:

$$\begin{aligned} TER &= TM / Population \\ &= 800,000 / 23,000,000 \\ &= .035 \text{ rounded to } .03 \text{ (to be conservative)} \end{aligned}$$

There is no table available for an ARIA of 15%. Inherent risk and control risk for inventory are greater than for accounts receivable. However, due to the inclusion of a component for analytical procedures risk, ARIA for inventory is not significantly greater than ARIA for accounts receivable. Because the book value of the population for inventory is much larger, the tolerable misstatement as a percent is much lower for inventory. As a result, the sample size for inventory should be larger than the sample size for accounts receivable in requirement a.

c. The same ARIA must be used for the entire combined test. It would be most prudent to use the lower of the ARIAs calculated for the separate tests, (i.e. 10% from the examples shown in requirements a and b).

Tolerable misstatement as a percent:

$$\begin{aligned} TER &= TM / Population \\ &= 800,000 / (12,000.000 + 23,000,000) \\ &= 800,000 / 35,000,000 \\ &= .023 \text{ (rounded to } .02) \end{aligned}$$

Sample size computed using **Table 14-7** (allows for a .005 exception rate -- an average of the expected misstatements for accounts receivable and inventory—and assumes misstatement percent of 100%):

n = 194

16-34 (Continued)

d. The generation of random numbers using Excel (P1634.XLS) to obtain the sample of 38 accounts receivable for confirmation would be obtained as follows:

Population book value = $12,000,000

Command to obtain each random number:

=RANDBETWEEN(1,12000000)

Once the formula is entered, it can be copied down to select additional random numbers. To obtain a sorted list, the list of random numbers should be copied to a separate column, and pasted as a value (use the "Paste Special" command and select "value"). Then use the "Data Sort" command to obtain a sorted list.

The command for selecting the random numbers can be entered directly onto the spreadsheet, or can be selected from the function menu (math & trig) functions. It may be necessary to add the analysis tool pack to access the RANDBETWEEN function.

A example prepared using Excel is included on the diskette under the filename P1634.XLS.

16-35 a. This nonstatistical (i.e., nonprobabilistic or judgmental) sample is a stratified sample. All 23 items over $10,000 were examined 100%. The remaining 7,297 items were tested with a sample of 77 items. Although this was not a probabilistic sample, GAAS require that in the auditor's judgment, it is a representative one. Accordingly, the results must be projected to the population and a judgment made about sampling risk, although sampling risk and precision cannot be measured.

Projection of the total population misstatement would be as follows:

Items over $10,000:

Projected Misstatement = Audited value - Recorded value
                                    = 432,000 - 465,000
                                    = (33,000) overstatement

Items under $10,000 - average misstatement amount method:

Projected Misstatement = Average sample misstatement x population size
                                    = [(4,350) / 77] x (7,320 - 23)
                                    = (56.49) x 7297
                                    = (412,207) overstatement

16-35 (Continued)

Items under $10,000 - proportional amount method:

Projected Misstatement = Sample misstatement ratio x population book value
= [(4,350) / 81,500] x (2,760,000 - 465,000)
= (.053) x 2,295,000
= (121,635) overstatement

Where sample misstatements are:

ITEM	AUDITED VALUE	RECORDED VALUE	MISSTATEMENT
12	4,820	5,120	(300)
19	385	485	(100)
33	250	1,250	(1,000)
35	3,875	3,975	(100)
51	1,825	1,850	(25)
59	3,780	4,200	(420)
74	0	2,405	(2,405)
Totals	14,935	19,285	(4,350)

Note that the sample misstatements are divided by the sample book value of $81,500 to calculate the sample misstatement ratio. The projected misstatement is significantly lower using the proportional amount method because the average account size in the sample is large than the average account size in the population.

Total misstatement is either:

(33,000) + (412,207) = (445,207) overstatement
or
(33,000) + (121,635) = (154,635) overstatement

In either case, the following can be said: There are a significant number of misstated items in the sample, and the amount is quite large. Since the sample is representative, it is clear that there is a material misstatement of the population. The amount of misstatement is not easily estimable from the sample. It could be significantly higher or lower than either point estimate. At this point, the best course of action would be to ask the client to make a study of their records for all population items to identify more accurately the misstatements that exist and correct them.

16-35 (Continued)

b. If this was a PPS sample, the sampled portion would be evaluated as follows:

Misstatement taintings:

ITEM	AUDITED VALUE	RECORDED VALUE	MISSTATEMENT	PERCENT
12	4,820	5,120	(300)	(.059)
19	385	485	(100)	(.206)
33	250	1,250	(1,000)	(.800)
35	3,875	3,975	(100)	(.025)
51	1,825	1,850	(25)	(.014)
59	3,780	4,200	(420)	(.100)
74	0	2,405	(2,405)	(1.000)

Calculation of overstatement bound:

OVERSTATEMENT	UPL	RECORDED VALUE	UNIT MISSTATEMENT ASSUMPTION	MISSTATEMENT BOUND PORTION
0 [1]	.039	2,295,000	1.0	89,505
1	.023	2,295,000	1.0	52,785
2	.020	2,295,000	.800	36,720
3	.018	2,295,000	.206	8,510
4	.018	2,295,000	.100	4,131
5	.017	2,295,000	.059	2,302
6	.017	2,295,000	.025	975
7	.017	2,295,000	.014	546

Overstatement bound from sample   195,474
Misstatement of 100% items   33,000
Total overstatement bound   228,474

[1] From **Table 14-8** using an ARIA of 5 percent and a sample size of 75.

16-35 (Continued)

An adjusted understatement bound is calculated as follows:

Initial understatement bound = .039 x 2,295,000
= 89,505

Point estimate for overstatements = sum of unit misstatement assumptions / sample size x recorded population amount

= 2.204 / 77 x 2,295,000
= 65,691

Adjusted understatement bound = initial bound - point estimate for overstatements

= 89,505 - 65,691
= 23,814

As would be expected, this is very small. Since all misstatements were overstatements, one wouldn't expect a net understatement to occur.

The result of a PPS sample indicate that the accounts receivable balance is overstated by as much as $228,474. This is about 8 percent of the recorded book amount. It is significantly greater than tolerable misstatement, indicating that the population is unacceptable and must be subject to more scrutiny either by the client and/or the auditor.

c. A template for the PPS portion of the problem is prepared using Excel on the Companion Website and on the diskette accompanying this manual. (Filename P1635.XLS.) This template is a complete worksheet for MUS, including appropriate tables for various exception rates and risk levels. You will note that the results are very similar to those computed manually, the differences being due to rounding.

Chapter 17

Audit of the Payroll and Personnel Cycle

■ **Review Questions**

17-1 General ledger accounts that are likely to be affected by the payroll and personnel cycle in most audits include the following:

Cash	Direct labor
Inventory	Salary expense
Construction in progress	Commission expense
Wages payable	Payroll tax expense
Payroll taxes withheld	
Accrued payroll taxes	

17-2 In companies where the payroll is a significant portion of inventory, as in manufacturing and construction companies, the improper account classification of payroll can significantly affect asset valuation for accounts such as work in process, finished goods, and construction in process. For example, if the salaries of administrative personnel are incorrectly charged to indirect manufacturing overhead, the overhead charged to inventory on the balance sheet can be overstated. Similarly, if the indirect labor cost of individual employees is charged to specific jobs or processes, the valuation of inventory is affected if labor is improperly classified. When some jobs are billed on a cost plus basis, revenue and the valuation of inventory are both affected by improperly classifying labor to jobs.

17-3 Five tests of controls that can be performed for the payroll and personnel cycle are:

1. *Examine time card for indication of approval to ensure that payroll payments are properly authorized.* The purpose of this test is to determine that recorded payroll payments are for work actually performed by existing employees (existence).
2. *Account for a sequence of payroll checks to ensure existing payroll payments are recorded.* The purpose of this test is to determine that existing payroll transactions are recorded (completeness).
3. *Examine time cards to ensure that recorded payroll payments are for work actually performed by existing employees.* The purpose of this test is the same as in item 1 above.
4. *Compare postings to the chart of accounts to ensure that payroll transactions are properly classified.* (Classification)
5. *Observe when recording takes place to ensure that payroll transactions are recorded on a timely basis.* (Timing)

17-4 The percentage of total audit time in the cycle devoted to performing tests of controls and substantive tests of transactions is usually far greater in the payroll and personnel cycle than for the sales and collection cycle because there is relatively little independent third party evidence, such as confirmation, to verify the related payroll accounts. In contrast, the accounts related to the sales and collection cycle can usually be verified for the most part by confirmations from customers. In addition, in the sales and collection cycle, verification of the realizability of receivables and sales cutoff tests are important and time consuming tasks.

17-5 The auditor should be concerned with whether the personnel department is following the proper hiring and termination procedures. An obvious reason for this would be to ensure that there are adequate safeguards against hiring and retaining incompetent and untrustworthy people. The ramifications of hiring such people can range from simple inefficiency and waste to outright fraud or theft. More important, though, it is necessary for the auditor to assure himself or herself that the client is hiring and terminating according to operations standards and procedures. It is necessary to see if the internal controls are working as planned before they can be effectively evaluated. To say that the auditor doesn't care who is hired and who is fired is to suggest that he or she doesn't care if the internal controls work according to any standards. Failure to follow proper termination procedures could lead to fraudulent payments for work not performed.

17-6 To trace a random sample of prenumbered time cards to the related payroll checks in the payroll register and compare the hours worked to the hours paid is to test if those employees who worked are being paid for their time actually worked. Employees are likely to inform management if they are not paid, or underpaid. To trace a random sample of payroll checks from the payroll register and compare the hours worked to the hours paid is to test if the recorded payroll payments are for work actually performed by existing employees. This test, in effect, attempts to discover nonexistent employees or duplicate payments, if there are any. For this reason, the second procedure is typically more important to the audit of payroll.

17-7 In auditing payroll withholding and payroll tax expense, the emphasis should normally be on evaluating the adequacy of the payroll tax return preparation procedures rather than the payroll tax liability, because a major reason for misstatements in the liability account is incorrect preparation of the returns in the past. If the preparation procedures are inadequate, and the amounts do not appear reasonable, then the auditor should expand his or her work and recompute the withholding and expense amounts to determine that the proper amount has been accrued. In addition, the auditor should consider the amount of penalties which may be assessed for inadequate withholdings and include these amounts in the accrual if they are significant.

17-8 Several analytical procedures for the payroll and personnel cycle and misstatements which might be indicated by significant fluctuations are as follows:

ANALYTICAL PROCEDURE	MISSTATEMENT TYPES
1. Comparison of payroll expense accounts to amounts in prior years.	Cutoff misstatements or improper amounts recorded in a period.
2. Direct labor divided by sales compared to industry standards in prior years.	Cutoff misstatements or amounts charged to improper payroll accounts.
3. Commission expense divided by sales compared to industry standards, prior years, or sales agreements.	Failure to record commission on sales, or recording the improper commission amount.
4. Payroll tax expense divided by salaries and wages compared to prior year balances adjusted for changes in the tax rate and not including officers' salaries.	Failure to record payroll taxes or recording of the improper amount.
5. Comparison of accrued payroll and payroll tax accounts to prior years.	Failure to record payroll accruals or recording improper amounts at the end of a period.
6. The percentage of labor included in work in process and finished goods inventories compared to prior years.	Use of improper labor standards, or classification misstatements.
7. Analysis of direct labor variances.	Use of improper labor standards, or classification misstatements.

17-9 An auditor should perform audit tests primarily designed to uncover fraud in the payroll and personnel cycle when he or she has determined that internal controls are weak (or the opportunity exists for management to override the internal controls) or when there are other reasons to suspect fraud. Audit procedures that are primarily for the detection of fraud in the payroll and personnel cycle include:

1. Examine cancelled payroll checks for employee name, authorized signature, and proper endorsement (especially for second endorsements) to discover checks going to nonexistent employees. The endorsement should be compared to signatures on W-4 forms.
2. Trace selected transactions recorded in the payroll journal to the personnel department files to determine whether the employees were actually employed during the period.
3. Select several terminated employees from payroll records to determine whether each former employee received his or her termination pay in accordance with company policy and to determine that the employee's pay was discontinued on the date of termination.

17-9 (Continued)
4. Examine the subsequent payroll periods of terminated employees to ascertain that the employees are no longer being paid.
5. Request a surprise payroll payoff to observe if any unclaimed checks result which will necessitate extensive investigation.

17-10 The *Payroll Master File* is maintained for each employee indicating the gross pay for each payment period, deductions from the gross pay, the net pay, the check number, and the date. The purpose of this record is to provide detailed information for federal and state income tax purposes, and to serve as the final record of what each employee was actually paid.

The *W-2 Form* is issued to each employee at the end of each calendar year and indicates his or her gross pay, income taxes withheld, and FICA withheld for the year. In serving as a summary of the employee's earnings record, the W-2 form conveniently provides information necessary for the employee to fill out his or her income tax returns.

A *Payroll Tax Return* is the form required by and submitted to the local, state and federal governments for the payment of withheld taxes and the employer's portion of FICA taxes and state and federal unemployment compensation taxes.

17-11 Where the primary objective is to detect fraud, the auditor will examine the following supporting documents and records:

1. Cancelled payroll checks for employee name, authorized signature and proper endorsement, watching specifically for unusual or recurring second endorsements.
2. Payroll journal, tracing transactions to the personnel files to determine whether the employees were actually employed during the payroll period.
3. Payroll journal and individual payroll records, selecting terminated employees to determine whether each terminated employee received his or her termination pay in accordance with company policy and whether each employee was paid in the subsequent payroll period.
4. Payroll checks, observing each employee as he or she picks up and signs for his or her checks.
5. Time cards, testing them for reasonableness or observing whether they are being punched by the proper employees.

17-12 Types of authorizations in the payroll and personnel cycle are:

1. Deduction authorization, without which the wrong amount (or no deduction) may be deducted from the employee's paycheck.
2. Rate authorizations, without which the employee may be getting paid at the wrong rate.
3. Time card authorization, without which the employee may be getting paid for the wrong quantity of hours worked.
4. Payroll check authorization, without which unauthorized funds may be paid out.
5. Commission rate authorization, without which the salespeople might be improperly compensated for their sales efforts.
6. Authorization to hire a new employee, without which nonexistent or unqualified personnel may be added to the payroll.

17-13 It is common to verify total officers' compensation even when the tests of controls and substantive tests of transactions results in payroll are excellent because the salaries and bonuses of officers must be included in the SEC's 10-K Report and the federal income tax return and because management may be in a position to pay themselves more than the authorized amount, since the controls over the officers' payroll are typically weaker and therefore easier to override than those of the normal payroll.

The usual audit procedure used to verify the officers' compensation is to obtain the authorized salary of each officer from the minutes of the board of directors and compare it to the related earnings record.

17-14 An imprest payroll account is a separate payroll bank account in which a constant balance, either zero or small, is maintained. When a payroll is paid, a check for the exact amount of the net payroll is transferred from the general account to the impressed account. The purpose and advantage of an imprest payroll account is that it limits the company's exposure to payroll fraud by limiting the amount which may be misappropriated.

17-15 Several audit procedures the auditor can use to determine whether recorded payroll transactions are recorded at the proper amount are:

1. Recompute hours worked from time cards.
2. Compare pay rates with union contract, approval by the board of directors, or other source.
3. Recompute gross pay.
4. Check withholdings by reference to tax tables and authorization forms in personnel files.
5. Recompute net pay.
6. Compare cancelled check with payroll journal for amount.

17-16 Attributes sampling can be used in the payroll and personnel cycle in performing tests of controls and substantive tests of transactions with the following objectives:

1. Time card hours agree with payroll computations.
2. Overtime hours are approved.
3. Foreman approves all time cards.
4. Hourly rates agree with personnel files and union contracts.
5. Gross pay calculation is verified.
6. Exemptions taken agree with W-4.
7. Income tax, other deductions, and net pay calculations are verified.
8. Authorizations are available for voluntary withholdings and miscellaneous deductions.
9. Paycheck endorsement is same as signature on W-4 form.

17-16 (Continued)

The frequency of control deviations or monetary errors and irregularities must be estimated prior to performing the tests. This estimate together with the acceptable risk of assessing control risk too low (ARACR) and the tolerable exception rate will enable the auditor to determine the sample size required. Once the tests are performed on the sample, evaluation of the results will indicate whether the exception rate is lower than, equal to, or higher than that anticipated. The auditor must then use this judgment to decide the appropriate action to take.

■ **Multiple Choice Questions From CPA Examinations**

17-17 a. (2)   b. (1)   c. (3)

17-18 a. (1)   b. (1)   c. (4)

■ **Discussion Questions and Problems**

17-19

TRANSACTION-RELATED AUDIT OBJECTIVE	TEST OF CONTROL	POTENTIAL MISSTATEMENT	SUBSTANTIVE AUDIT PROCEDURE
1. Recorded payroll transactions are stated at the proper pay rates (accuracy).	Examine authorizations in personnel files.	Employees are paid the wrong rate.	Compare rates in payroll journal to rates in personnel files.
2. Recorded payroll transactions exist (existence).	Examine personnel files for termination notices.	Employees are improperly terminated and payment continues.	Compare termination dates from personnel files to date of last paycheck.
3. Hours worked are correctly recorded (accuracy).	Examine time cards and observe preparation.	Incorrect recording of time.	Randomly sample workers and trace to time cards for hours worked.
4. Recorded payroll payments are for work actually performed by existing employees (existence).	Examine time cards for approval.	Incorrect times are used in computing employees' pay.	Analyze payroll records of a sample of employees for reasonableness.

17-19 (Continued)

TRANSACTION-RELATED AUDIT OBJECTIVE	TEST OF CONTROL	POTENTIAL MISSTATEMENT	SUBSTANTIVE AUDIT PROCEDURE
5. Recorded payroll transactions are for proper rate and amount (accuracy).	Examine payroll journal for indication of internal verification.	Employees pay is miscalculated.	Recompute employees' pay, compare pay rates to personnel files, and hours worked to time cards.
6. Time records are properly classified by job (classification).	Examine system of identifying jobs by number.	Direct labor is charged to wrong jobs.	Trace entries to job summaries to time cards, job cards, etc.
7. Recorded payroll checks are for work performed by existing employees (existence).	Observe and discuss payroll system with employees.	Payroll payments are made to nonexistent employees.	Trace payroll checks to employees, to determine if employee exists.
8. Payments are made to actual employees (existence).	Observe payments and discuss with employees.	Payments are made to wrong employees.	Examine cancelled checks for endorsements, and compare to personnel file.
9. Recorded payroll transactions are for work performed by existing employees (existence).	Observe distribution of paychecks and recording of unclaimed wages.	Unclaimed paychecks are cashed by the wrong people.	Examine cancelled checks for endorsements, and compare to personnel file.

TYPE OF TEST	TRANSACTION-RELATED AUDIT OBJECTIVE(S)
1. Substantive test of transactions	To determine if monthly payroll costs have been correctly allocated (accuracy).
2. Test of control	To determine if recorded payroll transactions are for work actually performed by existing employees (existence).
3. Substantive test of transactions	To determine if employees are paid for the hours they have worked (accuracy).
4. Substantive test of transactions	To determine if the appropriate person is paid and amount and time are correct (accuracy and timing).
5. Substantive test of transactions	To determine if the correct job is charged for labor and if the amount is recorded correctly for each job (classification and accuracy).
6. Test of control	To determine if all payroll checks are recorded (completeness).
7. Substantive test of transactions	To determine whether terminated employees were subsequently paid for work not performed (existence). To determine whether an obligation may exist for unpaid severance pay (completeness).

17-21

RECOMMENDED CONTROL	SUBSTANTIVE AUDIT PROCEDURE
1. Internal verification of classification.	Trace labor distribution to supporting job input forms.
2. Approval of time cards by foreman and observation of use of time clock by the foreman.	Observe employees punching in—only one card per employee—to see whether any employee punches two cards (normally not an effective or practical audit procedure).
3. Paychecks distributed by someone other than the foreman.	Perform payroll payoff, requiring identification from all employees prior to payment.
4. Pay employees only for time charged to jobs. Reconcile payroll expense to amounts charged to jobs.	Compare total hours worked from payroll journal to total hours worked as recorded on job cost tickets.
5. Payroll checks not returned to payroll clerk after signing.	Perform payoff as described in 3 above.
6. Internal verification of calculations and amounts.	Recompute federal withholding taxes and trace to employee earnings record.
7. Payroll checks are prenumbered and accounted for. Use an imprest bank account where the amount to be deposited is taken from the payroll journal.	Reconcile the disbursements in the payroll journal to the disbursements on the payroll bank statement.

17-22

	TYPE OF TEST	APPLICABLE TRANSACTION-RELATED OR BALANCE-RELATED AUDIT OBJECTIVE(S)
1.	(1)	Accuracy.
2.	(4)	Detail tie-in.
3.	(1)	Completeness.
4.	(2)	Posting and summarization.
5.	(4)	Completeness, accuracy and cutoff.
6.	(2)	Existence, timing and accuracy.
7.	(3)	N/A
8.	(1)	Accuracy.
9.	(3)	N/A
10.	(4)	Completeness.
11.	(3)	N/A
12.	(1)/(2) (1), (2) (if totals are compared)	Existence and accuracy (if totals are compared).

17-23 A flowchart of steps for each type of test is given below (requirements a, b, and c):

TESTS OF CONTROLS OR SUBSTANTIVE TESTS OF TRANSACTIONS	TESTS OF DETAILS OF BALANCES
6	2
5	9
3	7
8	4
	1

17-10

17-24 a. Brendin's approach to determining why this year's payroll tax expense was so high suffers from two serious deficiencies: First, it lacks relevance, and second, it is too narrowly focused. The approach lacks relevance in that he is testing payroll *withholding* which is not the same as payroll tax expense. Some payroll taxes are related to withholding such as FICA, but income tax withheld does not give rise to an expense, and certain payroll taxes, such as unemployment compensation, are not withheld. The approach is too narrowly focussed in that the analytical test results could have resulted from a misstatement of the payroll itself; Brendin does not appear to be considering this possibility.

b. A more suitable approach for determining whether payroll tax was properly stated in the current year would be to evaluate the reasonableness of the total payroll, reconcile the payroll to amounts shown on payroll tax reports, and check computations as shown on those reports for reasonableness.

17-25 The following audit procedures should be used to verify the payroll related accounts:

1. Accrued payroll:
   a. Review the company's policy for computing the accrual and whether it is consistent with the prior year.
   b. Assess whether 60 percent is a reasonable approximation of the portion of the subsequent payroll application to the current year.
   c. Test the subsequent payroll for cutoff and accuracy.
   d. Determine that the computation of the accrual is correct.
2. Withheld payroll taxes:
   a. Compare the balance in the liability account with the payroll journal.
   b. Reconcile the amount to subsequent payroll tax reports and cash disbursed.
   c. Review in light of the subsequent period's payroll.
3. Accrued payroll taxes:
   a. Trace FICA withheld from payroll journal to payroll tax reports.
   b. Review amounts on payroll tax reports for reasonableness.
   c. Reconcile accruals to payroll tax reports.
   d. Examine subsequent cash disbursed.

17-26 a. The purpose of a surprise payroll payoff is to determine whether or not nonexistent personnel are included in the payroll.

b. Procedures other than a surprise payroll payoff that can be used to discover nonexistent employees are:

1. Examine cancelled payroll checks for employee name, authorized signature, and proper endorsement which agrees with the employee's signed W-4 form.
2. Select several terminated employees from payroll records to determine whether each former employee received his or her termination pay in accordance with company policy and was not paid in subsequent payrolls.

17-26 (Continued)

c. When the payroll payoff is taking place, the client should observe these control procedures:

1. All employees must prove identity.
2. Unclaimed paychecks must be further investigated. Unclaimed paychecks might be accounted for by employees who are sick or on vacation. After all present employees have received their checks, the remaining paychecks should be traced to the personnel files to determine if these employees were ever employed by the client. Thereafter, if practical, the remaining checks should be held until the employees can be present with proper identification to claim the check.

d. See c.2 above.

17-27 a.

WEAKNESSES	LIKELY MISSTATEMENTS
1. The foreman has the ability to hire employees and enter their names into the pay system with no other approval.	Nonexistent or incompetent employees may be hired at the foreman's option.
2. The foreman may make changes to salary rates without approval of company management.	Employees or nonexistent employees may be paid at rates which are higher than their skill warrants.
3. No investigation of new employees to determine background experience and dependability is performed.	Dishonest or unqualified employees may be hired.
4. No control exists over time cards and the completion thereof.	Employees may report and be paid for time that they did not work.
5. No review or internal verification of the amount on the payroll checks is performed.	Misstatements made by the payroll clerks in favor of employees would likely not be discovered.
6. Payroll checks are not prenumbered or controlled by the payroll clerks.	The chief accountant could prepare, sign, and cash an extra payroll check without detection.

The emphasis in the audit of payroll for Kowal should be the determination that payroll is properly computed, that employees who are paid exist and have worked the time reported, and that employees have no previous experience which would indicate that they are dishonest. To accomplish these objectives, the following tests will be performed:

17-27 (Continued)

1. Clerical tests of the correct input of payroll hours.
2. A payroll payoff performed under the supervision of the auditor.
3. A sample of the personnel working at certain times during the day compared to the times reported for that period.
4. Investigation of a sample of employees to determine that their previous experience and training qualifies them for their present duties and they have no previous history of dishonesty.

b. The following changes may be made to improve the Kowal Manufacturing Company's internal control over payroll procedures:

1. A system of advice forms should be installed so that hirings, terminations, rate changes, etc., are reported to the payroll department in writing. Such forms should be approved by the foreman's superior.
2. Before an applicant is hired, his or her background should be investigated by contacting references to determine that he or she is not dishonest and has no other undesirable personal characteristics.
3. The supply of blank time cards should be removed. At the beginning of each week the payroll department should provide each worker with a time card stamped with his or her name.
4. A time clock should be installed and the workers required to punch in and out. A responsible employee should be stationed at the time clock to determine that workers are not punching the time cards of other workers who may be late or absent, or who may have left work early.
5. The foreman should collect the time cards at the end of the week, approve them, and turn them over to the payroll clerk. All time cards should be accounted for and any missing cards investigated.
6. If the company has a cost system that requires the workers to prepare production reports or to account for their time by work tickets, the time cards and the production reports or work tickets should be compared.
7. The payroll clerks' work should be arranged so that they check each other. Under the existing system of computing the payroll, the clerk who does not do the original computing should check the original work of the other clerk.
8. The payroll checks should be prenumbered to control their issuance.
9. The payroll checks should be distributed to the workers by a responsible person other than the foreman. Unclaimed checks should be held in safekeeping by the payroll department until claimed by the worker.
10. A responsible person other than the chief accountant and the payroll clerks should reconcile the payroll bank account.
11. From time to time an officer of the company should witness a payroll distribution on a surprise basis.

17-28 a. An audit program to verify sales commission expense is as follows:

1. Select a sample of office copies of sales invoices.
   a. Check commissions rate to commissions rate file.
   b. Check computation of sales commissions.
   c. Examine invoices for internal verification by accounts receivable clerk.
   d. Trace sales commission amounts to sales commission ledger.
2. Foot the sales commission ledger for one or more months, and trace the total to the general ledger.
3. Compare totals for periods in the sales commission ledger to period balances of sales commission expense.

b. An audit program to verify accrued sales commissions is:

1. Compare the accrual with that of the previous year. Investigate any significant change.
2. Compare the amount of commissions paid to the salesmen on the fifteenth of the month following year-end to the total accrued commissions at year-end. Obtain a reconciliation and explanation for any reconciling items.
3. Send confirmations to salesmen for the larger amounts of accrued commissions and a sample of the smaller amounts.

17-29 a. Mr. Brown's internal controls do not provide proper control of unclaimed wages. Commingling different funds weakens internal control because the custodian can cover up shortages by interfund cash transfers or other manipulations.

Furthermore, with no accountability for unclaimed wages, the custodian might take them and state they were paid to the wage earner.

The extent of responsibility that is vested in the custodian and other duties assigned to him are worthy of further consideration by the auditor. For example, does he participate in payroll preparation? Handle cash receipts?

b. Better internal control over unclaimed wages can be provided by modifying the payroll and accounting procedures. The payroll envelopes showing the employee's name and payroll details should be provided by the payroll department. Insertion of cash in the envelopes should be by a person other than the individual computing the payroll. The envelopes should be compared to the payroll records for details. All handling of payroll cash should be by persons whose duties are separate from petty cash or cash receipt functions.

Preferably, the distribution of envelopes to employees should be in the presence of a third party. Each employee should sign a receipt for his or her envelope. Unclaimed envelopes should be turned over to Mr. Brown or another responsible person at once.

17-29 (Continued)

At regular intervals the unclaimed wages should be deposited in the general cash account and an unclaimed wages account should be established as a current liability. Payment of any unclaimed wages from this account should require proper authorization. After a specified period the unclaimed wages should be returned to income or, if legally required, paid to the state.

The petty cash fund should be maintained on an imprest basis and, to lessen the number of reimbursements, consideration should be given to increasing the size of the fund.

17-30 a. To select a comprehensive sample representative of the whole payroll, the auditor should consider the following factors:

1. Quality of internal control.
2. Planned assessed control risk.
3. Number of departments (consider departmental wage rates).
4. Frequency of payrolls.
5. Total number of employees.
6. Types, functions and job classifications.

17-30 (Continued)

b.

COLUMN NUMBER	MEANS OF VERIFICATION
1, 2, & 3	Employment record maintained in personnel department.
4 & 5	Clock cards, time tickets, or timekeeper's report.
6	Union contract or personnel department.
7	1) Reference to union contract for premium time provision. 2) Extension of Column 6 x (Column 4 + Column 5).
8	1) Reference to employee earnings record to determine whether employee is subject to tax. 2) Extension of current rate x taxable portion of current earnings.
9	1) Reference to employee signed W-4 card for number of exemptions claimed. 2) Reference to an income tax withheld table.
10, 11 & 12	Employee signed withholding authorization.
13	Column 7 less Column 8, 9, 10, 11, and 12.
14	1) Review check numbers for sequence.
15 & 16	1) Trace gross amount of earnings to account posting in the general ledger on a sample basis. 2) From the job description indicated, determine the reasonableness of the account charged. (An example of unreasonableness would be: Job Classification--Sweeper; Account charged--Machine maintenance.)

c. Additional audit procedures that must be performed:

1. Examine check for alterations.
2. Compare name on payroll and payee.
3. Compare amounts paid.
4. Examine endorsements, paying careful attention to unusual second endorsements.
5. Compare signature on endorsement with signature on W-4 statement, looking for obvious differences.
6. Test payroll record footings and postings.
7. Reconcile the total payroll with tax reports.

17-30 (Continued)
8. Verify unclaimed wages.
9. Verify accrued wages and salaries.
10. Observe and perform a distribution of the payroll.
11. Perform payroll tests on salaried payroll and/or officers' salaries.
12. Verify liability for employee withholding (federal income tax, employee portion of FICA, union dues withheld, etc.)
13. Verify reconciliation of payroll bank accounts.
14. Reconcile labor distribution cost records and payroll.

17-31 a. Conventional forms and documents in a payroll system include the following:

- Personnel records
- Deduction authorization forms
- Rate authorization forms
- Time cards and job time tickets
- Payroll checks
- Payroll journal and labor distribution
- Earnings record
- W-2 form
- Payroll tax returns

In using the computer service center, it appears that there is no loss in documentation in substance; however, the *earnings record* is not printed out each pay period, thus, the current version is usually in *machine readable form*. (This assumes that authorization forms exist although they are not discussed in the case.) The fact that the earnings record is in magnetic form is not a problem, as long as the service bureau has adequate backup and recovery controls.

The above analysis reflects the fact that Leggert's internal controls in the payroll area are generally good. There is good segregation of duties between the President and Clark, assuming both are trustworthy, honest people. Procedures, forms, records, and reports are comprehensive and well-designed.

The only potential weakness in internal control is that errors in details could be made by the service bureau and not necessarily be caught. It is difficult to imagine that these would be material.

17-31 (Continued)

b.

PAYROLL TRANSACTION-RELATED AUDIT OBJECTIVE	PROCEDURES	TYPE OF PROCEDURE
1. Recorded payroll payments are for work performed by existing employees (existence).	a. Observe existence of personnel files in President's care.	Test of control
	b. Observe use of time clock and control of time cards by clerk.	Test of control
	c. Examine time cards for President's approval.	Test of control
	d. Observe distribution of payroll checks by President.	Test of control
	e. Examine cancelled checks for proper endorsement.	Substantive test of transactions
	f. Compare cancelled checks with personnel records.	Substantive test of transactions
	g. Examine cancelled check for President's signature.	Test of control
2. Existing payroll transactions are recorded (completeness).	a. Account for the numerical sequence of payroll checks.	Test of control and substantive test of transactions
	b. Observe preparation of payroll bank reconciliation by President.	Test of control
3. Recorded payroll transactions are for the amount of time actually worked and at the proper pay rate; withholdings are properly calculated (accuracy).	a. Observe the use of the time clock and control time cards by Clark.	Test of control
	b. Observe Clark rechecking hours.	Test of control
	c. Recompute gross pay, deductions and net pay.	Substantive test of transactions
	d. Trace rates and authorizations to personnel file.	Substantive test of transactions
	e. Examine payroll journal for approval by Clark.	Test of control
	f. Compare rates in payroll journal with personnel files to determine that rate actually paid is authorized.	Substantive test of transactions

17-31 (Continued)

PAYROLL TRANSACTION-RELATED AUDIT OBJECTIVE	PROCEDURES	TYPE OF PROCEDURE
4. Payroll transactions are properly classified (classification).	a. Review chart of accounts. b. Examine payroll journal for approval by Clark. c. Compare classification with chart of accounts or procedures manual.	Test of control Test of control Substantive test of transactions
5. Payroll transactions are recorded on the correct dates (timing).	a. Observe collection and processing of time cards by Clark. b. Examine payroll journal for approval by Clark. c. Observe posting of ledger by Clark. d. Observe preparation of payroll bank reconciliation by President. e. Compare date of check recorded in payroll journal with date on cancelled checks and time cards.	Test of control Test of control Test of control Test of control Substantive test of transactions
6. Payroll transactions are properly included in the employee earnings record; they are properly summarized.	a. Observe re-adding of payroll journal and posting by clerk. b. Examine payroll journal for approval by Clark. c. Observe posting of ledger by Clark. d. Trace postings from payroll journal to general ledger.	Test of control Test of control Test of control Substantive test of transactions

    c. Procedures in performance format:

       1. Make observations of the following activities by Mary Clark:
          a) Control, collection and processing of time cards.
          b) Rechecking of hours on time cards.
          c) Processing and approval of payroll journal.
          d) Posting of general ledger.
       2. Make observations of the following activities by the President:
          a) Maintenance of personnel files.
          b) Distribution of pay checks.
          c) Processing and approval of payroll journal.
          d) Posting of general ledger.

17-31 (Continued)

       3. Make observations of the following general matters and activities:
          a) Use of time clock by employees.
          b) Existence and use of adequate chart of accounts.
       4. Select a sample of payroll check numbers and:
          a) Account for existence and recording of pay checks.
          b) Examine pay checks for President's signature.
          c) Examine checks for proper endorsement.
          d) Compare cancelled checks with personnel records.
          e) Compare date on check with date recorded in payroll journal and on the time card.
       5. Select a sample of payroll entries from the payroll journal and perform the following steps:
          a) Obtain time cards, examine for President's approval, and trace hours to payroll journal.
          b) Examine personnel files and authorization for rates and deductions.
          c) Recompute gross pay, deductions, and net pay.
          d) Compare account classification with chart of accounts or procedures manual.
       6. Select a sample of payroll journals and perform the following steps:
          a) Examine payroll journal for approval by Clark.
          b) Trace postings to general ledger.

d. A sampling data sheet follows. Note that this sampling data sheet was prepared using attributes sampling. The only difference between this approach and a nonstatistical approach is the determination of sample size. Under nonstatistical sampling, students' sample sizes will vary.

17-31 (Continued)

DESCRIPTION OF ATTRIBUTES	PLANNED AUDIT EPER*	TER**	ARACR**	INITIAL SAMPLE SIZE***
1. Payroll check number accounted for	0%	5%	5%	59
2. Payroll check signed by President	0%	4%	5%	74
3. Time card approved by President	1%	6%	5%	78
4. Time card hours agree with payroll journal	1%	6%	5%	78
5. Personnel file is complete	0%	6%	5%	49
6. Pay rate and deductions supported by authorization	1%	4%	5%	156
7. Gross pay, deductions, and net pay correctly computed	0%	5%	5%	59

* These amounts are arbitrary to complete data sheet. Information to determine actual appropriate amounts is not given in problem.
** These amounts are judgments and are not the only acceptable amounts.
*** Determined from attributes sampling tables.

Chapter 18

Audit of the Acquisition and Payment Cycle: Tests of Controls, Substantive Tests of Transactions, and Accounts Payable

■ **Review Questions**

18-1 a. Asset accounts:

- Office supplies
- Delivery equipment
- Machinery and equipment
- Land
- Cash in bank
- Prepaid expenses

b. Liability accounts:

- Accounts payable
- Accrued property taxes
- Accrued insurance
- Other accrued liabilities

c. Expense accounts:

- Purchases, purchase returns & allowances, purchases discounts (COGS accounts)
- Rent expense
- Legal expense
- Fines and penalties
- Advertising expense
- Repairs and maintenance
- Depreciation expense
- Utilities expense
- Property tax expense
- Administrative expenses
- Income tax expense

TRANSACTION-RELATED AUDIT OBJECTIVE	POSSIBLE INTERNAL CONTROLS	COMMON TESTS OF CONTROLS
1. Recorded cash disbursements are for goods and services actually received (existence).	■ There is adequate segregation of duties between accounts payable and custody of signed checks. ■ Supporting documentation is examined before signing of checks by an authorized person. ■ Approval of payment on supporting documents at the time checks are signed.	■ Discuss with personnel and observe activities. ■ Discuss with personnel and observe activities. ■ Examine indication of approval.
2. Existing cash disbursement transactions are recorded (completeness).	■ Checks are pre-numbered and accounted for. ■ The bank reconciliation is prepared monthly by an employee independent of recording cash disbursements or custody of assets.	■ Account for a sequence of checks. ■ Examine bank reconciliations and observe their preparation.
3. Recorded cash disbursement transactions are accurate (accuracy).	■ Calculations and amounts are internally verified. ■ The bank reconciliation is prepared monthly by an independent person.	■ Examine indication of internal verification. ■ Examine bank reconciliations and observe their preparation.
4. Cash disbursement transactions are properly classified (classification).	■ An adequate chart of accounts is used. ■ Account classifications are internally verified.	■ Examine procedures manual and chart of accounts. ■ Examine indication of internal verification.

TRANSACTION-RELATED AUDIT OBJECTIVE	POSSIBLE INTERNAL CONTROLS	COMMON TESTS OF CONTROLS
5. Cash disbursement transactions are recorded on the correct dates (timing).	■ Procedures require recording of transactions as soon as possible after the check has been signed. ■ Dates are internally verified.	■ Examine procedures manual and observe whether unrecorded checks exist. ■ Examine indication of internal verification.
6. Cash disbursement transactions are properly included in the accounts payable master file and are properly summarized (posting and summarization).	■ Accounts payable master file contents are internally verified. ■ Accounts payable master file or trial balance totals are compared with general ledger balances.	■ Examine indication of internal verification. ■ Examine initials on general ledger accounts indicating comparison.

18-3

TRANSACTION-RELATED AUDIT OBJECTIVE	POSSIBLE INTERNAL CONTROLS	COMMON TESTS OF CONTROLS
1. Recorded acquisitions are for goods and services received, consistent with the best interests of the client (existence).	■ Purchase requisition, purchase order, receiving report, and vendor's invoice are attached to the voucher. ■ Acquisitions are approved at the proper level. ■ Computer accepts entry of purchases only from authorized vendors in the vendor master file. ■ Documents are cancelled to prevent their reuse. ■ Vendors' invoices, receiving reports, purchase orders, and purchase requisitions are internally verified.	■ Examine documents in voucher package for existence. ■ Examine indication of approval. ■ Attempt to input transactions with valid and invalid vendors. ■ Examine indication of cancellation. ■ Examine indication of internal verification.

TRANSACTION-RELATED AUDIT OBJECTIVE	POSSIBLE INTERNAL CONTROLS	COMMON TESTS OF CONTROLS
2. Existing acquisition transactions are recorded (completeness).	■ Purchase orders are prenumbered and accounted for. ■ Receiving reports are prenumbered and accounted for. ■ Vouchers are prenumbered and accounted for.	■ Account for a sequence of purchase orders. ■ Account for a sequence of receiving reports. ■ Account for a sequence of vouchers.
3. Recorded acquisition transactions are accurate (accuracy).	■ Calculations and amounts are internally verified. ■ Batch totals are compared with computer summary reports. ■ Acquisitions are approved for prices and discounts.	■ Examine indication of internal verification. ■ Examine file of batch totals for initials of data control clerk; compare totals to summary reports. ■ Examine indication of approval.
4. Acquisition transactions are properly classified (classification).	■ Adequate chart of accounts is used. ■ Account classifications are internally verified.	■ Examine procedures manual and chart of accounts. ■ Examine indication of internal verification.
5. Acquisition transactions are recorded on the correct dates (timing).	■ Procedures require recording transactions as soon as possible after the goods and services have been received. ■ Dates are internally verified.	■ Examine procedures manual and observe whether unrecorded vendors' invoices exist. ■ Examine indication of internal verification.
6. Acquisition transactions are properly included in the accounts payable and inventory master files, and are properly summarized (posting and summarization).	■ Accounts payable master file contents are internally verified. ■ Accounts payable master file or trial balance totals are compared with general ledger balances.	■ Examine indication of internal verification. ■ Examine initials on general ledger accounts indicating comparison.

18-4 Auditing standards require that the tests of controls and substantive tests of transactions cover the entire accounting period in order to determine that the system was operating in a consistent manner throughout the period. In selecting the number of items for testing, the auditor must determine the sample size, statistically or nonstatistically, such that it is likely to be representative of the actual conditions of the population of all transactions.

In testing items which are periodic procedures rather than individual transactions (such as monthly bank reconciliations), the auditor must determine the appropriate timing to determine that those procedures are operating properly.

18-5 The importance of cash discounts to the client is that the client can produce a substantial savings if it makes use of the cash discounts available. The auditor should examine vouchers and invoices to determine whether discounts are being taken in accordance with the terms available.

18-6 The difference in the purpose of the steps is that Procedure 1 ascertains whether all existing acquisitions are recorded properly (completeness and accuracy), whereas Procedure 2 is designed to determine whether recorded acquisitions are proper (existence and accuracy). Although the two procedures test opposite objectives (completeness and existence), they are similar in that each is designed to determine that the vendor's name, type of material and quantity purchased, and total amount of the acquisition agree with the receiving report, vendor's invoice, and acquisitions journal entries.

18-7 It is difficult to control blank or voided checks (as well as checks issued before they are mailed) without having a printed prenumbered system of blank checks. Without prenumbering, unauthorized and unrecorded checks may be more easily issued without detection until after they have cleared the bank. The auditor can compensate for poor control over checks by reconciling recorded cash disbursements with cash disbursements on the bank statement for a test period.

18-8 A voucher is a document used by an organization to establish a formal means of recording and controlling acquisitions. A voucher register is a journal for recording the vouchers for the acquisition of goods and services. The use of a voucher system improves control over the recording of purchases by facilitating the recording in numerical order at the earliest possible date, the point at which the invoice is received.

18-9 The point at which goods and services are received is ordinarily when title to the goods and services passes and a liability that should be included in the financial statements is established.

18-10 The acquisition and payment cycle is related to the inventory accounts in that normally all purchases of raw materials in the case of a manufacturing operation or merchandise in the case of a distribution company are recorded through this cycle. If the tests of internal controls of the acquisition and payment cycle indicate that proper controls exist to ensure that the proper cost is used in valuing the inventory and that new purchases of inventory are recorded at the proper time, in the proper amount, and in the proper account, tests concerned with the accuracy and cutoff of the inventory accounts may be reduced from that level required if the controls were not adequate.

18-11 The acquisition and payment cycle includes the recording of liabilities that are set up in the accounts payable account. If the auditor finds that the internal controls in the acquisition and payment cycle are sufficient to ensure that accounts payable are recorded in the proper amount and at the proper time, reconciling the vendors' statements and testing the cutoff as year-end procedures of the accounts payable balance may be greatly reduced.

18-12 The procedure will most likely uncover the misstatement in item b. The search for unrecorded invoices is designed to detect an understatement of accounts payable.

18-13 Unless evidence is discovered which indicates that a different approach should be followed, auditors traditionally follow a conservative approach in selecting vendors for accounts payable confirmations and customers for accounts receivable confirmations. The auditor assumes that the client is more likely to understate accounts payable, and therefore concentrates on the vendors with whom the client deals actively, especially if that vendor's balance appears to be lower than normal on the client's accounts payable listing at the confirmation date. In verifying accounts receivable, the auditor assumes that the client is more likely to overstate account balances; and for that reason concentrates more on the larger dollar balances and is not as concerned with "zero balances."

18-14 A vendor's invoice is sent with or at the same time as the order and states the amount of goods shipped, the price, and other details. This is the vendor's bill for the goods shipped. A vendor's statement contains the individual open items and the ending balance due in the account. A vendor's statement is not as meaningful as an invoice to verify individual transactions because a statement includes only the total amount of the transactions and not the details making up the shipment, such as unit price and freight. The vendor's statement can be used to verify the correct balance in accounts payable for an individual vendor. The statement contains the ending balance and the individual transactions required to reconcile the accounts payable listings and determine the propriety of the balances shown for individual vendors.

18-15 There are several reasons why it is not as common to confirm accounts payable at an interim date as accounts receivable:

- Less reliance is placed on accounts payable systems than accounts receivable systems for most audits. For accounts payable, it is common to rely heavily on the search for unrecorded accounts payable to test the balance. When control risk is assessed at the maximum, it is inappropriate to confirm at an interim date.
- In auditing accounts payable, it is common for the auditor to confirm only those accounts for which there are not vendors' statements available in the client's hands at year-end. Hence, the auditor will not know which accounts will be confirmed until the end of the year.
- Accounts payable confirmation is usually a less important and less time consuming task than confirmation of receivables; therefore, it is less important to perform the accounts payable early for purposes of reducing year-end audit time.

18-16 It is important that the cutoff of accounts payable be coordinated with that of the physical inventory to determine that they are established at the same point in time. If these cutoffs are not consistent, goods may be counted in the physical inventory for which no liability in accounts payable has been recorded, or vice versa. Such a situation would result in an understatement of accounts payable and cost of goods sold or an overstatement of these two accounts, respectively. During the physical inventory, the auditor should gather cutoff information (such as the last several receiving reports and shipping documents) to assist in the determination that an accurate cutoff was established.

18-17 F.O.B. destination means that the title to the goods passes when they are received by the purchaser. F.O.B. origin signifies that the title passes to the buyer when the goods are shipped by the seller.

The auditor should be aware that the client may receive inventory subsequent to year-end that legally was the property of the client at year-end. When receiving reports near year-end are being examined and tested in connection with inventory cutoff tests, the auditor should search for goods that were shipped prior to year-end F.O.B. origin and received after the closing date. Examination of bills of lading will substantiate the date of shipment.

■ Multiple Choice Questions From CPA Examinations

18-18 a. (3)   b. (4)   c. (4)

18-19 a. (4)   b. (3)   c. (3)

■ Discussion Questions and Problems

18-20

QUESTION	a. TRANSACTION-RELATED AUDIT OBJECTIVE(S)	b. TEST OF CONTROL	c. POTENTIAL MISSTATEMENT(S)	d. SUBSTANTIVE PROCEDURE
1	Recorded acquisitions and payments are for goods and services received, consistent with the best interests of the client (existence).	Observe and inquire about personnel performing purchasing, shipping, payables and disbursing functions.	Goods received and not recorded or recorded and not received. Disbursements made for goods not received.	Vendor statement reconciliation. Review of physical inventory shortages.

18-20 (Continued)

QUESTION	a. TRANSACTION-RELATED AUDIT OBJECTIVE(S)	b. TEST OF CONTROL	c. POTENTIAL MISSTATEMENT(S)	d. SUBSTANTIVE PROCEDURE
2	Acquisitions are recorded on the correct dates (timing). Existing acquisitions are recorded (completeness).	Observe and inquire about the procedure performed by mail clerk. Compare date mail is received to date accounting received invoices.	Late recording or non-recording of liabilities to suppliers.	Vendor statement reconciliation. Search for unrecorded liabilities.
3	Existing acquisitions are recorded (completeness).	Account for numerical sequence of receiving reports and determine that all were recorded.	Receiving reports are misplaced and acquisitions not recorded.	Vendor statement reconciliation.
4	Acquisitions are recorded at the proper amounts (accuracy).	Examine cancelled invoices for indication of checking for clerical accuracy.	Acquisitions from vendors are recorded at improper amounts.	Test extensions, footings, discounts, and freight terms on vendors' invoices.
5	Acquisition transactions are properly classified (classification).	Examine indication of approval.	Acquisitions are recorded in the wrong account.	Examine supporting invoice for reasonableness of accounting distribution.
6	Payments are recorded on the correct dates (timing). Existing payments are recorded (completeness).	Observe whether the system automatically posts checks when they are prepared.	Checks are disbursed and not recorded.	Examine checks clearing the bank prior to year-end to determine that they were recorded in the cash disbursements journal prior to year-end.

18-8

18-20 (Continued)

QUESTION	a. TRANSACTION-RELATED AUDIT OBJECTIVE(S)	b. TEST OF CONTROL	c. POTENTIAL MISSTATEMENT(S)	d. SUBSTANTIVE PROCEDURE
7	Acquisitions are for goods and services received, consistent with the best interests of the client (existence).	Examine invoices for which checks have been disbursed to determine that they have been cancelled.	Invoices are recorded and paid more than once.	Examine vendor statements, noting any unrecorded payments appearing on the statement.
8	Recorded cash disbursements are for goods and services actually received (existence).	Observe and inquire about the handling of checks from the time they are mailed to suppliers.	Checks are disbursed and no merchandise is received. Checks are received by other than the supplier for whom they are intended.	Trace checks to supporting invoice and determine reasonableness of expenditure. Reconcile vendors' statements.

18-21

QUESTION	a. TYPE OF TEST	b. PURPOSE OF PROCEDURE
1	Both (test of authorization is a test of control)	■ To determine that the amount recorded in the acquisitions journal is correct (accuracy). ■ To determine that recorded purchases are for goods and services actually received (existence).
2	Both (accounting for sequence is a test of control)	■ To determine that all receiving reports were eventually entered into the system as liabilities (completeness). ■ To determine that acquisitions were recorded at the proper amounts, considering the goods received (accuracy).
3	Substantive test of transactions	To determine that the amount recorded is accurate, that the classification is proper, and that the acquisition is for goods and services received, consistent with the best interests of the company (accuracy, classification and existence).
4	Test of control	To determine that the vendors' invoices are approved for payment, and that receiving reports and purchase orders are all attached (existence).
5	Substantive test of transactions	To determine that postings to the cash disbursements journal are properly summarized and posted to the general ledger and are posted to the accounts payable master file (posting and summarization).
6	Test of control	To determine that all check numbers are included to the cash disbursements journal, no check number is included more than once and voided checks are accounted for (completeness and existence).
7	Substantive test of transactions	To determine that the proper amount of cash disbursements are recorded during the test month. Checks are not recorded more than once and checks are not omitted (accuracy, existence and completeness).
8	Substantive test of transactions	To determine that checks are recorded on the correct dates (timing).

18-10

18-22

MISSTATE-MENT	TRANSACTION-RELATED AUDIT OBJECTIVE NOT MET	PREVENTIVE CONTROL	SUBSTANTIVE PROCEDURE
1	Acquisition transactions are properly classified (classification).	Account distributions are reviewed by a responsible individual prior to entry into the system.	Examination of supporting invoices for entries into the repairs and maintenance account to verify the proper account distribution.
2	Acquisition transactions are recorded on the correct dates (timing).	Receiving reports to be delivered to accounting at the end of the day on which the raw materials are received. Accounting department accounts for numerical sequence of receiving reports after obtaining the last number used from receiving personnel.	At the date on which the cutoff test is to be performed, the auditor obtains the number of the last receiving report(s) that should have been recorded and accounts for the numerical sequence of all previous receiving report(s) which should have been recorded.
3	Recorded cash disbursements are for goods and services actually received (existence).	Once checks are signed by the treasurer, they are returned to someone independent of purchasing and accounts payable for mailing. All supporting documents are cancelled to prevent reuse.	Review physical inventory shortages for unusual or inconsistent occurrences. Compare payee on the check to the company name on the vendor's invoice.

18-22 (Continued)

MISSTATE-MENT	TRANSACTION-RELATED AUDIT OBJECTIVE NOT MET	PREVENTIVE CONTROL	SUBSTANTIVE PROCEDURE
4	Recorded cash disbursement transactions are correctly stated (accuracy).	Checks are prepared using a computer process which assures simultaneous preparation of check and journal. Reconcile bank account on a timely basis at the end of each month.	Compare check amounts to entries in the cash disbursements journal. Test bank reconciliation.
5	Cash disbursement transactions are recorded on the correct dates (timing).	Transactions are recorded automatically using a computer process with the same information as the check preparation.	Trace last checks written to cash disbursements journal. Examine date checks cancelled at bank to determine if checks were held by the client.
6	Recorded acquisitions are for goods and services received, consistent with the best interests of the client (existence).	Require that an authorized purchase order and/or approval of each invoice by the ordering department head be required before payments are made for goods received.	Examine underlying documents for reasonableness and authenticity.

18-12

18-23 a. The type of audit evidence used for each procedure is as follows:

AUDIT PROCEDURE	TYPE OF AUDIT EVIDENCE
1	Internal and external documentation.
2	Analytical procedure.
3	Internal documentation.
4	External documentation (exchange rate); reperformance.
5	Inquiries of client.
6	External documentation.
7	Confirmation.
8	Reperformance.

b.

AUDIT PROCEDURE	Detail tie-in	Existence	Completeness	Accuracy	Classification	Cutoff	Obligations	Presentation and disclosure
1			X			X		
2		X	X			X		
3					X			X
4				X				
5					X			X
6		X	X	X		X		
7		X	X	X		X		
8	X							

Note: Rights and Realizable value are not applicable to accounts payable.

18-23 (Continued)

    c. Generally accepted auditing standards require that all audit objectives be met by gathering sufficient competent evidence. Auditor judgment is required to determine the appropriate evidence to satisfy each objective. For example, where an objective is contributed to by an audit procedure that uses less reliable evidence, the audit objective will not be completely met. In such a case, additional evidence will be gathered using other audit procedures.

        In this case, the evidence used in procedure 5 is from inquiries of the client, which is generally a weak form of evidence. Thus, the classification and presentation and disclosure objectives could require more reliable evidence from other audit procedures to be fully met.

        Procedure 3 uses internal documentation as its primary evidence. The reliability of this procedure would depend on the effectiveness of the client's internal controls in producing the internal documents.

18-24

EXCEPTION	TYPE OF EXCEPTION	TRANSACTION-RELATED AUDIT OBJECTIVE NOT MET	AUDIT IMPORTANCE	FOLLOW-UP	EFFECT ON AUDIT	PREVENTIVE CONTROLS
1	Monetary misstatement	Acquisition transactions are properly classified (classification).	Indicates that no one is effectively reviewing the accounting distribution. Auditor must consider the effect of the exceptions on determining the amount of reliance which he or she may place on the system.	Determine the significance of the misclassifications and plan any required additional steps which are deemed appropriate.	If considered significant, the exceptions could prevent reliance on the system of internal controls and require the auditor to perform additional tests of the classification of items within the financial statements.	Have someone review the account distribution of invoices which enter the system.
2	Control deviation	Recorded acquisitions and related cash disbursements are for goods and services received, consistent with the best interests of the client (existence).	Indicates that the controller is not following the procedure of initialing invoices. This may indicate that he or she is not effectively reviewing invoices and other supporting documents prior to payment.	Determine whether or not the controller is effectively reviewing invoices and other supporting documents.	If determination is made that controller does not review supporting documents, the audit tests should be increased to determine the significance of the weakness.	A competent independent person should review supporting documents for approval of controller and test items to determine effectiveness of controller's review.

18-15

18-24 (Continued)

EXCEPTION	TYPE OF EXCEPTION	TRANSACTION-RELATED AUDIT OBJECTIVE NOT MET	AUDIT IMPORTANCE	FOLLOW-UP	EFFECT ON AUDIT	PREVENTIVE CONTROLS
3	Monetary misstatement	Acquisition transactions are recorded on the correct dates (timing).	At the date of the physical inventory, this situation will be critical in that any items counted in physical inventory and not recorded in the acquisitions journal will cause an understated cost of sales and accounts payable.	Determine whether or not this situation persists through-out the year and whether it is rectified at physical inventory date and year-end.	Require expansion of purchase cutoff work at physical inventory date and year-end.	Require that copies of all receiving reports be routed directly to accounting and that accounting account for numerical sequence of receiving reports on a regular basis.
4	Monetary misstatement	Recorded cash disbursements are for goods and services actually received (existence).	It could be a fraudulent payment or it could result in an overstatement of perpetual inventory records. If the payment is fraudulent, there are serious audit ramifications. If it is unintentional, the situation is wasteful of company assets and must be brought to the client's attention.	First determine whether it is fraudulent. If not, investigate the frequency of occurrence of duplicate payments to determine their significance.	The duplicate payments result in recording of non-existent inventory. If the company performs an interim physical inventory, the auditor could experience a problem relying on the system of internal control between the physical inventory date and year-end.	Invoices must be matched with an original receiving report and purchase order prior to approval for payment. All duplicate invoices are marked "duplicate" upon receipt.

18-16

18-24 (Continued)

EXCEPTION	TYPE OF EXCEPTION	TRANSACTION-RELATED AUDIT OBJECTIVE NOT MET	AUDIT IMPORTANCE	FOLLOW-UP	EFFECT ON AUDIT	PREVENTIVE CONTROLS
5	Monetary misstatement	Recorded cash disbursement transactions are correctly stated (accuracy).	Results in $100 liability which may or may not be recorded on the books.	Investigate the exception rate to determine the possible effect of unrecorded liabilities on the financial statements.	Probably none, since occurrence rate is low. If amount is significant, then expansion of reconciliation of vendor statements may be appropriate.	An independent person should compare checks to invoice amount prior to signing checks.
6	Control deviation	Existing cash disbursement transactions are recorded (completeness).	The check may not actually have been voided. It could represent the disbursement of cash if a check was prepared.	Determine company policy for voided checks and evaluate the potential for unrecorded checks.	Auditor should examine the bank cutoff statement for the possibility that the voided check and other checks may have been issued and cashed but not recorded.	Require that all voided checks be properly voided and saved.

18-17

18-24 (Continued)

EXCEPTION	TYPE OF EXCEPTION	TRANSACTION-RELATED AUDIT OBJECTIVE NOT MET	AUDIT IMPORTANCE	FOLLOW-UP	EFFECT ON AUDIT	PREVENTIVE CONTROLS
7	Control deviation and Monetary misstatement	Recorded acquisitions are for goods and services received, consistent with the best interests of the client (existence). Recorded acquisition transactions are correctly stated (accuracy).	Absence of receiving reports prevents the auditor from determining whether or not the goods were received and processed on a timely basis. The extension error indicates that the clerical accuracy of invoice tests are ineffective.	Obtain bill of lading copy from vendor to determine whether or not the merchandise was received. Determine if the absence of receiver indicates that they are not compared to the invoice. Determine the exception rate by expanding the tests if the misstatement noted is considered significant.	If either of the problems is considered significant to the auditor, he or she should expand the scope of his or her tests of controls or substantive tests of transactions to determine the effect on the financial statements.	Require that copies of receiving reports must be present before invoices are approved for payment. Have an independent person test extensions to determine that the clerical tests are effective.

NOTE: For all monetary misstatements that are potential frauds, the auditor should evaluate whether a fraud occurred. Even one fraud is sufficient for the auditor to consider the potential impact on the audit, primarily because materiality is normally smaller for fraud than for errors.

18-18

18-25

INSTRUCTION	EVALUATION	APPLICATION DIFFICULTIES
1	If the vast majority of transactions exceed this amount, the limit is appropriate. Otherwise, a sample of smaller amounts should also be included.	For attributes sampling, the sample must be randomly selected from the total population. This limitation would prevent the use of attributes sampling or at least force the auditor to generalize only to those transactions exceeding $100 rather than to the overall system.
2	If raw materials is the most significant account included in the accounts tested, this stratification of the judgmental sample is appropriate.	To use such a stratification, the population would have to be divided into raw materials and others, and the sample size computed and results evaluated for each population separately.
3	Such elimination of vendors from repeat selections fulfills no purpose in the test and eliminates the possibility of selecting more sample items from vendors with whom the client does considerable business.	The sample would not be random and the auditor could not statistically generalize to the population.
4	When invoices are not located they should not simply be replaced. The fact that they were not located must be taken into account in the evaluation of the results of the test.	The evaluation of results makes little sense if transactions with missing documents are omitted from the sample.
5	This is an appropriate way to perform the test as long as the sample size used is sufficient to cover all tests performed.	There would be no difficulty in application.
6	No sample which meets the above requirements can be random. The random selection of this sample will not provide results which may be evaluated statistically.	See response 3 above.

18-26 a. The auditor must conduct the audit in accordance with generally accepted auditing standards. It is more difficult to discover embezzlements than most types of errors, but the auditor still has significant responsibility. In this situation, the weaknesses of internal control are such that it should alert the auditor to the potential for fraud. On the other hand, the fraud may be immaterial and therefore not be of major concern.

b.

1. The person who reconciles the bank account does not compare payees on checks to the cash disbursements journal.
2. The president signs blank checks, thus providing no control over expenditures.
3. No one checks invoices to determine that they are cancelled when paid.

c.

1. Comparison of payee on checks to cash disbursements journal.
2. Follow up all outstanding checks which did not clear the bank during the engagement until they clear the bank. Compare payee to cash disbursements journal.

18-27 a. The fact that the client made a journal entry to record vendors' invoices which were received late should simplify the CPA's test for unrecorded liabilities and reduce the possibility of a need for a further adjustment, but the CPA's test is nevertheless required. Clients normally are expected to make necessary adjustments to their books so that the CPA may audit financial statements that the client believes are complete and correct. If the client has not recorded late invoices, the CPA is compelled in his or her testing to substantiate what will ultimately be recorded as an adjusting entry. In this audit, the CPA should test entries in the 2000 voucher register to ascertain that all items that were applicable to 1999 have been included in the journal entry recorded by the client.

b. No. The CPA should obtain a letter in which responsible executives of the client's organization represent that to the best of their knowledge all liabilities have been recognized. However, this is done as a normal audit procedure to remind the client of his or her responsibilities and the statements that have been made. It does not relieve the CPA of the responsibility for making his or her own tests.

c. Whenever a CPA is justified in relying on work done by an internal auditor he or she can reduce (but not eliminate) his or her own audit work. In this case, the CPA should have determined early in his or her audit that Ozine's internal auditor is qualified by being both technically competent and reasonably independent. Once satisfied as to these points, the CPA should discuss the nature and scope of the internal audit program with the internal auditor and review his or her working papers in order that the CPA may properly coordinate his or her own program with that of the internal auditor. If the Ozine internal auditor is qualified and has made tests for unrecorded liabilities, the CPA may limit his or her work to a less extensive test in this audit area if the results of the internal auditor's tests were satisfactory.

18-27 (Continued)
- d. Work done by an auditor for a federal agency will normally have no effect on the scope of the CPA's audit, since the concern of government auditors is usually limited to matters which are unrelated to the financial statements. Nevertheless, the CPA should discuss the government auditor's work program with him or her, as there are isolated situations where specific procedures followed to a satisfactory conclusion by a government auditor will furnish the CPA with added assurance and therefore permit him or her to reduce certain work in an area. However, government auditors are usually interested primarily in substantiating as valid and allowable those costs which a company has allocated against specific government contracts or sales to the government, and consequently there is little likelihood that the auditor for a federal agency at Ozine would check for unrecorded liabilities.

    (Another reason for discussing the federal auditors results with him or her is that his or her findings may affect the financial statements in other ways.)
- e. In addition to the 2000 acquisitions journal, the CPA should consider the following sources for possible unrecorded liabilities:

    1. If a separate cash disbursements journal exists, examine underlying documentation for disbursements recorded during the first part of 2000. Determine if any of the disbursements relate to acquisitions that should have been recorded in 1999.
    2. Vendors' invoices that have not been entered in the acquisitions journal.
    3. Status of tax returns for prior years still open.
    4. Discussions with employees.
    5. Representations from management.
    6. Comparison of account balances with preceding year.
    7. Examination of individual accounts during the audit.
    8. Existing contracts and agreements.
    9. Minutes.
    10. Attorneys' bills and letters of representation.
    11. Status of renegotiable business.
    12. Correspondence with principal suppliers.
    13. Audit testing of cutoff date for reciprocal accounts, e.g., inventory and fixed assets.

18-28
- a. The acquisitions journal is a good source of information on transactions for tests of acquisitions and cash disbursements for the current year. If an acquisitions journal were used, the auditor would select items from this journal for these tests. The lack of this journal will force the auditor to locate a different source of information.
- b. In performing tests of acquisitions, the auditor should use prenumbered receiving documents as the sampling unit for tests of completeness, and cash disbursement entries for other tests (e.g., existence and classification).
- c. If there are no misstatements discovered in the auditor's tests of controls and substantive tests of transactions for acquisitions and cash disbursements, the auditor may be able to reduce the scope of his or her tests for existence, accuracy and classification of accounts payable.

18-28 (Continued)

    d. The client's request for early completion of the audit will present a problem for the auditor to evaluate the propriety of the purchase cutoff. Since no acquisitions journal exists, the auditor is likely to conclude that there is an important weakness in internal controls for the recording of accounts payable. To compensate for this lack of internal control, the auditor will need to perform an extensive search for unrecorded liabilities at the end of the year. The earlier the audit is completed, the less time the auditor will have to obtain vendors' statements and invoices as evidence in determining the appropriateness of the accounts payable balance.

    e. The year-end audit of accounts payable should include the following audit procedures (to satisfy cutoff objective):

1. Reconcile vendors' statements to the accounting records as of year-end.
2. Examine invoices that are paid subsequent to year-end to determine whether or not they should have been included in accounts payable at year-end. If these invoices indicate that the purchases were received prior to year-end, the auditor should search the accounts payable listing for these items. If they do not appear on the accounts payable listing, they represent unrecorded liabilities and should be recorded by the client at year-end.
3. Examine all invoices which are unpaid at the end of the audit to determine whether or not they should have been recorded at year-end. For any of these items which were liabilities at year-end, the auditor should follow the same procedures followed in 2. above.

    f. The auditor must satisfy himself or herself that this audit has been sufficient to determine that the financial statements are fairly stated. If the auditor is able to achieve this and complete his or her engagement by the date requested by the client, then it is possible to conduct an adequate audit in these circumstances. Otherwise, it is not possible.

18-29 a. The most important balance-related audit objectives for accounts payable are:

1. Accounts payable in the accounts payable list agree with related master file and the total is correctly added and agrees with the general ledger (detail tie-in).
2. Existing accounts payable are in the accounts payable list (completeness).
3. Transactions in the acquisition and payment cycle are recorded in the proper period (cutoff).

Other objectives which must also be met, but generally receive less emphasis are:

4. Accounts payable in the accounts payable list are exist.
5. Accounts payable in the accounts payable list are correctly stated.
6. Accounts payable in the accounts payable list are properly classified.
7. Accounts in the acquisition and payment cycle are properly presented and disclosed.

18-29 (Continued)

b. Mincin is not required to use accounts payable confirmation procedures. The auditor is required to obtain confirmation of accounts receivable, since the primary audit test is for possible material overstatements and generally the client has available only internal documents such as sales invoices. For accounts payable the auditor can examine external evidence such as vendor invoices and vendor statements which substantiate the accounts payable balance. Although not required, the accounts payable confirmation is often used. The auditor might consider such use when:

1. Internal controls are weak.
2. The company is in a "tight" cash position and billpaying is slow.
3. Physical inventories exceed general ledger inventory balances by significant amounts.
4. Certain vendors do not send statements.
5. Vendor accounts are pledged by assets.
6. Vendor accounts include unusual transactions.

c. A selection technique using the large dollar balances of accounts is generally used when the primary objective is to test for overstatements (often for accounts receivable confirmation). Accounts with zero balances or relatively small balances would not be subjected to selection under such an approach. When auditing accounts payable, the auditor is primarily concerned with the possibility of unrecorded payables or understatement of recorded payables. Selection of accounts with relatively small or no balances for confirmation is the more efficient direction of testing since understatements are more likely to be detected when examining such accounts.

When selecting accounts payable for confirmation the following procedures could be followed:

1. Analyze the accounts payable population and stratify it into accounts with large balances, accounts with small balances, accounts with zero balances, etc.
2. Use a sample technique that selects items based on criteria other than the dollar amounts of the items (select based on terminal digits, select every n^{th} item based on predetermined interval, etc.)
3. Design a sampling plan that will place more emphasis on selecting accounts with zero balances or relatively small balances, especially when the client has had substantial transactions with such vendors during the year.
4. Select prior-year vendors who are no longer used.
5. Select new vendors used in the subsequent period.
6. Select vendors that do not provide periodic statements.
7. Select accounts reflecting unusual transactions during the year.
8. Select accounts secured by pledging assets.

18-30 a. It is an appropriate procedure to have the client perform the reconciliations of vendors' statements as long as the auditor maintains control over the statements which have been received directly from the vendor and the auditor performs adequate tests to determine that the reconciling items shown on the reconciliations are proper.

b. On Statement 1, the auditor must determine that the payment was recorded on the company's books prior to June 30. The auditor may also want to examine the cutoff bank statement to determine if the check to this vendor cleared the bank within a reasonable amount of time.

On Statement 2, the auditor must determine that the payment was recorded on the company's records prior to June 30 and investigate the reason that the vendor had not received the payment at the time his or her statement was prepared. The auditor must determine whether or not the goods represented on the invoices which Milner had not received were in the company's inventory at June 30. This may be accomplished by requesting that the vendor send proof of shipment for the goods invoiced.

For Statement 3, the auditor should request that the vendor provide additional details of the account balance. Otherwise, the auditor will not be able to use the vendor's statement and will have to include the $5,735.69 as a potential misstatement.

For Statement 4, the auditor must determine whether or not the item for which the credit memo was issued by the vendor on July 15 was appropriately recorded on the company's records at June 30, including consideration of inventory.

The Statement 5 reconciliation is incorrect. The payment by Milner on July 3 should not have been deducted from the accounts payable balance per the master file. The auditor should investigate the unlocated difference, since it could be comprised of two much larger offsetting amounts that the auditor may wish to test.

c. The auditor must consider whether the coverage achieved by the 18 confirmations which were received directly from the vendors is sufficient outside verification of the accounts payable balance at June 30. If the auditor is satisfied with this coverage, he or she may wish to support the four nonresponses by examining vendor invoices in support of the amount recorded in the master file. If the client has received vendor statements from any of these four suppliers, the auditor may wish to reconcile these statements.

18-31 a. It is essential to coordinate the cutoff tests with the physical observation of inventory. If the cutoff is inconsistent with the physical inventory there can be significant misstatements in the income statement and the balance sheet. For example, assume an inventory acquisition for $40,000 is received late in the afternoon of December 31, after the physical inventory is completed. If the acquisition is included in accounts payable and purchases but excluded from inventory, the result is an understatement of net earnings of $40,000. On the other hand, if the acquisition is excluded from both inventory and accounts payable, there is a misstatement in the balance sheet, but the income statement is correct.

18-31 (Continued)

b.

RECEIVING REPORT NO.	DESCRIPTION OF MISSTATEMENT(S)	ADJUSTING ENTRY DEBIT ACCOUNT	AMOUNT	CREDIT ACCOUNT	AMOUNT
2631	None				
2632	Received prior to year-end and not recorded	Inventory	3,709.16	Accounts payable	3,709.16
2633	Included in accounts payable and not inventory	Inventory	5,182.31	Purchases	5,182.31
2634	Received prior to year-end and not recorded	Inventory	6,403.00	Accounts payable	6,403.00
2635	Included in accounts payable and not inventory	Inventory	8,484.91	Purchases	8,484.91
2636	None				
2637	Title passed prior to year-end and not recorded	Inventory	7,515.50	Accounts payable	7,515.50
2638	None				

c. Typically, misstatements which have an effect on earnings are most important because of the importance of earnings to users of financial statements. Receiving report numbers 2633 and 2635 affect earnings. In addition, these misstatements are more important because they represent the recording of part of the entry. If they are not adjusted, the inventory balance the following year will be understated by $13,667.22 (5,182.31 + 8,484.91). For the other three items (receiving report numbers 2632, 2634 and 2637), the misstatement is less important because they would be recorded the following year and the account balances would then be proper.

18-32 a.

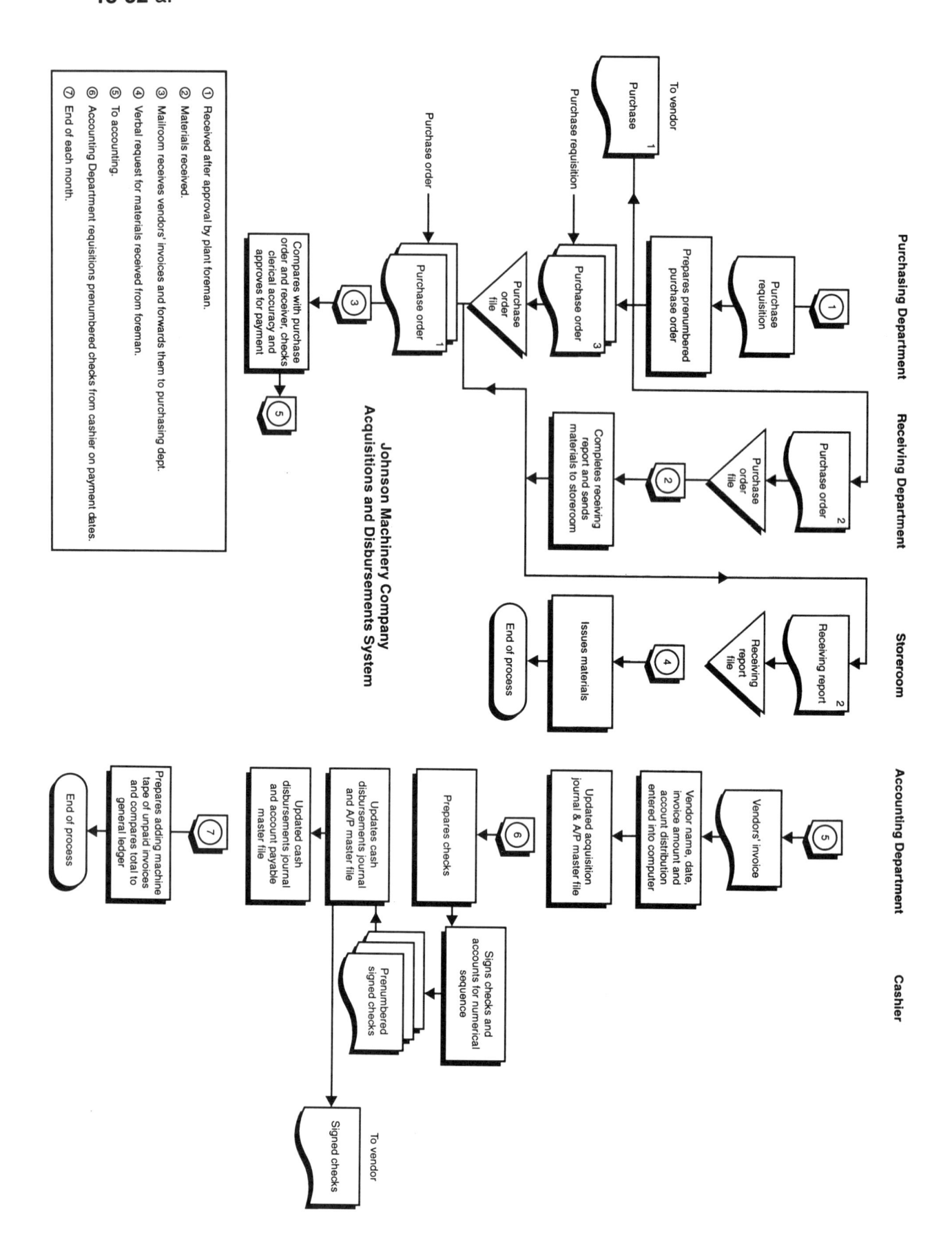

Johnson Machinery Company
Acquisitions and Disbursements System

Purchasing Department
① Purchase requisition → Prepares prenumbered purchase order → Purchase order (3 copies)
- Copy 1: To vendor
- Purchase order file
- Purchase order → ③ Compares with purchase order and receiver, checks clerical accuracy and approves for payment → ⑤

Receiving Department
Purchase order 2 → Purchase order file → ② Completes receiving report and sends materials to storeroom

Storeroom
Receiving report 2 → Receiving report file → ④ Issues materials → End of process

Accounting Department
⑤ Vendors' invoice → Vendor name, date, invoice amount and account distribution entered into computer → Updated acquisition journal & A/P master file → ⑥ Prepares checks → Updates cash disbursements journal and account payable master file → Updated cash disbursements journal and A/P master file → ⑦ Prepares adding machine tape of unpaid invoices and compares total to general ledger → End of process

Cashier
Signs checks and accounts for numerical sequence → Prenumbered signed checks → Signed checks → To vendor

---

① Received after approval by plant foreman.
② Materials received.
③ Mailroom receives vendors' invoices and forwards them to purchasing dept.
④ Verbal request for materials received from foreman.
⑤ To accounting.
⑥ Accounting Department requisitions prenumbered checks from cashier on payment dates.
⑦ End of each month.

18-26

18-32 (Continued)

b. and c.

TRANSACTION-RELATED AUDIT OBJECTIVE	CONTROLS IN EXISTENCE	TEST OF CONTROL
1. Recorded acquisitions are for goods and services received, consistent with the best interests of the client (existence).	■ Existence of purchase requisitions, purchase order, receiving report, and vendor's invoice attached together. ■ Approval of purchase requisitions and invoices for payment. ■ Internal verification of vendors' invoices. ■ Approval of purchase requisitions.	■ Examine documents for existence. ■ Examine documents for indication of approval. ■ Examine invoices for indication of test of clerical accuracy. ■ Examine requisitions for approval.
2. Existing acquisition transactions are recorded (completeness).	Purchase orders are prenumbered and accounted for.	Account for numerical purchase orders.
3. Recorded acquisition transactions are correctly stated (accuracy).	Invoices are tested for clerical accuracy.	Examine invoices for indication of test of clerical accuracy.
4. Acquisition transactions are properly classified (classification).	None	N/A
5. Acquisitions are recorded on the correct dates (timing).	None	N/A
7. Acquisition transactions are properly included in the accounts payable and inventory master files; they are properly summarized (posting and summarization).	At month end unpaid invoices are added and the total is reconciled to the general ledger balance.	Test reconciliation of accounts payable master file to general ledger.

18-32 (Continued)

d. Weaknesses in acquisitions and cash disbursements are as follows:

1. Documents are not cancelled to prevent their reuse.
2. Duplicate invoices are not marked to prevent their processing and duplicate payment.
3. Receiving reports are not prenumbered and therefore cannot be accounted for.
4. No internal verification of the classification to which invoices are charged is performed.
5. No procedures are enforced to ensure the recording of transactions as soon as possible after the goods and services have been received.
6. Signed checks are returned to accounting.

e. An audit program to test the internal controls is as follows:

1. Obtain the acquisitions journal for the year and perform the following procedures:
   a) Foot the journal for one month and reconcile to the general ledger.
   b) Account for the numerical sequence of purchase requisitions, purchase orders, and checks.
   c) From the acquisitions journal select a sample of vendors' invoices and examine each of them as follows:
      1) See that a purchase order and receiving report exist.
      2) Compare the quantities on the purchase order, receiving report, and invoice to determine that the goods received are the same (quantity and description) as those ordered and billed.
      3) Compare the price on the purchase order to that on the invoice to determine that the price billed is the same as that approved.
      4) Examine purchase requisition for foreman approval.
      5) Examine vendor's invoice for indication of test of clerical accuracy and approval for payment.
      6) Examine the cancelled check, compare payee, amount, and date to the cash disbursements journal. Compare the check signer to the list of authorized signers.
      7) Examine the invoice to determine that the account classification is proper.
2. From the receiving report file in the storeroom select a sample of receiving reports and determine that each was eventually recorded. Compare the date received to the date recorded as accounts payable to determine whether or not receipts are recorded on a timely basis.
3. Obtain the month-end reconciliation of the listing of accounts payable to the general ledger. Test the entries on the reconciliation for propriety.

18-32 (Continued)

Part 2

The following comments apply to the procedures for confirming accounts payable:

1. Step 1 is appropriate.
2. The selection of accounts to confirm concentrates on the larger account balances. It is appropriate to select vendors with whom the client does a significant volume; however, those are not necessarily the accounts with the larger balances. The auditor may wish to select the larger dollar balances and at the same time make a selection from the accounts below the $2,000 limit. It is common in accounts payable confirmation to confirm some zero balances.
3. It is appropriate to have the accounts payable clerk prepare the confirmations; however, presenting that individual with a list which indicates the account selection procedure may enable the client to negate the effectiveness of the selection procedure in future years.
4. Normally, accounts payable confirmations consist of a request for a vendor statement rather than providing the vendor with a balance.
5. Step 3 is appropriate where the balance is indicated on the confirmation.
6. Step 4 is appropriate.
7. By allowing the accounts payable clerk to insert the confirmations in the envelopes, the auditor provides an opportunity for this person to switch the confirmation with a fraudulent one.
8. The auditor should mail the confirmations.

18-33

Computer Solution. Computer prepared data sheets using Excel are contained on the Companion Website and on the diskette accompanying this manual. (Filename P1833.XLS.)

Application of audit sampling is not appropriate for Procedures 1-9 due to the nature of the procedures. In this case, audit sampling is also not appropriate for Procedure 11 because the sampling unit is a line item in the cash disbursements journal. The sampling data sheet that follows represents an attributes sampling approach. The only differences between this approach and a nonstatistical sampling approach are the estimate of ARACR and the determination of sample sizes. See the footnotes to the sampling data sheet for further explanations. A sampling data sheet using attributes sampling follows:

18-33 (Continued)

	DESCRIPTION OF ATTRIBUTE	PLANNED AUDIT			
		EPER	TER	ARACR*	INITIAL SAMPLE SIZE**
10.a.	Entry in CD journal agrees with details on cancelled check.	0%	6%	10%	38
10.b.(1)	All supporting documents attached to vendors invoice.	1%	5%	10%	77
10.b.(2)	Documents agree with disbursements.	0%	6%	10%	38
10.b.(3)	Entry in CD journal agrees with details on vendor's invoice.	0%	6%	10%	38
10.b.(4)	Discount was taken as appropriate.	0%	6%	10%	38
10.b.(5)	Vendor's invoice initialed.	1%	5%	10%	77
10.b.(6)	Account costing reasonable.	0%	6%	10%	38
10.b.(7)	Purchases approved by Ward.	1%	5%	10%	77
10.b.(8)	P.O. or P.R. properly approved.	1%	5%	10%	77
10.b.(9)	Prices, footings and extensions are correct.	0%	6%	10%	38
10.b.(10)	Details on supporting documents agree.	0%	6%	10%	38
10.b.(11)	Documents properly completed and cancelled upon payment.	1%	5%	10%	77

*   For a nonstatistical sampling data sheet, ARACR columns should indicate "medium" for all attributes.

** For a nonstatistical sampling data sheet, students' determination of sample size will vary. While no one answer is correct, the sample size chosen for each attribute should reflect the EPER, TER and ARACR for that attribute.

18-33 (Continued)
Part 2

a. *Attributes sampling approach*: The results portion of the sampling data sheet are as follows:

ATTRIBUTE NO.		SAMPLE SIZE	EXCEPTIONS	EXCEPTION RATE	CUER
10.a.		50	0	0	4.5%
10.b.	(1)	50	1*	2%	7.6%
	(2)	50	0	0	4.5%
	(3)	50	0	0	4.5%
	(4)	50	0	0	4.5%
	(5)	50	6*	12%	over 17.8%
	(6)	50	3**	6%	12.9%
	(7)	50	0	0	4.5%
	(8)	50	0	0	4.5%
	(9)	50	0	0	4.5%
	(10)	50	0	0	4.5%
	(11)	50	0	0	4.5%

* Control deviations
** Monetary misstatements

Nonstatistical approach: Because CUER under nonstatistical sampling is estimated using auditor judgment, students' answers to this question will vary. They will most likely be similar to the CUERs calculated using attributes sampling.

Because the SER is zero for attributes 10.a., 10.b.(2)-(4), and 10.b.(7)-(11), it is unlikely that students will estimate CUER greater than the TER of 5% (tests of controls) or 6% (substantive tests of transactions). For attribute 10.b.(5) students should conclude that the results are not acceptable because the SER of 12% clearly exceeds the TER of 5%. For attribute 10.b.(6), even though the SER equals the TER of 6%, the results are not acceptable because sampling error must be considered in determining CUER. For attribute 10.b.(1), students' estimates of CUER will be more variable since the SER is only 2%. Some students will find the results acceptable, and some will not, depending on their estimates of sampling error.

b. Exception 1 is not an exception, and has no effect on tests of details of accounts payable.

Exception 2 is a control deviation. Even though it is not a monetary misstatement, controls require the presence of all supporting documents before a purchase and the related disbursement are processed. If an invalid purchase is recorded, the liability and the related debited account may be overstated. If an invalid disbursement is recorded, accounts payable may be inappropriately reduced. Thus, misstatements in existence of those transactions could actually result in both overstatements and understatements of accounts payable. Tests for existence include tracing

18-33 (Continued)

items on the accounts payable listing to supporting documents and confirmation of accounts payable and reconciliation to vendor's statements.

Exception 3 is a control deviation where one-half of those items also contain monetary misstatements. Misclassification is a serious misstatement. However, it relates to the debit entry, not the credit to accounts payable. Tests supporting charges to assets and expense accounts will need to be increased, but tests of accounts payable will probably not be affected.

c. Following is an audit program for accounts payable. The balance-related audit objectives tested by each procedure are indicated. Because the appropriate audit risk for accounts payable is high and inherent risk low, and because analytical review procedures were excellent, detailed tests should be held to a minimum. The exception to this is for procedure 3; this has not been reduced because of the exception in procedure 10.b.(1).

18-33 (Continued)

	\multicolumn{8}{c	}{BALANCE-RELATED AUDIT OBJECTIVES}
	Detail tie-in	Existence	Completeness	Accuracy	Classification	Cutoff	Obligations	Presentation and disclosure
1. Obtain list of accounts payable. Foot the list and agree to general ledger.	X							
2. Trace all items on the list over $10,000 to vendor's invoice and supporting documents.		X		X				
3. Obtain vendor's statements for 20 vendors with greatest volume of purchases, plus 10 others, by confirmation. Reconcile statements to accounts payable list.		X	X	X		X		
4. Examine all subsequent period disbursements and payments in process of amounts over $5,000 to determine if they were recorded in the proper period.			X			X		
5. Review the list of accounts payable for proper classification of accounts due to related parties, debit balances, or items with unusual terms.					X			X

Note: Rights and Realizable value are not applicable to accounts payable. No audit work was considered necessary for obligations.

18-33

Chapter 19

Completing the Tests in the Acquisition and Payment Cycle: Verification of Selected Accounts

■ Review Questions

19-1 Since the source of the debits in the asset account is the acquisitions journal (or similar record), the current period acquisitions of property, plant and equipment have already been partially verified as part of the acquisition and payment cycle. The disposal of assets, depreciation and accumulated depreciation are not tested as a part of the acquisition and payment cycle.

19-2 The reason for the emphasis in auditing property, plant and equipment in the current period is that there is an expectation that permanent assets will be kept and maintained on the records for several years. The assets carried over from the preceding years can be assumed to have been verified in the prior years' audits.

If it cannot be shown through tests of controls and substantive tests of transactions that all disposals have been recorded, additional testing of the prior balance could be required. A first year audit also necessitates tests of the beginning balance.

19-3 Many clients may accidentally or intentionally record purchases of assets in the repair and maintenance account. The misstatement is caused by a lack of understanding of generally accepted accounting principles and some clients' desire to avoid income taxes. Repair and maintenance accounts are verified primarily to uncover unrecorded property purchases.

The auditor typically vouches the larger amounts debited to those expense accounts at the same time that property accounts are being audited.

19-4 The audit procedures which may be applied to determine that all property, plant and equipment retirements have been recorded are as follows:

1. Review whether newly acquired assets replace existing assets. If so, inquire as to whether the old asset has been removed from the books.
2. Analyze gains on the disposal of assets and miscellaneous income for receipts from the disposal of assets. Compare these to property, plant and equipment accounts to see whether the asset has been removed from the books.
3. Review planned modification and changes in product lines, taxes, or insurance coverage for indications of deletions of equipment.
4. Make inquiries of management and production personnel about the disposal of assets.

19-5 The two considerations to be kept in mind in auditing depreciation expense are:

1. Whether the client is following a consistent depreciation policy from period to period.
2. The accuracy of the client's calculations.

An overall reasonableness test can be made by calculating the depreciation rate for the year times the undepreciated fixed assets. In addition, it is desirable to check the accuracy of the depreciation calculation. The extent of the accuracy tests will vary depending on the engagement circumstances.

19-6 Since the source of the debits to prepaid insurance is the acquisitions journal or similar record (assuming all insurance premiums are charged to prepaid insurance rather than insurance expense), the current period premiums have already been partially verified as a part of the acquisition and payment cycle. The allocation of the premium between prepaid insurance is not tested as a part of the acquisition and payment cycle.

19-7 The audit of prepaid insurance should ordinarily take a relatively small amount of audit time because:

1. The balance in prepaid insurance is normally immaterial;
2. There are ordinarily few transactions during the year and most transactions are immaterial;
3. The transactions are ordinarily not complex.

19-8 The evaluation of the adequacy of insurance is a test of reasonable protection against the loss of existing assets. The verification of prepaid insurance is performed to determine whether:

1. The balances represent proper charges against future operations.
2. The additions represent charges to these accounts and are reflected at actual cost.
3. Amortization or write-off is reasonable under the circumstances.

The evaluation of adequacy of insurance coverage is more important because of the potential loss due to under-insurance. Verification of prepaid insurance usually involves an immaterial amount and is not emphasized in most audits.

19-9 The audit of prepaid expenses differs from the audit of other asset accounts, such as accounts receivable or property, plant, and equipment, because prepaid expenses are often immaterial. Analytical procedures are often sufficient for auditing prepaid expenses, while tests of details of balances are usually required for the other accounts listed above.

19-10 Debits to accrued rent arise from the cash disbursements journal, which is verified as a part of tests of controls and substantive tests of transactions for cash disbursements. The credits typically arise from the general journal and may not have been verified as a part of these tests. Furthermore, tests of controls and substantive tests of transactions do not include verification of the inclusion of accruals on all existing property and verification of the consistent treatment of the accruals from year to year.

19-11 Property tax accruals take little audit time for most audits, and since there are relatively few transactions to test and they are typically material in amount, it is common to verify the accounts 100 percent. On the other hand, accounts payable takes quite a bit of audit time and since there are usually a large number of transactions to test and they are typically varied in amount, it is common to verify the account on a test basis.

19-12 The following documents will be used to verify prepaid property taxes and related expense accounts:

1. Deeds to properties
2. Property tax returns
3. Cancelled checks
4. Invoices from the taxing authority

19-13 Three expense accounts that are tested as part of the acquisition and payment cycle or the payroll and personnel cycle are:

1. Property tax expense
2. Payroll expense
3. Rent expense

Three expense accounts that are not directly verified as part of either of these cycles are:

1. Depreciation expense
2. Amortization of patents
3. Year-end bonuses to officers

19-14 The analysis of expense accounts is a procedure by which selected expense accounts are verified by examining underlying supporting vendors' invoices or other documentation to determine if the transactions making up the total are correctly stated. The emphasis in most expense account analysis is on existence of recorded amounts, accuracy, and classification.

Potentially the same objectives are accomplished in tests of controls and substantive tests of transactions as for expense account analysis. The major differences are that tests of controls and substantive tests of transactions are selected from all of the acquisitions and cash disbursements journals for the entire period whereas transactions examined for expense analysis are limited to the account being analyzed. Nevertheless, the procedures are closely related, and if the tests of controls and substantive tests of transactions procedures results are satisfactory, reduced expense account analysis is implied.

19-15 The approach for verifying depreciation expense should emphasize the consistency of the method of depreciation used and the related computations, since these aspects of depreciation expense are the main determinants of the account balance. The use of analytical procedures and reperformance tests is important for depreciation expense.

19-15 (Continued)
In verifying repair expense, the emphasis should be on vouching transactions which may be capital items; therefore, examining supporting documentation for transactions from months with unusually large totals or transactions that are themselves large or unusual is the normal audit approach followed.

The approach is different because in repairs and maintenance the primary objective is to locate improperly classified fixed assets, whereas in depreciation the emphasis is on consistency from period to period and accurate depreciation calculations.

19-16 The factors that should affect the auditor's decision whether or not to analyze an account balance are:

1. The analytical procedures indicate there is a high likelihood of misstatement in an account.
2. The tests of controls and substantive tests of transactions indicate there is a high likelihood of misstatement in an account.
3. The account is likely to contain misstatements because it is difficult for the client to properly classify or value the transactions.
4. The auditor knows that the account is frequently subject to abuse or misstatement.
5. The analysis of the account might disclose a contingency.
6. Tax returns and the SEC require the disclosure of certain information which the account is likely to provide.

Four expense accounts that are commonly analyzed in audit engagements are:

1. Legal expense
2. Travel and entertainment expense
3. Tax expense
4. Repair and maintenance expense

■ Multiple Choice Questions From CPA Examinations

19-17 a. (1)   b. (1)   c. (4)

19-18 a. (3)   b. (4)   c. (4)

19-19 a. (1)   b. (2)

19-20 a. (2)   b. (4)   c. (4)

Discussion Questions and Problems

19-21

ITEM NO.	INTERNAL CONTROL	SUBSTANTIVE AUDIT PROCEDURE
1	Use of government study depreciation tables.	Compare to government study depreciation table.
2	Establish a policy for deciding which items require capitalization and establish an internal verification procedure.	Test all expense charges to these accounts that exceed a certain amount.
3	Have construction foreman periodically report to the accounting department whether or not there have been abandonments or replacements.	Trace from equipment recorded on the accounting records to the equipment.
4	Internally verify charges for depreciation expenses.	Compare depreciation expense for administration and manufacturing to previous years.
5	Assign tools to individual foreman and periodically count the tools.	Check the client's physical count of the tools.
6	Require internal verification in the recording of property acquisitions.	Compare supporting documentation on property acquisitions to the recorded value.
7	Require the deposit of all cash directly into the bank account.	(1) Confirm loans with the bank and perform other tests for unrecorded loans. (2) Examine plant asset additions and determine whether they are recorded.

19-22

PURPOSE	TEST OF CONTROL TO TEST FOR EXISTENCE OF CONTROL	SUBSTANTIVE PROCEDURE TO TEST FOR MISSTATEMENTS
1. To assure that recording misstatements are minimized. (Existence, completeness)	Verify that master file exists and is used.	Physically examine fixed assets and trace to master file.
2. To minimize accounting classification misstatements. (Classification)	Verify that written policies exist.	Examine supporting documentation for transactions to determine if policies are followed for account classification.
3. To minimize improper purchases. (Existence)	Examine a sample of purchase invoices of fixed assets in excess of $20,000 for Board of Directors' approval.	Examine a sample of purchase invoices of fixed assets for propriety and reasonableness.
4. To provide a record of fixed assets and protect against their loss. (Completeness and existence)	Examine the company's physical count of equipment that compares tags on the equipment to records of tags.	Trace a sample of recorded equipment to the related equipment to make sure it exists.
5. To minimize depreciation calculation and recording misstatements. (Accuracy)	Examine records for indication of periodic verification of master file.	Test calculations and postings of depreciation charges.

19-6

19-23

ITEM NO.	TYPE OF EVIDENCE USED	TYPE OF PROCEDURE	OBJECTIVE(S)
1	Analytical procedure.	Analytical procedure.	Not applicable
2	Confirmation.	Test of details of balances.	Existence Completeness Accuracy Cutoff
3	Internal documentation.	Test of control.	Completeness
4	Physical examination.	Test of details of balances.	Existence Accuracy
5	Reperformance.	Substantive test of transactions.	Posting and summarization
6	Analytical procedure.	Analytical procedure.	Not applicable
7	Inquiry of client.	Test of details of balances.	Completeness Accuracy Presentation and disclosure
8	External documentation (cancelled checks) and internal documentation (journal).	Substantive test of transactions.	Completeness Timing Accuracy
9	External documentation.	Substantive test of transactions.	Existence Accuracy Timing Classification
10	External documentation.	Test of details of balances.	Completeness Cutoff Accuracy
11	Reperformance.	Test of details of balances.	Accuracy
12	Observation.	Test of control.	Existence

19-24 a. No. In a first audit the auditor's attention cannot be confined to activity in the year under audit because (1) some balance sheet accounts include material amounts which originated in prior years, (2) some income and expense accounts include entries which are based on decisions or transactions of prior years, and (3) consistency over the years in the application of generally accepted accounting principles is necessary for fairly presented financial statements. Also, some audit testing of a nonrecurring nature will be necessary in an initial engagement because the auditor does not have the benefits of (1) familiarity with the company's history, personnel, system and operations, (2) information regarding the composition and reliability of beginning of the year balances, and (3) preceding year's audit working papers. Consequently, in the first audit the auditor will require such corporation documents as bylaws, articles of incorporation, minutes since incorporation, organization charts and flowcharts, and must comprehensively obtain an understanding of internal control and assess control risk to determine the scope of audit testing.

b. The audit program procedures which the auditor should use to verify the January 1, 2000, balances in the land, building and equipment, and accumulated depreciation accounts of Hardware Manufacturing Company should include the following:

1. Read the minutes since incorporation in 1996 to ascertain that for major property transactions approved, all transactions were recorded in the accounts, and recorded transactions were properly approved.
2. Scan activity in the general ledger accounts since incorporation in 1996 for both fixed assets and accumulated depreciation to identify items of large amount and unusual nature which will warrant further investigation.
3. Examine support for principal property additions to ascertain that the capitalization includes costs of freight-in, installation, and major improvements and labor, and overhead on self-constructed assets.
4. Ascertain that fixed assets donated by stockholders were recorded at fair market value on the date of donation and that contributed capital was properly credited.
5. Compare the yearly totals of repairs and maintenance account balances and test abnormally high amounts to see that they do not include assets charged to expense.
6. Examine recorded deeds supporting ownership of buildings and determine that any encumbrance was properly reported in the financial statements.
7. Examine support (asset and accumulated depreciation) for recorded disposals or abandonments of material amounts.
8. Tour the plants and account for major property items on hand to substantiate the reasonableness of fixed asset master file records and to ascertain that idle, obsolete or worthless assets are not being reported at more than their fair value in the financial statements.
9. Test the assigned lives of depreciable assets and the bases, methods and computations of accumulated depreciation for propriety and consistency.

19-24 (Continued)

10. Review charges to the accumulated depreciation accounts to determine that they properly represent disposals, abandonments or extraordinary repairs.
11. Review the gains and losses on property disposals as an additional means of assurance that the depreciation lives and methods used are reasonable.
12. Scan federal income tax returns of prior years and revenue agents' reports pertaining to them to determine whether adjustments made for tax purposes should also be made on the books.
13. Determine that transactions involving the investment credit were properly recorded and that generally accepted accounting principles of income tax allocation are being used for differences between tax depreciation and financial statement depreciation.
14. Inspect real estate and property tax bills to further substantiate ownership and valuation of fixed assets.

19-25

PURPOSE	EVALUATION OF ADEQUACY
1. To assure that the clients' detailed schedule equals the total in the general ledger. (Detail tie-in)	This procedure is necessary as a starting point to perform detailed tests.
2. To assure that taxes on property included on the schedule of prepaid taxes are not over- or underpaid. (Accuracy)	This procedure is adequate for its purpose.
3. To assure that the prepaid account is correctly stated. (Accuracy)	This procedure is adequate for its purpose.

Overall, the program fails to emphasize the possibility of omitted property from the list. The key to an adequate audit of accrued property taxes is making sure all owned property and only owned property is included and on the list.

19-26

LIABILITY THAT COULD BE UNCOVERED	AUDIT PROCEDURE TO UNCOVER LIABILITY
a. Lawsuit	Review minutes of the Board of Directors' meetings.
b. Building used as collateral for a loan	Examine documents of ownership to determine if the loan is collateralized and send confirmations to major banks.
c. Unrecorded lease	Examine lease agreements.
d. Note payable	Examine underlying records for loans related to the interest expense and send confirmations to major banks.
e. Policy loan	Obtain a confirmation from the life insurance company.
f. Note payable	Obtain confirmation from bank for loans.
g. Income taxes payable for nondeductible expenses	Examine a sample of travel and expense reports to make sure they comply with IRS requirements.

19-27 The banker has failed to recognize that the audit tests discussed relate as much to the income statement as to the balance sheet. For example, obtaining an understanding of internal control and the tests of controls and substantive tests of transactions are heavily income statement oriented, analytical procedures are more closely related to the income statement than to the balance sheet, and even tests of details of the balance sheet help to uncover misstatements in the income statement. The typical audit recognizes the interrelationship between the income statement and the balance sheet and uses this interrelationship to help design more effective tests to uncover misstatements in both statements. The auditor is and should be greatly concerned about the fair presentation of the income statement.

19-28 a. Day's approach of using repair and maintenance as a model to verifying interest and legal expense is improper because the objectives of each of the three accounts are different. In repair and maintenance, the primary objective is to evaluate whether material capital items have been improperly included as an expense. Therefore, it is appropriate to examine supporting documentation for all transactions over a specified amount, such as $500.

The objective of analyzing interest expense is to search for unrecorded notes payable or similar liabilities (the auditor is looking for payments of interest for which no principal is recorded). The primary objective of analyzing legal expense is to uncover a contingent liability such as a lawsuit. Given these objectives, it is not appropriate to limit the items verified to those transactions over $500 as was done for repair and maintenance.

19-28 (Continued)

    b.   *Interest expense.* (1) Perform ratio and trend analysis by recomputing interest expense on the basis of prevailing interest rates for the client and the average monthly outstanding debt. (2) Examine the cash disbursements journal for the payee for each note or contract interest payment. For each payee send a confirmation if there is any question about the possibility of an unrecorded or misstated liability or related collateral. (3) For each payee examine underlying records to verify such things as interest rates, accrued interest, and the principal liability.

        Legal expense. Analyze all of the transactions for the year and examine underlying documentation for every transaction. Request letters from attorneys who have performed legal services connected in any way with the client's actual or potential lawsuits or other contingent liabilities.

19-29 a. Other considerations in the audit that should affect the auditor's decision as to which accounts to analyze are:

1. The analytical procedures indicate there is a high likelihood of misstatement in certain accounts.
2. Certain accounts are likely to contain misstatements because it is difficult for the client to properly classify or value their expense items.
3. Certain accounts are frequently subject to abuse or misstatement.
4. The analysis of certain accounts might disclose contingencies.
5. Tax returns and the SEC require the disclosure of information which certain accounts are likely to provide.
6. Prior years' audits revealed problems in certain accounts.

    b. In general, the auditor's decision to reduce but not eliminate expense account analysis is a good one on the grounds that the likelihood of misstatement is reduced when there is good internal control and the other considerations affecting the expectation of misstatement indicate that there are likely to be no material misstatements.

        It is questionable, however, whether there should be a reduction in the analysis of legal expense. It is common practice to examine supporting documentation for every legal expense transaction for the year because one expenditure might bring to light a highly material lawsuit or other contingency. On the other hand, the analysis of any transactions in utilities expense seems unwarranted unless there is a specific reason for doing it that is not mentioned in the problem.

    c. The decision to eliminate account analysis for acquisition of raw materials, supplies expense, and insurance expense is probably a good one unless there were other indications of potential misstatements.

        The decision to eliminate the analysis of current period additions to fixed assets is probably not a good one. Ordinarily, current period fixed additions are tested because they are material in amount, they affect the financial statements for several years in the future, and they often require considerable professional judgment to correctly record them.

19-30 a. The tests of acquisition and cash disbursement transactions have two purposes: to determine whether related internal accounting controls are functioning (tests of controls), and to determine whether the transactions actually contain any monetary misstatements (substantive). The results of the tests apply to the population of all acquisitions and cash disbursements, including plant and equipment and lease acquisitions and cash disbursements, even though the specific sample tested does not include any such transaction. Thus, if the results of the tests are favorable, it is concluded that there is a lower expectation of misstatements in plant and equipment and lease transactions, and vice-versa.

b. A summary of the results from tests of controls and substantive tests of transactions for acquisitions and cash disbursements from Case 18-33 is: all transaction-related audit objectives are being met at a satisfactory level except:

1. All supporting documents are not always attached to the vendor's invoice. *Note: Students using a **nonstatistical** approach to Case 18-33 may not conclude that the results for this attribute [10.b.(1)] are unacceptable, depending on their estimate of CUER. However, most students will likely conclude that the results are unacceptable.*
2. All vendors invoices are not initialed for internal verification. Half of those not initialed had account classification errors.

The impact of these results and the results from items 1 through 7 affect the balance-related audit objectives for plant and equipment in the following way:

19-30 (Continued)

BALANCE-RELATED AUDIT OBJECTIVE	RESULTS OF TESTS OF CONTROLS AND SUBSTANTIVE TESTS OF TRANSACTIONS	RESULTS FROM CONCLUSIONS 1-7
Detail tie-in	Misstatements unlikely	—
Existence	Misstatements moderately likely	—
Completeness	Misstatements unlikely	Conclusion 1 supports
Accuracy	Misstatements moderately likely	Conclusion 4 indicates a need for additional evidence
Classification	Misstatements highly likely	Conclusion 6 indicates a need for additional evidence
Cutoff	Misstatements unlikely	—
Realizable value	No significant evidence provided	Conclusion 3 indicates a need for additional evidence
Rights and obligations	Misstatements unlikely	—
Presentation and disclosure	No evidence provided	Conclusion 4 indicates a need for additional evidence

    Conclusions 3, 5, and 7 indicate a need for more extensive auditing for existence, completeness, accuracy, and classification. All large items should be verified and samples should be larger than normal. All other tests can be performed at minimum levels.

c. The results of tests of controls and substantive tests of transactions are directly related to the tests of many expense accounts, primarily through tests for account classification, but also through tests of accuracy and existence. For example, if the auditor concludes that the internal controls are effective for recording acquisition transactions, the likelihood of misstatements for accounts such as supplies, purchases, and repairs and maintenance is greatly reduced. The auditor must keep in mind, however, that certain expense accounts are not usually verified as a part of tests of controls and substantive tests of transactions. An example is depreciation expense. Similarly, certain accounts may have a higher inherent risk such as legal expense and therefore require additional testing even if tests of controls and substantive tests of transactions results are satisfactory. Also, analytical procedures and tests of details of balances for balance sheet accounts results affect the extent of auditing needed for expense accounts.

19-30 (Continued)
    d. The results of tests of controls and substantive tests of transactions indicate the potential for significant classification misstatements. (See the results for Audit Procedure 10b(5) for classification in Part 2 of Problem 17-33.) This potential for misclassification misstatement combined with the analytical procedures results in Conclusion 6 indicate a need for more extensive account analysis for repairs and maintenance, small tools expense, and the three other accounts where there are significant changes from prior years. No other conclusions should cause the auditor significant concern in the audit of expense accounts.

19-31 a. Items 1 through 6 would have been found in the following way:

1. The company's policies for depreciating equipment are available from several sources:
   a) The prior year's audit working papers and permanent file.
   b) Footnote disclosure in the annual report and SEC Form 10-K.
   c) Company procedures manuals.
   d) Detailed fixed asset records.
2. The ten-year lease contract would be found when supporting data for current year's equipment additions were examined. Also, it may be found by a review of company lease files, contract files, or minutes of meetings of the board of directors. The calculations would likely be shown on a supporting schedule and can be traced to the general journal.
3. The building wing addition would be apparent by the addition to buildings during the year. The use of the low construction bid amount would be found when support for the addition was examined. When it was determined that this inappropriate method was followed, the actual costs could be determined by reference to construction work orders and supporting data. The wing could also be examined.
4. The paving and fencing could be discovered when support was examined for the addition to land.
5. The details of the retirement transactions could be determined by examining the sales agreement, cash receipts documentation, and related detailed fixed asset record. This examination would be instigated by the recording of the retirement in the machinery account or the review of cash receipts records.
6. The auditor would become apprised of a new plant in several ways:
   a) Volume would increase.
   b) Account details such as cash, inventory, prepaid expenses, and payroll would be attributed to the new location.
   c) The transaction may be indicated in documents such as the minutes of the board, press releases, and reports to stockholders.
   d) Property tax and insurance bills examined show the new plant.

One or more of these occurrences should lead the auditor to investigate the reasons and circumstances involved. Documents from the city and appraisals could be examined to determine the details involved.

19-31 (Continued)

b. The appropriate adjusting journal entries are as follows:

1. No entry necessary.

2. This is an operating lease and should not have been capitalized.

Prepaid rent	$ 5,000	
Lease liability	35,400	
Allowance for depreciation—machinery and equipment	2,020	
Machinery and equipment		$40,400
Depreciation expense		2,020

   To correct initial recording of lease:

Equipment rent expense	$ 3,750	
Prepaid rent		$ 3,750

   To record nine months rent:

   9/12 x $5,000 = $3,750

3. The wing should have been recorded at its cost to the company.

(Accounts originally credited)	$ 1,500	
Buildings		$ 1,500

   To correct initial recording of new wing:

Depreciation expense	$ 317	
Allowance for depreciation—buildings		$ 317

   To correct depreciation for excess cost.

   Depreciation on beginning balance
   120,000/25 = 4,800

   Depreciation recorded on addition
   5,150 - 4,800 = 350

   Correct depreciation for addition:

   Remaining useful life of addition is 12 years
   (60,000/120,000 x 25 = 12-1/2 years; 12-1/2 - ½ = 12 years)

   Depreciation = $16,000/12 x ½ = $667
   Correction = $667 - $350 = $317

19-31 (Continued)

4. The paving and fencing are land improvements and should be depreciated over their useful lives.

Land improvements (may be combined with buildings with buildings account—buildings and improvements)	$ 5,000	
Land		$ 5,000

   To correct initial recording of paving and fencing:

Depreciation expense	$ 250	
Allowance for depreciation—Land Improvements		$ 250

   To record first year's depreciation on paving and fencing:

   $5,000/10 x ½ = $250

5. The cost and allowance for depreciation should have been removed from the accounts and a gain or loss on sale recorded.

Cost of asset		$48,000
Allowance for depreciation:		
To 12/31/99 - 48,000/10 x 3-1/2	16,800	
For 2000 - 48,000/10 x ½	2,400	
	19,200	
Net book value	28,800	
Cash proceeds	26,000	
Loss on sale	$ 2,800	

   The correcting entry is:

Allowance for depreciation—Machinery and Equipment	$20,300	
Loss on sale of assets	2,800	
Machinery and Equipment		$22,000
Depreciation expense		1,100

19-16

19-31 (Continued)

6. Donated property should be capitalized at its fair market value.

Land	$10,000	
Buildings	40,000	
Contributed capital- Donated Property		$50,000

To record land and building for new plant donated by Crux City:

Depreciation expense	$ 800	
Allowance for depreciation— Buildings		$ 800

To record depreciation on new plant:

$40,000/25 x ½ = $800

19-32 a.

    To: In-Charge Auditor

    From: Audit Manager

    Subject: Concerns about the schedule prepared by staff assistant in the audit of Vernal Manufacturing Company

The analytical procedures schedule for the audit of Vernal Manufacturing Company is completely inadequate and needs to be redone. There are several deficiencies:

1. The headings, references, and indexing on the working paper are incomplete. It appears that the schedule was prepared by the client, but it is not possible to determine from the working paper.

2. A classified income statement would provide more useful information than the single-step statement provided.

3. The schedule should include the additional columns showing the percent of net sales for 12-31-99 and 12-31-00. This information would permit us to more effectively evaluate the relative change in each account.

4. There is no indication that the general ledger totals were compared to general ledger balances or that calculations were tested.

5. There is no identification of accounts which we are concerned may be materially misstated. For example, the $1,381 change in insurance expense appears immaterial but the 427% change in other expense may be significant.

6. There is no indication of specific accounts that require additional investigation and the nature of such investigation.

7. There is no indication that the client's explanations have been evaluated and supported by evidence. Management inquiry is a weak form of evidence and unsatisfactory by itself.

19-32 (Continued)

b. For every explanation provided by the client, an alternative possibility is a misstatement in the financial statements. The auditor must be satisfied that significant differences are not material misstatements. The following are a few examples:

ACCOUNT	POSSIBLE MISSTATEMENT
Sales	Cutoff error for sales
Sales returns and allowances	Returns due to technological deficiencies in products that may indicate obsolete inventory
Miscellaneous income	Including proceeds of the sale of equipment as income rather than decreasing the equipment account
Cost of goods sold	Small increase in cost of goods sold compared to net sales may indicate an overstatement of ending inventory or understatement of any of the accounts making up cost of goods sold

c. To perform a meaningful determination of the most important variances, an alternative design of the working paper follows. It is much easier to determine relevant variances with an adequate analytical procedures working paper.

19-32 (Continued)

	PER G/L 12-31-99	PERCENT 12-31-99	PER G/L 12-31-00	PERCENT 12-31-00	CHANGE AMOUNT	PERCENT
Sales	$8,467,312	100.8%	$9,845,231	102.5%	$1,377,919	16.3%
Sales returns and allowances	(64,895)	(0.8%)	(243,561)	(2.5%)	(178,666)	275.3%
Net Sales	8,402,417	100.0%	9,601,670	100.0%	1,199,253	14.3%
Cost of goods sold:						
Beginning inventory	1,487,666	17.7%	1,389,034	14.5%	(98,632)	(6.6%)
Purchases	2,564,451	30.5%	3,430,865	35.7%	866,414	33.8%
Freight-in	45,332	0.5%	65,782	0.7%	20,450	45.1%
Purchase returns	(76,310)	(0.9%)	(57,643)	(0.6%)	18,667	(24.5%)
Factory wages	986,755	11.7%	1,145,467	11.9%	158,712	16.1%
Factory benefits	197,652	2.4%	201,343	2.1%	3,691	1.9%
Factory overhead	478,659	5.7%	490,765	5.1%	12,106	2.5%
Factory depreciation	344,112	4.1%	314,553	3.3%	(29,559)	(8.6%)
Ending inventory	(1,389,034)	(16.5%)	(2,156,003)	(22.5%)	(766,969)	55.2%
Total	4,639,283	55.2%	4,824,163	50.2%	184,880	4.0%
Gross margin	3,763,134	44.8%	4,777,507	49.8%	1,014,373	27.0%
Selling, general and administrative:						
Executive salaries	167,459	2.0%	174,562	1.8%	7,103	4.2%
Executive benefits	32,321	0.4%	34,488	0.4%	2,167	6.7%
Office salaries	95,675	1.1%	98,540	1.0%	2,865	3.0%
Office benefits	19,888	0.2%	21,778	0.2%	1,890	9.5%
Travel and entertainment	56,845	0.7%	75,583	0.8%	18,738	33.0%
Advertising	130,878	1.6%	156,680	1.6%	25,802	19.7%
Other sales expense	34,880	0.4%	42,334	0.4%	7,454	21.4%
Stationery and supplies	38,221	0.5%	21,554	0.2%	(16,667)	(43.6%)
Postage	14,657	0.2%	18,756	0.2%	4,099	28.0%
Telephone	36,551	0.4%	67,822	0.7%	31,271	85.6%
Dues and memberships	3,644	0.0%	4,522	0.0%	878	24.1%
Rent	15,607	0.2%	15,607	0.2%	0	0.0%
Legal fees	14,154	0.2%	35,460	0.4%	21,306	150.5%
Accounting fees	16,700	0.2%	18,650	0.2%	1,950	11.7%
Depreciation, SG&A	73,450	0.9%	69,500	0.7%	(3,950)	(5.4%)
Bad debt expense	166,454	2.0%	143,871	1.5%	(22,583)	(13.6%)
Insurance	44,321	0.5%	45,702	0.5%	1,381	3.1%
	961,705	11.4%	1,045,409	10.9%	83,704	8.7%
Total operating income	2,801,429	33.3%	3,732,098	38.9%	930,669	33.2%
Other expenses:						
Interest expense	120,432	1.4%	137,922	1.4%	17,490	14.5%
Other	5,455	0.1%	28,762	0.3%	23,307	427.3%
Total	125,887	1.5%	166,684	1.7%	40,797	32.4%
Other income:						
Gain on sale of assets	43,222	0.5%	(143,200)	(1.5%)	(186,422)	(431.3%)
Interest income	243	0.0%	223	0.0%	(20)	(8.2%)
Miscellaneous income	6,365	0.1%	25,478	0.3%	19,113	300.3%
Total	49,830	0.6%	(117,499)	(1.2%)	(167,329)	(335.8%)
Income before taxes	2,725,372	32.4%	3,447,915	35.9%	722,543	26.5%
Income taxes	926,626	11.0%	1,020,600	10.6%	93,974	10.1%
Net income	$1,798,746	21.4%	$2,427,315	25.3%	$ 628,569	34.9%

19-32 (Continued)

The following are variances of special significance to the audit that have been determined from the revised analytical procedures worksheet included in the solution to Part a. Before doing additional work, there should be further discussion with knowledgeable management about the variances identified. After investigating management's explanations, the following additional audit procedures may be appropriate:

ACCOUNT	POTENTIAL ADDITIONAL AUDIT PROCEDURES
1. Sales	Perform extensive cutoff tests and other tests for possible overstatements.
2. Sales returns and allowances	Examine supporting documents for the largest sales returns and allowances and consider the effect on inventory valuation.
3. Cost of goods sold. Cost of goods sold increased only $185,000, but sales increased 1.2 million.	Do careful tests of physical counts, costing, cutoff, inventory, and tests for obsolescence.
4. Travel and entertainment	Examine supporting documentation for large travel and entertainment expenses.
5. Telephone	Compare telephone expense by month to determine the possibility of a misclassification.
6. Legal expense	Analyze legal expense to determine the possibility of lawsuits or other legal actions that might affect the financial statements.
7. Depreciation expense	Compare depreciation by month to determine the possibility of the failure to record one month's depreciation.
8. Bad debt expense	Performed detailed analytical procedures and other tests of accounts receivable to evaluate the adequacy of the allowance for uncollectible accounts.
9. Other expense	Analyze other expense to determine the nature of other expense and the possibility of misclassification or incorrect accounting.
10. Gain on the sale of assets	Analyze the account to determine the nature of the transactions and the misclassification or incorrect accounting.

Chapter 20

Audit of the Inventory and Warehousing Cycle

■ **Review Questions**

20-1 Inventory is often the most difficult and time consuming part of many audit engagements because:

1. Inventory is generally a major item on the balance sheet and often the largest item making up the accounts included in working capital.
2. The need for organizations to have the inventory in diverse locations makes the physical control and counting of the inventory difficult.
3. Inventory takes many different forms which are difficult for the auditor to fully understand.
4. The consistent application of different valuation methods can be fairly complicated.
5. The valuation of inventory is difficult due to such factors as the large number of different items involved, the need to allocate the manufacturing costs to inventory, and obsolescence.

20-2 The acquisition and payment cycle includes the system for purchasing all goods and services, including raw materials and purchased parts for producing finished goods. Purchase requisitions are used to notify the purchasing department to place orders for inventory items. When inventory reaches a predetermined level or automatic reorder point, requisitions may be initiated by stockroom personnel or by computer. In other systems, orders may be placed for the materials required to produce a customer order, or orders may be initiated upon periodic evaluation of the situation in light of the prior experience of inventory activity. After receiving the materials ordered, as part of the acquisition and payment cycle, the materials are inspected with a copy of the receiving document used to book perpetual inventory. In a standard cost inventory system, the acquisition and payment cycle computes any inventory purchase variances, which then enter the inventory system.

The following audit procedures in the acquisition and payment cycle illustrate the relationship between that cycle and the inventory and warehousing cycle.

1. Compare the inventory cost entered into the inventory system to the supporting invoice to determine that it was properly recorded and the purchase variance (standard cost system), if any, was properly reflected.
2. Test the purchase cutoff at the physical inventory date and year-end to determine whether or not the physical inventory and year-end inventory cutoffs are proper from a purchase standpoint.

20-3 Cost accounting records are those which are concerned with the processing and storage of raw materials, work in process, and finished goods, insofar as these activities constitute internal transfers within the inventory and warehousing cycle. These records include computerized files, ledgers, worksheets and reports which accumulate material, labor, and overhead costs by job or process as the costs are incurred.

Cost accounting records are important in conducting an audit because they indicate the relative profitability of the various products for management planning and control, and determine the valuation of inventories for financial statement purposes.

20-4 The most important tests of the perpetual records the auditor must make before assessed control risk can be reduced, which may permit a reduction in other audit tests are:

1. Tests of the purchases of raw materials and pricing thereof.
2. Tests of the cost accounting documents and records by verifying the reduction of the raw material inventory for use in production and the increase in the quantity of finished goods inventory when goods have been manufactured.
3. Tests of the reduction in the finished goods inventory through the sale of goods to customers.

Assuming the perpetuals are determined to be effective, physical inventory tests may be reduced, as well as tests of inventory cutoff. In addition, an effective perpetual inventory will allow the company to test the physical inventory prior to the balance sheet date.

20-5 The continuation of shipping operations during the physical inventory will require the auditor to perform additional procedures to insure that a proper cutoff is achieved. The auditor must conclude that merchandise shipped is either included in the physical count or recorded as a sale, but not both.

Since no second count is taken, the auditor must increase the number of test counts to determine that the counts recorded are accurate.

20-6 The auditor must not give the controller a copy of his or her test counts. The auditor's test counts are the only means of controlling the original counts recorded by the company. If the controller knows which items were test counted, he or she will be able to adjust other uncounted items without detection by the auditor.

20-7 The most important audit procedures to test for the ownership of inventory during the observation of the physical counts and as a part of subsequent valuation tests are:

1. Discuss with the client.
2. Obtain an understanding of the client's operations.
3. Be alert for inventory set aside or specially marked.
4. Review contracts with suppliers and customers to test for the possibility of consigned inventory or inventory owned by others that is in the client's shop for repair or some other purpose.
5. Examine vendor invoices indicating that merchandise on hand was sold to the company.

20-7 (Continued)

6. Test recorded sales just before and just after the physical inventory to determine that the items were or were not on hand at the physical inventory date and that a proper cutoff was achieved.

20-8 Auditing procedures to determine whether slow-moving or obsolete items have been included in inventory are:

1. Obtain a sufficient understanding of the client's business to aid in recognizing inventory that is no longer useful in the client's business.
2. Review the perpetual records for slow-moving items.
3. Discuss the quality of the inventory with management.
4. Ask questions of production personnel during physical inventory observation about the extent of the use or nonuse of inventory items.
5. Make observations during the physical inventory for rust, damaged inventory, inventory in unusual locations, and unusual amounts of dust on the inventory.
6. Be aware of inventory that is tagged obsolete, spoiled, or damaged, or is set aside because it is obsolete or damaged.
7. Examine obsolescence reports, scrap sales, and other records in subsequent periods that may indicate the existence of inventory that should have been excluded from the physical inventory or included at a reduced cost.
8. Calculate inventory ratios, by type of inventory if possible, and compare them to previous years or industry standards.

20-9 The auditor could have uncovered the misstatement if there were adequate controls over the use of inventory tags. More specifically, the auditor should have assured himself or herself that the client had accounted for all used and unused tag numbers by examining all tags, if necessary. In addition, the auditor should have selected certain tags (especially larger items) and had the client show him or her where the goods were stored. The tag numbers used and unused should have been recorded in the auditor's working papers for subsequent follow-up. As part of substantive procedures, the auditor could have performed analytical tests on the inventory and cost of sales. A comparison of ratios such as gross margin percentage and inventory turnover could have indicated that a problem was present.

20-10 A proper cutoff of purchases and sales is heavily dependent on the physical inventory observation because a proper cutoff of sales requires that finished goods inventory included in the physical count be excluded from sales and all inventory received be included in purchases.

To make sure the cutoff for sales is accurate, the following information should be obtained during the taking of the physical inventory:

1. The last shipping document number should be recorded in the working papers for subsequent follow-up to sales records.
2. A review should be made of shipping to test for the possibility of shipments set aside for shipping and not counted or other potential cutoff problems.

20-10 (Continued)

3. When prenumbered shipping documents are not used, a careful review of the client's method of getting a proper sales cutoff is the first step in testing the cutoff.
4. A list of the most recent shipments should be included in the working papers for subsequent follow-up to sales records.

For the purchase cutoff, the following information should be noted:

1. The last receiving report number should be noted in the working papers for subsequent follow-up to purchase records.
2. A review should be made of the receiving department to make sure all inventory has been properly included in the physical inventory.

20-11 Compilation tests are the tests of the summarization of physical counts, the extension of price times quantity, footing the inventory summary, and tracing the totals to the general ledger.

Several examples of audit procedures to verify compilation are:

1. Trace the tag numbers used to the final inventory summary to make sure they were properly included and the numbers not used to the final inventory summary to make sure no tag numbers have been added.
2. Trace the test counts recorded in the working papers to the final inventory summary to make sure they are correctly included.
3. Trace inventory items on the final inventory list to the tags as a test of the existence of recorded inventory.
4. Test the extensions and footings of the physical inventory summary.

20-12

ANALYTICAL PROCEDURE	TYPE OF POTENTIAL MISSTATEMENT
1. Compare gross margin percentage with previous years.	Overstatement or understatement of inventory amounts (prices and/or quantities).
2. Compare inventory turnover with previous years.	Obsolete inventory.
3. Compare unit costs with previous years.	Overstatement or understatement of unit costs.
4. Compare extended inventory value with previous years.	Errors in compilation, unit costs, or extensions.
5. Compare current year manufacturing costs with previous years.	Misstatement of unit costs of inventory, especially direct labor and manufacturing overhead.

20-13

DATE	PURCHASE QUANTITY	PRICE	TO BE INCLUDED IN 12-31-99 INVENTORY	EXTENSION
11-26-99	2,400	$2.07	700 @ $2.07	$1,449.00
12-06-99	1,900	$2.28	1,900 @ $2.28	4,332.00
				$5,781.00

Assuming FIFO inventory valuation, the 12-31-99 inventory should be valued at $5,781, and is thus currently overstated by $121.

If the 1-26-00 purchase was for 2,300 binders at $2.12 each, the 12-31-96 inventory should be valued at $5,477.00 (1,900 @ $2.12 + 700 @ $2.07) and is thus currently overstated by $425. The reason is the lower of cost or market rule, with the $2.12 being the replacement cost.

20-14 The direct labor hours for an individual inventory item would be verified by examining engineering specifications or similar information to determine whether the number of hours to complete a unit of finished goods was correctly computed. Ordinarily it is difficult to test the number of hours to an independent source.

The manufacturing overhead rate is calculated by dividing the total annual number of labor hours into total manufacturing overhead. These two totals are verified as a part of the payroll and personnel and acquisition and payment cycles.

Once these two numbers are verified (overhead rate per direct labor hour and the number of direct labor hours per unit of each type of inventory), it is not difficult to verify the overhead cost in inventory.

20-15 With a job cost system, labor charged to a specific job is accumulated on a job cost sheet. The direct labor dollars included on the job cost sheet can be traced to the employee "job time sheet" to make sure the hours are correctly included on the job cost sheet. The labor rate can be verified by comparing it to the amount on the employee's earnings record.

20-16 Assuming the auditor properly documents receiving report numbers as a part of the physical inventory observation procedures, the auditor should verify the proper cutoff of purchases as a part of subsequent tests by examining each invoice to see if a receiving report is attached. If the receiving report is dated on or before the inventory date and the last recorded number, the received inventory must have been included in the physical inventory; therefore the invoice should be included in accounts payable. Those invoices which are received after the balance sheet date but shipped F.O.B. shipping point on or before the close of the year would indicate merchandise in transit.

■ **Multiple Choice Questions From CPA Examinations**

20-17 a. (2)   b. (4)   c. (1)

20-18 a. (4)   b. (2)   c. (1)

20-19 a. (4)   b. (4)   c. (2)

Discussion Questions and Problems

20-20

PURPOSE OF INTERNAL CONTROL	TEST OF CONTROL	POTENTIAL FINANCIAL MISSTATEMENT	SUBSTANTIVE AUDIT PROCEDURE
1. To ensure inventory is recorded when received, payments made are for goods received, and quantities and descriptions are accurate. (Completeness, existence and accuracy)	Account for a numerical sequence of receiving reports and observe matching invoices received from vendors.	Understatement of inventory or payment for goods not received.	Trace quantity and description on vendor's invoice to receiving report.
2. To minimize theft or unrecorded shipments of inventory. (Existence)	Discuss with client and observe whether personnel prepare shipping documents.	Overstatement of inventory.	Compare physical count to perpetual records.
3. To ensure inventory shipments are recorded as sales. (Completeness)	Account for a numerical sequence of shipping orders.	Understatement of sales.	Trace quantity and description on bills of lading to recorded sales.
4. For a proper valuation of inventory. (Accuracy)	Examine receiving and requisition documents, trace to perpetual records.	Misstatement of inventory.	Compare physical count to perpetual inventory record.
5. To make sure physical inventory counts are accurate. (Accuracy, existence and completeness)	Observe counting personnel and discuss with client.	Misstatement of inventory.	Compare physical count to perpetual inventory record.

20-20 (Continued)

PURPOSE OF INTERNAL CONTROL	TEST OF CONTROL	POTENTIAL FINANCIAL MISSTATEMENT	SUBSTANTIVE AUDIT PROCEDURE
6. To assure reasonable costs are used for inventory and cost of goods sold. (Accuracy)	Review procedures for determining standard costs.	Misstatement of inventory.	Trace costs from supporting documents to development of standards.
7. To make sure obsolete goods are classified as such. (Accuracy)	Read policy and discuss procedures with client.	Misstatement of inventory.	Analytical procedures for inventory.
8. To make sure inventory compilation is accurate. (Accuracy)	Observe who compiles the inventory and discuss with client.	Misstatement of inventory.	Reperform clerical tests of inventory compilation.

20-21 a. It is important to review the cost accounting records and test their accuracy for the following reasons:

   1. The cost accounting records determine unit costs which are applied to derive inventory values. Since inventory is usually material, unit costs must be verified.
   2. In many companies, there are many types of inventory items with complex cost structures. The potential for misstatement is great in determining costs. The auditor would need to go to an extreme effort to verify such costs without being able to rely on the cost accounting records which provides the costs, (i.e., it is far more efficient to test the cost accounting records than the costs themselves).
   3. The cost accounting records also deal with transferring inventories through the production cycle and then from finished goods for sales. These transfers must be handled accurately for inventory to be properly stated.

   b. 1. Examine engineering specifications for expected (standard) labor hours. Examine time records for hours worked on part during measured period. Divide by units produced to test reasonableness of standard.
   2. Review specifications for types of labor required to produce parts, or observe production. Review union contracts or earnings records to develop reasonable rate for this labor mix.

20-21 (Continued)

3. Identify appropriate overhead accounts, paying careful attention to consistent application. Determine amounts for these accounts for a measured period. Determine direct labor hours from payable records from the same period. Compute the overhead rate per direct labor hour.
4. Review engineering specifications. Review material usage variance.
5. Trace to vendor's invoices. Review material price variance.
6. Sum individual components.

20-22

AUDIT PROCEDURE	TYPE OF TEST	PURPOSE
1	Substantive Test of Transactions	To test the accuracy of the client's perpetual inventory records. (Existence, completeness, and accuracy)
2	Substantive Test of Transactions	To test client's final inventory compilation. (Existence, completeness, accuracy and classification)
3	Substantive Test of Transactions	To test that the final inventory was valued at its proper cost. (Accuracy)
4	Test of Control	To make sure that proper controls exist and are being followed in the taking of the physical inventory. (Existence, completeness, accuracy and classification)
5	Test of Control	To ensure that no raw material was issued without proper approval. (Existence)
6	Test of Control or Substantive Test of Transactions	To ensure that additions recorded on the finished goods perpetual records were recorded on the books as completed production. (Accuracy and classification)
7	Substantive Test of Transactions	To ensure that all inventory represented by an inventory tag actually exists. (Existence)

20-23

MISSTATEMENT	CONTROL THAT SHOULD HAVE PREVENTED THE MISSTATEMENT FROM OCCURRING	SUBSTANTIVE AUDIT PROCEDURE THAT COULD BE USED TO UNCOVER THE MISSTATEMENT
1	Internal verification by another person.	Examine vendors' invoices in support of prices used.
2	Keep a record of the last shipping report number shipped before the inventory count.	Examine bills of lading for first shipments recorded after the physical inventory to determine that they were shipped after year-end.
3	Perform independent second counts on all merchandise. All persons responsible for inventory tags and compilation of physical inventory should be independent of custody of perpetual inventory records.	Record test counts and trace to compiled inventory.
4	Use of prenumbered tags and accounting for numerical sequence.	Account for all prenumbered tags during the physical examination and during compilation tests.
5	Internal verification of perpetual inventory prices.	Compare vendor invoice prices to perpetual inventory prices.
6	Segregation of obsolete inventory.	Perform net realizable value and lower of cost or market tests of inventory, including tests of the perpetual inventory.
7	Periodic review of reasonableness of manufacturing overhead rate.	Test reasonableness of manufacturing overhead rate.

20-24 a. When the inventory is a material item in the financial statements that the CPA is auditing, his or her observation of the taking of the physical inventory is in compliance with the auditing standard pertaining to field work that requires obtaining sufficient competent evidential matter to afford a reasonable basis for an opinion regarding the financial statements. Observation is a generally accepted auditing procedure applied in the audit of the physical inventory.

20-24 (Continued)

By observing the taking of the physical inventory, the CPA is seeking to satisfy himself or herself as to the effectiveness and application of the methods of inventory taking and as to the measure of reliance which may be placed upon the client's inventory records and its representations as to inventory quantities. He or she must ascertain that the physical inventory actually exists, that the inventory quantities are being determined by reasonably accurate methods, that the inventory is in a salable or usable condition, and that consigned goods are not commingled with owned goods.

b. The CPA makes test counts of inventory quantities during observation of the taking of the physical inventory to satisfy himself or herself that an accurate count is being made by the individuals taking the inventory. The extent of test counting will be determined by the inventory taking procedures; for example, the number of test counts would be reduced if there were two teams, one checking the other, taking the inventory. On the other hand, the test counts would be expanded if misstatements were found in the inventory counts.

Some test counts are recorded by the CPA for the purpose of subsequent comparison with the client's compilation of the inventory. The comparison procedure goes beyond the mere determination that quantities have been accurately transcribed. In addition, the CPA seeks assurance that the description and condition of the inventory items is accurate for pricing purposes and that the quantity information, such as dozen, gross, cartons, etc., is proper.

Another reason for recording test counts in the working papers is to provide evidence of the extent of tests in the event that audit procedures are questioned at some future date.

c.

1. The CPA does not regard the inventory certificate as a satisfactory substitute for his or her own audit of the inventory. The service company has merely assumed the client's function of taking the physical inventory, pricing it, and making the necessary extensions. To the extent that the service company is competent, the system of internal control with regard to the inventory has been strengthened. Nevertheless, as the CPA would under other strong systems of internal control, he or she would investigate the system to determine that it is operating in a satisfactory manner. The CPA's investigation would necessarily entail an observation of the taking of the inventory and testing the pricing and calculation of the inventory.

2. The inventory certificate of the outside specialists would have no effect upon the CPA's report. The auditor must be satisfied that the inventory was fairly stated by observing the taking of the inventory and testing the pricing and compilation of the inventory.

On the other hand, if the taking of the inventory was not observed and no audit tests were applied to the computation of the inventory, the CPA would be compelled to disclaim an opinion on the financial statements as a whole if the amount of the inventory is material.

20-24 (Continued)

If it is impractical or impossible for the CPA to observe the taking of the physical inventory, but he or she is able to determine that inventory is fairly stated by the application of other auditing procedures, the CPA would be able to issue an unqualified opinion.

3. The CPA would make no reference to the certificate of the outside specialists in his report. The outside specialists are serving as adjuncts of the company's staff of permanent employees. The outside specialists are not independent.

20-25 a. The auditor in this situation should observe the recording of the shipments on the day of occurrence and record these details in the working papers so a determination can be made as to whether the shipments affected the physical inventory count.

b.

1. There is no clear-cut answer to sample size for inventory counts. The answer to the question depends on additional factors, such as the randomness of your test counts and whether the values of the merchandise are relatively stratified. It also depends on inherent risk for inventory physical counts and the materiality of inventory compared to total assets.
2. Request a recount by the client or greatly expand your tests to determine whether a material misstatement exists.

c. The auditor should determine how this inventory is valued and after discussion with the client it may be well to classify it as obsolete. In all cases, the auditor must specifically identify the merchandise in the working papers for subsequent evaluation. The auditor should also be aware that this could be an indication of widespread obsolescence problems in other parts of the inventory.

d. One of the important tasks the auditor undertakes during the observation is to determine that inventory tags are physically controlled. This assures that the inventory is not understated because tags are lost, or overstated because falsified tags are added. In this situation, the auditor should recover the discarded tags and request that the practice be stopped, and that control of tags be established under the auditor's direct observation.

20-26 The following procedures should be established to insure that the inventory count includes all items that should be included and that nothing is counted twice:

1. All materials should be cleared from the receiving area and stored in the appropriate space before the count.
2. Incoming shipments of unassembled parts and supplies should be held in the receiving area until the end of the day and then inventoried.
3. If possible, the day's shipments of finished appliances should be taken to the shipping area before the count. (Unshipped items remaining in the shipping area should be inventoried at the end of the day.)

20-26 (Continued)

4. Great care must be exercised over goods removed from the warehouse itself. These may be unassembled parts and supplies requisitioned on an emergency basis or unscheduled shipments of finished appliances. Alternative methods for recording these removals are:
   a) Keep a list of all items removed and indicate on the list whether the item had been counted.
   b) Record the removal on the inventory tag if the item has been inventoried.
   c) Indicate on the material requisition or the shipping order that the item had been inventoried. For any of these alternatives, a warehouse employee or the perpetual inventory clerk must adjust the recorded counts.
5. The finished appliances remaining in the warehouse should be inventoried at the end of the day.
6. The warehouse should be instructed to date all documents as of the day the materials are received, issued, or shipped.
7. The inventory clerk should post the May 31 production and shipment of finished goods to the inventory record based upon the dates shown on the plant production report and the shipping report. This will provide a proper cutoff because provisions have been made to adjust all counts for goods manufactured and shipped on May 31.
8. The listing of inventory differences should be reviewed by the controller and warehouse supervisor prior to booking the adjustment. Abnormal differences should be investigated, and recounts (with appropriate reconciliation) should be made where appropriate.

20-27

Computer Solution. Computer solutions in Excel are contained on the Companion Website and on the diskette accompanying this manual. (Filename is P2027.XLS.)

a.

	1999	1998	1997	1996
Gross margin %	26.3%	22.6%	22.4%	22.4%
Inventory turnover	6.6	7.6	7.6	7.9

b. Logical causes of the changes in the gross margin as a percent of sales include:

1. Selling prices were raised without a corresponding increase in cost of sales.
2. The method of accounting for inventory was changed, causing a higher ending inventory (more expenses absorbed into inventory) and lower cost of sales.
3. Inventory cutoff was improper, causing sales to be recorded without the corresponding entry to cost of sales.
4. The product mix of the company changed. More high markup items were sold than in previous years.

20-27 (Continued)

5. An improper journal entry was recorded which adjusted the gross margin upward.

Logical causes of the changes in the inventory turnover include:

1. The increased selling prices which caused the gross margin percent to increase, reduced demand for the product, and decreased the inventory turnover.
2. The company is building its inventory supply in anticipation of increased sales in the future.
3. The company's inventory contains obsolete or unsalable merchandise which is affecting the turnover rate.

c. 26.3% - 22.6% = 3.7% increase of gross margin %
3.7% x sales of $23.2 million = $858,000 potential misstatement

$17.1 million (1999 COGS) ÷ 7.6 (1998) inventory turnover = $2.25 million
$2.9 million - 2.25 million = $650,000 potential misstatement

Both calculations indicate a potential misstatement exceeding $500,000.

d. The auditor should discuss the two changes with the client and obtain a reasonable explanation for them. He or she should then perform appropriate procedures to verify the validity of the explanation. Ultimately, the auditor must be confident the change does not result from a misstatement in the financial statements.

20-28 a.
1. Exclude
2. Exclude
3. Include
4. Include
5. Exclude

b.
1. This merchandise would be excluded because title does not pass to buyer on an F.O.B. destination shipment until delivery to the buyer. Since it was not received until January 2000, there is no basis for including it in inventory.
2. Goods held "on consignment" do not belong to the consignee, and should not be included in inventory.
3. Normally title to a stock item does not pass to the customer until shipment, even though it has been set aside. Therefore it should be included in inventory.
4. Title to goods shipped F.O.B. shipping point normally passes to the buyer on delivery to the transportation agency, and in this instance the goods belong to your client at December 31, 1999. There is an error in recording the acquisition.

20-28 (Continued)

5. Since this machine is fabricated to the customer's order, title to customer made-merchandise passes to the buyer as materials and labor are appropriated to the job. When the job is completed and ready for shipment as in this case, it may be considered as a completed sale.

20-29 a.

1. Extension errors are as follows:

DESCRIPTION	EXTENSION AS RECORDED	ACTUAL EXTENSION	OVER (UNDER) STATEMENT
Wood	$ 5.58	$ 55.80	$ (50.22)
Metal cutting tool	670.00	870.00	(200.00)
Cutting fluid	529.00	640.00	(111.00)
Sandpaper	258.00	2.85	255.15
			$ (106.07)

2. The differences in the previous year's and this year's cost indicate a problem. The auditor should attempt to obtain support for the current year's cost if the effect of the differences noted seems significant (considering that the test only covered 20% of the dollar items). A review for reasonableness indicates the following:
   a) Precision cutting torches are expensive. Maybe $500 each is a reasonable price. Examine a vendor's invoice or a price list.
   b) Aluminum scrap values may fluctuate significantly. The two prices may be reasonable. Look at sales invoices for the two years.
   c) Lubricating oil cost appears unreasonable for this year and for the previous year. The auditor should examine invoices for both years.
   If the previous year's costs were incorrect, determination of the effect of the misstatements on the prior year's and this year's financial statements must be completed to determine the need for disclosure of the misstatements.
3. Investigate the reasons for the omission of these tags from final inventory compilation. If it is determined that the omission of two tags is significant based on the number of tags used and tested, the auditor should account for all tags to determine the total extent of omissions.
4. Page total footing errors are as follows:

PAGE NO.	CLIENT TOTAL	CORRECT TOTAL	OVER- (UNDER-) STATEMENT
14	$1,375.12	$1,375.08	$ 0.04
82	8,721.18	8,521.18	200.00
			$200.04

20-29 (Continued)

b. First, the auditor should keep in mind that only 20% of the inventory was tested. If sampling was random, a direct extrapolation would magnify projected misstatements by five. In addition, the auditor must consider sampling error.

The net effect of the misstatements for which we were able to compute the actual misstatement was an overstatement of inventory by $93.97, a small amount (see items 1 and 4). However, the exceptions resulted from various causes including incorrect decimal placement, mathematical errors, and unit of measure errors. The auditor should determine that the net effect of the misstatements is not significant; in addition, to insure against other individual misstatements which might be significant, the auditor should review the extensions and other computations for reasonableness and obvious misstatements.

For the items for which the amount of the misstatement could not be determined, the auditor should follow up as described in 2 and 3 above. From the results of the follow-up, the effect of the misstatements noted should be assessed and determination made as to the need for expansion of scope for the tests considered.

c. Prior to compiling the inventory next year, Martin Manufacturing should implement the following internal controls:

1. The compilation of inventory should be computerized. If not, all extensions and footings should be recomputed by a second person.
2. Someone familiar with the inventory should review the compilation schedules for reasonableness of quantities, prices, and extensions.
3. All inventory tags should be accounted for prior to posting to the compilation schedules and a control total compared to the total on the compilation sheets after the compilation is complete.

20-30 a. Necessary adjustments to client's physical inventory:

Material in Car #AR38162—received in warehouse on January 2, 2000	$ 8,120
Materials stranded en route (Sales price $19,270/125%)	15,416
Total	23,536
Less unsalable inventory	1,250 *
Total adjustment	$22,286

* If freight charges have been included in the client's inventory, the amount would be $1,600 and the amount of the total adjustment would be $21,936. Journal entry 6 probably would have a credit to purchases of $1,600 in this case.

20-30 (Continued)

b. Auditor's worksheet adjusting entries:

1. | | | |
    |---|---|---|
    | Purchases | $ 2,183 | |
    | Accounts Payable | | $ 2,183 |

    To record goods in warehouse but not invoiced-received on RR 1060.

2. No entry required. Title to goods had passed.

3. | | | |
    |---|---|---|
    | Accounts receivable | 12,700 | |
    | Sales | | 12,700 |

    To record goods as sold which were loaded on December 31 and not inventories-SI 968.

4. | | | |
    |---|---|---|
    | Sales | 19,270 | |
    | Accounts receivable | | 19,270 |

    To reverse out of sales material included in both sales (SI 966) and in physical inventory (after adjustment).

5. No adjustment required.

6. | | | |
    |---|---|---|
    | Claims receivable | 1,600 | |
    | Purchases | | 1,250 |
    | Freight In | | 350 |

    To record claim against carrier for merchandise damaged in transit.

7. | | | |
    |---|---|---|
    | Inventory | 22,286 | |
    | Cost of goods sold | | 22,286 |

    To adjust accounts for changes in physical inventory quantities.

8. | | | |
    |---|---|---|
    | Sales | 15,773 | |
    | Accounts receivable | | 15,773 |

    To reverse out of sales invoices #969, 970, 97l. The sales book was held open too long. This merchandise was in warehouse at time of physical count and so included therein.

20-31 a. The advantage of using difference estimation instead of nonstatistical sampling is that sampling risk is quantified when an auditor uses difference estimation. Under nonstatistical sampling methods, the auditor must estimate sampling risk using professional judgment.

b. Sample size is determined as follows:

$$n = \left[\frac{SD^* \cdot (Z_A + Z_R) \cdot TM}{TM - E^*}\right]^2$$

where n = initial sample size
N = population size
Z_A = confidence coefficient for acceptable risk of incorrect acceptance (Beta risk)
Z_R = confidence coefficient for acceptable risk of incorrect rejection (Alpha risk)
SD^* = advanced estimate of the standard deviation
TM = tolerable misstatement for the population (materiality)
E^* = estimated point estimate of the population misstatement

Thus:

$$n = \left[\frac{30 \cdot (1.64 + 0) \cdot 2{,}000}{16{,}000 - 4{,}000}\right]^2$$

$$= (8.2)^2$$

$$= 67$$

20-31 (Continued)

c. Sample statistics are as follows:

ITEM NO.	e_j DIFFERENCE	$(e_j)^2$ DIFFERENCE SQUARED
1	$19	361
2	11	121
3	(19)	361
4	40	1,600
5	90	8,100
6	38	1,444
7	(90)	8,100
8	70	4,900
9	(85)	7,225
Totals	$74	32,212

Mean:

$$\bar{e} = \frac{\sum e_j}{n} = \frac{74}{60} = 1.23$$

Standard Deviation:

$$SD = \sqrt{\frac{\sum (e_j)^2 - n(\bar{e})^2}{n - 1}}$$

$$= \sqrt{\frac{32,212 - 60(1.23)^2}{60 - 1}}$$

$$= 23.3$$

Statistical estimates for population:

Point Estimate:

$$\hat{E} = N \cdot \bar{e} = 2,000 \cdot 1.23 = \$2,460$$

20-18

20-31 (Continued)

Computed Precision Interval at 90% reliability (confidence level) associated with a 5% Beta risk:

$$CPI = N \cdot Z_A \cdot \frac{SD}{\sqrt{n}} \cdot \sqrt{\frac{N-n}{N}}$$

$$= 2,000 \cdot 1.64 \cdot \frac{23.3}{\sqrt{60}} \cdot \sqrt{\frac{2,000-60}{2,000}}$$

$$= \$9,715$$

Upper Confidence Limit:

$$UCL = \hat{E} + CPI$$

$$= \$2,460 + \$9,715$$

$$= \$12,175$$

d. The confidence limits are within tolerable misstatement because the actual standard deviation is less than the preliminary estimates used to determine sample size.

20-32

Computer Solution. Computer solutions in Excel are contained on the Companion Website and on the diskette accompanying this manual. (Filename P2032.XLS.)

A. A price of $8 is proper for pricing L37 spars at 12-31-99 since the next shipment of spars was not received until 1-06-00. However, the next invoice shows a lower cost which indicates a decline in the value of this product. If the net realizable value (selling price less cost to sell) is less than the $8 per meter cost, the spars should be revalued to net realizable value at 12-31-99.

B. The total is 10,000/12 feet times $1.20 per foot = $1,000. In addition, the freight of $200 should have been as follows:

$$\frac{\$200}{(12,800 \text{ inches } / \text{ 12 inches per foot})} = \$0.1875 \text{ per ft}$$

Total inventory cost should be ($1.20 + 0.1875 per foot) times 10,000/12 feet = $1,156.25 or an overstatement of inventory by $10,844.21.

20-32 (Continued)

C. FIFO value would be:

Voucher 12-61	1,000 yards at $10.00 per yard	= $10,000
Voucher 11-81	500 yards at $ 9.50 per yard	= 4,750
Inventory is overstated by $250		$14,750

Voucher number 12-81 is not used because the receiving date is after year-end.

D. FIFO value would be:

Voucher 12-61	800 feet at $8.00 per foot	= $6,400
Voucher 11-81	200 feet at $8.20 per foot	= 1,640
		$8,040

Inventory is understated by $40. However, if the reduction in cost on voucher #12-61 indicates that the net realizable value of the struts is below the cost on voucher #10-81, then the net realizable value of the struts should be used as the cost.

E. Pricing is correct if the item is for inventory. It is possible that this item should be capitalized.

F. Proper FIFO cost is 40 pair times 2 = 80 springs times $69.00 each = $5,520. Inventory is understated by $5,244.

G. Pricing is correct. However, the fasteners were purchased in 1994 five years ago, and only eleven or 14% have been used. Consideration should be given as to whether net realizable value is less than cost.

20-32 (Continued)

SEA GULL AIRFRAMES, INC.
SUMMARY OF INVENTORY MISSTATEMENTS

Item No. and Description	Quantity Per Inventory	Quantity Correct	Quantity Difference	Price Per Inventory	Price Correct	Price Difference	Recorded Amount	Correct Amount	Amount of Misstatement
A. L37 Spars	3,000	3,000	0	8.00	8.00	0.00	24,000.00	24,000.00	0.00
B. B68 Metal Formers	10,000	833	9,167	1.20	1.3875	-0.1875	12,000.00	1,155.79	-10,844.21
C. R01 Metal Ribs	1,500	1,500	0	10.00	10/9.50	.50	15,000.00	14,750.00	-250.00
D. St26 Struts	1,000	1,000	0	8.00	8/8.20	-.20	8,000.00	8,040.00	40.00
E. Industrial hand drills	45	45	0	20.00	20.00	0.00	900.00	900.00	0.00
F. L803 Steel Leaf Springs	40	80	-40	69.00	69.00	0.00	276.00	5,520.00	5,244.00
G. V16 Fasteners	5.50	5.50	0	10.00	10.00	0.00	55.00	55.00	0.00
Total misstatement									-5,810.21
Items over $5,000									-11,054.21
Items under $5,000									5,244.00
									-5,810.21

CONCLUSION: (see next page for calculations)

There is a material potential misstatement due to the number and size of misstatements found relative to the sample chosen. In order to determine a more accurate estimate of the actual misstatement, additional tests are necessary.

REMARKS

A. NRV [assumed] exceeds cost.
B. Quantity based on inches, not feet; freight not included.
C. 500 yards overpriced.
D. 200 feet underpriced. NRV [assumed] O.K.
E. [Assumed] not capitalizable.
F. Includes extension error in inventory.
G. Consider separately for obsolescence.

20-32 (Continued)

PROJECTED MISSTATEMENTS

Dollars tested

Sample items	Over 5,000	Under $5,000
No exceptions	360,000	2,600
A	24,000	
B	12,000	
C	15,000	
D	8,000	
E		900
F		276
G		55
Dollars tested	419,000	3,831

PROJECTED MISSTATEMENT IGNORING SAMPLING ERROR*

$$\text{More than } \$5,000 \quad \frac{4,150,000}{419,000} \times -11,054.21 = -\$109,486$$

$$\text{Less than } \$5,000 \quad \frac{4,125,000}{3,831} \times 5,244 = \$5,646,436$$

* Used ratio estimation for projected misstatement. Difference estimation results are equally unacceptable.

20-33 a. Cutoff misstatements will exist for accounts payable whenever the liability for a purchase is recorded in the wrong period. The following rules should be followed for recording purchases:

1. Record as of date received when shipped FOB destination.
2. Record as of date shipped when shipped FOB origin.

On this basis, the receiving reports would be evaluated as follows:

RECEIVING REPORT NO.	AMOUNT	DATE SHIPPED	DATE RECEIVED	FOB POINT	SHOULD BE RECORDED IN AUGUST	WAS RECORDED IN AUGUST
41,679	$ 860	8-29	8-31	Dest.	Yes	Yes
41,680	1,211	8-27	9-01	Orig.	Yes	Yes
41,681	193	8-20	9-01	Orig.	Yes	Yes
41,682	4,674	8-27	9-01	Dest.	No	Yes
41,683	450	8-30	9-02	Dest.	No	No
41,684	106	8-30	9-02	Orig.	Yes	No
41,685	2,800	9-02	9-02	Orig.	No	No
41,686	686	8-30	9-02	Dest.	No	No

The entry to adjust the records as of August 31 for cutoff misstatements in accounts payables is as follows:

Dr. Accounts payable $4,568
    Cr. Purchases $4,568

To adjust accounts payable for cutoff misstatements in recording inventory purchases:

RR No. 41,682 $4,674
RR No. 41,684   (106)
                        $4,568

b. Sales should be recorded as of the date shipped. The following shipping documents were dated on September 1 and recorded in August:

    109,311 $ 56
    109,312   3,194
    109,313   635
    109,314   193
                       $4,078

These result in the following entry:

Dr. Sales $4,078
    Cr. Accounts receivable $4,078

To adjust sales for cutoff misstatements at August 31.

20-33 (Continued)

c.
1. Inventory received near the balance sheet date should be included in inventory if it is recorded as a purchase and excluded if it is not recorded as a purchase.
2. Inventory shipped near the balance sheet date should be excluded from inventory if it is recorded as a sale and included if it has not been recorded as a sale.

These principles lead to the following analysis.

Receipt of Goods

1. Inventory for all receiving reports up to 41,684 are included in inventory.
2. Using the analysis in part a, column 6, inventory for all receiving reports up to 41,684, except 41,682 and 41,683, should be included in accounts payable and inventory.

REPORT NO.	AMOUNT	SHOULD BE INCLUDED IN PURCHASES AND INVENTORY	WAS INCLUDED IN INVENTORY
41,679	860	Yes	Yes
41,680	1,211	Yes	Yes
41,681	193	Yes	Yes
41,682*	4,674	No	Yes
41,683*	450	No	Yes
41,684	106	Yes	Yes
41,685	2,800	No	No
41,686	686	No	No

*Requires removal from inventory.

3. Inventory for receiving reports 41,682 and 41,683 should therefore be removed from the physical count:

	Amount
41,682	4,674
41,683	450
	5,124

Shipment of Goods

1. Inventory for shipping documents 109,314 to 109,317 were included in inventory. All inventory for documents 109,313 and earlier were excluded.
2. Sales, after adjustments, were included only for shipments 109,310 and those preceding, as shown in the analysis in part b.

20-33 (Continued)

3. Inventory for shipping documents 109,311 to 109,313 should therefore be added to inventory. The amount of the cost of the inventory cannot be determined without reference to inventory costs. Presumably, cost will be less than the sales value shown in part b.

SHIPPING DOCUMENT NO.	INCLUDED IN PHYSICAL	RECORDED AS SALE AFTER ADJUSTMENTS IN PART b
109,310	No	Yes
109,311*	No	No
109,312*	No	No
109,313*	No	No
109,314	Yes	No
109,315	Yes	No
109,316	Yes	No
109,317	Yes	No
109,318	Yes	No

*Requires addition to inventory at cost.

SHIPPING DOCUMENT NO.	SELLING PRICE
109,311	$ 56
109,312	3,194
109,313	635
Inventory cost	3,885
(70% of selling price)	2,719

Summary

Reduction of inventory due to physical count error resulting from receipt of goods.	$5,124.00
Increase of inventory due to physical count error resulting from shipment of goods.	2,719.50
Net reduction of inventory required	$2,404.50

d. The accuracy about September 1 receipts and shipments of goods could be verified by reference to bills of lading.

20-25

Chapter 21

Audit of the Capital Acquisition and Repayment Cycle

■ Review Questions

21-1 Four examples of interest bearing liability accounts commonly found on balance sheets are:

1. Notes payable
2. Contracts payable
3. Mortgages payable
4. Bonds payable

These liabilities have the following characteristics in common:

1. Relatively few transactions affect the account balance, but each transaction is often highly material in amount.
2. The exclusion of a single transaction could be material in itself.
3. There is a legal relationship between the client entity and the holder of the stock, bond, or similar ownership document.
4. There is a direct relationship between interest and dividend accounts and debt and equity.

These liabilities differ in what they represent and the nature of their respective liabilities.

21-2 The characteristics of the liability accounts in the capital acquisition and repayment cycle that result in a different auditing approach than the approach followed in the audit of accounts payable are:

1. Relatively few transactions affect the account balance, but each transaction is often highly material in amount.
2. The exclusion of a single transaction could be material in itself.
3. There is a legal relationship between the client entity and the holder of the stock, bond, or similar ownership document.
4. There is a direct relationship between interest and dividend accounts and debt and equity.

21-3 It is common to audit the balance in notes payable in conjunction with the audit of interest expense and interest payable because it minimizes the verification time and reduces the likelihood of overlooking misstatements in the balance. Once the auditor is satisfied with the balance in notes payable the related interest rates and due dates for each note, it is easy to test the accuracy of accrued interest. If the interest expense for the year is also tested at the same time, the likelihood of omitting a note from notes payable for which interest has been paid is minimized. When there are a large number of notes or a large number of transactions during the year, it is usually too time consuming to completely tie out interest expense as a part of the audit of the notes payable and related accrued interest. Normally, however, there are only a few notes and few transactions during the year.

21-4 The most important controls the auditor should be concerned about in the audit of notes payable are:

1. The proper authorization for the issuance of new notes (or renewals) to insure that the company is not being committed to debt arrangements that are not authorized.
2. Controls over the repayment of principal and interest to insure that the proper amounts are paid.
3. Proper records and procedures to insure that all amounts in all transactions are properly recorded.
4. Periodic independent verification to insure that all the controls over notes payable are working.

21-5 The most important analytical procedures used to verify notes payable is a test of interest expense. By the use of this test, auditors can uncover misstatements in interest calculations or possible unrecorded notes payable.

21-6 It is more important to search for unrecorded notes payable than unrecorded notes receivable because the omission of an asset is less likely to occur than the omission of a debt. Several audit procedures the auditor can use to uncover unrecorded notes payable are:

1. Examine the notes paid after year-end to determine whether they were liabilities at the balance sheet date.
2. Obtain a standard bank confirmation which included specific reference to the existence of notes payable from all banks with whom the client does business.
3. Review the bank reconciliation for new notes credited directly to the bank account by the bank.
4. Obtain confirmation from creditors who have held notes from the client in the past and are not currently included in the notes payable schedule.
5. Analyze interest expense to uncover a payment to a creditor who is not included on the notes payable schedule.
6. Review the minutes of the board of directors for authorized but unrecorded notes.

21-7 The primary purpose of analyzing interest expense is to uncover a payment to a creditor who is not included on the notes payable schedule. The primary considerations the auditor should keep in mind when doing the analysis are:

1. Is the payee for the interest payment listed in the cash disbursements journal also included in the notes payable list?
2. Has a confirmation for notes payable been received from the payee?

21-8 The tests of controls and substantive tests of transactions for liability accounts in the capital acquisition and repayment cycle consists of tests of the control and substantive tests over the payment of principal and interest and the issuance of new notes or other liabilities, whereas the tests of details of balances concern the balance of the liabilities, interest payable, and interest expense. A unique aspect of the capital acquisition and repayment cycle is that auditors normally verify the transactions and balances in the account at the same time, as described in the solution to Review Question 21-3.

21-9 Four types of restrictions long-term creditors often put on companies in granting them a loan are:

1. Financial ratio restrictions
2. Payment of dividends restrictions
3. Operations restrictions
4. Issue of additional debt restrictions

The auditor can find out about these restrictions by examining the loan agreement and related correspondence associated with the loan, and by confirmation. The auditor must perform calculations and observe activities to determine whether the client has observed the restrictions.

21-10 The primary objectives in the audit of owners' equity accounts are to determine whether:

1. The internal controls over capital stock and related dividends are adequate.
2. Owners' equity transactions are recorded properly, as defined by the following six transaction-related audit objectives:

    - Existence
    - Completeness
    - Accuracy
    - Classification
    - Timing
    - Posting and summarization

3. Owners' equity balances are properly presented and disclosed as defined by the following balance-related audit objectives:
    - Detail tie-in
    - Existence
    - Completeness
    - Accuracy
    - Classification
    - Cutoff
    - Presentation and disclosure

21-11 Although the corporate charter and bylaws are legal documents, their legal nature is not being judged by the auditor. They are being used only to reference transactions being tested by the auditor and provide insight into some of the key control features of the company. The auditor should consult an attorney if the information the auditor needs from the documents is not clear or if a legal interpretation is needed.

21-12 The major internal control over owners' equity are:

1. Proper authorization of transactions
2. Proper record keeping
3. Adequate segregation of duties between maintaining owners' equity records and handling cash and stock certificates
4. The use of an independent registrar and stock transfer agent

21-13 The audit of owners' equity for a closely held corporation differs from that for a publicly held corporation in that the amount of time spent in verifying owners' equity in a closely held corporation is usually minimal because of the relatively few transactions for capital stock accounts that occur during the year. For publicly held corporations, the audit of owners' equity is more complex due to the existence of a larger number of shareholders and frequent changes in the individuals holding stock.

The audits are not significantly different in regard to whether the transactions in the equity accounts are properly authorized and recorded and whether the amounts in the accounts are properly classified, described, and stated in accordance with generally accepted accounting principles.

21-14 The duties of a stock registrar are to make sure that stock is issued by a corporation in accordance with the capital authorization of the board of directors, to sign all newly issued stock certificates, and to make sure old certificates are received and cancelled before a replacement certificate is issued when there is a change in the ownership of the stock.

The duties of a transfer agent are to maintain the stockholder records, and in some cases, disburse cash dividends to shareholders.

The use of the services of a stock registrar improves the effectiveness of the client's internal controls by preventing the improper issuance of stock certificates. Along similar lines, the use of the services of an independent transfer agent improves the control over the stock records by putting them in the hands of an independent organization.

21-15 The number of shares outstanding, the correct valuation of capital stock transactions, and par value can all be confirmed with a transfer agent. The balance can then be easily recalculated from this information.

21-16 Since it is important to verify that properly authorized dividends have been paid to owners of stock as of the dividend record date, a comparison of a random sample of cancelled dividend checks to a dividend list prepared by management would be inadequate. Such an audit step is useless unless the dividend list has first been verified to include all stockholders of record at the dividend record date. A better test is to determine the total number of shares outstanding at the dividend date from the stock registrar and recompute the total dividends that should have been paid for comparison with

21-16 (Continued)

the total amount actually paid. A random sample of cancelled checks should then be compared to the independent registrar's records to verify that the payments were actually made to valid shareholders.

21-17 If a transfer agent disburses dividends for a client, the total dividends declared can be verified by tracing the amount to a cash disbursement entry to the agent and also confirming the amount. There should ordinarily be no need to test individual dividend disbursement transactions if a stock transfer agent is used.

21-18 The major emphasis in auditing the retained earnings account should be on the recorded changes that have taken place during the year, such as net earnings for the year, dividends declared, prior period adjustments, extraordinary items charged or credited directly to retained earnings, or setting up or elimination of appropriations. Except for dividends declared, the other items should be verified during other parts of the engagement. This is especially true of the net earnings for the year. Therefore, the audit of retained earnings primarily consists of an analysis of the changes in retained earnings and the verification of the authorization and accuracy of the underlying transactions.

21-19 For auditing owners' equity and calculating earnings per share, it is crucial to verify that the number of shares used in each is accurate. Earnings are verified as an integral part of the entire audit and should require no additional verification as a part of owners' equity. The most important auditing considerations in verifying the earnings per share figure are the accounting principles prescribed by APB 15 and the descriptions of the various classes of stock in the corporate charter and minutes of the board of directors.

■ **Multiple Choice Questions From CPA Examinations**

21-20 a. (2)   b. (1)   c. (3)

21-21 a. (4)   b. (3)   c. (1)

Discussion Questions and Problems

21-22

a. PURPOSE OF CONTROL	b. POTENTIAL FINANCIAL STATEMENT MISSTATEMENT	c. AUDIT PROCEDURE TO DETERMINE EXISTENCE OF MATERIAL MISSTATEMENT
1. To insure that all note liabilities are actual liabilities of the company.	Loss of assets through payment of excess interest rates or the diversion of cash to unauthorized persons.	Examine note request forms for proper authorization and discuss terms of note with appropriate management personnel.
2. To insure that note transactions are recorded in full and in detail.	Improper disclosure or misstatements in notes payable through duplication.	Reconcile detailed contents of master file or other records to control account.
3. To prevent misuse of notes and funds earmarked for notes.	Misstatement of liabilities and cash.	Perform all substantive procedures on extended basis. Trace from paid notes file to cash receipts to determine that the appropriate amount of cash was received when the note was issued.
4. To insure that notes are not paid more than once.	Loss of cash.	Examine outstanding notes and paid notes for similarities and the potential for reusing the notes.
5. To insure that all note-related transactions agree with account balances.	Misstatement of notes payable.	Reconcile master file with outstanding notes payable.
6. To insure that only the proper interest amount is paid and recorded.	Misstatement of interest expense and related accrual.	Recompute interest on a test basis.

21-23 a.

AUDIT PROCEDURE	PURPOSE
1	To determine the nature of restrictions on client as a means of verifying whether the restrictions have been met and to insure they are adequately disclosed.
2	To insure that the bonds are not subject to unnecessary early retirement by bondholders and that proper disclosures are made.
3	To determine if the account balances are reasonable as related to each other and to examine for unreasonable changes in the account balances.
4	To determine if the calculations are correct and accounts are accurate.
5	To obtain independent confirmation of bond indebtedness and collateral.

b. The auditor should be alert for the following provisions in the bond indenture agreement:

1. Restrictions on payment of dividends
2. Convertibility provisions
3. Provisions for repayment
4. Restrictions on additional borrowing
5. Required maintenance of specified financial ratios

c. The auditor can determine whether the above provisions have been met by the following procedures:

1. Audit of payments of dividends
2. Determine if the appropriate stock authorizations are adequate
3. Determine if sinking fund is adequate
4. Search for other liabilities
5. Calculate ratios and compare to agreement

d. The auditor should verify the unamortized bond discount or premium on a bond that was in force at the beginning of the year by recalculation. This is done by dividing the premium or discount by the number of total months the bonds will be outstanding and multiplying by the number of months remaining. For bonds issued in the current year, the bond premium or discount must first be verified. The monthly premium or discount is then calculated and multiplied by the number of months still outstanding.

21-23 (Continued)

    e. The following information should be requested from the bondholder in the confirmation of bonds payable:

      1. Amount of bond
      2. Maturity date
      3. Interest rate
      4. Payment dates
      5. Payment amounts
      6. Assets pledged as security
      7. Restrictions on client activities

21-24 Any or all of the following items, which would be of interest to the auditor, might be found in a trust indenture:

1. An exact description of the bonds, including the authorized issue and the exact title given the bonds. This would be of interest in determining that the bonds outstanding do not exceed the authorized amount and to fully describe the issue on the balance sheet.
2. Interest rate and interest provisions. This information is desirable in determining the amount and correct treatment of accrued interest. It is also necessary for determining the correctness of the entry separating interest from principal at the date of sale.
3. The trust indenture will state the maturity date of the bonds and the conversion or redemption features, if any. The auditor determines that the significant parts of such data have been disclosed on the balance sheet and would use the data as conversion or redemption to determine the acceptability of any transactions entered into in accordance with such provisions.
4. The trust indenture will contain any existing provisions as to the establishment of a sinking fund for redemption of the bonds and for surplus reservation, if any, and will state the manner in which final repayment of the bonds must be carried out. The auditor uses this information in connection with his or her verification of sinking fund and surplus reserve transactions and balances. The information as to final repayment is needed to determine the proper accounting treatment of deposits made for purpose of repayment.
5. The name of the trustee and the duties and rights of the trustee are included as part of the agreement. The auditor corresponds with the trustee as of each audit date for confirmation of bonds outstanding and status of the issue.
6. Any special reports that must be prepared for the trustee are enumerated in the indenture as well as any special provisions as to methods of accounting. The auditor uses this information to assist the client in complying with the terms of the indenture.
7. The indenture will contain the description of any property pledged as security for repayment of the bonds. The auditor must disclose the existence of such a pledge.
8. The indenture may contain provisions as to expenditures for maintenance and/or replacement of property. The auditor must determine the correctness of the classification of entries to such accounts as made by the company.

21-24 (Continued)

9. The indenture may include provisions regarding amounts of working capital, definitions of inclusions in working capital, and ratios of short-term borrowings to various other balance sheet amounts. The auditor will assist the client in properly reporting under such requirements.
10. The indenture may contain restrictions on dividend payments. The auditor must disclose the existence of such covenants when certifying financial statements.
11. The indenture may contain provisions regarding insurance coverage. The auditor will determine compliance with such requirements and report on any failure to comply.

The following items would normally be included in a confirmation obtained from a trustee under a bond indenture:

1. The amount of bonds authorized and outstanding at the balance sheet date together with changes during the year. This procedure affords evidence as to the correct liability and would disclose certain kinds of unrecorded transactions.
2. The status of interest payments, if the trustee acts as paying agent. The auditor considers such information as a part of his or her evidence supporting the accrual of interest.
3. Status of sinking fund, if any such fund is provided for by the agreement. This is the auditor's principal evidence as to the balance and operation of such a fund.
4. Information as to the date, due date (or term), and description of the issue may also be obtained from the trustee. These items have been included previously under the indenture.
5. Information as to any default under the agreement. A default may subject the company to various penalties which might require disclosure.

21-25
a. The auditing necessary for notes payable and related interest accounts in these circumstances would be minimal. Aside from checking interest calculations and postings to the proper accounts as a matter of audit routine, the only major audit procedure would be to confirm the amount and provisions of the note with the bank.
b. If Fox was unprofitable, had a need for additional financing, and had weak internal controls, it would be necessary to search for unrecorded notes. This could be done by obtaining standard bank confirmations with specific reference to the existence of notes payable, reviewing the bank statements and reconciliations for new notes credited directly to the bank account by the bank, and analyzing interest expense to uncover a payment to a creditor who is not included on the notes payable schedule.

21-26 a. The emphasis in the verification of notes payable in this situation should be in determining whether all existing notes are included in the client's records. The four audit procedures listed do not satisfy this emphasis.

b.

AUDIT PROCEDURE	PURPOSE
1	To determine if the notes payable list reconciles to the general ledger.
2	To determine if the notes payable on the list are correctly recorded and disclosed.
3	To verify that all recorded notes payable are properly recorded and disclosed.
4	To insure that interest expense is properly recorded on the books.

c. Procedure 2 is not necessary in light of procedure 3. They both perform the same function and the confirmation is from an independent source. The sample sizes for the procedures are probably appropriate, considering the deficiencies in record keeping procedures.

d. In addition to the procedures mentioned, the following ones are essential because there must be a search for unrecorded notes:

1. Analyze interest expense and send a confirmation for notes payable to all payees not receiving a confirmation for notes.
2. Confirm the balance in notes payable to payees included in last year's notes payable list but not confirmed in the current year.
3. Examine notes paid after year-end to determine whether they were liabilities at the balance sheet date.
4. Obtain a standard bank confirmation which includes a specific reference to notes payable from all banks with which the client does business.
5. Review the minutes of the board of directors.

21-27 In each case, any actual failure to comply would have to be reported in a footnote to the statements in view of the possible serious consequences of advancing the maturity date of the loan. The individual audit steps that should be taken are as follows:

a. Calculate the working capital ratio at the beginning of and through the previous fiscal year. If it is under 2 to 1, determine compensation of officers for compliance with the limitation.
b. Examine the client's copies of insurance policies or certificates of insurance for compliance with the covenant, preparing a schedule of book value, appraised or estimated value, and coverage for the report. Confirm policies held with trustee.

21-27 (Continued)

    c. Examine vouchers supporting tax payments on all property covered by the indenture. By reference to the local tax laws and the vouchers, determine that all taxes have been paid before the penalty-free period expired. If the vouchers in any case are inadequate, confirm with the trustee who holds the tax receipts.

    d. Vouch the payments to the sinking fund. Confirm bond purchases and sinking fund balance with trustee. Observe evidence of destruction of bonds for bonds cancelled. Report the fund as an asset, preferably giving the composition as to cash and bonds held alive, if any.

21-28 a. It is desirable to prepare a working paper for the permanent file for the mortgage so that the appropriate information concerning the mortgage will be conveniently available for future years' audits. This information should include all the provisions of the mortgage as well as the purchase price, date of purchase, and a list of items pledged as collateral. It may also contain an amortization schedule of principal and interest (especially if the auditor has access to a computer program for preparation of such a schedule).

    b. The audit of mortgage payable, interest expense, and interest payable should all be done together since these accounts are related and the results of testing each account have a bearing on the other accounts. The likelihood of misstatement in the client's records is determined faster and more effectively by doing them together.

    c. The audit procedures that should ordinarily be performed to verify the issue of the mortgage, the balance in the mortgage and interest payable, and the balance in the interest expense accounts are:

1. Determine if the mortgage was properly authorized.
2. Obtain the mortgage agreement and schedule the pertinent provisions in the permanent file, including the face amount, payments, interest rate, restrictions, and collateral.
3. Confirm the mortgage amount, terms, and collateral with the lending institution.
4. Recompute interest payable at the balance sheet date and reconcile interest expense to the decrease in principal and the payments made.
5. Test interest expense for reasonableness.

21-29

a. PURPOSE OF CONTROL	b. POTENTIAL FINANCIAL STATEMENT MISSTATEMENT	c. AUDIT PROCEDURES TO DETERMINE EXISTENCE OF MATERIAL MISSTATEMENT
1. To insure that records are properly maintained.	Misstatement of owners' equity and the disbursement of dividends and capital to the wrong people.	Determine if company uses services of an independent registrar, or transfer agent. Confirm details of equity accounts with them.
2. To insure that stock is issued and retired only at the discretion of the board.	Illegal payments of cash and issue of shares.	Examine cancelled shares and newly issued ones to make sure they are included in the board of directors minutes.
3. To insure that records are properly maintained.	Misstatement of owners' equity and earnings per share.	Account for all unissued certificates and account for all cancelled certificates and their mutilation.
4. To insure that the general ledger reflects the balance of supporting records.	Misstatement of owners' equity and earnings per share.	Trace postings from master file and stock certificates into general ledger. Reconcile master file to general ledger.
5. To insure that the dividends declared are paid to the proper individuals.	Misstatement of dividends declared on balance sheet or payment to the wrong people which could result in a liability.	Obtain confirmation of paid dividends from independent transfer agent.
6. To insure that all shares issued or retired are properly authorized.	Misstatement of dividends declared on balance sheet or payment to the wrong people which could result in a liability.	Verify authenticity of all changes in owners' equity account.

21-30

a. PURPOSE OF AUDIT PROCEDURES	b. MISSTATEMENTS THAT MAY BE UNCOVERED
1. To determine what type of stock may be issued, under what circumstances, and its description.	Unauthorized outstanding stock or improper description of stock.
2. To determine if any stock issues, retirements, or dividends were authorized.	Unauthorized or omitted equity transactions.
3. To determine the propriety of changes in the accounts and to verify their accuracy.	The issuance or retirement of stock without proper authorization, improper valuation, or incorrect dividend calculations.
4. To determine if there were any shares issued or retired during year, or if any certificates are missing.	Unrecorded or unauthorized transactions, or transactions not handled in a legal manner.
5. To determine if all retired stock has been cancelled.	Same as 4.
6. To verify that earnings per share has been correctly computed.	Incorrect earnings per share computation.
7. To determine that dividends are legal and disclosure in the financial statements is proper.	Illegal payments of dividends and improper disclosure of the information in the financial statements.

21-31 The proposal for the limitation of procedure is not justified by the stated facts. Although the transfer agent and the registrar know the number of shares issued, they do not necessarily know the number of shares outstanding. Furthermore, the audit of capital stock includes more than determining the number of shares outstanding. For example, the auditor must determine what authorizations exist for the issuance of shares, what assets were received in payment of shares, how the transactions were recorded, and what subscription contracts have been entered into. Confirmation from the registrar could not help in determining these things.

In addition to confirmation from the registrar, the audit of capital stock might include the following procedures, the purposes of which are briefly indicated:

1. Examine the corporation charter--to determine the number of shares authorized and the special provisions for each class of stock if more than one class is authorized.
2. Examine minutes of stockholders' and directors' meetings--to determine authorization for appointments of the registrar and the transfer agent; to determine authorization for the issuance or reacquisition of shares.

21-31 (Continued)

3. Examine provisions regarding capital stock in the corporation law of the state of incorporation—to determine any special provisions, such as those for the issuance of no par stock.
4. Analyze the capital stock accounts to obtain an orderly picture of stock transactions for use as a guide to other auditing procedures and as a permanent record.
5. Trace the consideration received for capital stock into the records—to determine what consideration has been received and how it has been recorded.
6. Examine and schedule treasury stock and review entries for treasury stock—to determine the existence of treasury stock as authorized and to determine that a proper record has been made.
7. Review registrar's invoices and cash disbursements—to determine that original issue taxes have been paid.
8. Compare dividends with stock outstanding at dividend dates—to determine that dividends have been properly paid and also to substantiate the stock outstanding.
9. Review subscription and option contracts, etc.—to determine the facts in regard to subscriptions and options and to determine that these facts have been properly recorded and that they are adequately disclosed.

21-32
a. The approach followed by the auditor is effective in assuring that the amount used for dividends is in agreement with calculations based on stock that should have been properly authorized. However, because the chief accountant, who is also a stockholder, has the unsegregated duties of preparing dividend checks, recording them in the dividend journal and reconciling the bank account, it is possible for him or her to prepare and send dividend checks without recording them and cover the use of funds by falsifying the bank reconciliation. It is also possible to pay some stockholders an incorrect amount of dividends and thereby pay himself or herself or others more.

b. To verify dividends in this situation, it would be necessary for the auditor to verify the bank reconciliation to insure that no funds are being used for more than the declared amounts of dividends. In addition, it would be desirable to prepare a proof of cash for the year to make sure all dividends were disbursed. Next, the amount of some dividend checks should be recomputed considering the number of shares held and dividend rate to make sure the correct amount was paid. Finally, all checks paid to the chief accountant should be totaled and the amount should be recomputed by multiplying the annual dividend times the number of shares he or she holds.

21-33 a. The audit program for the audit of Pate Corporation's capital stock account would include the following procedures:

1. Examine the articles of incorporation, the bylaws, and the minutes of the board of directors from the inception of the corporation to determine the provisions or decisions regarding the capital stock, such as classes of stock, par value or stated value, authorized number of shares, authorization for the sale of new issues or additional sales of unissued stock, declarations of stock splits and dividends in the form of cash or stock, and granting of stock options or stock rights. Determine that the accounting records are in accordance with these provisions or decisions and that appropriate disclosure is made by footnote if necessary. Extract pertinent data for the auditor's permanent file.
2. Examine the stock certificate stub book and determine whether the total of the open stubs agrees with the Capital Stock account in the general ledger. Examine cancelled stock certificates which are generally attached to the corresponding stub.
   Information on the stubs regarding the number of shares, date, etc. for both outstanding and cancelled stock certificates should be compared with the Capital Stock account. All certificate numbers should be accounted for and, if the CPA deems it necessary, confirmation of the number of certificates printed should be obtained from the printer. A test check should be made to determine that the proper amounts of original issue and capital stock transfer taxes have been affixed to the stubs and the cancelled certificates. The stockholders shown in the stock certificate stub book should be compared with the stockholders' master file if one is maintained.
3. Analyze the Capital Stock account from the corporation's inception and verify all entries. Trace all transactions involving the transfer of cash either to the cash receipts or the cash disbursements records. If property other than cash was received in exchange for capital stock, trace the recording of the property to the proper asset account and consider the reasonableness of the valuation placed on the property. Transactions showing the sale of stock at a discount or premium should be traced to the Capital Contributed in Excess of Par Value account. If capital stock has been sold at a discount, consideration should be given to the possible violation of state laws and the client's attention should be directed to the matter. Should the analysis of the Capital Stock account disclose that the corporation has engaged in treasury stock transactions, determine that the increase or decrease in net assets resulting from these transactions has not been placed in the Retained Earnings account.
   The audit procedures to be applied to the audit of the Capital Contributed in Excess of Par Value account are usually applied at the same time that the Capital Stock account is being audited because the two accounts are interrelated. The accounts should be analyzed and the entries verified when the related entries in the Capital Stock account are verified. If an entry is not related to Capital Stock account entries, as in the case of a write-off of a deficit as the result of a quasi-reorganization, authorization for the entry and the supporting material should be examined.

21-33 (Continued)

4. The following audit procedures would be applied to the Retained Earnings account:
   a) Analyze the account from its inception. Consider the validity of the amounts representing income or loss that were closed from the Profit and Loss account. Amounts representing appraisal increments or writing up of assets should be considered for reasonableness, and the increase should be reported separately from retained earnings in the stockholders' equity section of the balance sheet.
   b) Any extraordinary gains or losses carried directly to the Retained Earnings account should be investigated and their treatment reviewed in relation to generally accepted accounting principles.
   c) Entries recording the appropriation of retained earnings or the return of such appropriations should be reviewed for reasonableness, and authorization for the entries should be traced to the proper authority. Similarly, actions of the board of directors that affected retained earnings should be traced to the account analysis.
   d) Conditions such as loan covenants or contingent liabilities that were uncovered during the audit that might require or make desirable the placing of restrictions on retained earnings should be reviewed for proper disclosure in the financial statements.
   e) Entries recording cash or stock dividends should be traced to the minutes of the board of directors for authorization and traced to the Cash account or the Capital Stock account. A separate computation should be made by the CPA of the total amount of dividends paid based upon his or her schedules of outstanding stock as an overall test of the existence of the distributions. If stock dividends have been distributed, the amount removed from retained earnings should be reviewed for compliance with generally accepted accounting principles.

b. In conducting his or her audit, the CPA verifies retained earnings as he or she does other items on the balance sheet for several reasons. A principal reason is that the verification is an assurance or double check that no important item was overlooked in the audit of the accounts that were the contra or balancing part of the entry recorded in retained earnings. An example of an important item that may be overlooked would be a balance sheet account that was closed during the year under audit and the ledger card for the account removed from the general ledger current file. Another reason is that, though the entry in the contra account may have been examined, the auditor may have overlooked that the balancing part of the entry was to retained earnings, a treatment that may have been contrary to generally accepted accounting principles; his or her audit of retained earnings would bring this noncompliance to his or her attention.

Still another reason for verifying the retained earnings account is to determine whether any portion of the balance in the account may be subject to restriction by state law or other authority. Since the account is the basis for the payment of dividends, it is important to determine that the balance is composed of income realized from transactions free from any restrictions.

Chapter 22

Audit of Cash Balances

■ **Review Questions**

22-1 The appropriate tests for the ending balance in the cash accounts depend heavily on the initial assessment of control risk, tests of controls, and substantive tests of transactions for cash receipts. The company's controls over cash receipts assist the auditor in determining that cash received is promptly deposited, that receipts recorded are proper, that customer accounts are promptly updated, and that the cash cutoff at year-end is proper. If the results of the evaluation of internal control, the tests of controls, and the substantive tests of transactions are adequate, it is appropriate to reduce the tests of details of balances for cash, especially for the detailed tests of bank reconciliations. On the other hand, if the tests indicate that the client's controls are inadequate, extensive year-end testing may be necessary.

22-2 The appropriate tests for the ending balance in the cash accounts depend heavily on the initial assessment of control risk, tests of controls, and substantive tests of transactions for cash disbursements. The company's controls over cash disbursements assist the auditor in determining that cash disbursed is for approved company purposes, that cash disbursements are promptly recorded in the proper amount, and that cash cutoff at year-end is proper. If the results of the evaluation of internal control, the tests of controls, and the substantive tests of transactions are adequate, it is appropriate to reduce the tests of details of balances for cash, especially for the detailed tests of bank reconciliations. On the other hand, if the tests indicate that the client's controls are inadequate, extensive year-end testing may be necessary.

An example in which the conclusions reached about the controls in cash disbursements would affect the tests of cash balances would be:

> If controls over the issuance of blank checks, the review of payees, amounts, and supporting documentation, the signing of checks, and the reconciliation of bank statements and vendors' statements are adequate, the auditor's review of outstanding checks on the year-end bank reconciliation may be greatly reduced. The year-end outstanding checks can be verified by testing a sample of checks returned with the cutoff bank statement rather than tracing all paid outstanding checks and the final monthly checks in the cash disbursements journal to the last month's cleared checks and the bank reconciliation.

22-3 The monthly reconciliation of bank accounts by an independent person is an important internal control over cash balances because it provides an opportunity for an internal verification of the cash receipts and cash disbursements transactions, investigation of reconciling items on the bank reconciliation, and the verification of the ending cash balance. Anyone responsible for the following duties would not be considered independent for the purposes of preparing monthly bank reconciliations:

22-3 (Continued)
- Issuance of checks
- Receipt and deposit of cash
- Other handling of cash
- Record keeping

22-4 The controller's approach is to reconcile until the balance agrees. The shortcoming of this approach is that it does not include a review of the items which flow through the account and it opens the door for the processing of improper items. Such items as checks payable to an improper parties, reissuance of outstanding checks to improper parties, and kiting of funds would not be discovered with the controller's approach. The controller's procedures should include the following:

a. Examination of all checks clearing with the statement (including those on previous month's outstanding check list) and comparison of payee and amount to the cash disbursements journal.
b. Test of cash receipts to determine that they are deposited within a reasonable amount of time.
c. Follow-up on old outstanding checks so that they can be recognized as income after it is determined that they will not be cashed, and no liability exists.

22-5 Bank confirmations differ from positive confirmations of accounts receivable in that bank confirmations request several specific items of information, namely:

1. The balances in all bank accounts.
2. Restrictions on withdrawals.
3. The interest rate on interest-bearing accounts.
4. Information on liabilities to the bank for notes, mortgages, or other debt.

Positive confirmations of accounts receivable request of the buyer to confirm an account balance stated on the confirmation form or designate a different amount with an explanation. The auditor anticipates few exceptions to accounts receivable confirmations, whereas with bank confirmations he expects differences which the client must reconcile. Bank confirmations should be requested for all bank accounts, but positive confirmations of accounts receivable are normally requested only for a sample of accounts. If bank confirmations are not returned, they must be pursued until the auditor is satisfied as to what the requested information is. If positive confirmations of accounts receivable are not returned, second and maybe third requests may be made, but thereafter, follow-ups are not likely to be pursued. Alternative procedures, such as examination of subsequent payments or other support of customers' accounts may then be used.

The reason why more importance is placed on bank confirmations than accounts receivable confirmations is that cash, being the most liquid of assets, must be more closely controlled than accounts receivable. In addition, other information-- such as liabilities to the bank—must be known for purposes of the financial statements. Finally, there are usually only a few bank accounts and most bank accounts have a large volume of transactions during the year.

22-6 This is a good auditing procedure that attempts to discover if any accounts that should have been closed are still being used, such as by a company employee to deposit customer remittances. The procedure may also discover unrecorded and contingent liabilities.

22-7 A cutoff bank statement is a partial period bank statement with the related cancelled checks, duplicate deposit slips, and other documents included in bank statements, which is mailed by the bank directly to the auditor. The purpose of the cutoff bank statement is to verify the reconciling items on the client's year-end reconciliation with evidence that is inaccessible to the client.

22-8 Auditors are usually less concerned about the client's cash receipts cutoff than the cutoff for sales, because the cutoff of cash receipts affects only cash and accounts receivable and not the income statement, whereas a misstatement in the cutoff of sales affects accounts receivable and the income statement.

For the purpose of detecting a cash receipt cutoff misstatement, there are two useful audit procedures. The first is to trace the deposits in transit to the cutoff bank statement to determine the date they were deposited in the bank account. Since the recorded cash will have to be included as deposits in transit on the bank reconciliation, the auditor can test for the number of days it took for the in-transit items to be deposited. If there is more than a two or three day delay between the balance sheet date and the subsequent deposit of all deposits in transit, there is an indication of a cutoff misstatement. The second audit procedure requires being on the premises at the balance sheet date and counting all cash and checks on hand and recording the amount in the working papers. When the bank reconciliation is tested, the auditor can then check whether the deposits in transit equal the amount recorded.

22-9 An imprest bank account for a branch operation is one in which a fixed balance is maintained. After authorized branch personnel use the funds for proper disbursements, they make an accounting to the home office. After the expenditures have been approved by the home office, a reimbursement is made to the branch account from the home office's general account for the total of the cash disbursements. The purpose of using this type of account is to provide controls over cash receipts and cash disbursements by preventing the branch operators from disbursing their cash receipts directly, and by providing review and approval of cash disbursements before more cash is made available.

22-10 The purpose of the four-column proof of cash is to verify:

- Whether all recorded cash receipts were deposited.
- Whether all deposits in the bank were recorded in the accounting records.
- Whether all recorded cash disbursements were paid by the bank.
- Whether all amounts that were paid by the bank were recorded as cash disbursements in the accounting records.

Two types of misstatements that the four-column proof of cash is meant to uncover are:

- Cash received that was not recorded in the cash receipts journal
- Checks that cleared the bank but have not been recorded in the cash disbursements journal

22-11 Whenever a cutoff bank statement is not received directly from the bank, the auditor may verify the bank statement for the month subsequent to year-end. The audit procedures used for the verification are as follows:

1. Foot all of the cancelled checks, debit memos, deposits, and credit memos.
2. Check to see that the bank statement balances when the totals in 1 are used.
3. Review the items included in 1 to make sure they were cancelled by the bank in the proper period and do not include any erasures or alterations.

The purpose of this verification is to test whether the client's employees have omitted, added, or altered any of the documents accompanying the statement.

22-12 Lapping is a defalcation in which a cash shortage is concealed by delaying the crediting of cash receipts to the proper accounts receivable. The first step in the fraud is to withhold cash remitted by a customer from a bank deposit. A few days later, because the customer must receive credit for the remittance, the first customer's account is credited with an amount from a remittance made by a second customer. The process requires the continuous shifting of shortages from account to account and the crediting of subsequent receipts to the wrong accounts receivable.

Kiting is a procedure used to conceal cash shortages from employers and auditors, to conceal bank overdrafts from the bank or banks affected, or to pad a cash position. All kiting procedures are designed to take advantage of the "float" period during which a check is in transit between banks.

A shortage in the cash in bank account may be concealed by depositing in the bank a transfer check drawn on another bank. The transfer check, not recorded as a deposit or a cash disbursement, brings the bank account into agreement with the books of account. The check is recorded a few days later and the shortage "reappears" unless the process is repeated. A similar effect may be obtained by depositing unrecorded fictitious N.S.F. checks.

If a depositor desires to write a check for which he does not have funds on deposit, he can deposit a transfer check large enough to cover the payment, even though the transfer check itself creates an overdraft. The transfer process may be repeated indefinitely or may be terminated by a deposit of sufficient funds to cover the overdraft. Since the purpose of this procedure is to conceal an overdraft from the bank, the transfer check may or may not be recorded on the books on the date that it was drawn.

Kiting to pad a cash position typically occurs at the end of a fiscal period; a check transferring funds from one bank to another is deposited and recorded on the date drawn but is not recorded as a cash disbursement until the following period. In this case, the credit on the books would probably be made to a revenue account and the subsequent debit to an expense account.

The following audit procedures would be used to uncover lapping:

22-12 (Continued)

- Confirm accounts receivable and give close attention to exceptions made by customers about payment dates. The confirmation procedure is better applied as a surprise at an interim date so that if a person is engaged in lapping, he or she will not have been able to bring the "lapped" accounts up to date. If the confirmations are always prepared at year-end, the audit step may be anticipated by the person doing the lapping and the shortage given a different form such as kiting of checks.
- Make a surprise count of the cash and customers' checks on hand. The deposit of these funds should be made under the auditor's control, and the details of the deposit should later be compared with the cash receipts book and the accounts receivable records.
- Compare the details of remittance lists (if prepared), stamped duplicate deposit slips, and entries in the cash receipts book. Since deposit slips are easily altered, some auditors prepare duplicate deposit slips for deposits made a few days before and after the audit date and have these slips authenticated by the bank. These authenticated duplicate deposit slips are compared to remittance lists and to entries in the cash book.
- Compare the check vouchers received with the customers' checks with stamped duplicate deposit slips, the entries in the cash book, and postings to the accounts receivable records. If the client stamps the voucher with the date it was received, the auditor should make a careful comparisons of the stamped dates to the dates recorded in the cash receipts journal.

Kiting might be uncovered by the following audit procedures:

- As a surprise count of cash and customers' checks on hand is made as a test for lapping, determine that checks representing transfers of funds are properly recorded on the books.
- Prepare a schedule of the interbank transfers made for a few days before and after the audit date. The schedule should show, for each check, the date that the cash disbursement was recorded on the books, and the dates of withdrawal and deposit shown on the bank statements.
- Obtain cutoff bank statements directly from the bank covering the seven to ten day period after the balance sheet date. Examine the checks returned with the cutoff statements and pay attention to dates of the transactions stamped by the banks on the backs of the checks. These stamped dates should not be earlier than the dates of the checks or the dates of cash disbursements recorded on the books. Protested (N.S.F.) checks should be investigated to determine they are not fictitious checks deposited temporarily to cover a shortage.

22-13 Assuming a client with excellent internal controls uses an imprest payroll bank account, the verification of the payroll bank reconciliation ordinarily takes less time than the tests of the general bank account even though the number of payroll checks exceeds those written on the general account because an imprest payroll account has no activity other than payroll checks drawn and deposits made to reestablish the standard minimum account balance. Furthermore, most employees cash their checks quickly, so there usually are few outstanding checks, especially older ones, and no other reconciling items. On the other hand, the general bank account will include all

22-13 (Continued)
regular activity plus bank charges, notes, other liabilities, etc., that must be reconciled and verified.

22-14 The verification of petty cash reimbursements consists of footing the petty cash vouchers supporting the amounts of the reimbursements, accounting for a sequence of petty cash vouchers, examining the petty cash vouchers for authorization and cancellation, and examining the supporting documentation attached to the vouchers for reasonableness. The balance in the fund is verified by a count of the petty cash. Testing of petty cash transactions is more important than the ending balance in the account, because even if the amount of the petty cash fund is small, there is potential for a large number of improper transactions if the fund is frequently reimbursed.

22-15 There is a greater emphasis on the detection of fraud in tests of details of cash balances than for other balance sheet accounts because the amount of cash flowing into and out of the cash account is frequently larger than for any other account in the financial statements. Furthermore, the susceptibility of cash to misappropriation is greater than other types of assets because most other assets must be converted to cash to make them usable.

This emphasis affects the auditor's evidence accumulation in auditing year-end cash as in these examples:

- Verifying whether cash transactions are properly recorded
- Testing of bank reconciliations
- Obtaining bank confirmations

22-16 The misstatements that are of the greatest concern to auditors in bank reconciliations are intentional ones to cover up a cash shortage, usually resulting from a defalcation. A fraudulent deposit in transit or an omitted outstanding check will both cover up a cash shortage. Omitted deposits in transit or inclusion of a nonexistent outstanding check are likely misstatements only when the bank balance, after reconciling items are accounted for, is greater than the book balance, a highly unlikely occurrence.

■ **Multiple Choice Questions From CPA Examinations**

22-17 a. (3)   b. (1)   c. (2)

22-18 a. (3)   b. (3)   c. (4)

Discussion Question And Problems

22-19

MOTIVATION	INTERNAL CONTROL	AUDIT PROCEDURE
1. To cover a shortage.	Internal verification of bank reconciliation, including accounting for all checks recorded in the cash disbursements journal as cleared or still outstanding.	Trace all checks dated on or before June 30 that cleared with the cutoff bank statement to the June 30 outstanding check list.
2. Same as 1.	Same as 1.	Verify the bank reconciliation by tracing checks dated on or before June 30 in the cash disbursements journal to checks clearing with the June 30 bank statement. Any checks not clearing should be included on the June 30 outstanding check list.
3. Hold open books to improve cash position.	Independent bank reconciliation.	Trace deposits in transit to cutoff bank statements to determine deposit date.
4. To cover a cash shortage or to improve the current ratio.	Independent bank reconciliation.	Obtain bank confirmation.
5. Original check was unauthorized and illegal. Outstanding check made the bank reconcile.	Independent bank reconciliation that includes accounting for all cash disbursement transactions.	Verify the bank reconciliation, including cash disbursements for all material uncleared outstanding checks.
6. Kiting-covering a defalcation or padding a cash position.	Independent bank reconciliation.	Trace all interbank transfers to accounting records.
7. To cover a shortage.	Internal verification of bank reconciliation.	Foot outstanding check list.

22-20

SUBSTANTIVE AUDIT PROCEDURE	TYPE OF TEST
1. Prepare an interim period proof of cash.	Substantive test of transactions
2. Trace prelisting of cash receipts to cash receipts book.	Substantive test of transactions
3. Examine bank cancellation date for checks clearing near the end of the year; obtain the last check number issued directly from the client.	Test of details of cash balances.
4. Compare recorded cash disbursements to receiving reports.	Substantive test of transactions
5. Examine invoices for discounts not taken.	Substantive test of transactions
6. Trace deposits in transit to the cash receipts journal for the current item.	Test of details of cash balances.
7. Prepare an interim proof of cash.	Substantive test of transactions

22-21 The objectives of each of the audit procedures are:

1. To determine if there is a cutoff misstatement in cash disbursements.
2. To make sure the cash receipts were recorded by the bank shortly after the beginning of the new year *and* recorded in the current year's cash receipts journal. A misstatement in either of these could indicate the cover-up of a cash shortage or a cash receipts cutoff misstatement.
3. To ascertain all cash balances and liabilities to banks that might exist. The verification includes amounts and descriptions.
4. To assure that the client is using the correct balance from the bank in preparing its reconciliation.
5. To determine which checks on the outstanding check list have since cleared and to uncover checks that should have been included on the outstanding check list, but were not. These could represent a cover-up of a cash shortage.
6. To create a list of outstanding checks for follow-up to determine why they have not cleared and to investigate the possibility of a misstatement of cash and accounts payable.
7. To assure that all loans, terms, and arrangements with the bank were properly authorized by the board of directors and are disclosed in the financial statements.
8. To reconcile the recording of cash receipts and cash disbursements between the bank and the client's books and to prepare a bank reconciliation at the same time. This may disclose existence, completeness, accuracy, cutoff, or posting and summarization misstatements.

22-22 a. Bank reconciliation:

Balance per bank	$ 696
Add:	
Deposits in transit	1,000
Check erroneously charged to Pittsburgh Supply	396
	2,092
Less: outstanding checks	(1,394)
Adjusted bank balance	$ 698
Balance per books before adjustments	$ 8,256
Adjustments to books:	
July bank service charge	(87)
Note payment (5,800 principal, 300 interest)	(6,100)
NSF check	(311)
Unrecorded check	(1,060)
Balance per books after adjustments	$ 698

(1)
6/30 DIT	$ 600
July deposits per books	25,456
July deposits per bank	(25,056)
7/31 DIT	$ 1,000

(2)
6/30 O/S checks	$ 1,742
July checks per books	21,811
July checks clear	(23,615)
Erroneous check charged	396
Unrecorded check	$ 1,060
7/31 O/S checks	$ 1,394

b. Adjusting entry:

Miscellaneous expense	$ 87	
Interest expense	300	
Note payable	5,800	
Allowance for doubtful accounts	311	
Purchases	1,060*	
Cash in bank		$7,558

To record adjustments arising from 7/31/99 bank reconciliation.

*Will require reversal on August 1 because of recording in cash disbursements journal.

22-22 (Continued)

c.

RECONCILING ITEM	AUDIT PROCEDURE
1. Deposits in transit	Trace to duplicate deposit slip and entry on cutoff bank statement.
2. Erroneous check	Examine correction notice in August charge received from bank.
3. Outstanding checks	Obtain cutoff bank statement. Trace enclosed checks to outstanding check list. Trace uncleared items to supporting documentation.
4. Bank service charge	Examine advice returned with July bank statement.
5. Note payment	Examine cancelled note. Recompute interest. Check for absence of note on 7/31 bank confirmation.
6. NSF check	Examine advice returned with July bank statement. Examine other related evidence from credit manager to determine if account is uncollectible.
7. Unrecorded check	Examine check returned with July bank statement. Trace number to absence in July cash disbursements journal and recording in August. Examine supporting documentation. Investigate why unrecorded.

d. The correct cash balance for the financial statements is $698.

22-23 a. In verifying the interbank transfers, the following audit procedures should be performed:

1. List interbank transfers made a few days before and after the balance sheet date (already done).
2. Trace these interbank transfers to the appropriate accounting records, bank reconciliations, and bank records to verify proper recording.

22-23 (Continued)

b. **For December 1999**

Cash in bank	$14,000	
Branch bank clearing account		14,000
Cash in bank	15,000	
Branch bank clearing account		15,000
Cash in bank	28,000	
Branch bank clearing account		28,000

Only the first entry is essential because the same entry is also being made on the branch bank for the other two entries.

For January 2000

Eliminate corresponding entries already made for the above.

c. **For December 1999**

Home office clearing account	$26,000	
Cash in bank		26,000
Home office clearing account	15,000	
Cash in bank		15,000
Home office clearing account	28,000	
Cash in bank		28,000

For January 2000

Eliminate corresponding entries already made for the above.

d. and e.

HOME OFFICE RECORDS		BRANCH ACCOUNT RECORDS
12,000	No DIT*	No OC**
26,000	No DIT	No OC
14,000	No DIT	No OC
11,000	No DIT	OC
15,000	No DIT	No OC
28,000	No DIT	OC
37,000	No DIT	No OC

*DIT = Deposit in transit
**OC = Outstanding check

22-24 a.

CORRECTED RECONCILIATION
December 31, 1999

Balance per bank 12-31-99		$16,996.76
Add:		
Deposits in transit		2,662.25
Less: Outstanding checks*		(2,467.75)
Balance per bank - adjusted		$17,191.26
Balance per books - before adjustments		$17,174.86
Add: proceeds of note collected by bank		400.00
Less:		
Dishonored check	$200.00	
Unrecorded bank service charge	5.50	
Error in recording check	178.10	(383.60)
Balance per books - adjusted		$17,191.26

*List of checks totals $2,467.75, not $2,267.75.

b.

Cash	$400.00	
Notes receivable		400.00
To record collection of a note left for collection.		
Accounts receivable	200.00	
Cash		200.00
To charge dishonored check to accounts receivable.		
Miscellaneous expense	5.50	
Cash		5.50
To charge December bank service charge to expense.		
Accounts payable	178.10	
Cash		178.10
To charge to accounts payable (or to receivables) the actual amount of a check drawn which was recorded for a lower amount.		

22-25 a.

	9/30/99	Cash Receipts	Cash Disbursements	10/31/99
Balance per bank	$5,411	$26,536	$25,217	$6,730
Deposits in transit				
9/30/99	3,611	(3,611)		
10/31/99		693		693
Outstanding checks				
9/30/99	(916)		(916)	
10/31/99			1,278	(1,278)
Bank error-check charged to wrong account			(407)	407
NSF checks		(300)	(609)	309
Balance per bank - adjusted	$8,106	$23,318	$24,563	$6,861
Balance per books unadjusted	$8,106	$19,711	$23,967	$3,850
Adjustments to be made				
Interest charged			596	(596)
Note proceeds		3,607		3,607
Balance per books - adjusted	$8,106	$23,318	$24,563	$6,861

  b. Adjusting journal entries:

Dr. Cash in bank	$ 3,607	
Cr. Notes receivable		3,300
Cr. Interest income		307
Dr. Interest expense	596	
Cr. Cash in Bank		596

To record adjustments resulting from Oct.31, 1999 reconciliation of bank account.

22-26

Tuck Company
RECONCILIATION OF CASH RECEIPTS, CASH DISBURSEMENTS AND BANK ACCOUNT
For the Month of December 1999

	11/30/99 Beginning Reconciliation	Cash Receipts	Cash Disbursements	12/31/99 Ending Reconciliation
Per bank statement	$19,400	$148,700	$132,500	$35,600
Deposits in transit:				
11/30/99	1,100	(1,100)		
12/31/99		2,400		2,400
Outstanding checks:				
11/30/99	(2,300)		(2,300)	
12/31/99			4,000	(4,000)
Check of Tucker Co. charged in error			(300)	300
Dishonored checks returned during December		(400)	(400)	
Adjusted bank amounts	$18,200	$149,600	$133,500	$34,300
Per books before adjustment	$18,200	$149,690	$124,885	$43,005
Correction of recording of check #1501			(675)	675
Cancellation of check #1504			(800)	800
Counter check drawn by president			200	(200)
Postdated check #1575 presented for payment			10,000	(10,000)
Correction of recording of note proceeds		(90)		(90)
Bank service charges made in December			30	(30)
Adjustment for check #2540			(140)	140
Adjusted book amounts	$18,200	$149,600	$133,500	$34,300

Chapter 23

Completing the Audit

■ **Review Questions**

23-1 A contingent liability is a potential future obligation to an outside party for an unknown amount resulting from activities that have already taken place. Some examples would be:

- Pending litigation
- Income tax disputes
- Product warranties
- Notes receivable discounted
- Guarantees of obligations of others
- Unused balances of outstanding letters of credit

An actual liability is a real future obligation to an outside party for a known amount from activities that have already taken place. Some examples would be:

- Notes payable
- Accounts payable
- Accrued interest payable
- Income taxes payable
- Payroll withholding liabilities
- Accrued salaries and wages

23-2 If you are concerned about the possibility of contingent liabilities for income tax disputes, there are various procedures you could use for an intensive investigation in that area. One good approach would be an analysis of income tax expense. Unusual or nonrecurring amounts should be investigated further to determine if they represent situations of potential tax liability. Another helpful procedure for uncovering potential tax liabilities is to review the general correspondence file for communication with attorneys or internal revenue agents. This might give an indication that the potential for a liability exists even though no actual litigation has begun. Finally, an examination of internal revenue agent reports from prior years may provide the most obvious indication of disputed tax matters.

23-3 The auditor would be interested in a client's future commitments to purchase raw materials at a fixed price so that this information could be disclosed in the financial statements. The commitment may be of interest to an investor as it is compared to the future price movements of the material. A future commitment to purchase raw materials at a fixed price may result in the client paying more or less than the market price at a future time.

23-4 The analysis of legal expense is an essential part of every audit engagement because it may give an indication of contingent liabilities which may become actual liabilities in the future and require disclosure in the current financial statements. Since any single contingency could be material, it is important to verify all legal transactions, even if the amounts are small. After the analysis of legal expense is completed, the attorneys to whom payment was made should be considered for letters of confirmation for contingencies (attorney letters).

23-5 Pyson should determine the materiality of the lawsuits by requesting from Merrill's attorneys an assessment of the legal situations and the probable liabilities involved. In addition, Pyson may have his own attorney assess the situations. Proper disclosure in the financial statements will depend on the attorneys' evaluations of the probable liabilities involved. If the evaluations indicate highly probable, material amounts, disclosure will be necessary in the form of a footnote, assuming the amount of the probable material loss cannot be reasonably estimated. If the client refuses to make adequate disclosure of the contingencies, a qualified or adverse opinion may be necessary.

23-6 An asserted claim is an existing legal action that has been taken against the client, whereas an unasserted claim represents a *potential* legal action. The client's attorney may not reveal an unasserted claim for fear that the disclosure of this information may precipitate a lawsuit that would be damaging to the client, and that would otherwise not be filed.

23-7 If an attorney refuses to provide the auditor with information about material existing lawsuits or likely material unasserted claims, the audit opinion would have to be modified to reflect the lack of available evidence. This is required by SAS 12 (AU 337), and has the effect of requiring management to give its attorneys permission to provide contingent liability information to auditors and to encourage attorneys to cooperate with auditors in obtaining information about contingencies.

23-8 The first type of subsequent event is one that has a direct effect on the financial statements and requires adjustment. Examples of this type of subsequent event are as follows:

- Declaration of bankruptcy by a customer with an outstanding accounts receivable balance due to the deteriorating financial condition
- Settlement of a litigation for an amount different from the amount recorded on the books
- Disposal of equipment not being used in operations at a price below the current book value
- Sale of investments at a price below recorded cost
- Sale of raw material as scrap in the period subsequent to the balance sheet date

23-8 (Continued)

The second type of subsequent event is one that has no direct effect on the financial statements but for which disclosure is advisable. Examples include the following:

- Decline in the market value of securities held for temporary investment or resale
- Issuance of bonds or equity securities
- Decline in the market value of inventory as a consequence of government action barring further sale of a product
- Uninsured loss of inventories as a result of fire

23-9 Malano's approach does not take into consideration the need to obtain letters from attorneys as near the end of field work as possible. If the letters are received near the balance sheet date, the period from the balance sheet to the end of the auditor's field work will not be included in the attorneys' letters. His procedure would not obtain the most current information regarding contingent liabilities, and would not provide adequate information for disclosure of pertinent subsequent events.

23-10 The major considerations the auditor should take into account in determining how extensive the subsequent events review should be are:

- The company's financial strength and stability of earnings
- The effectiveness of the company's internal controls
- The number and significance of the adjustments made by the auditor
- The length of time between the balance sheet date and the completion of the audit
- Changes in key personnel

23-11 Audit procedures normally performed as a part of the review for subsequent events are:

- Cutoff and valuation tests of various balances and related transactions; e.g., sales cutoff tests
- Inquire of management
- Correspond with attorneys
- Review internal statements prepared subsequent to the balance sheet date
- Review records prepared subsequent to the balance sheet date
- Examine minutes of meetings of board of directors and stockholders subsequent to the balance sheet date
- Obtain a letter of representation

23-12 Subsequent events occurring between the balance sheet date and the date of the auditor's report are those transactions and events which might affect the financial statements being audited (either adjustment, disclosure, or both). Examples of these types of events would be:

- Declaration of bankruptcy by a customer with an outstanding accounts receivable balance due because of a deteriorating financial condition
- Settlement of a litigation for an amount different from the amount recorded on the books
- Disposal of equipment not being used in operations at a price below the current book value
- Sale of investments at a price below recorded cost
- Sale of raw material as scrap in the period subsequent to the balance sheet date
- Decline in the market value of securities held for temporary investment or resale
- Issuance of bonds or equity securities
- Decline in the market value of inventory as a consequence of government action barring further sale of a product
- Uninsured loss of inventories as a result of fire

If these events and transactions have a material effect on the financial statements, they may require adjustment of the current period financial statements or disclosure.

The subsequent discovery of facts existing at the date of the auditor's report occurs when the auditor becomes aware that some information included in the financial statements was materially misleading after the audited financial statements have been issued. Some examples of such facts would be:

- Subsequent discovery of the inclusion of fraudulent sales
- Subsequent discovery of the failure to write-off obsolete inventory
- Omission of an essential footnote

In such cases when the auditor discovers the statements to be misleading, he or she should request the client to issue a revised set of financial statements as soon as possible containing a new audit report and an explanation of the reasons for the revisions to the financial statements.

23-13 The weakness in Lawson's approach is the danger of discovering an inadequacy in one audit area which could affect other areas of the audit. For example, if misstatements were discovered as part of the tests of controls for sales, the initial plans for the tests of details of balances for accounts receivable may have been insufficient and should have been revised. Similarly, the audit of fixed assets is related to the contracts and notes payable whenever fixed assets are used as collateral.

Another difficulty with Lawson's approach is that there is no combining of the misstatements in different audit areas to determine if the combined misstatements are material. If the combined misstatements are considered material, it may be necessary to expand the testing in certain areas or require adjusting entries to some balances.

23-14 The accumulation of audit evidence is crucial to the auditor in determining whether the financial statements are stated in accordance with generally accepted accounting principles, applied on a basis consistent with the preceding year. The evaluation of the adequacy of the disclosures in financial statements is made to determine that the account balances on the trial balance are properly aggregated and disclosed on the financial statements.

Examples where adequate disclosure could depend heavily upon the accumulation of evidence are:

- The disclosure of declines in inventory values below cost
- The segregation of current from noncurrent receivables
- The segregation of trade accounts receivable from amounts due from affiliates
- The disclosure of contingent liabilities that the auditor has not been informed of by the client

Examples where audit evidence does not normally significantly affect the adequacy of the disclosure are:

- Deciding whether a disposal of equipment should be recorded as an extraordinary item
- The disclosure of an acquisition as a pooling of interests or a purchase
- The disclosure of contingencies that the auditor was informed of by the client

23-15 A letter of representation is a written communication from the client to the auditor which formalizes statements that the client has made about matters pertinent to the audit. The five categories of items with examples in each category follow (refer students to SAS 85—AU 333—for a comprehensive list):

1. *Financial statements*
   - Management's acknowledgment of its responsibility for the fair presentation in the financial statements of financial position, results of operations, and cash flows in conformity with generally accepted accounting principles
   - Management's belief that the financial statements are fairly presented in conformity with generally accepted accounting principles
2. *Completeness of information*
   - Availability of all financial records and related data
   - Absence of unrecorded transactions
3. *Recognition, measurement, and disclosure*
   - Information concerning fraud involving (1) management, (2) employees who have significant roles in internal control, or (3) others where the fraud could have a material effect on the financial statements
   - Information concerning related party transactions and amounts receivable from or payable to related parties

23-15 (Continued)

4. *Significant risks and uncertainties*
   - Unasserted claims or assessments that the entity's lawyer has advised are probable of assertion and must be disclosed in accordance with Financial Accounting Standards Board (FASB) Statement No. 5, *Accounting for Contingencies*
   - Satisfactory title to assets, liens or encumbrances on assets, and assets pledged as collateral
   - Compliance with aspects of contractual agreements that may affect the financial statements

5. *Subsequent events*
   - Subsequent events that have a direct effect on the financial statements and require adjustment
   - Subsequent events that have no direct effect on the financial statements but for which disclosure is advisable

A management letter is a letter directed to the client to inform management of certain recommendations about the business which the CPA believes would be beneficial to the client.

Items that might be included in a management letter are:

- Recommendation to switch inventory valuation methods
- Recommendation to install a formal security system
- Recommendation to prepare more timely bank reconciliations
- Recommendation to segregate duties
- Recommendation to have certain types of transactions authorized by specific individuals

23-16 SAS 8 (AU 550) requires the auditor to read information in annual reports containing audited financial statements for consistency with the financial statements and the auditor's report. Types of information the auditor examines include statements about financial condition in the president's letter and displays and summaries of statistical financial information.

23-17 A regular working paper review is the one that is done by someone who is knowledgeable about the client and the unique circumstances in the audit. The purposes of this review are to:

- Evaluate the performance of inexperienced personnel
- To make sure that the audit meets the CPA firm's standard of performance
- To counteract the bias that frequently enters into the auditor's judgment.

Examples of important potential findings in a regular working paper review are:

- Incorrect computations
- Inadequate scope
- Lack of proper documentation for audit decisions

23-17 (Continue)

An independent review is one done by a completely independent person who has no experience on the engagement. The purpose is to have a competent professional from within the firm who has not been biased by the ongoing relationship between the regular auditors and the client perform an independent review. Examples of important potential findings in an independent review are:

- A number of small adjustments waived which should have been accumulated into an adjusting journal entry due to materiality
- Too narrow and too biased of a scope in an audit area
- Inadequate disclosure of contingencies

Multiple Choice Questions From CPA Examination

23-18 a. (3) b. (1) c. (3)

23-19 a. (4) b. (3) c. (1) d. (4)

23-20 a. (3) b. (1) c. (2) d. (1)

Discussion Questions And Problems

23-21 a. A contingent liability is a potential future obligation to an outside party for an unknown amount arising from activities that have already taken place. A commitment is an agreement to commit the entity to a set of fixed conditions in the future, regardless of what happens to profits or the economy as a whole.

Knowledge of both contingencies and commitments is extremely important to users of financial statements because they represent the encumbrance of potentially material amounts of resources during future periods, and thus affect the future cash flows available to creditors and investors. Because of this, generally accepted accounting principles require that material contingencies and commitments be disclosed. The auditor has an obligation to discover the existence of such items to determine that they are properly disclosed in order to have complied with generally accepted auditing standards.

b. Three useful audit procedures for uncovering contingencies that Johnson would likely perform in the normal conduct of the audit, even if she had no responsibility for uncovering contingencies, are:

- Review internal revenue agent reports of income tax settlements
- Review minutes of meetings of board of directors and stockholders
- Confirm used and unused balances of lines of credit

c. Three other procedures Johnson is likely to perform specifically for the purpose of identifying undisclosed contingencies are:

- Make inquiries of management
- Analyze legal expenses for indication of contingent liabilities
- Request letters from attorneys regarding the existence and status of litigation and other potential contingent liabilities

23-22 a. A contingent liability is a potential future obligation to an outside party for an unknown amount resulting from activities that have already taken place. The most important characteristic of a contingent liability is the uncertainty of the amount; if the amount were known it would be included in the financial statements as an actual liability rather than as a contingency.

b. Audit procedures to learn about these items would be as follows:

The following procedures apply to all three items:

- Discuss the existence and nature of possible contingent liabilities with management and obtain appropriate written representations.
- Review the minutes of directors' and stockholders' meetings for indication of lawsuits or other contingencies.
- Analyze legal expense for the period under audit and review invoices and statements of legal counsel for indications of contingent liabilities.
- Obtain letters from all major attorneys performing legal services for the client as to the status of pending litigation or other contingent liabilities.

The following are additional procedures for individual items:

Guarantee of interest payments
- Discuss, specifically, any related party transactions with management and include information in letter of representation.
- Review financial statements of affiliate, and where related party transactions are apparent, make direct inquiries of affiliate management, and perhaps even examine records of affiliate if necessary.

Lawsuit Judgment - no additional procedures; see above list of procedures applicable to all three items.

Stock dividend
- Confirm details of stock transactions with registrar and transfer agent.
- Review records for unusual journal entries subsequent to year-end.

c. Nature of adjusting entries or disclosure, if any, would be as follows:

1. If payment by Newart is uncertain, the $3,750 interest liability for the period June 2 through December 1, 1999, could be reflected in the Marco Corporation's accounting records by the following entry:

Interest Payments for Newart Company $3,750
    Accrued Interest Payable - Newart Bonds $3,750

23-22 (Continued)

The debit entry should be included as other assets. Collection is uncertain and the Marco Corporation may not have a right against the Newart Company until all interest payments have been met and the bonds retired. If this treatment is followed, the balance sheet should be footnoted to the effect that the Marco Corporation is contingently liable for future interest payments on Newart Company bonds in the amount of $60,000.

If the interest has been paid by the time the audit is completed, or if for other reasons it seems certain that the payment will be made by Newart on January 15, no entry should be made by Marco. In this circumstance a footnote disclosing the contingent liability of $63,750 and the facts as to the $3,750 should be included with the statements.

2. The lawsuit should be described in a footnote to the balance sheet. In view of the court decision, retained earnings may be restricted for $40,000, the amount of the first court decision. Also, in view of the court decision any reasonable estimate of the amount the company expects to pay as a result of the suit might be used in lieu of the $40,000. A current liability will be set up as soon as a final decision is rendered or if an agreement as to damages is reached. If liability is admitted to by Marco, and only the amount is in dispute, a liability can be set up for the amount admitted to by the company with a corresponding charge to expense or shown as an extraordinary item if the amount is material.

3. The declaration of such a dividend does not create a liability which affects the aggregate net worth in any way. The distribution of the dividend will cause a reduction in retained earnings and an increase in capital stock. No entry is necessary, but an indication of the action taken, and that such a transfer will subsequently be made, should be shown as a footnote or as a memorandum to Retained Earnings and Common Stock in the balance sheet.

23-23
a. 4 - The amount appeared collectable at the end of the field work.
b. 1 - The uncollectible amount was determined before end of field work.
c. 3 - Amount should have been determined to be uncollectible before end of field work, but it was discovered after the issuance of the statements. The financial statements should have been known to be misstated on 8-19-99.
d. 2 - The cause of the bankruptcy took place after the balance sheet date, therefore the balance sheet was fairly stated at 6-30-99. Most auditors would probably require that the account be written off as uncollectible at 6-30-99, but they are not required to do so. Footnote disclosure is necessary because the subsequent event is material.
e. 2 - The sale took place after the balance sheet date but, since the loss was material and will affect future profits, footnote disclosure is necessary.
f. 2 - The lawsuit originated in the current year, but the amount of the loss is unknown.
g. 1 - The settlement should be reflected in the 6-30-99 financial statement as an adjustment of current period income and not a prior period adjustment.
h. 4 - The financial statements were believed to be fairly stated on 6-30-99 and 8-19-99.

23-23 (Continued)

    i. 2 - The cause of the lawsuit occurred before the balance sheet date and the lawsuit should be included in the 6-30-99 footnotes. Note: If the loss is both probable and can be reasonably estimated, then answer 4 is correct - adjust the 6-30-99 financial statements for the amount of the expected loss.

23-24 a. The practice of reviewing the working papers of subordinates on a continuing basis rather than when the audit is completed is a good one because it enables the auditor to refine the audit approach based on the information provided from the working papers that are reviewed. In addition, since many areas of the audit relate to each other, reviewing the working papers on a continuing basis gives the auditor a more integrated picture of the company's operations. It is also an excellent practice from a supervisory point of view.

    b. It is acceptable for Adams to prepare the financial statements provided he obtained sufficient audit evidence to warrant their fair presentation. This is a common practice on many audits because the CPA has greater expertise in financial statement presentation than the client.

    c. By not having a review of the working papers by another partner in the firm, there is no check against any bias and unintentional error that may exist on the part of the auditor. Except for some degree of independence and technical competence, Adams is in much the same position as the typical controller. An independent review is essential in this case.

23-25 a. It is desirable to have a letter of representation in spite of the accumulated audit evidence to impress upon management its responsibility for the representations in the financial statements and to formally document the responses from the client to inquiries about various aspects of the audit.

    b. The letter of representation is not very useful as audit evidence since it is a written statement from a nonindependent source. In effect, the client being audited makes certain representations related to the audit of itself.

    c. Several categories of information commonly included in a letter of representation with examples in each category follow (See SAS 85—AU 333— for a complete list):

1. *Financial statements*
   - Management's acknowledgment of its responsibility for the fair presentation in the financial statements of financial position, results of operations, and cash flows in conformity with generally accepted accounting principles
   - Management's belief that the financial statements are fairly presented in conformity with generally accepted accounting principles
2. *Completeness of information*
   - Availability of all financial records and related data
   - Absence of unrecorded transactions

23-25 (Continued)
3. *Recognition, measurement, and disclosure*
   - Information concerning fraud involving (1) management, (2) employees who have significant roles in internal control, or (3) others where the fraud could have a material effect on the financial statements
   - Information concerning related party transactions and amounts receivable from or payable to related parties
4. *Significant risks and uncertainties*
   - Unasserted claims or assessments that the entity's lawyer has advised are probable of assertion and must be disclosed in accordance with Financial Accounting Standards Board (FASB) Statement No. 5, *Accounting for Contingencies*
   - Satisfactory title to assets, liens or encumbrances on assets, and assets pledged as collateral
   - Compliance with aspects of contractual agreements that may affect the financial statements
5. *Subsequent events*
   - Subsequent events that have a direct effect on the financial statements and require adjustment
   - Subsequent events that have no direct effect on the financial statements but for which disclosure is advisable

23-26 a. Schwartz's legal and professional responsibility in the issuance of management letters is only to make sound recommendations based on his professional interpretation of the audit evidence accumulated and to not omit information of serious systems weaknesses. He must follow due care in management letters and management services in the same manner as is required for audits.

b. Major considerations which will determine whether Schwartz is liable in this situation are whether the client installed the system according to Schwartz's instructions or whether they deviated from his instructions and whether they could have foreseen the possibility of the erased master file based on their understanding of the system. Another major consideration is the degree to which Schwartz followed due care considering the needs of the client and the competence of existing employees of Cline Wholesale Co.

23-27 1. The state government's approval of a plan for the construction of an express highway would have come to the CPA's attention through inquiries of officers and key personnel, review of the minutes of the meetings of the board of directors and stockholders, and reading of local newspapers. The details of the item would not have to be disclosed as a separate footnote because all fixed assets of the corporation, including the right to the condemnation award, were to be sold as of March 1, 2000 (see item 6).

23-27 (Continued)

2. It is improbable that the CPA would learn the source of the $25,000 unless it were revealed in a discussion with the president or his personal accountant or unless the auditor prepared the president's personal income tax return. In the latter case, the interest charges would have lead the CPA to investigate the use to which the funds were put. Setting out the loan in the balance sheet as a loan from an officer would be sufficient disclosure. The source from which the officer obtained the funds would not be disclosed because it is the officer's personal business and has no effect upon the corporation's financial statements. Furthermore, disclosure of the funds' source might be construed as detrimental to the officer.

3. The additional liability for the ore shipment would have been revealed to the CPA in scanning January transactions. Regular examination of 1999 transactions and related documents such as purchase contracts would have caused the CPA to note the time for subsequent follow up to determine the final liability. In addition the client's letter of representation might have mentioned the potential liability. The item would not require separate disclosure, but would be handled by adjusting the financial statement amounts for purchases, ending raw materials inventory, and accounts payable by the amount of the additional charge, $9,064. [(72 - 50)/50 = .44; .44 x 20,600 = 9,064)

4. The CPA might learn of the agreement to purchase the treasurer's stock ownership through inquiries of management and legal counsel, review of the minutes of the meetings of the board of directors and stockholders, and subsequent reading of the stock purchase agreement. The absence of the treasurer might also arouse the CPA's curiosity. The details of the agreement would be disclosed in a footnote because the use of company cash for the repurchase of stock and the change in the amount of stock held by stockholders might have a heavy impact on subsequent years' financial statements. Usually, a management change, such as the treasurer's resignation, does not require disclosure in the financial statements. The details underlying the separation (personal disagreements and divorce) should not be disclosed because they are personal matters.

5. Through inquiries of management, review of financial statements for January, scanning of transactions, and observations, the CPA would learn of the reduced sales and of the strike. Disclosure would not be made in the financial statements of these conditions because such disclosure might create doubt as to the reasons therefore and misleading inferences might be drawn.

6. The contract with Mammoth Industries would come to the CPA's attention through inquiries of management and legal counsel, reading of the minutes of the meetings of the board of directors and stockholders, and examination of the contract. All important details of the contract should be disclosed in a footnote because of the great effect upon the corporation's future. The factors contributing to the entry into the contract need not be disclosed in statements; while they might be of interest to readers, they are by no means essential to make the statements fairly presented.

23-28 1. A retroactive pay increase could be uncovered by reading the minutes of the board of directors' or stockholders' meetings, examining contracts, holding discussions with management, reading the local newspaper, and analyzing internal financial statements prepared subsequent to the balance sheet date.

   Granting of a retroactive pay increase is likely to create a liability at the balance sheet date for the earned but unpaid wages in the year under audit. A liability clearly exists if a union contract was under negotiation at the balance sheet date but not settled until later. If the retroactive pay increase was unexpected at the balance sheet date, the expense could be related to the date of the settlement, but even then, most auditors would require that retroactive wages be accrued at the balance sheet date. The liability and related expense that should be accrued at the balance sheet date is the amount of unpaid wages existing at the balance sheet date assuming the pay increase is accrued. No mention in the audit report is necessary.

2. An additional tax assessment could be uncovered by examining subsequent cash disbursements, review of the minutes of the board of directors or stockholders, examining internal revenue agent reports for all expenses not cleared by the Internal Revenue Service, requesting letters from attorneys near the end of the field work, and through discussions with management.

   The tax assessment should be accrued as a tax expense and a liability for the year under audit and clearly disclosed if the amount is material. If the tax assessment is accrued and adequately disclosed, no audit report modification is necessary.

3. The antitrust suit may have been uncovered through inquiries of the client, the client representation letter, or letters from client's legal counsel. The antitrust suit should be disclosed in a footnote.

4. The declaration of a stock dividend subsequent to the balance sheet date could be uncovered by reading the minutes of the board of directors or stockholders subsequent to the balance sheet date, by confirmation with the independent stock registrar, or through discussion with management.

   The stock dividend should be disclosed in a footnote, including the date of declaration, the percent of the stock dividend, and the effect on issued shares, capital stock, paid-in capital and retained earnings. No audit report modification is necessary.

5. The sale of a major fixed asset at a substantial profit could be uncovered by reviewing minutes of the board of directors or stockholders, reviewing correspondence files, reviewing cash receipts records of the subsequent period, or through discussions with management.

   The sale should be disclosed in a footnote, and the explanation should include the amount of the gain and the effect, if any, on future operations of the company. No audit report modification is necessary.

23-29 a. The fallacy of Hatton's argument is that it fails to allow for the possibility that a subsequent transaction may shed additional light on transactions or evaluations that were made in the year of the audit report. The audit of subsequent transactions is also necessary for determining the proper cutoff for the current year.

23-29 (Continued)

    b. Examples of information obtained by examining subsequent events which are essential to the current period audit are:

- Sale of inventory as scrap
- Write-offs of a large account receivable due to bankruptcy
- Discovery of oil on the land
- Realization of the unmarketability of a product
- New knowledge regarding a tax dispute
- Discovery of watered stock
- Settlement of a labor dispute resulting in a retroactive wage adjustment
- Partial or complete destruction of uninsured property due to a fire

23-30 a. In this situation, Little need only send requests for letters to those attorneys who are involved with legal matters directly affecting the financial statements. The letters should be sent reasonably near to the completion of the field work, but the follow-up on nonresponses and unsatisfactory responses should not be deferred until the last day of field work. She should have examined the letters when they were returned and performed follow-up work at that time. Furthermore, the third letter should have addressed the lawsuit if the client informed the auditor of its existence.

    b. The auditor would be required to follow up on the first attorney's letter by sending a second request or calling the attorney to solicit a response. The second letter would not require any additional follow-up due to the nature of the work performed by this attorney. Regarding the third attorney's letter, it is necessary to have a conference with the attorney, client, and auditor to determine the nature and significance of the lawsuit.

       It would be a serious violation of due care to ignore the information in the third attorney's letter. In rare circumstances, a disclaimer of opinion is necessary if the information cannot be obtained.

23-31 a. See the "Summary of Possible Adjustments" on the page 23-16.

    b. Aviary's management may refuse to make some or all of the proposed adjustments because all of the adjustments except (4) reduce net income. Management will most likely be reluctant to make any adjustments that will make the company look less profitable. Aviary's management may also refuse to make some or all of the proposed entries because they do not want to admit that their records contain misstatements.

    c. As indicated on the "Summary of Possible Adjustments" on page 23-16, you should attempt to have Aviary's management record all of the potential adjustments found. However, at a minimum, entries (5) and (6) should be recorded. One positive way for you to convince Aviary's management to make these entries would be to stress that (1) considerable judgment is required to determine the allowances for inventory obsolescence and doubtful accounts and (2) it is not uncommon for auditors to assist clients in adjusting these accounts. This may help minimize management's reluctance to admit making a mistake.

23-31 (Continued)

You should also stress that it would be wise to adjust the allowance accounts in a year with substantial net income. The allowance accounts will most likely increase in future years, especially if entries (5) and (6) are not made in the current year. Since management cannot be sure that the company will generate substantial net income in future years, it would be best to adjust the allowance accounts in the current year and avoid a substantial reduction to net income in a future year that is not as profitable as the current year.

23-31 a.

Client Name Aviary Industries

SUMMARY OF POSSIBLE ADJUSTMENTS

Year-ended December 31, 1999

Description	A/C Dr. A/C Cr.	Total Amount	Possible Adjustments - Dr (CR)					
			Current Assets	Non-Current Assets	Current Liabilities	Non-Current Liabilities	Beginning Equity	Income	Expenses
(1) Unrecorded credit memos*	Sales R&A / A/R	23,529	(23,529)					23,529	
(2) Unrecorded inventory purchases	Purchases / A/P	22,357			(22,357)				22,357
(3) Sales recorded in wrong period	Sales / A/R	36,022	(36,022)					36,022	
(4) Held checks	Cash / A/P	48,336	48,336		(48,336)				
(5) Obsolete inventory**	Loss A/C / Inventory Allow. A/C	20,000	(20,000)						20,000
(6) AFDA understated**	Bad debt exp. / AFDA	25,000	(25,000)						25,000
Totals			(56,215)		(70,693)			59,551	67,357

Conclusions:

The net effect of the above items is as follows:

Working capital $126,908 decrease
Total assets: $ 56,215 decrease
Net income: $126,908 decrease

Opinion as to need for AJE: Preliminary materiality was $100,000. However, revised materiality based on 5% of <u>actual</u> income before taxes = $1,652,867 x 5% = $82,643. Rounded = $82,500. The combined effect of the above proposed entries on net income exceeds revised materiality. Propose that all entries be recorded. However, at a minimum, entries (5) and (6) should be recorded in order to decrease the effect of the above entries to a level below revised materiality of $82,500. Entry (1) or (2) may also have to be recorded in order to have some cushion between the net income misstatement and revised materiality after recording entries (5) and (6).

*   Entry assumes that the prior year effect is ignored because ending retained earnings is misstated by the amount of the current year misstatement. Another approach would be to consider the offsetting effect of the prior year's misstatement on net income. Under this approach, the entry would reflect a reduction of opening equity by $14,333 and a reduction of net income by $9,166 ($23,529 - $14,333). Current asset misstatement would be unchanged. Entry also assumes that items were returned prior to 12-31-99 and counted in inventory at year-end (no COGS/inventory misstatement).

**   Because entry deals with an accounting estimate, the lower end of the range would be sufficient.

23-16

23-32 a. Reportable conditions are matters coming to the auditor's attention that, in his or her judgment, should be communicated to the client's audit committee, or similar body, because they represent significant deficiencies in the design or operation of the company's internal control.

Item 1 This is a reportable condition item, as it represents a situation that causes sales to be recorded in the wrong period. A sample occurrence rate of 7 percent is considered significant.

Item 2 This could be a reportable condition if it is concluded that the frequency and amount of disputed items is significant. Otherwise, it would be a management letter item.

Item 3 This is a management letter item. It is not accounting control related, but affects the efficiency of the Company's production system.

Item 4 This could be a reportable condition if it is concluded that the inventory items are obsolete and their revaluation would be significant. Otherwise, it probably not be included in either letter.

Item 5 This is a management letter item. It is not accounting control related, but affects the Company's ability to deal with a potential fire in the inventory area.

Item 6 This is probably a management letter item. It is accounting control related, but is not systemic or significant in amount. However, it reflects on the integrity of the clerk involved and requires some specific action by the Oakridge manager. Whether it would be included in the letter is a matter of judgment in the circumstances.

Item 7 This is a reportable condition. Timely reconciliation of all bank accounts is an important control.

Item 8 This is a management letter item, and dealing with this problem in an effective manner could result in significant savings to the Company.

b. No specific solution is provided for this requirement as each student's letter will reflect his or her answers to Requirement a and their personal writing style.

c. No specific solution is provided for this requirement as each student's letter will reflect his or her answers to Requirement a and their personal writing style.

23-32 (Continued)

TEMPLATE FOR REPORTABLE CONDITIONS LETTER

[FIRM LETTERHEAD]

[Date]

[Client addressee - Audit Committee or other similar body]

Dear [   ]:

In planning and performing our audit of **[Client Name]** for the year ended **[Audit Date]**, we considered its internal control in order to determine our auditing procedures for the purpose of expressing our opinion on the financial statements and not to provide assurance on internal control. However, we noted certain matters involving internal control and its operation that we consider to be a reportable condition under standards established by the American Institute of Certified Public Accountants. Reportable conditions involve matters coming to our attention relating to significant deficiencies in the design or operation of internal control that, in our judgment, could adversely affect the organization's ability to record, process, summarize, and report financial data consistent with the assertions of management in the financial statements. The matters we noted are listed below.

[Audit Area]

Finding [*Item No. and descriptive title*] [Detailed description of item.]

Potential impact [Describe potential impact on financial statements. Indicate both nature and magnitude, to the extent possible.]

Recommended action [Present recommendation(s) for correction/improvement. Indicate potential cost of implementation and operation of recommendations to the extent possible.]

We will be happy to discuss these matters with you in more detail at your request and convenience, and we stand ready to assist you in the implementation of our recommendations should you desire such assistance.

Please be aware that this report is intended solely for the information and use of the audit committee [**or similar body**], management, and others in **[Client Name]**.

Very truly yours,

[Firm Name and Signature]

23-32 (Continued)

TEMPLATE FOR MANAGEMENT LETTER

[FIRM LETTERHEAD]

[Date]

[Client addressee - Chief Executive Officer or other appropriate addressee]

Dear [   ]:

In addition to the items included in our letter to your audit committee **[or similar body]** of **[Date of Reportable Conditions letter],** which we considered reportable conditions, we also noted a number of other matters that we would like to bring to your attention. These may be internal control related matters that we believe may be improved, but are not of the significance of reportable conditions, or more general operating matters. We have presented these below along with our recommendations for improvement.

[Audit Area]

Finding **[Item No. and descriptive title]** **[Detailed description of item.]**

Potential benefit(s) from improvement **[Describe potential benefit(s) that could result from improvement. Indicate both nature and magnitude, to the extent possible.]**

Recommended action **[Present recommendation(s) for correction/improvement. Indicate potential cost of implementation and operation of recommendations to the extent possible, and relate to potential benefits.]**

We will be happy to discuss these matters with you in more detail at your request and convenience, and we stand ready to assist you in the implementation of our recommendations should you desire such assistance.

Very truly yours,

[Firm Name and Signature]

■ Internet Problem Solution: Subsequent Events

23-1 What subsequent events did Goss Graphic Systems Inc. report in its 10-K405 filed with the SEC on January 14, 1999? [Hint 1: SEC EDGAR® site (http://www.sec.gov). Hint 2: Look at footnotes #21 and 22]. Classify the subsequent events as either type 1 (direct effect) or type 2 (no direct effect).

Answer: The actual footnotes follow for Goss Graphic. Note that Goss's fiscal year-end is September 30.

21. INVESTMENT IN AFFILIATE

In November 1997, the Company made a $5.0 million, or 15%, equity investment in DALiM Gmbh, a pre-press software specialist. The Company made additional investments of $2.5 million in fiscal year 1998, increasing its equity participation to more than 20%. In 1998, the Company also recorded equity losses of $0.7 million, including related goodwill amortization.

On November 18, 1998, DALiM filed for bankruptcy due to insolvency. As a result, the Company determined that its net investment was impaired and the balance of $6.8 million was written off in fiscal 1998. [*Type 1 - direct effect on financial statements*]

22. SUBSEQUENT EVENTS

The Company's operating loss for fiscal year 1998 has caused it to utilize a substantial portion of its available liquidity. As a result, the Company has taken certain actions subsequent to September 30, 1998 intended to increase its profitability and the availability of liquidity, including senior management changes, a revised business plan, workforce reductions, a sale of $35.6 million in accounts receivable, a renegotiation of its Revolving Credit Facility (see Note 10 for a summary of the Amendment), and a commitment by an affiliate of Stonington to make a capital contribution of at least $35 million. The capital contribution is expected to be made in the form of the receivables previously guaranteed by Stonington. While the Company's management believes that these actions will result in improved profitability and the ability to obtain necessary liquidity, there can be no assurances that they will be successful. [*Type 2 - no direct effect on financial statements*]

On November 19, 1998, the Company announced a five percent reduction of its worldwide workforce. This reduction, which affected both salaried and hourly jobs, refocused efforts on improving process flow associated with new product manufacturing and customer service. The major emphasis involved realignment of the North American operation, which serves the Company's largest installed customer base. The severance cost relating to this workforce reduction is approximately $6.7 million and will be charged to expense during the quarter ending December 31, 1998. [*Type 2 - no direct effect on financial statements*]

Chapter 24

Other Audit, Attestation Services, and Compilation Engagements

■ **Review Questions**

24-1 Levels of assurance represent the degree of certainty the practitioner has attained, and wishes to convey, that the conclusions stated in his or her report are correct.

Audits of historical financial statements prepared in accordance with generally accepted accounting principles are one type of examination. They are governed by generally accepted auditing standards. An audit results in a conclusion that is in a positive form. In this type of report, the practitioner makes a direct statement as to whether the presentation of the assertions, taken as a whole, conform with the applicable criteria. The level of assurance is high.

In a review, the practitioner provides a conclusion in the form of a negative assurance. In this form, the practitioner's report states whether any information came to the practitioner's attention to indicate that the assertions are not presented in all material respects in conformity with the applicable criteria. The level of assurance is moderate.

A compilation is defined in SSARS as presenting, in the form of financial statements, information that is the representation of management *without undertaking to express any assurance* on the statements.

24-2 A negative assurance states, along with factual statements, that nothing came to the auditor's attention that would lead the auditor to believe that the financial statements were not prepared in accordance with GAAP or other comprehensive basis of accounting. The reason for including such a statement in a review report is to provide financial statement users with some level of assurance that the financial statements are fairly stated. The level of assurance is less than that for an audit of historical financial statements, but more than the level of assurance for a compilation (very minimal assurance).

24-3 Compilation is defined in SSARS No. 1 as presenting in the form of financial statements, information that is the representation of management, without undertaking to express any assurance on the statements. Review is defined by SSARS No. 1 as performing inquiry and analytical procedures that provide the accountant with a reasonable basis for expressing limited assurance that there are no material modifications that should be made to the statements in order for them to be in conformity with GAAP.

The level of assurance for compilation is extremely low. Reviews provide limited assurance, but considerably less than a typical audit.

24-4 One of three forms of compilation can be provided to clients:

- *Compilation With Full Disclosure* Compilation of this type requires disclosures in accordance with generally accepted accounting principles, the same as for audited statements.

- *Compilation That Omits Substantially All Disclosures* This type of compilation is acceptable if *the report indicates the lack of disclosures* and the absence of disclosures is not, to the CPA's knowledge, undertaken with the intent to mislead users.

- *Compilation Without Independence* A CPA firm can issue a compilation report even if it is not independent with respect to the client, as defined by the *Code of Professional Conduct*. However, the CPA firm must state its lack of independence in the report.

24-5 The following five things are required by SSARS No. 1 for compilation. The preparer of the statements must:

- Know something about the accounting principles and practices of the client's industry.
- Know the client, the nature of its business transactions, accounting records and employees, and the basis, form, and content of the financial statements.
- Make inquiries to determine if the client's information is satisfactory.
- Read the compiled financial statements and be alert for any obvious omissions or errors in arithmetic and generally accepted accounting principles.
- Disclose in the report any omissions or departures from generally accepted accounting principles of which the accountant is aware. This requirement does not apply to a compilation that omits substantially all disclosures.

24-6 For a compilation, the accountant does not have to make inquiries or perform other procedures to verify information supplied by the entity beyond those identified in the answer to Review Question 24-5. But if the auditor becomes aware that the statements are not fairly presented, he or she should obtain additional information. If the client refuses to provide the information, the auditor should withdraw from the compilation engagement.

24-7 The following types of procedures are emphasized for review services:

- Obtain knowledge of the accounting principles and practices of the client's industry. The level of knowledge for reviews should be somewhat higher than that for compilation.
- Obtain knowledge of the client. The information should be about the nature of the client's business transactions, its accounting records and employees, and the basis, form, and content of the financial statements. The level of knowledge should be higher than that for compilation.

24-7 (Continued)
- Make inquiries of management. The objective of these inquiries is to determine whether the financial statements are fairly presented, assuming that management does not intend to deceive the accountant. Inquiry is the most important of the review procedures. The following are illustrative inquiries:
  - Inquire as to the company's procedures for recording, classifying, and summarizing transactions, and disclosing information in the statements.
  - Inquire into actions taken at meetings of stockholders and board of directors.
  - Inquire of persons having responsibility for financial and accounting matters whether the financial statements have been prepared in conformity with generally accepted accounting principles consistently applied.
- Perform analytical procedures. The analytical procedures are meant to identify relationships and individual items that appear to be unusual. The appropriate analytical procedures are no different from the ones already studied in Chapter 7 and in those chapters dealing with tests of details of balances.

24-8 For review services, if a client fails to follow generally accepted accounting principles, a modification of the report is needed. The accountant is not required to determine the *effect of a departure* if management has not done so, but that fact must also be disclosed in the report. For example, the use of replacement cost rather than FIFO for inventory valuation would have to be disclosed, but the effect of the departure on net earnings does not require disclosure.

24-9 Compilations and reviews under SSARS No. 1 can only be issued for nonpublic companies for which an audit has not been performed. They may be for monthly, quarterly, or annual statements.

Reviews under SAS 71 (AU 722) are issued on quarterly information of publicly held companies as a part of the client's reporting requirements to the SEC. Although there are some minor differences in the wording on a review report and an SAS 71 report, they are substantively the same.

24-10 The review procedures are essentially the same for SAS 71 (AU 722) and SSARS 1 reviews. SAS 71 does require one procedure not required by SSARS 1: read the minutes of directors and stockholders (versus inquiring).

In addition, the following factors probably result in SAS 71 reviews having a higher level of assurance than SSARS No. 1 reviews:

- The level of knowledge the accountant has about the client's accounting system and business is likely to be higher for SAS 71 reviews. Because an annual audit is done for companies that have SAS 71 reviews, the accountant is already knowledgeable about such things as the client's accounting and reporting practices, the internal controls, and specialized industry problems.
- The auditor's knowledge of the results of the audit procedures performed during the annual audit will affect the scope of the procedures performed during the review of interim financial information.

24-10 (Continued)
- The accountant will also have a good idea whether the quarterly statements were accurate after the annual audit is complete. This information will be useful in determining the review procedures in subsequent years.

24-11 The purpose of an engagement of specified elements, accounts, or items is like that of an ordinary audit, but it is limited only to certain accounts or parts of the financial statements. An example is the audit of the sales account for a retail store in a shopping mall.

The following are four specific requirements for reports on specified elements, accounts, or items:

- The specified elements, accounts, or items must be identified.
- The basis on which the specified elements, accounts, or items are presented and the agreements specifying the basis must be described.
- The source of significant interpretations made by the client about the provisions of a relevant agreement must be indicated and described.
- If the specified element, account, or item is presented on a basis that is not in conformity with GAAP or another comprehensive basis of accounting, a paragraph that restricts the distribution of the report to those within the entity and the parties to the contract or agreement must be added.

24-12 The reporting requirements for statements prepared on a basis other than GAAP include the following paragraphs: introductory, scope, middle, opinion, and restriction of distribution paragraph. The introductory, scope, and opinion paragraphs are essentially the same as for statements prepared in conformity with GAAP. The middle paragraph states the basis of presentation and refers to a note to the financial statements that describes the basis of accounting followed. The restriction of distribution (final) paragraph is used when the financial statements are prepared in conformity with requirements of a governmental regulatory agency. Distribution of the report is then restricted to those within the entity and for filing with the regulatory agency.

24-13 It would be appropriate for Germany to provide a report to Northern State Bank on all of the conditions except the competency of management. Reports on the working capital ratio, dividends paid on preferred stock, and aging of accounts receivable are factual matters within a normal auditor's competence. Reporting on the competence of management is highly subjective and should not ordinarily be in a debt compliance letter.

24-14 Information accompanying basic financial statements is any and all information prepared for management or outside users included with the basic financial statements. Examples include detailed comparative statements supporting control totals in the basic statements, supplementary information required by the SEC, statistical data such as ratios and trends, and specific comments on the changes that have taken place in the financial statements.

The auditor can provide one of two levels of assurance for information accompanying basic financial statements. The auditor may issue a positive opinion indicating a high level of assurance, or a disclaimer indicating no assurance.

24-15 Attestation standards provide a general framework for and set reasonable boundaries around the attestation function. They provide guidance to AICPA standard-setting bodies for establishing detailed standards and interpretations of standards for specific types of services. They also provide practitioners useful guidance in performing new and evolving attestation services where no specific guidance exists.

The attestation standards, therefore, provide a conceptual framework for various types of services. Generally accepted auditing standards do the same thing for the conduct of the ordinary audit of financial statements prepared in accordance with generally accepted accounting principles.

24-16 A *prospective financial statement* is a predicted or expected financial statement in some future period or at some future date. There are two general types of prospective financial statements: forecasts and projections. A *forecast* is a prospective financial statement that presents an entity's expected financial position, results of operations, and cash flows for future periods, to the best of the responsible party's knowledge and belief. A *projection* is a prospective financial statement that present an entity's financial position, results of operations, and cash flows, to the best of the responsible party's knowledge and belief, given one or more hypothetical assumptions.

An examination of prospective financial statements involves:

- Evaluating the preparation of the prospective financial statements.
- Evaluating the support underlying assumptions.
- Evaluating the presentation of the prospective financial statements for conformity with AICPA presentation guidelines.
- Issuing an examination report.

24-17 An engagement to report on internal control involves the auditor's obtaining an understanding of the design of all or part of a client's internal controls in effect as of a specified date or during a specified period. This is followed by the performance of tests of controls, the evaluation of the results of the understanding and the tests of controls, and the issuance of a report thereon. When an auditor performs an audit of financial statements, the scope of the understanding of internal control and the related tests of controls depend on the extent to which the auditor intends to reduce assessed control risk in determining the nature, timing, and extent of related substantive tests. Thus, where no reduction is planned, the scope of the understanding and the tests of controls will be less in an audit than in a special engagement to report on internal control.

24-18 The five steps for obtaining an understanding of internal control and the performance of tests of controls are:

- Plan the scope of the engagement.
- Obtain an understanding of internal control.
- Evaluate the design effectiveness of controls.
- Test and evaluate the operating effectiveness of controls.
- Form an opinion about management's assertion regarding the effectiveness of internal control.

24-19 Service organization auditors may issue two types of reports (SAS 70, AU 324):

- Report on controls placed in operation
- Report on controls placed in operation and tests of operating effectiveness

The user organization's auditor can use the report on controls placed in operation and tests of operating effectiveness to reduce control risk. A report on controls placed in operation can be used by the user organization's auditor in obtaining an understanding of internal control to plan the audit. However, evidence concerning the operating effectiveness of controls is necessary to assess control risk below the maximum.

■ Multiple Choice Questions From CPA Examinations

24-20 a. (4)   b. (3)   c. (2)   d. (1)   e. (2)   f. (3)

24-21 a. (1)   b. (1)   c. (1)   d. (1)

24-22 a. (4)   b. (3)   c. (2)   d. (1)

24-23 a. (2)   b. (3)   c. (1)

■ Discussion Questions And Problems

24-24 a. A typical additional information report includes the financial statements associated with a short-form report plus additional information likely to be useful to management and other statement users. The statements included with short form audit reports are defined by the profession, but the additional information included in additional information reports varies considerably.
b. The purpose of additional information reports is to provide management and other users information that is useful for their decision making that has not been included in the basic financial statements.
c. It would be appropriate to include all of the items as additional information except the following:

  2. The adequacy of insurance coverage. The auditor is not an insurance professional, and any comments about the insurance coverage should be factual. For example, it would be appropriate to state that the insurance coverage is less than the recorded book value.
  5. Adequacy of the allowance for uncollectible accounts. Comments that an account balance is correctly stated are inappropriate. The auditor has already issued an auditor's opinion on the statements as a whole. If an opinion on a specific account balance is desired, it should be done in accordance with a special report.
  7. Material weaknesses in internal control. These should be identified and communicated to management as a part of a reportable conditions letter.

24-24 (Continued)

    d. The following could also be included as additional information:

- Detailed breakdown of sales and expenses by month
- Detailed financial statements making up cost of goods sold, selling and administrative expenses
- A detailed breakdown of inventory

    e. The following would be added to the standard audit report:

Our audit was made for the purpose of forming an opinion on the basic financial statements taken as a whole. The accompanying information on pages x through y is presented for purposes of additional analysis and is not a required part of the basic financial statements. Such information has not been subjected to the auditing procedures applied in the audit of the basic financial statements, and, accordingly, we express no opinion on it.

24-25 a. The purpose of a debt compliance letter is to provide the lender with an independent opinion of the existence or nonexistence of some condition. The lender usually will request a CPA to determine whether certain loan covenants are being adhered to by the debtor.

    b. An audit of the company is necessary before a debt compliance letter is issued because a compliance letter would be difficult to prepare without an audit. This stems from the fact that the CPA is usually concerned with financial balances and ratios of the company when preparing a debt compliance letter. An audit is virtually required in order to verify these amounts.

    c. A CPA firm could issue a debt compliance letter on the amount of the current ratio and the owner's equity. The firm may report on these two aspects since it is qualified to evaluate such matters. However, the other three requests require legal expertise and subjective judgment that a CPA firm does not claim to possess. Therefore, the CPA should restrict the debt compliance letter to the two quantitative requests.

24-26 a. The additional information commonly includes some or all of the following kinds of materials in addition to those commonly included in a short-form report:

- Detailed comparative statements supporting the control totals on the basic financial statements
- Supplementary information required by the FASB or the SEC
- Statistical data
- A schedule of insurance coverage
- Specific comments on the changes that have taken place in the statements

    b. Yes, the auditor assumes the same degree of responsibility for additional information that he or she assumes for individual items in the customary basic financial statements in the absence of a statement by the auditor to the contrary; that is, that they are fairly stated in all material respects in relation to the basic financial statements, taken as a whole.

24-26 (Continued)

The report shall either contain an expression of an opinion regarding the financial statements, taken as a whole, or an assertion to the effect that an opinion cannot be expressed. When an overall opinion cannot be expressed, the reasons therefore should be stated. In all cases where an auditor's name is associated with financial statements, the report should contain a clear-cut indication of the character of the audit, if any, and the degree of responsibility the auditor is taking.

The concept that "the report should contain a clear cut indication of the character of the audit, if any, and the degree of responsibility the auditor is taking," is applicable to both short-form and additional information reports.

24-27 The accountant is responsible for the care in the preparation of compiled financial statements. The accountant must perform all five steps identified in the answer in Review Question 24-5 with due care. The report must also be properly prepared and reflect the findings of the accountant.

Users other than management are not prohibited from using compiled financial statements. They can expect the accountant to meet the standards set by the profession.

The courts have not established the responsibilities of accountants for compilations. Presumably, the responsibilities should be far less than for audits and somewhat less than for reviews. Responsibilities exist, but the level has yet to be finalized.

24-28

PROCEDURE	a. REQUIRED ON A REVIEW ENGAGEMENT	b. REQUIRED ON A COMPILATION ENGAGEMENT
1.	X	X
2.	X	
3.	X	X
4.		
5.	X	
6.		
7.	X	
8.	X	
9.		

X = Required procedure

24-29 a. The requirements are the same as for audited statements. The company must use a historical cost method, including lower of cost or market and the valuation method must be specified on the statements.

b. The CPA firm is apparently associating itself with financial statements that are not in accordance with generally accepted accounting principles. In addition, the firm could be signing a tax return that violates the tax laws.

Unless the facts are fully disclosed in the statements and tax returns, the firm could be in violation of Rule 203 of the Rules of Conduct. There is also potential liability from financial statement users and the Internal Revenue Service.

c. There are three categories of procedures that the accountant should follow.

- Understand the client's business. If the accountant understands the nature of the client's inventory needs, an assessment of the amount that is likely to be on hand is more likely.
- Analytical procedures. The use of ratio analysis--including inventory turnover, gross margin, and inventory as a percent of current assets--should be useful in this case.
- Inquiries of management. Appendix A of SSARS 1 provides guidance as to the appropriate inquiries for inventories.
  - Have inventories been physically counted? If not, how have inventories been determined?
  - Have general ledger control accounts been adjusted to agree with physical inventories?
  - If physical inventories are taken at a date other than the balance sheet date, what procedures were used to record the change in inventory between the date of the physical inventory and the balance sheet date?
  - Were consignments in or out considered in taking physical inventories?
  - What is the basis of valuation?
  - Does inventory cost include material, labor, and overhead where applicable?
  - Have write-downs for obsolescence or cost in excess of net realizable value been made?
  - Have proper cutoffs of purchases, goods in transit, and returned goods been made?
  - Are there any inventory encumbrances?

d. The problem is serious because the statements appear not to be acceptable as stated. The client is not following generally accepted accounting principles and the tax returns apparently are not being prepared correctly. On the basis of the information provided, it is questionable whether a CPA firm can sign the tax return. Materiality is a critical consideration.

The most important course of action is for the staff person to talk to the partner and see what he or she says. The staff person is obligated to the firm to express the viewpoint that the statements are not correctly prepared.

24-29 (Continued)

ALTERNATIVES	COST - BENEFIT
1. Convince the client to prepare proper financial statements by convincing management of potential consequences. Also convince the client of benefits of properly prepared statements.	This is the best alternative, but the firm may lose the client.
2. Prepare review as the statements now exist, but include appropriate report qualifications. Do not do or sign tax return.	The firm will probably lose the client, but it is an appropriate action.
3. Withdraw.	Loss of client, but will potentially save the firm from a lawsuit or IRS action.
4. Change to a compilation with full disclosure.	This alternative is identical to No. 2 and requires disclosure. The firm still cannot sign the tax return.

24-30 a. In addition to the inquiries listed, the accountant must understand the client's business to facilitate evaluating whether the statements are reasonable. Analytical procedures must also be performed. It may also be appropriate to inquire about such things as the possibility of unbilled sales, authorization procedures for sales, whether the accounts receivable control account has been reconciled with the master file records, and the possible inclusion of consignment shipments as sales.

b. In reviews, no procedures such as tests of controls, substantive tests of transactions, cutoff tests, or confirmation requests are done. The only things that are done are inquiries and analytical tests. An examination of the procedures for sales and receivables discussed in Chapters 13 and 15 shows that there is considerable difference between an audit and those review procedures listed in this problem.

c. Inquiries would ordinarily be made of the chief financial officer in a small or large business. Ordinarily the chief financial officer in a small business is the owner, but it may also be a controller or vice-president.

d. Additional procedures should be performed when the accountant believes, based on the information obtained through inquiry and analytical procedures, that the financial statements may be materially misstated. Examples where this could be the case are:

- A material increase in the gross margin percent
- A material decrease in allowance for uncollectible accounts divided by accounts receivable
- A statement by a bookkeeper that leads the accountant to believe the client's personnel do not fully understand correct sales cutoff procedures

24-30 (Continued)

e. The achieved level of assurance for audits is ordinarily much higher than for reviews. The differences in the procedures identified in this problem and those studied in Chapters 13 and 15 are significant and result in large differences in the achieved levels of assurance.

24-31 a. It is *not* appropriate to do a review service for a publicly held company. Review service engagements are restricted to nonpublic companies. Annual statements of public companies must either be audited or unaudited in accordance with generally accepted auditing standards and requirements of the Securities and Exchange Commission. This provides a clearer definition in the level of assurance for the financial statements of public companies. However, a review-type service can be provided for interim financial statements of public companies (an SAS 71 review).

b. There are some deficiencies in the approach taken:

- Since Tidwell is a high risk client, indicating a high likelihood of misstatement, and since the required review procedures include inquiries and analytical procedure, the review should, at least in part, be performed by the more experienced member of the engagement team, and not be so completely delegated.
- Since there are some differences between an SSARS 1 review and an SAS 71 review, use of the firm's standard procedures for SSARS reviews without modification is inappropriate. Additional procedures to be performed include (at a minimum):

  - Relating inquiries to findings in the recent audit
  - Reading minutes

c. The following problems exist with regard to the report:

- Pages should be marked "unaudited" not "reviewed."
- The report should be addressed to the client, not the Securities and Exchange Commission.
- The wording of the report should be changed from the SSARS review to the SAS 71 wording.

24-32 a. We have audited, in accordance with generally accepted auditing standards, the balance sheet of Pollution Control Devices, Inc. as of___, and the related statements of income, retained earnings, and cash flows for the year then ended, and have issued our report thereon dated ___.

In connection with our audit, nothing came to our attention that caused us to believe that the Company failed to comply with any of the provisions of the indenture dated ____with _(lender)_ insofar as they relate to accounting matters. However, our audit was not directed primarily toward obtaining knowledge of such noncompliance.

This report is intended solely for the information of the boards of directors and managements of Pollution Control Devices, Inc. and _(lender)_ and should not be used for any other purpose.

24-32 (Continued)

    b. The supplemental report would have to state that the company was not in compliance with the provisions of the indenture because net earnings did not exceed dividends by at least $1,000,000.

    c. The supplemental report would be the same as discussed in b. Assuming that a default in the provisions of the indenture results in the loan becoming due immediately, the auditor's report would have to include either an adverse or qualified opinion depending upon the materiality of the misstatement. Since the mortgage is for $4 million, which is material to the client, violation of the indenture and potential default cannot be dismissed as being immaterial.

    d. Contingencies due to a lawsuit may affect the liabilities of the client which will affect the indenture provisions. The auditor will be unable to express an opinion in the debt compliance letter because of this uncertainty. This should be disclosed in the supplemental report.

24-33 a. There are two aspects of the audit that are affected because of the special audit of royalties. First, the allowable materiality for royalties must be lower than ordinary. Second, the resolution of the dispute is desirable because of the effect it will have on the special report.

       It will probably be necessary for the auditor to do the following due to the special report:

- Increase the sample size for tests of sales transactions.
- Test more sales cutoff transactions than normal because of the importance of sales.
- Verify the existence, accuracy, and classification of the four types of disputed sales.

    b. A standard unqualified report is appropriate for the financial statements unless a $9,000 (12% of 75,000) disputed amount is considered material.

    c. We have audited the account, royalties expense, and the five related accounts identified in paragraph three below, applicable to Ronnie Johnson for writing CPA Review Materials for Quality CPA Review for the year ended December 31, 1999 under the terms of the licensing agreement between Ronnie Johnson and Quality CPA Review. These accounts are the responsibility of Quality CPA Review's management. Our responsibility is to express an opinion on the account, royalty expense, and the five related accounts based on our audit.

       We conducted our audit in accordance with generally accepted auditing standards. Those standards require that we plan and perform the audit to obtain reasonable assurance about whether the account, royalties expense, is free of material misstatement. An audit includes examining, on a test basis, evidence supporting the amounts and disclosures for the account. An audit also includes assessing the accounting principles used and significant estimates made by management, as well as evaluating the overall account presentation. We believe that our audit provides a reasonable basis for our opinion.

24-33 (Continued)

We have been informed that, under Quality CPA Review's interpretation of the contract, royalties are to be paid on the basis of 12% of gross sales which specifically exclude royalties on any of the following four accounts:

- Materials sent to instructors for promotion
- Uncollected fees due to bad debts
- Candidates who paid no fee because they performed administrative duties during the course
- Refunds to customers who were dissatisfied with the course

In our opinion, the account, royalties expense, presents fairly, in all material aspects, the amount of royalties applicable for the CPA materials sold by Quality CPA Review during the year-ended December 31, 1999, under the interpretation of the royalty agreement as stated above.

In our opinion, gross sales and the four accounts identified in paragraph three on which royalties have not been paid are fairly stated, in all material respects, for the year-ended December 31, 1999 as presented in Schedule Three on page four of the financial statements.

This report is intended solely for the information and use of the board of directors and management of Quality CPA Review and Ronnie Johnson, and should not be used for any other purpose.

24-34 a. Jones will probably have to conduct additional audit tests in order to report on these items individually. It will be necessary for Jones to accumulate additional evidence since the materiality of the individual items is much lower than for the overall financial statements. The additional evidence will enable the auditor to obtain a higher level of assurance regarding the items than is attained without expanding the audit procedures. The individual items have a lower level of materiality because their magnitude is less than the overall financial statements. Therefore, an amount that is not considered material to the financial statements as a whole may be material when applied to the three accounts being considered.

b. The following additional tests are likely to be needed before the special report can be issued:

Sales
- Cutoff tests of sales may be expanded
- Depending upon the previous results, tests of controls and substantive tests of transactions for sales may be increased

Net fixed assets
- Examine physical existence of a sample of fixed assets
- Determine if fixed assets are still on the books but not being used
- Recalculate depreciation
- Increase vouching of additions in the current year

Inventory
- Increase the price test coverage of inventory value

24-34 (Continued)

It should be noted that the extent of these tests depends on the results attained in these areas in the audit, the amount of evidence gathered in the audit, and the client's internal controls. The audit procedures above are vague because of this and are intended to be illustrative of the type of procedures that should be considered. After-the-fact auditing has limitations in that some information cannot feasibly be recreated. For instance, the auditor cannot extend test counts of inventory in order to verify the quantity of inventory. In these cases the auditor must attempt to satisfy the objective by alternative methods.

c. We have audited the schedules of sales, net fixed assets, and inventory valued at FIFO (as defined in the lease agreement dated ____ between (lessor) and Sarack Lumber Supply Co.) of Sarack Lumber Supply Co. for the year-ended ____. These schedules are the responsibility of Sarack Lumber Supply Co's. management. Our responsibility is to express an opinion on the schedules based on our audit.

We conducted our audit in accordance with generally accepted auditing standards. Those standards require that we plan and perform the audit to obtain reasonable assurance about whether the schedules of sales, net fixed assets, and inventory valued at FIFO are free of material misstatement. An audit includes examining, on a test basis, evidence supporting the amounts and disclosures in the schedules. An audit also includes assessing the accounting principles used and significant estimates made by management, as well as evaluating the overall schedule presentation. We believe that our audit provides a reasonable basis for our opinion.

In our opinion, the schedules of sales, net fixed assets, and inventory valued at FIFO present fairly, in all material respects, the sales, net fixed assets, and inventory valued at FIFO of Sarack Lumber Supply Co. for the year-ended ___, on the basis specified in the lease agreement referred to above.

This report is intended solely for the information and use of the boards of directors and managements of Sarack Lumber Supply Co. and (lessor) and should not be used for any other purpose.

24-35 a. It would be acceptable to undertake the engagement only if all of the following conditions exist:

- The accountant has sufficient competence to properly complete an examination of the forecasted financial statements.
- The client is willing to take responsibility for preparation (with the accountant's assistance) of the forecast in accordance with guidelines, established by the AICPA in *Statements on Standards for Accountant's Services on Prospective Financial Statements*.
- The accountant believes a reasonably accurate forecast is practicable in the circumstances.
- The client understands and agrees to the examination procedures and reporting requirements the accountant must comply with.

24-35 (Continued)

b. If Monson believes the accountant can issue an opinion about the achievability of the forecast, but later finds that such an opinion cannot be given, Monson is likely to be unhappy. The result would be a loss of fee, loss of a client for other services, and perhaps even a lawsuit. Similarly, Monson must understand his responsibilities concerning the forecast of the assumptions and other aspects of the report, again to avoid a misunderstanding later.

c. The primary information the CPA firm will need to help in completing the forecast are the following:

- Audited financial statements for the past several years. (Easily available because Monson is an audit client.)
- Information about the economic conditions of the industry. The CPA firm will likely need knowledge beyond that required for performing the audits.
- Information about the offer he has made for the new business and the offer he has received for the existing assets. Since the financial statements will be a forecast, and not a projection, it is necessary to determine that there is a reasonable likelihood of the transaction being completed and the forecasted result, assuming both transactions are finalized.

d. The report will be a report on a forecast and will include the following components:

- An identification of the prospective financial statements presented.
- A statement that the examination of the prospective financial statements was made in accordance with AICPA standards and a brief description of the nature of such examination.
- The accountant's opinion that the prospective financial statements are presented in conformity with AICPA presentation guidelines and that the underlying assumptions provide a reasonable basis for the forecast.
- A caveat that the prospective results may not be achieved.
- A statement that the accountant assumes no responsibility to update the report for events and circumstances occurring after the date of the report.

24-36 a. Warren can accept the attest engagement to examine and report on management's assertion about the effectiveness of Veridyne's internal control if the following conditions are met:

- Veridyne's management accepts responsibility for the internal control structure and has evaluated its effectiveness using appropriate established criteria.
- Management presents its written assertion of the effectiveness of internal control based on the established criteria.
- Sufficient evidential matter exists or can be developed to support management's assertion.

24-36 (Continued)

    b. The engagement activities to report on management's assertion about the effectiveness of internal control are similar to the procedures for assessing control risk on an audit. These activities include:

        1. *Plan the engagement.* The practitioner and client should agree on the areas to be covered and timing of the study.
        2. *Obtain an understanding of internal control.* These procedures to learn about the transactions, their flow through the system, and control activities are similar to the procedure performed in obtaining an understanding of internal control during an audit.
        3. *Evaluate the design effectiveness of controls.* The practitioner should evaluate whether the controls are suitably designed to prevent or detect misstatements in specific financial statement assertions.
        4. *Test and evaluate the operating effectiveness of the controls.* These tests are concerned with how the control was applied and its consistency of application. The methodology for these procedures is similar to the procedures for completing tests of controls.
        5. *Form an opinion about management's assertion regarding the effectiveness of internal control.* The results of the tests of controls and any identified control deficiencies are evaluated to determine whether management's assertion about the effectiveness of internal control is fairly stated.

    c. Warren could also perform an agreed-upon procedures engagement related to management's assertion about the effectiveness of internal control. Warren's report would then be in the form of procedures and findings.

Chapter 25

Internal and Governmental Financial Auditing and Operational Auditing

■ Review Questions

25-1 Internal auditors who perform financial auditing are responsible for evaluating whether their company's internal controls are designed and operated effectively and whether the financial statements are fairly presented. This responsibility is essentially the same as the responsibility of external auditors who perform financial audits. The two types of auditors are also similar in that they both must be competent and must remain objective in performing their work and reporting their results. Despite these similarities, the role of the internal auditor in financial auditing differs from that of an external auditor in the following ways:

- Because internal auditors spend all of their time with one company, their knowledge about the company's operations and internal controls is much greater that the external auditor's knowledge.
- Guidelines for performing internal audits are not as well defined as the guidelines for external auditors.
- Internal auditors are responsible to the management of the companies that they work for, while external auditors are responsible to financial statement users.
- Because internal auditors are responsible to management, their decisions about materiality and risks may differ from the decisions of external auditors.

25-2 The five parts of the scope of the internal auditor's work, according to *Standards for the Practice of Internal Auditing* are as follows:

- Internal auditors should review the reliability and integrity of financial and operating information and the means used to identify, measure, classify, and report such information.
- Internal auditors should review the systems established to ensure compliance with those policies, plans, procedures, laws, and regulations that could have a significant impact on operations and reports and should determine whether the organization is in compliance.
- Internal auditors should review the means of safeguarding assets and, as appropriate, verify the existence of such assets.
- Internal auditors should appraise the economy and efficiency with which resources are employed.
- Internal auditors should review operations or programs to ascertain whether results are consistent with established objectives and goals and whether the operations or programs are being carried out as planned.

25-3 External auditors are considered more independent than internal auditors for the audit of historical financial statements because their audit report is intended for the use of external users. From an internal user's perspective, internal auditors are employees of the company being audited.

Internal auditors can achieve independence by reporting to the board of directors or president. The responsibilities of internal auditors affect their independence. The internal auditor should not be responsible for performing operating functions in a company or for correcting deficiencies when ineffective or inefficient operations are found.

25-4 Governmental financial audits are similar to audits of commercial companies in that both types of audits require the auditor to be independent, to accumulate and evaluate evidence, and to apply generally accepted auditing standards (GAAS). The two types of audits are different because governmental financial audits also require the auditor to apply generally accepted governmental auditing standards (GAGAS), which are broader than GAAS and include testing for compliance with laws and regulations. Governmental financial auditing can be done either by auditors employed by federal and state governments (governmental auditors) or by CPA firms.

25-5 The Single Audit Act was created in 1984 to eliminate redundancy in the audits of governmental agencies. The Single Audit Act provides for a single coordinated audit to satisfy the audit requirements of all federal funding agencies.

25-6 The auditing standards of the Yellow Book are consistent with the ten generally accepted auditing standards of the AICPA.

Some important additions and modifications are as follows:

- *Materiality and significance* The Yellow Book recognizes that acceptable audit risk and tolerable misstatement may be lower in governmental audits than in audits of commercial enterprises.
- *Quality control* Organizations that audit government entities must have an appropriate system of internal quality control and must participate in an external quality control review program.
- *Compliance auditing.* The Yellow Book requires that the audit be designed to provide reasonable assurance of detecting material misstatements resulting from noncompliance with provisions of contracts or grant agreements that have a material and direct effect on the financial statements.
- *Working papers.* The Yellow Book indicates that working papers should contain sufficient information to enable an experienced reviewer with no previous connection to the audit to ascertain from the working papers evidence that supports the auditors' significant conclusions and judgments.
- *Reporting.* The audit report must state that the audit was made in accordance with generally accepted government auditing standards. In addition, the report on financial statements must describe the scope of the auditors' testing of compliance with laws and regulations and internal controls and present the results of those tests, or refer to a separate report containing that information.

25-7 The primary specific objectives which must be incorporated into the design of audit tests under the Single Audit Act are as follows:

- Amounts reported as expenditures were for allowable services.
- Records indicate that those who received services or benefits were eligible to receive them.
- Matching requirements, levels of effort, and earmarking limitations were met.
- Federal financial reports and claims for advances and reimbursements contain information that is supported by the records from which financial statements were prepared.
- Amounts claimed or used for matching were determined in accordance with relevant OMB Circulars.

25-8 The revised OMB Circular A-133 greatly simplified reporting under the Single Audit Act. The following reports are required:

1. An opinion on whether the financial statements are in accordance with GAAP, and an opinion as to whether the schedule of Federal awards is presented fairly in all material respects in relation to the financial statements as a whole.
2. A report on internal control related to the financial statements and major programs.
3. A report on compliance with laws, regulations and the provisions of contracts or grant agreements, noncompliance with which could have a material effect on the financial statements. This report can be combined with the report on internal control.
4. A schedule of findings and questioned costs.

25-9 An operational audit is the review of any part of an organization's operating procedures and methods for the purpose of evaluating efficiency and effectiveness.

25-10 The three major differences between financial and operational auditing are:

- *Purpose of the audit* Financial auditing emphasizes whether historical information was correctly recorded. Operational auditing emphasizes effectiveness and efficiency. The financial audit is oriented to the past, whereas an operational audit concerns operating performance for the future.
- *Distribution of the reports* For financial auditing, the report is typically distributed to many users of financial statements, such as stockholders and bankers. Operational audit reports are intended primarily for management.
- *Inclusion of nonfinancial areas* Operational audits cover any aspect of efficiency and effectiveness in an organization and can therefore involve a wide variety of activities. Financial audits are limited to matters that directly affect the fairness of financial statement presentations.

25-11 Effectiveness refers to the accomplishment of objectives, whereas efficiency refers to the resources used to achieve those objectives. An example of an operational audit for effectiveness would be to assess whether a governmental agency has met its assigned objective of achieving elevator safety in a city. An example of efficiency is when two different production processes manufacture a product of identical quality, the process with the least cost is considered to be most efficient.

25-12 The following are the distinctions between the three kinds of operational audits and an example of each for a not-for-profit hospital:

TYPES OF OPERATIONAL AUDIT	EXAMPLE FOR A HOSPITAL
Functional Functions are a means of categorizing the activities of a business, such as the billing function or production function. A functional operational audit deals with any of these functions.	Review of the payroll department to determine if the operations are effectively and efficiently performed.
Organizational An operational audit of an organization deals with an entire organizational unit, such as a department, branch, or subsidiary.	Review of the entire hospital for inefficiencies found in any department in the hospital.
Special assignment Special operational auditing assignments arise at the request of management for anything of concern to management.	Review of the IT system for failure to bill insurance companies for reimbursable charges.

25-13 Internal auditors are in a unique position to perform operational audits. They spend all of their time working for the company they are auditing. They therefore develop considerable knowledge about the company and its business, which is essential to effective operational auditing.

25-14 Different federal and state government auditors perform operational auditing, often as a part of doing financial audits. The most widely recognized government auditors group is the United States General Accounting Office (GAO). In addition, each state has an Auditor General's office that has similar responsibilities to the GAO. There are also auditors for most state treasury departments and various other state government auditors.

There are no significant differences between internal and governmental auditors' roles and opportunities for operational auditing. Internal auditors ordinarily do operational audits of for-profit organizations, whereas governmental auditors perform the same role for governmental units.

25-15 It is common, as a part of doing an audit of historical financial statements, for CPA firms to also identify operational problems and make recommendations that may benefit the audit client. The recommendations can be made orally, but they are typically made by use of a *management letter*.

It is also common for the client to engage a CPA firm to do operational auditing of one or more specific parts of its business. Usually, such an engagement would occur only if the company does not have an internal audit staff or if the internal audit staff lacks expertise in a certain area. In most cases, specialized management services staff of the CPA firm, rather than the auditing staff, performs these services. For example, a company may ask the CPA firm to evaluate the efficiency and effectiveness of its computer systems.

25-16 Criteria for evaluating efficiency and effectiveness in operational auditing means deciding the specific objectives that should have been achieved in the operation being audited. Usually, it is insufficient to state that the criteria is efficient and effective operations. More specific criteria are usually described. The following are five possible specific criteria for evaluating effectiveness of an IT system for payroll:

- Was payroll completed and computer generated payroll checks prepared at least twelve hours before the payroll distribution deadline in each of the past 26 weeks?
- Were there two or less complaints by employees each week in the past 26 weeks concerning incorrect paychecks that are attributable to the IT system?
- Is there a weekly review of the completed payroll by a person who is qualified to evaluate whether the payroll is reasonable?
- Is the weekly error listing reviewed by the payroll system's analyst to evaluate whether the payroll system should be changed?
- Does the IT payroll system for each branch office include the specific application controls for payroll that are recommended by the home office?

25-17 The three phases of operational auditing are planning, evidence accumulation and evaluation, and reporting and follow-up. These phases have equivalents in historical financial statement audits, but each phase is, of course, somewhat different.

25-18 Planning in an operational audit is similar to the audit of historical financial statements. Like audits of financial statements, the operational auditor must determine the scope of the engagement and communicate that to the organizational unit. It is also necessary to properly staff the engagement, obtain background information about the organizational unit, evaluate internal controls, and decide the appropriate evidence to accumulate.

The major difference between planning an operational audit and a financial audit is the extreme diversity in operational audits. Because of the diversity, it is often difficult to decide on specific objectives of an operational audit. Another difference is that staffing is often more complicated in an operational audit than in a financial audit. This is because the areas covered by operational audits are diverse and often require special technical skills.

25-19 Two major differences in operational and financial auditing reports affect operational auditing reports. First, in operational audits, the report is usually sent only to management, with a copy to the unit being audited. The lack of third party users reduces the need for standardized wording in operational auditing reports. Second, the diversity of operational audits requires a tailoring of each report to address the scope of the audit, findings, and recommendations.

■ **Multiple Choice Questions from CPA Examinations**

25-20 a. (3) b. (4) c. (2) d. (4)

25-21 a. (3) b. (3) c. (1) d. (3)

25-22 a. (4) b. (1) c. (5) d. (3)

25-23 a. (2) b. (4) c. (3)

■ Discussion Questions and Problems

25-24 a. 1. The strength of the Board's objectives include:

- appraising the cost and revenue estimation of each project.
- verifying that appropriate controls exist and are used to monitor the progress of projects.
- reviewing the preparation of financial reports.

2. Modification and/or additions needed to improve the set of objectives established by the Board include:

- an appraisal of goals to determine whether the research department's projects are consistent with organizational goals.
- protection of assets by identifying fixed assets and materials entrusted to the research department and determining whether proper controls exist for their usage and physical safekeeping.

b. Procedures that would be suitable for performing the audit of the research department include the following:

- Study written goals and objectives of the research department.
- Review the organizational chart.
- Review and test the adequacy and reliability of internal controls.
- Review each project to see who is responsible for the project and whether the proposal is properly documented.
- Review those projects which required corrective action by management.
- Evaluate the usage of resources in the research department by conducting tests as necessary to collect evidence.

c. Some of the documents that members of the hospital's internal audit staff would be expected to review during the audit and the purpose for reviewing these documents are discussed as follows:

25-24 (Continued)

DOCUMENT	AUDIT PURPOSE
Organization chart	The organization chart will identify the key staff members of the department and acquaint the auditors with the organizational structure of the department. This provides a quick means of verifying names that appear on various department documents.
Department and project budgets	The budgets will provide the auditor with insight on how the department has allocated expenditures among project generation, project planning, and project research.
Project proposal	A project proposal will describe the project and indicate the amount of time, people, and funding authorized. It will state the objectives of research and the expected completion dates. Project proposals also could be viewed as a means of identifying deviations.

25-25 a. Objectivity means that the internal auditor must have, and maintain, an unbiased and independent viewpoint in the performance of audit tests, evaluation of the results, and issuance of the audit findings. Objectivity would not exist if the internal auditor were to audit his/her own work. Objectivity implies no subordination of judgment to another and a lack of influence by others over the internal auditor.

   b.
   1. Objectivity is not impaired. Development of written policies and procedures to guide Lajod's staff is a responsibility of the internal audit staff. The internal auditors are responsible for the independent evaluation and verification of proper internal controls.
   2. Objectivity is impaired. The preparation of bank reconciliations is an internal check over cash. In order to maintain objectivity, the auditor should not perform assignments that are included as part of the independent evaluation and verification of proper internal controls. Separation of duties should be maintained.
   3. Objectivity is not impaired in the review of the budget for reasonableness if the internal auditor has no responsibility for establishing or implementing the budget. Objectivity is also not impaired if the internal auditor merely reviews budget variances and explanations for those variances. Objectivity would be impaired, however, if the internal auditor makes managerial decisions concerning performance in the review of variances.
   4. Objectivity is impaired in that the internal auditor will be called upon to evaluate the design and implementation of the system in which the auditor played a significant role. Testing of the internal controls would not impair objectivity because this activity is necessary for determining the adequacy of accounting and administrative controls.
   5. Objectivity is impaired. The internal auditors should not be involved in the record keeping process.

25-25 (Continued)

    c.
1. Yes, the reporting relationship results in an objectivity problem. The controller is responsible for the accounting system and related transactions.

   The internal audit staff is responsible for independent and objective review of the accounting system and related transactions. Independence and objectivity may not exist because the internal audit staff is responsible for reviewing the work of the corporate controller, the person to whom it reports.

2. No, the responses for requirement b would not be affected by the internal audit staff reporting to an audit committee rather than the controller. In order to maintain objectivity, the internal audit staff should refrain from performing non-audit functions such as management decision-making, design and installation of systems, record keeping, etc. Ideally, the internal audit staff should perform only audit functions to avoid being called upon to evaluate its own performance. This is true without regard to organizational reporting relationships.

25-26 a. Additional steps that ordinarily should be taken by Lado Corporation's internal auditors as a consequence of finding excessive turnover in a department of White Division are categorized and explained below.

Field Work The department turnover rate should be compared with rates in other departments of White Division, other divisions of Lado Corporation, and industry rates if available. The present department turnover rate should be compared with previous rates in the department.

The nature of skills needed in the department should be reviewed and compared to job descriptions, if job descriptions exist. The hiring procedures employed by the personnel department should be reviewed as well as Lado's wages and benefits to determine if they are competitive.

The labor efficiency variance should be examined in an attempt to determine the portion attributable to inadequate training. Multiple standards or a new standard may be appropriate. Present and former departmental workers should also be interviewed in an attempt to get additional points of view on the problems of the department.

Recommendations The information gathered during the performance of field work would form the basis for any recommendations. Audit findings would be included in the audit report and unfavorable findings would lead, in most cases, to recommendations. Recommendations likely to result from the audit findings might include the preparation/revision of job descriptions and the establishment of formal training programs.

Operating Management Review The internal auditors should adopt a participatory or problem-solving approach in reviewing audit findings and making recommendations to the department being reviewed. The report should be discussed with the departmental supervisor before the report is finalized. The comments and suggestions of the supervisor should be considered and, if appropriate, included in the report.

25-26 (Continued)

    b. The participation of the Internal Audit Department in the computer feasibility study, including advising and concurring with the system selected, creates an objectivity problem. The Internal Audit Department could not accept an audit assignment involving the problems of the existing computer system without placing themselves in a position of conflict of interest.

        To eliminate the existing objectivity problem, outside consultants should be used to study the problems with the computer system. To reduce future objectivity problems, the Internal Audit Department should not perform functions that may place it in a position of auditing its own work. Auditors should not assume a decision making role as this will negate their future independence from those decisions.

    c.

        1. The location of Lado Corporation's Internal Audit Department is inappropriate. Independence is the key to the work of the internal auditor and is achieved through organizational status and objectivity. A Director of Internal Auditing should report to a high level management executive in order to promote independence, ensure adequate audit coverage, and to assure the proper consideration of audit reports.

            Having the Director of Internal Audits directly report to the Corporate Controller is inappropriate. A major portion of the internal auditor's responsibility involves the review of the accounting function. Thus, the Director may be far less than objective in evaluating the work of a superior.

        2. Reports of Lado's Internal Audit Department should be distributed to all those having a direct interest in the audit, including:

- the executive to whom the internal audit function reports.
- persons from whom replies to the report are required.
- persons responsible for the activity or activities reviewed (auditees and superiors).

25-27 Issues that must be addressed and procedures that should be used by Haskin's Internal Audit Department (IAD) in the audit review of Burlington Plant's 1999 capital expenditure project include the following:

a.

ISSUES
1. The criteria used by the Capital Budgeting Group (CBG) need to be evaluated to determine whether they are consistent with Haskin's long-term goals and objectives.
2. The internal controls in the capital budgeting process need to be evaluated to determine whether the CBG applied the criteria consistently.
3. The ROI (hurdle rate) must be tested for reasonableness to be sure the appropriate projects are selected.
4. The IAD must determine how well the project is now doing as compared to the original analysis.

25-27 (Continued)
    b.

PROCEDURES

1. Review Haskin's long-term goals and objectives to determine the appropriateness of each evaluation criterion being employed by the CBG.

2. Review, test and evaluate the internal controls associated with the capital budgeting process. This would include a review of the capital budgeting procedures manual, if one exists, and preparing a flowchart for the capital budgeting process.

3. Review how the hurdle rate is determined now and was determined in 1998. Determine if a risk adjustment was incorporated into the decision process by such means as increasing the hurdle rate or decreasing estimated cash flows.

4. Interview and evaluate the competence of the available participants in the decision, including the originator of the CBG. Read the minutes of the CBG's meetings and review all status reports for the project from inception through its completion. Review the quantitative analysis used by the CBG to determine if data were valid, assumptions and estimates reasonable, only relevant costs were considered, and cost behavior (fixed and variable) was correctly perceived.

5. Review Haskin's internal accounting controls to assure that all acquisition and installation costs for the machines are capitalized and that operating and maintenance costs for the machines are recorded accurately and expensed. Review documents related to the acquisition of other machines and determine the actual amount of investment. Review accounting, maintenance, and production records, and other documentary evidence to determine actual operating costs and actual contribution for each machine.

25-28

WEAKNESSES/ INEFFICIENCIES	RECOMMENDATIONS
1. Quantities of materials received are not verified by the materials manager.	Besides inspecting all incoming goods to ensure that quality standards are met, the materials manager should verify quantities received by actual physical count. All material receipts do not have to be counted for a verification program to be effective. Systematically verifying one or several receipts from each vendor during a given time period can identify those receipts which are the most troublesome. Once identified, efforts can be directed to correcting the problem. The verification process is performed by comparing receiving document quantities to actual physical counts to ensure invoice totals are correct.
2. The materials manager prepares purchasing requests based on product schedules and not on requisitions received from operating departments.	Purchasing requests prepared by the materials manager are to be based on requisitions received from operating departments and not production schedules for a four month period. Production schedules could be outdated and not reflect current sales trends. Operating departments are constantly adjusting production levels to account for changes. To improve budgetary control over expenditures, the controller's office also should review the requests in conjunction with forward planning to ensure expenditures are consistent with company sales projections. Once an analysis of inventory flows is complete the economic order quantity can be applied to determine the reorder point and to minimize inventories.
3. The majority of Lecimore's requirements for a critical raw material is supplied by a single vendor.	It is best to develop alternate sources of supply for critical materials. The obvious benefits are reduced reliability on a single vendor, and the reduced possibility of lost production because of material shortages and/or other interruptions in the operation due to a single vendor. Encouragement of competition by the effective allocation of material requirements between vendors is also another benefit that can be expected to materialize if an effective program is implemented. Other benefits such as improved vendor services and technical assistance may also result as vendors attempt to gain increased shares of the goods provided the user company.

25-12

25-28 (Continued)

WEAKNESSES/ INEFFICIENCIES	RECOMMENDATIONS
4. Rush and expedite orders are made by production directly to the purchasing department without consulting the materials managers.	Rush and expedite orders should be reviewed by the materials manager to determine if any of the orders can be filled using existing inventories.
5. The purchasing department is held responsible for the cost of special orders which can be clearly identified by requesting departments.	The direct association of special order costs with responsible departments is necessary in order to exercise proper control. Responsibility accounting obligates departments to exercise judgment and prudence over those costs they are held accountable for. Through responsibility reporting, excessive costs are highlighted so that corrective actions can be implemented.
6. Engineering changes are not discussed with other departments before the materials needed to implement the change are ordered.	A general policy outlining the authority and responsibility for implementing engineering changes must be established. The proposed changes should be reviewed thoroughly by various company departments before an order is placed. The controller's office would review the proposal in light of incremental costs or cost savings that are expected to result. The manufacturing departments would review the change from an adaptability point of view. Before placing an order, purchasing would have to receive approval from the reviewing departments. Once approval is obtained, the vendor selection process can begin.
7. Accounting is not notified by the materials manager of the receipt of partial shipments.	Besides notifying the purchasing department of the receipt of partial shipments, the materials manager should also inform the accounting department so that vendor invoices can be processed correctly. Receiving reports clearly identifying the receipt as a partial shipment is the most effective means of communicating this information. By appropriately annotating the receiving report, vendors will not be paid for materials the company has not received.

WEAKNESSES	RECOMMENDATIONS
1. An authorization document which describes the item to be acquired indicates the benefits to be derived, and estimates its cost, is not prepared and reviewed with management.	To obtain approval for the purchase of machinery and equipment, an appropriations request should be prepared, describing the item, indicating why it is needed, and estimating its expected costs and benefits. The document also could include the item's accounting classification, expected useful life, depreciation method and rate, and name the approving company executives.
2. There is no control over authorized acquisitions. The purchase requisitions and purchase orders for fixed assets are interspersed with other requisitions and purchase orders and handled through normal purchasing procedures.	Authorized acquisitions should be processed using special procedures and purchase orders. These purchase orders should be subjected to numerical control. Copies of purchase orders should be distributed to all appropriate departments so that the acquisition can be monitored.
3. Plant engineering does not appear to be inspecting machinery and equipment upon receipt.	Purchases of machinery and equipment should be subject to normal receiving inspection routines. In the case of machinery and equipment, plant engineering is usually responsible for reviewing the receipt to make certain the correct item was delivered and that it was not damaged in transit. All new machinery and equipment would be assigned a control number and tagged at the time of receipt.
4. The lapse schedules are not reconciled periodically to general ledger control accounts to verify agreement.	At least once each year, machinery and equipment lapse schedules, which provide information on asset cost and accumulated depreciation, should be reconciled to general ledger control accounts. Furthermore, an actual physical inventory of existing fixed assets should be taken periodically and reconciled to the lapse schedules and general ledger control account to assure accuracy.
5. Machinery and equipment accounting policies, including depreciation, have not been updated to make certain that the most desirable methods are being used.	Machinery and equipment accounting procedures, including depreciation, must be updated periodically to reflect actual experience, and changes in accounting pronouncements and income tax legislation.